The
Cult of
Counterterrorism

Other Books by Neil C. Livingstone

*The War against Terrorism**

Fighting Back: Winning the War against Terrorism
(with Terrell E. Arnold)*

America the Vulnerable: The Threat of Chemical/Biological
Warfare (with Joseph D. Douglass, Jr.)*

Beyond the Iran-Contra Crisis: The Shape of U.S.
Anti-Terrorism Policy in the Post-Reagan Era
(with Terrell E. Arnold)*

*The Complete Security Guide for Executives**

Inside the PLO: Secret Funds, Covert Units, and its War
against Israel and the United States (with David Halevy)

*Available from Lexington Books

The Cult of Counterterrorism

The "Weird World" of Spooks,
Counterterrorists, Adventurers,
and the Not-Quite Professionals

NEIL C. LIVINGSTONE

Lexington Books

D.C. Heath and Company • Lexington, Massachusetts • Toronto

This book is published as part of Lexington Books
Issues in Low-Intensity Conflict series, Neil C. Livingstone, consulting editor.

Library of Congress Cataloging-in-Publication Data

Livingstone, Neil C.
The cult of counterterrorism
The "weird world" of spooks, counterterrorists,
adventurers, and not quite professionals / Neil Livingstone.
p.   cm.
Includes index.
ISBN 0-669-21407-8 (alk. paper)
1. Terrorism. 2. Terrorism—Prevention. 3. Commando troops.
4. Spies. 5. Secret service. I.Title. II. Title:
Counterterrorists, adventurers, and the not quite professionals.
HV6431.L583   1989
363.3'2—dc20   89-12488
CIP

Published simultaneously in Canada
Printed in the United States of America
International Standard Book Number: 0-669-21407-8
Library of Congress Catalog Card Number: 89-12488

The paper used in this publication meets
the minimum requirements of American National Standard
for Information Sciences—Permanence of Paper
for Printed Library Materials, ANSI Z39.48-1984.

Year and number of this printing

89 90 91 92 8 7 6 5 4 3 2 1

*To Susan, who has lived on the edge
of the "weird world" without complaint
for twenty-one years*

Contents

Only those who have walked by night
know the beauty of the stars
—Former CIA counterterrorist

Introduction

T HE Special Forces Club is located on a quiet residential
street off Hans Crescent in the Knightsbridge section of
London. There is no sign; simply an address. You ring the bell
and a voice asks, "May I help you?" After confirming your
identity, the door buzzes open.

Across the entrance hall an inviting fire burns in a small book-
lined study. On the activities board at the base of the stairs is
a notice—what the French call the roll of honor—listing members that have died during the past month, with special notations beside the names of those killed in action. The steep stair-
case is lined with portraits of distinguished members of the club,
including those of a number of American and British agents
killed behind the lines during World War II.

On the second floor is a cozy bar, presided over by a portrait
of the Queen Mother, who is the chief patron of the Special
Forces Club. Not only does she occasionally come to lunch at the
club, she is usually in attendance on special days and for celebra-
tions. Once or twice a year she invites club members to a reception at her official residence. The bar is permeated with the scent
of curry from the dining room on the third floor, harking back
to the era when the cuisine in most British military clubs had a
distinctly Indian army flavor.

There are a dozen rooms on the top floor available on a night-
by-night basis to club members. Former CIA director and
former OSS (Office of Strategic Services) operator Bill Casey
was one of the many prominent members who enjoyed passing a

night or two at the Special Forces Club when he was in London. Indeed, the club was founded in the aftermath of World War II, chiefly by former OSS and British secret agents, and has grown over the years to include about 3,000 active members, representing the West's most elite special operations, counterterrorist, and intelligence (operations side) organizations. Most U.S. members are former OSS officers or from Delta Force, SEAL Team 6, or the CIA operations directorate. British members hail from the SAS (Special Air Service), SBS (Special Boat Service), or Scotland Yard's antiterrorism division, or are retired members of the operations directorate of the spy agency MI-6. France, Belgium, Canada, Australia, New Zealand, and other Western nations are also represented; no West Germans have been admitted, however, in deference to the World War II–era members.

In the mid-1970s the club fell on hard times, and an extraordinary meeting was called in London to save the club and put it back on a sound financial footing. Those in attendance read like a "Who's Who" of famous spies and special operators. Bill Casey spearheaded the rescue effort in the United States. Substantial funds were raised, and each of the major Western contingents agreed to be responsible for maintaining a room in the club. It was also decided to expand the membership, and thereby infuse the club with the youth needed to carry on in the future. In view of the fact that "every modern police force and army does, to a greater or lesser degree, retain some sort of specialist anti-terrorist capability," emphasis was placed on recruiting members from such units who were thought to possess the skills and attributes worthy of membership. As a result of such efforts, longtime members say that the club has never been in better shape than it is today.

On this occasion, the club is surprisingly quiet. No one looks like he has been bitten by a rabid dog. There is little idle chatter about golf or crabgrass that you find at many other private clubs. The vernacular of the Special Forces Club is war stories, and conversation mingles current events with what Wordsworth called "Old, unhappy, far-off things, and battles long ago."

Tonight's chief topic is the killing of three IRA terrorists by the SAS in Gibraltar. There is general agreement about the result; however, one former SAS man voices his belief that the British government should have announced its new "rules of engagement" ahead of the operation.

It is also the day before Camerone, the most significant annual event celebrated by the French Foreign Legion, and at least one of those present is planning to join some ex-Legionnaires the following day to raise their glasses to the memory of Captain Danjou after gathering at the Marshal Foch statue near Victoria Station.

Genesis of the Counterterrorist

During the second week of May 1988, surviving members of the Jedburgh Teams, or "Jed Teams," rendezvoused in Washington, D.C., for the second time since World War II. The Jed Teams were three-man units that parachuted behind enemy lines in occupied France or elsewhere in Europe to help organize and arm resistance groups. Each team consisted of a member of the British Special Operations Executive (SOE) or the U.S. OSS, an allied national from the country being infiltrated, and a U.S. or British serviceman. Among those in attendance at the Washington ceremonies was former "Jed Team" member William Colby, a past director of the CIA.

The reunion of the Jedburgh Teams, more than forty years after the war, is a reminder that virtually all modern-day Western special operations units, including their counterterrorist components, trace their origins to World War II, especially to the many groups and units established by the SOE and OSS to undertake a variety of espionage and sabotage activities behind enemy lines. This combination of intelligence and military requirements and missions persists to this day and is what gives special operations units much of their mystique.

Since World War II, the globe's conflict landscape has been dominated by what generally is referred to as LIC (pronounced "lick"), otherwise known as low-intensity conflict. It is LIC that is the milieu of today's special operators, who tend to be deployed more often in peacetime than in war. First, there were the wars of decolonization, where special operations forces were used by the French, British, Belgians, and other European powers to combat the insurgencies that gave shape and momentum to national liberation movements. Subsequently, Western special operations units have intervened in the violence endemic to the developing countries in recent years, both to shore up allies beset by insurgencies and discontent, and as a means of projecting power. For the United States, Vietnam and the war in Southeast Asia was the most recent major test for its special operations forces, and while it brought such units temporarily into disfavor, there are few today who doubt their utility. Special operations forces have been on the cutting edge of the conflict between the superpowers, and consequently, the Soviet-bloc nations have also placed great emphasis on developing such units and capabilities. Indeed, the Soviet invasions of Czechoslovakia (1968) and Afghanistan (1979) were spearheaded by special operations forces.

Currently, the most publicized mission of special operations forces is to combat terrorism. Such units, however, represent just one, albeit the most dramatic, dimension of the war against terrorism. Our popular fiction and movies celebrate the role and mystique of counterterrorist commandos. But the field of counterterrorism embraces far more than just elite commando units—it involves academicians, writers, spies, commercial firms and industry, media savants, politicians and policymakers, and architects and engineers. And with the growing interest in undermining the logistical and financial underpinnings of terrorist organizations, even accountants have become front-line combatants.

In many respects, the Special Forces Club represents a microcosm of the special operations community and is an appropriate place to begin any book about counterterrorism. In this connection, it is one of the most elite clubs in the world. Membership is not conferred or purchased, it is earned and conveys the unspoken sense of fraternity and camaraderie characteristic of those who have shared extraordinary risks and experiences. Most of its members have traveled to the heart of darkness and back again, veterans of unsung battles and twilight wars. In a world dominated by long-distance, often "faceless," combat and the so-called electronic battlefield, many club members have killed at close range. Violence and mind-numbing risk are not abstract concepts but are, or once were, their stock-in-trade. It is a world of unspoken bonds and unwritten codes of behavior, even between adversaries.

Because of the risks they take and the skills they have mastered, members of the club often find it difficult to adjust to the normal rhythms of daily life, to ordinary relationships with those who have not shared the same special background. Thus, they seek the company of their own kind at the club.

This sense of superiority is common among the globe's elite special operations units and can be found, for example, among the members of SEAL Team 6, the secretive counterterrorist unit maintained by the U.S. Navy, who informally refer to themselves as the "Jedi," after "Luke Skywalker" and the race of mythical warriors dedicated to combating evil in the *Star Wars* trilogy. These are men of zeal and intensity, addicted to action, who in Greek times would probably have been described as gods come to earth in the likeness of men.

My purpose in writing this book is to take the reader into the often cloistered and always shrouded world of counterterrorism. It is a world that admits few outsiders and is characterized by its own folkways and rituals, not unlike those of a religious brotherhood. From the Special Forces Club in London to the CIA's training facility, known as "the farm," near Williamsburg, Virginia, or the secluded chateau outside of Paris that houses the elite French counterterrorism unit RAID, the reader will be given a tour of the sites and locales that form the backdrop to the war against terrorism and are such a large part of the collective memory of so many individuals in the field. Much of it is uncharted terrain from the standpoint of previous scholarship, or even popular literature.

The reader will meet, or at least glimpse, many of the unique personalities one encounters in the world of counterterrorism, some with such remarkable skills and courage as to be beyond belief, others as phony as a three-dollar bill. In short, this book represents the first comprehensive survey of the counterterrorism field: the people, the places, the exploits, the skills and technologies, and the idioms and imagery that are so much a part of its mystique. Attention also will be paid to those who write and publish about the subject, renegade counterterrorists that employ their unique skills for evil instead of good, and the death squads and atrocities committed by some in the name of antiterrorism.

1

Counterterrorism Hype

Welcome to the weird world.

—Special Operator

W E LIVE in an age of terrorism. Far too frequently it dominates our headlines, our fears, our thoughts, our popular culture. A bomb goes off in Europe or a plane is hijacked, and the bottom drops out of the travel business. In the wake of the U.S. bombing raid on Libya in April 1986, some travel agencies reported bookings to Europe were down by as much as 75 percent. But for those intrepid travelers who press on regardless of the danger, there is *The Terrorism Survival Guide,* which offers readers "101 Travel Tips on How Not to Become a Victim." "Take Away the Fear and Put Back the Pleasure in Your Traveling," the dust jacket promises.[1]

Although Iran's late Ayatollah Khomeini and Libya's erratic strongman Colonel Muammar Qaddafi have threatened to sponsor terrorist attacks against the United States itself, what little terrorism this nation has experienced on its own soil has been chiefly of the home-grown variety and not particularly menacing. Nevertheless, the attempted bombing in March 1989 of a van driven by Sharon Rogers, wife of the captain of the U.S. warship that mistakenly shot down an Iranian passenger jet over the Persian Gulf, may be a portent of things to come. Despite the lack of a real statewide threat, concrete barriers shield the White House and other government buildings in Washington from terrorist vehicle bombs, replacing the buses and trucks that sufficed until more permanent barriers could be installed. Concrete "Jersey" barriers now protecting the White House, however, are scheduled to be replaced along Pennsylvania Avenue by 274 bollards, or concrete posts joined by chains. The Smithsonian is so frightened by the prospect of cars filled with explosives that it has closed the underground parking garage of the Air and Space Museum to visitors. The bus tunnels beneath the Pentagon also have been closed, and the building has been surrounded by sentry houses and pop-up vehicle barriers. A visitor without prior clearance approaching the Pentagon's River Entrance in a cab must exit the vehicle at the sentry station and walk the final hundred yards to the doors. While we are not surprised that shoppers in Belfast, Northern Ireland, are routinely stopped at checkpoints and searched for guns and explosives, who would have thought a quarter century ago that travelers at airports around the world would uncomplainingly walk through metal detectors, have their hand luggage X-rayed, and even submit to the indignity of an occasional pat-down body search by a beefy matron or security guard?

At the U.S. Capitol, once the very embodiment of this nation's open society, tough security measures have replaced the casual attitudes and patronage cops of the past. Congressional lawmakers have mandated counterterrorist training for their private praetorian guard, the Capitol Police Force, although liberals seek to block monies for similar training for Latin American police units, arguing that such training will contribute to human rights abuses. Staff members as well as lobbyists are required to wear color-coded identification badges, and everyone must pass through metal detectors while their bags and briefcases are checked. The Capitol plaza, once traversed by vehicles, has security gate houses at each entrance, and the U.S. Senate wants to eliminate all parking from the plaza. Former House Speaker Jim Wright, however, resisted the Senate proposal. Lest anyone think the U.S. House of Representatives is lax on the subject of terrorism, it should be noted that the House recently mandated that bulletproof metal plates be inserted in the backs of members' chairs in the House chamber to make terrorist attacks from the Visitors Gallery, such as that which occurred in 1954, more difficult.[2] On the other hand, the shrubbery planted in the heavy concrete planters intended as vehicle barriers on the Capitol plaza had to be pulled out because they blocked the view of oncoming cars and were a traffic hazard.

There may be a real basis, however, for the increased security at the Capitol. Indeed, the Capitol police reported that they seized 1,162 weapons in 1987, including an Uzi submachine gun, representing a 147-percent increase over 1986, when only 470 weapons were confiscated. They were, however, quick to point out that many of the weapons were discovered on "constituents who were unaware of Capitol gun-control restrictions and had no criminal intent."[3] One wonders, however, if some of the increase was not attributable to people being angrier at Congress than ever before.

New orders have gone out to all of the armed services to increase security at U.S. military installations. A 1987 order issued by the Chief of Naval Operations directed the "restructuring of the Navy's security forces to strengthen ability to deter, detect, and defeat terrorist attacks against service members, dependents and resources." In a related development, following successful tests involving 18 geese, the U.S. Army announced that it is going to deploy some 900 geese as guard birds to detect terrorist infiltration attempts at American military installations in Europe.

Meanwhile, the State Department has created an "Overseas Security Club" to promote security awareness among American children living overseas. A contest was held in which kids were asked to submit their ideas for a club logo. Participants were first required to view a State Department film entitled, "Are you A-OK?", which supposedly is shorthand for "Are You Alert Overseas Kids?" John Kim, a sixth grader at the Seoul American Elementary School, won the contest with his design of a thumbs-up hand in an circle, and was invited to Washington to present President Reagan with his honorary membership card in the Overseas Security Club.

Terrorism is also interfering with the affections of America's

servicemen. After the terrorist bombing of a local Chinese restaurant in 1987, U.S. military authorities declared the city of
Comayagua, Honduras, a popular R&R venue, off limits. In
response, twelve brothel owners, all female, who described
themselves as "proprietors of houses of tolerance," protested
the action to the U.S. Southern Command in Panama. Similarly, a curfew was placed on American military personnel at
Clark Air Base in the Philippines after three Americans were
slain by Marxist terrorists, an action that sent shock waves
throughout nearby Angeles City, which boasts 7,500 "bar
girls" and 500 nightspots.

The public is obsessed with terrorism. A tabloid newspaper
headline asks, "Are Terrorists Really Aliens From Outer
Space?" Dozens of films and books cast terrorists in the role of
heavies, and if the United States has trouble dealing with terrorists in real life, movie heroes like Chuck Norris and Sylvester
Stallone wreak vengeance on America's terrorist adversaries on
the silver screen. The trend has gone so far that the bad guys in
Steven Spielberg's recent comedy *Back to the Future* are a group
of Libyan gunmen in a Volkswagen minibus. The 1985 film
Brazil portrays a surrealistic world where terrorist attacks are so
commonplace that the patrons of a cafe that is bombed barely
look up from their coffee when an explosion rocks the place. One
of the most entertaining, if flawed, examples of the current crop
of antiterrorist films was *Let's Get Harry,* which tells the story of
four plumbers from Chicago who travel to South America to
save a buddy who has been kidnapped by terrorists. In preparation for his role as the veteran mercenary hired by the plumbers
to lead them on their odyssey, actor Robert Duvall reportedly
attended a school for mercenaries in Alabama and the Soldier of
Fortune convention in Las Vegas.

Superwriter Tom Clancy abandoned high-tech warfare in *Patriot Games* for the comparatively low-tech world of terrorism.
The dust jackets of several current pulp fiction thrillers are
indicative of the nation's reading tastes: "Political extremism
runs rampant in Spain, unleashing a savage tidal wave of death
and destruction. But when sixty innocents, including the family

of a U.S. Senator, are brutally massacred in the terrorist ambush of a tourist train, Phoenix Force is dispatched to Madrid
on a mission of bloody retribution.''[4]

Or, if the Phoenix Force is busy in Spain, one can always call
Able Team. ''Able Team is in between missions when a call
from Toni Blancanales puts them on the next flight to Britain,''
reads the lurid dust jacket prose:

> Communist-backed terrorists are sabotaging the British com-
> puter industry, but its [*sic*] not their only target. When Able
> Team realizes it's up against Aya Jishin, an old enemy, the
> Team knows America's next. Able Team's on its own for this
> one—the President won't take the threat seriously and he won't
> sanction the group's actions outside of the country. Carl Lyons
> and his men don't let this stop them. They will locate, identify
> and destroy—or die trying.[5]

One wonders if Carl Lyons is not another of Lt. Colonel Oliver
North's aliases.

There's even an annual guide called *Who's Who in Terrorism,*
and for only $50 you, too, can have ''over one thousand listings
of left and right wing organizations country by country, hundreds of fringe groups, in-depth reports on the most active
groups and their leadership,'' not to mention ''dozens of photos
and charts.'' Just think how impressed your friends and
business associates will be to learn that you were listed in *Who's
Who in Terrorism.* Books on terrorism have proliferated all out of
proportion to the problem. It is such an overwritten field, says
one observer, that ''The academics have begun to write about
what other academics are writing about terrorism.''[6]

''Have You Killed a Terrorist Today?''[7]

Guns are back in, after having been out during the ''sensitive
seventies.'' Because of impending changes in the National
Firearms Act of 1934, the Bureau of Alcohol, Tobacco and
Firearms (BATF) received more than 100,000 applications from

Americans desiring to own machine guns in April and May of 1986, more than had been received in the previous fifty years combined.[8] BATF officials attributed the three-foot-high stack of applications to the popularity of the film *Rambo* and the television series "Miami Vice."[9] A group of handgunners, the Citizens Committee for the Right to Keep and Bear Arms, has petitioned the Vatican to declare a nineteenth-century Italian priest who drove brigands away from his village with a brace of handguns the patron saint of handgun owners. Shooting ranges are springing up around the country, and a recent article in a leading southern newspaper advised that, in the gift category, "Fathers might prefer assault rifles over ties." The article goes on to say that one southern Florida gun shop even has an annual Father's Day sale.

Another gift idea for the weapons lover, which combines guns and soft porn, is the video entitled "Sexy Girls and Sexy Guns," featuring "Fourteen outrageous, sexy, southern California beauties firing some of the sexiest machine guns ever produced." The promotional literature, which suggests that the 60-minute video is "bound to become a classic," goes on to say that the girls are attired in string bikinis and high heels as they blast away with their Uzis, MAC-10s, AK-47s, and other automatic weapons. "It's something you just have to see," concludes the overenthusiastic advertisement.

Old Town Armory in Alexandria, Virginia, even sends out a "June Madness Flyer!!" advertising its latest weapons sale. "Our previous flyer generated so much interest in silenced guns that we made every effort possible to acquire some new and *very* interesting guns!" the flyer gushes, above pictures of various silenced rifles and pistols. The brochure notes that one $595 silencer, or "can" in counterterrorist parlance, "screws right onto your personal AR-15 or M-16" assault rifle. And if you're concerned about the legal requirements of owning a silenced gun, not to worry. "We have the necessary paperwork right here," Old Town Armory reassures the would-be buyer. "There is a one time $200.00 federal tax stamp and approximately a 3 month wait for processing the paperwork. A small price to pay for the years of satisfaction these guns will bring!'' For those who want a real conversation piece, under the heading ''Last Chance for a Machine gun,'' there's a 600-round M-60 machine gun for only $5,500. Taking a line from Coca-Cola, the ad boasts, ''This is the real thing!'' In 1978, the Irish Republican Army (IRA) was so proud of its acquisition of several stolen M-60s that it called a news conference to display one of the weapons to the media. Think how much trouble it would have saved the IRA if they had simply shopped at Old Town Armory; after all, ''Remember, NON-RESIDENTS are welcome to purchase from us!''

As an indication of just how heavily armed Americans are today, one company recently ran a full-page ad headlined, ''Need a place to put your machine gun?'' The subhead read: ''Buy a half-track,'' featuring a picture of a military half-track available from Ermco, a Tennessee firm. If one does not already have the machine gun, Ermco will sell that to you as well. ''The .50 cal. is alive and well in Nashville, Tennessee,'' announces another Ermco ad, ''Let us add one to your collection.'' Yet another advertisement, from a Pennsylvania company, offered a U.S. Army M76 ''Otter'' amphibious cargo/personnel carrier, with its original olive drab paint, for only $11,500. Being a full-track vehicle, it is hell on paved streets, but you can be assured that no one else in your neighborhood has one.

Many of those armed to the teeth cite terrorism, along with rising crime, as the motivation for their acquisition of weapons and explosives technology. There is a strong belief in survivalist circles, for examples, that a massive wave of international terrorist violence will soon sweep across North America. A teenager arrested in Winnipeg, Canada, in 1981 for possessing a small arsenal of weapons, including a homemade bazooka and a rocket launcher, claimed he was training to kill Russians and terrorists. And in Fairfax, Virginia, forty-one local seventh- and eighth-grade students created a brouhaha by making crossbows capable of shooting steel-tipped arrows more than eighty yards in shop class.

Ever on the lookout for new ways to attract the foreign currency needed to fund its modernization program, the People's Republic of China has converted a former People's Liberation Army (PLA) firing range "for the use of overseas sports fans." For a minimum fee of $200, the shooting ranges will allow the would-be "Rambo" to fire assault rifles, pistols, submachine guns, heavy machine guns, and even anti-tank rockets at targets such as old tanks, balloons, concrete structures, and human silhouette targets.[10] Bianchi, the holster manufacturer, is running a series of ads for its product line long on mystique and short on the technical data. Beneath pictures of gun-packing, tough, handsome middle-aged men in Banana Republic garb accompanied by compliant, come-hither, Oriental women, framed against various exotic backdrops, is the legend "Bianchi: Share the Adventure." One ad goes on to say, "From Hong Kong to Zaire, Bianchi International is on the side of active adventurers. People who rely on high-performance holsters as if their lives depended on it . . . . Firearms protection that holds its own in the rising heat of a jungle or on a dusty backtrack in Afghanistan." And if you are bored by old-time bull's-eye targets or human silhouettes, there is a firm selling exploding targets: "Hit the bull's-eye (with .22 cal. or larger) and the explosion will blow you away!"

The tragic 1988 murder of five schoolchildren in a Stockton, California, schoolyard by Patrick Prudy, a deranged ex-felon armed with a Kalashnikov semi-automatic assault rifle, created a national furor over military-style assault rifles. Legislation has been introduced to make such weapons illegal, and even President George Bush has publicly supported restrictions on ownership of such weapons. However, fears that assault-style weapons would no longer be available resulted in a "run" on Kalashnikovs and Uzis at gunshops around the nation.

Our national obsession with terrorism has created a general public fascination with terrorist instruments of violence. Contemporary publications are full of lurid stories about terrorist mayhem and speculation about how they plan on doing us in. As if nail-studded car bombs were not enough to worry about, Jack Anderson's column warns readers that the "CIA Discovers

Terrorists Have 'Invisible Bomb.'"[11] The *American Legion Magazine,* in an article about plastic explosives and the largely plastic Glock 17 pistol, speculates on "Plastic Terror: Is There A Defense?"[12] *Time* wonders aloud if the next terrorist attack won't come from a malefactor with a backpack "nuke."[13] The *Washington Times* says that the Palestine Liberation Organization (PLO) is developing its own fighter plane (yes, but will it fly?),[14] and dozens of publications offer frightening stories about either Libyans or Iranians assembling kamikaze boat fleets filled with explosives. Japanese terrorists are building homemade rockets, and speculation runs rampant that a poisoned bottle of "Liquid Gravy" might be connected to a terrorist plot. On the low-tech side, the *Washington Post* reports on a suicide bomber in Lebanon riding a mule and on the world's first coconut bomb, "made entirely of coconut oil byproducts," discovered in the Philippines.[15] And in the communist nation of Romania, even the humble typewriter was declared by the government a possible terrorist weapon in 1983; which it is, as mayhem writer John Minnery so ably demonstrated in his book *How to Kill,* volume four, if you hit someone with it.[16]

The Counterterrorist Bandwagon

It seems like everyone is getting into the act. Even former CIA Director Stansfield Turner, blamed by many for dismantling the Agency's covert capabilities, is hawking a videocassette "On Understanding and Countering Terrorism." This is the same Stansfield Turner who usually has a sharp or critical comment about any antiterrorist operation. But a buck is a buck, especially when it's a fast buck made by jumping on the counterterrorist bandwagon.

The terrorist is the contemporary villain we love to hate. Who can forget the ski mask–clad figure on the balcony at Munich during the 1972 Olympics or the wild-eyed young Shiite gunman holding a pistol to pilot John Testrake's head in the cockpit of TWA flight 847 after it had been forced to Beirut in 1985. And of all the terrorists the American public hates, Libya's mercurial leader, Colonel Muammar Qaddafi, is at the top of the list. A U.S. firm that calls itself Frustration Relief, Inc., markets "Mad Dog" golf balls, featuring a likeness of Qaddafi, so that would-be counterterrorists on the links can "tee off" by clobbering Qaddafi's face. In the wake of the U.S. air raid on Libya in April 1986, billboards went up around the country asking motorists to "Honk if you want to blow away Qaddafi," and a classified ad appeared in a number of magazines for a book entitled *Kill Kaddafi,* which posed the question, "Is this book fiction? Or can it really happen?"[17] The public obsession with the assassination of any other leader would be considered in bad taste, at the very least, but Qaddafi has a special knack for getting the American "goat" and so authorities take a rather laissez-faire attitude about public discussions of the Colonel's demise.

Terrorism intruded on the Olympics again in 1988. As the Calgary Winter Olympics was set to open, South Korea's Ambassador to Canada drew censure from International Olympic Committee president Juan Antonio Samaranch for publicly speculating that North Korea was likely to try to disrupt the summer games in Seoul with acts of "state-sponsored terrorism." Ever since the Munich disaster, the Olympics generally has boasted more security people than athletes. Similarly, U.S. Army troops, FBI agents, the Indiana State Police, local police and security personnel, and even elements of the elite U.S. counterterrorist Delta Force all contributed to the security of the 1987 Pan American Games in Indianapolis.

Terrorism even becomes a campaign issue periodically, as it did during the 1988 Republican primary campaign when former televangelist Pat Robertson alleged that his Christian Broadcasting Network (CBN) knew the location of all of the American hostages being held in Beirut during the 1985 TWA 847 hijacking crisis. He went on to suggest that if Reagan administration antiterrorism specialists had just watched CBN, they could have mounted a rescue operation. Although Robertson's remarks were patently absurd, President Reagan reacted angrily, wondering aloud why Robertson, if he actually had it, did not communicate such vital information directly to the White House. Even CBN's Beirut bureau chief, Gus Hashim, contradicted Robertson, saying that while he knew the identity of the hijackers, he did not know the location of the hostages.

Interestingly, according to the Democratic polling firm of Marttila & Kiley, the public by a 2 to 1 margin believes that the Republicans would do a better job than the Democrats in dealing with terrorism.[18]

The 1988 Philip C. Jessup International Law Moot Court Competition was a case concerning terrorism. The hypothetical case between two mythical nations known as the Republic of Yokum and the Confederation of Shangri, involving the seizure of an unarmed cruise ship by PACM (People's Armed Conflict Movement) terrorists, was a thinly disguised rendering of the 1985 *Achille Lauro* seajacking incident designed to challenge student competitors on a variety of issues relating to extradition and other germane questions.

Dressed to Kill

Perhaps one of the best indicators of the popular mores and attitudes of society at any moment can be ascertained by studying those walking billboards, the tee-shirt wearers of America, to learn what slogans and illustrations are "in." Today, an informal survey discovers more "I'd Rather Be Killing Terrorists" tee-shirts than "Save the Whales," along with such expressions of brotherly love as "Big Mac Attack" (featuring a picture of a MAC-10 submachine gun), "U.S. Navy SEALS," "Long Distance . . . reach out and touch someone" (with a silkscreen illustration of a sniper and set of cross hairs), "Terrorism Stops Here" (with a terrorist in rifle cross hairs), "Visit Lebanon: Help a Syrian Meet Allah," "Central Intelligence Agency, Instructor, Camp Peary," "S.A.S.: Britain's Best," "Mercenaries Don't Die . . . They Just Go to Hell to Regroup!", "Delta Force," "Hey, we just stepped in some Shiite!", "Terrorists are Sick . . . and I've got the Cure" (showing a man with a blazing MAC-10), "When Diplomacy Fails" (with a B-52 bomber streaking across a moonlit night sky), and that all-time favorite, the "Kadaffy Duck" tee-shirt. Another variation on the Qaddafi theme is a tee-shirt with the Libyan dictator's picture on it and the caption, "Libyan Pharmacist?" in the wake of Libya's claims that its chemical weapons production facility at Rabta is, in actuality, a pharmaceutical plant. One of the current favorites, of course, is "Ollie North for President," which comes in literally dozens of variations. Incidentally, this was not a poll conducted around a military reservation like Fort Bragg—where the tee-shirt tastes, quite frankly, are a good deal tamer and generally predisposed to football and baseball team emblems and beer endorsements—but in the trendy boutiques and upscale environments of Georgetown (Washington, D.C.), Beverly Hills, and even that New Age bastion, Boulder, Colorado.

While on the subject of clothing, the current "look" falls someplace between early white hunter and modern-day antiterrorist commando. Capitalizing on the trend, a chain of popular stores known as The Banana Republic has grown by leaps and bounds during the past decade, and now boasts stores across the nation, not to mention a highly successful mail-order catalogue business. Dozens of other catalogues purvey everything from desert camouflage fatigues to S.W.A.T. duty coveralls, sinister black Ninja uniforms complete with combination mask and hood (try making a deposit at your bank in this), the Israeli Defense Forces antiterrorist special Commando Vest (complete with a built-in holster, a place for extra ammo clips, a gas/smoke grenade pouch, shotgun shell loops, combat/survival knife sheath, and even pen loops for your cammie patterned pen), sniper face masks, Israeli Defense Forces berets, and fingerless wool gloves for sniping. Incidentally, among the accessories that can be purchased through the mail along with your Ninja outfit are throwing knives, steel throwing stars, push-dagger key rings, 14-inch throwing hatchets, swords, and what is described as a "mysterious looking bag" to carry your martial arts equipment in.

As one of Fawn Hall's "top ten turn-ons," late-night television host David Letterman announced "anything in camouflage."[19] Almost everything comes in camouflage coloring these days, from the pickup trucks advertised by former Washington Redskin running back John Riggins to ladies' garters. The advertisement for the camouflage garter freely admits that "yes, it's ridiculous," but at least you can take solace in the fact that it is "made in the U.S.A." Japanese cars, cameras, and television sets are flooding the United States, and our response is to proudly advertise that we still sell camouflage garters made in this country. There is even something called "Hide-a-Wipe," camouflage toilet tissue, for the commando who is afraid that a flash of white might draw enemy fire.

Military underwear is back in also, in case you had not noticed, or missed it the first time around. Just think what a turn-on it will be when your date sees you strip down to your camouflage briefs, "either bikini or high-rise cuts," your choice of woodland or desert camouflage patterns. And for those of you who remember brown U.S. Army briefs nostalgically, they are still available, along with matching tee-shirts. One ad notes that they are "anti-infra-red treated." Now there's a feature Jockey doesn't give you; no one's going to be able to pick you out with an infrared scope while you're running around the forest at night in your knickers. And for the women, how about Ollie North panties, emblazoned with "We're behind you, Ollie" on the seat? Not your typical Bloomies, but then again, they're not for your typical woman.

And for the little Ranger in your life, there's even camouflage children's wear, in tiger-stripe camouflage or standard BDU style. "Fits both boys and girls," advises the non-sexist ad. The ad also upbraids indifferent parents with, "Did you give your son or nephew a camouflage uniform last Christmas?" Among the other items available for kids are Special Forces or Airborne tee-shirts, the "Junior Sarge T-Shirt," the "Camouflage Youth Muscle Shirt," "Kid's Jump Boots," and even camouflage-patterned infant diaper covers, toddler shorts, and toddler elastic-waist pants. And once your boys and girls outgrow their olive-drab teddy bears outfitted in cammies, they can play

counterterrorist com' .ndo with their neighborhood friends using the "Young Enthusiast's Crossbow," which fires plastic
darts with rubber suction cups, and something called the "Combat Weapons Set," described as the "ultimate combat set":
"Includes M-16 rifle, battle helmet with adjustable strap,
binoculars, play combat watch, working compass, rubber knife,
and a soft plastic grenade. The M-16 features safe 'click action'
sound. The most play pieces for the most play options!"

You do not have to be a kid, though, to play with commando
toys these days. The Sharper Image, an unabashedly yuppie gift
store for adults, until recently sold a full range of expensive
water guns that looked so much like real Uzis and Berettas that
law enforcement officials report they were used in the commission of a number of crimes. As a result, The Sharper Image
discontinued the items, but they are still being sold by numerous
other stores. Also in the gift department, for the man who has
everything, there's the "Time Bomb Clock"—an alarm clock
attached to three sticks of (non-explosive) dynamite.

The Counterterrorism Mystique

The latest in contemporary yuppie chic, for those grown bored
by tennis camps, Club Med vacations, and running the Colorado River in rubber rafts, is a week at a counterterrorist training school where you purportedly are taught to drive like a
Hollywood stuntman and shoot it out with Carlos. The skills
taught by many such camps are highly suspect, however, and
may be more of a threat to the individual who might try to apply
them in real life than to any terrorist. The "terrorism on the
brain" syndrome can also be glimpsed in the Virginia State
Defense Force, a citizen militia last called up in 1940, which
recently conducted an "antiterrorist" training exercise in which
middle-aged housewives and their husbands guarded a
Culpeper waste water plant, which was substituting for one of
the state's 53 armories, from terrorists. It is a rare college or
university that does not offer some kind of course on terrorism
or political violence, or instruction in such related fields as

special operations and the craft of intelligence. And if your trenchcoat is back from the cleaners, until recently it was possible to sign up for "Careers in Covert Operations," a course offered by a Washington continuing education program and taught by a distinguished former CIA official, the late David Atlee Phillips.

The lecture circuit is also lucrative turf for speakers on terrorism. G. Gordon Liddy, of Watergate fame, is perhaps "King of the Counterterrorists" on the lecture stump. Liddy, who purports to be head of a counterterrorist commando team for hire known as the Hurricane Force, is said to make $1.5 million a year speaking an average of four times a week, mostly to college students, at $7,500 a crack. A number of the Iran/Contra figures are presently on the lecture circuit, including Major General (ret.) Richard Secord, who ran the Contra resupply effort; North's courier Robert Owen; and Michael Ledeen, the former National Security Council terrorism consultant who served as a middleman between the Israelis and the United States during the initial stages of the Iran initiative. Secord's asking price is $15,000 plus expenses per speech, though his fee reportedly is subject to negotiation, while Ledeen pulls down anywhere from a few thousand to $10,000.

Nothing better proves Andy Warhol's maxim that "in the future everyone will be famous for fifteen minutes" than terrorist incidents. Thanks to media, we often become intimately acquainted not only with the terrorists, but with their victims as well. Protracted hijacking dramas like the 17-day seizure of TWA flight 847 by Shiite gunmen give unusual prominence to otherwise ordinary men and women who simply have the misfortune of being in the wrong place at the wrong time. Like the often-sequeled *Airport* movies, we are introduced to the cool and unflappable pilot, the heroic priest, the elderly grandmother on her way to visit the grandchildren she has never seen (and maybe will never see), the newlyweds with their whole lives ahead of them, the suicidal man who thinks he has nothing to live for, the coward who rises above his fears and becomes a hero, and the hero whose nerve fails him in the crisis. In the stampede for news, no matter how trivial, we are inundated with the professional and hometown histories of every hostage, details of their personal lives and rubbernecking shirttail relatives and friends from the supermarket checkout line. Was there anyone in America that did not learn more than he or she ever wanted to know about TWA 847 hostage "spokesman" Allyn Conwell, his divorced wife and his child, his work history, and his insufferable views on what he perceived as America's misguided Middle East policy?

The label "former hostage" seems to be a part of the baggage that many victims will carry with them for the rest of their lives. It is likely to overshadow all of their other accomplishments and be the central focus of their obituaries. Some former hostages want nothing more than to fade back into the anonymity from whence they came. For others, the instant fame conferred on them by their hostage experience opens up new opportunities or careers. Retired Major General James Dozier, held hostage in Italy by the Red Brigades, ran for Congress in Florida. John Testrake, the pilot of TWA 847, was approached in 1987 by Republican leaders in Missouri about running for public office, but after "a good deal of consideration and prayer," he rejected the notion, at least for the time being. Although common wisdom says that once you are held hostage, your career as a foreign service office is over, Ambassador Diego Asencio (now retired), a hostage of M-19 terrorists in Colombia for 61 days, went on to become Assistant Secretary of State and subsequently U.S. ambassador to Brazil. Today he is much in demand as a public speaker on terrorism and heads a major congressional commission. Flight purser Uli Derickson, whose courage and effort to shield the Jewish passengers from the terrorists on TWA flight 847 has been accorded many honors and has seen herself portrayed heroically on the motion picture screen. On the other hand, some former hostages never seem to fade entirely away: they just become TV commentators during each subsequent hostage crisis. In 1988, former hostage in Lebanon David Jacobsen was back in the news for his campaign to run paid valentines to the eight remaining U.S. hostages in a West Beirut newspaper.

In January 1988, a dozen former American hostages from Iran held a poignant reunion to commemorate the seventh anniversary of their freedom. According to former hostage L. Bruce Laingen, planning has already commenced regarding an effort to reunite all 52 hostages sometime during the tenth anniversary of their ordeal. Another former Iran hostage, Moorhead "Mike" Kennedy, has co-authored a high school text on terrorism as a way of provoking more thought on the subject by young people.

And if there is a surfeit of anything in this world, it must be conferences on terrorism. Every week brings a new circular in the mail for a conference, seminar, meeting, private briefing, or congress on terrorism, nearly all featuring roughly the same speakers and presenters. For exaggerated prose, a recent ad for CD '87, the Asian International Civil Defense and Disaster Relief exhibition scheduled to be held in Kuala Lumpur, cannot be beat:

SOUTH EAST ASIA—A HOT SEAT WHERE NATURAL AND MAN–MADE DISASTERS AND CATASTROPHES ABOUND. TYPHOONS, VOLCANIC ERUPTIONS, HURRICANES, FLOODS, TERRORIST BOMBINGS, RIOTS, FIRES AND OTHERS KEEP SOUTH EAST ASIAN COUNTRIES ON THEIR TOES WITH UP-TO-DATE COUNTER AND PREVENTION MEASURES. IT IS A MARKET YET UNTAPPED MILLIONS OF DOLLARS ARE UP FOR GRABS FOR THE ENTERPRISING BUSINESSMAN WHO CAN CATER TO THE NEVER ENDING DEMANDS FOR CIVIL DEFENCE EQUIPMENT AND SYSTEMS.

Conservative fund-raiser Carl "Spitz" Channel, who pleaded guilty to conspiracy in the Iran/Contra affair, clearly recognized the drawing power of terrorism when he named one of his principal political action committees "The Anti-Terrorism American Committee."

Even something called the American Institute of Metaphysics Studies, which produces New Age "intuitive therapists," and offers instruction on such things as Atlantean Tarot (cards),

Karma, and "What It Means If You Know A Person Whose Name Has An X, Y, or Z," finds it necessary to mention terrorism in its brochure. Apparently terrorism was one of the manifestations of the upheaval the "Earth began to feel" as it moved from "its long stay in Pisces . . . into its 2,000 year term in Aquarius."

The security industry, fueled by public concern over terrorism, crime, and personal protection, is—according to some observers—the fastest growing industry in the United States, if not the Western world. Firms concentrating on executive protection, audio countermeasures, polygraph testing, home and business alarm systems, security guards, teaching aggressive driving techniques, crisis management, and a host of other products and services are springing up like mushrooms after a spring rain. Staid companies like Western Union are also getting into the act, offering a new service called "Crisis Communication Planning." CCS Communication Control, which advertises heavily in airline magazines and operates a string of so-called Spy Shops, has carried technological fetishism to new heights, with hundreds of heavily marked-up security and antiterrorist gadgets, including the ever-popular $10,000 "bionic briefcase," the CCS-II "Covert Spy Camera," and the CCX 1,000 bomb "sniffer." Ours is such an insecure society that a number of trendy catalogues sell so-called tap detectors, which allegedly will detect a tap on your phone. "When you're talking, who's listening?" asks The Sharper Image catalogue, which sells a $49 device. Of course, such devices can only detect the most obvious "taps" and are hardly reliable if a sophisticated foreign intelligence service wants to listen in on your calls.

Seemingly innocent and innocuous products are finding new applications in the rarefied world of conterterrorism. Take, for example, the "Car Finder," developed by a young Washington, D.C., inventor. The Car Finder was designed to help people locate their cars in crowded shopping center parking lots. Actually a small transmitter on a key chain, the Car Finder sends a signal to a receiver located beneath the dash and hooked into the electrical system of your car, causing the horn to honk and the lights to flash. It soon became clear, however, that many of the Car Finder's customers were using it, with only slight modification, as a remote starting device to thwart bombs wired to a vehicle's ignition. So successful was the Car Finder that the inventor, Mark Gottlieb, now produces Secure-A-Start for those customers fearful of turning the key in a booby-trapped vehicle.

Perhaps the only positive spin-off of terrorism that can be found is a report that doctors in Northern Ireland have had so much practice treating terrorist kneecappings—individuals either shot in the knees or who had their kneecaps reamed with a power drill—that they have perfected a number of new techniques for treating knee injuries. And, in the wake of a series of tavern bombings during the 1970s, doctors have apparently developed new methods for measuring cranial pressure and fabricating skull plates that are being utilized today to treat patients with everyday cranial injuries.[20]

Defining the Undefinable

In 1987, the Prime Minister of Malaysia, Dr. Mahathir Mohamad, rounded up ninety-one political opponents, using a law designed for "subversives and terrorists." From all indications, none of those arrested and jailed was involved in the commission of violent acts against the government or the people of Malaysia. Along the same lines, South Africa regularly brands all opponents of the government as "terrorists" and tries those arrested under provisions of a 1967 Terrorism Act. By any reasonable interpretation, the Terrorism Act is used to punish dissidents and opponents of apartheid rather than to combat terrorism. Although there was little actual terrorism involved in the massive popular uprising in Nicaragua that brought the Sandinistas to power, embattled dictator Anastasio "Tacho" Somoza regularly described his enemies as "terrorists." In a letter to a member of the U.S. Congress, Somoza's ambassador to Washington, Guillermo Sevilla Sacasa, blamed the country's ills on "agents of terrorism."[21] Then there was the anti-Castro exile who defined a terrorist as "a man who sets a bomb off and doesn't care who he kills. A revolutionary is a man who uses the methods and equipment available to him at the moment to hit Fidel Castro. We are revolutionaries." In other words, so long as one's target is Fidel Castro, anything is permissible.

Terrorism has become one of the cant words of our time, used to justify all manner of sin on the part of governments seeking to discredit or oppress their political opposition. By characterizing one's opponents as "terrorists," even the most venal and thuggish governments know that they are likely to win some international support on the part of those who unquestioningly leap to the defense of any state confronted by "terrorism." So powerful is public revulsion to terrorism in the West that there is also a tendency to ignore the methods employed in some countries to combat "terrorism."

The promiscuous use of the term terrorism, however, is not a one-way street. Cuba has been identified as a terrorist-sponsoring nation by the Reagan administration. In response, Cuban strongman Fidel Castro has called President Reagan "the worst terrorist in the history of mankind," as well as "a madman, an imbecile and a bum."[22] Similarly, Nicaraguan leader Daniel Ortega has accused the United States of "state terrorism" because of its support for the Contras.[23] Even Libya rejects the notion that it sponsors terrorism. "Our religion, our Arab values and morals, do not allow us to support terrorism," says Muammar Qaddafi's deputy, Major Abdul Salam Jalloud. Jalloud went on to say that Libya pledged to "combat all forms of terrorism and condemns it." It is the United States that is the real purveyor of terrorism, he continued, when it sends its aircraft carriers to intimidate people, withholds its wheat from the world's starving masses, and uses the CIA to carry out assassinations.[24] Senator Robert Byrd engaged in the same sloppy thinking when he branded the U.S. mining of Nicaragua's harbors "an act of terrorism." The CIA's mining of Nicaragua's harbors was many things, including ill considered, but it was not terrorism. As the word has entered the general lexicon, it is misused more and more often. One New York writer, complaining about the failure of government to take adequate steps to address the issue of the homeless, has complained of "state terrorism as social-welfare policy."[25]

Nearly all terrorists deny that they are terrorists, not wanting to be branded with such a negative, menacing, and pejorative term. Even the Palestinian pirates who seized the cruise ship *Achille Lauro* in 1985 and murdered an elderly Jewish wheelchair-bound passenger, Leon Klinghoffer, rejected any thought that they were terrorists at their trial in Genoa, Italy. "We are Palestinian fighters," announced Youssef Magied al-Molqi. "We are not terrorists."[26] Or as another Palestinian hijacker put it in 1980: "We are neither terrorists nor outlaws but a reform-minded political group fighting for justice and equality." Palestine Liberation Organization (PLO) leader Yasir Arafat set the standard for such doubletalk years ago. "Those who call us terrorists wish to prevent world public opinion from discovering the truth about us and from seeing the justice in our faces," said Arafat. "They seek to hide the terrorism and tyranny of their acts, and our own posture of self-defense." Even Qaddafi claims that he is not a terrorist: "Terrorism in the true sense of the word is rejected. I do not think any reasonable man would support terrorism. The problem is that the imperialists deliberately link the activities of freedom fighters—whom we support—with terrorists. They have caused a misunderstanding." Some misunderstanding!

Thus, the question remains: What is terrorism? It is clearly more than just a question of semantics or of whose ox is getting gored at any particular moment. There is always the urge to paraphrase Justice White's quip about pornography: that he can't define it but he knows it when he sees it. But unless it can be broken down into its basic elements and defined, it will be impossible to achieve widespread consensus among Western governments concerning its control and suppression.

Incidentally, don't wait for the United Nations to come up with a working definition: the General Assembly has been arguing over what constitutes terrorism for more than a decade and a half. Former Secretary of Defense Caspar Weinberger's 1984 suggestion that the United States call upon the United Nations to deal with the terrorism problem seems even more ludicrous today than it did then in light of the fact that the General Assembly, in 1987, named Libya chairman of the International Law Committee and, you guessed it, the committee's first task was to define terrorism.[27] An example of the bizarre definitions that can be expected from the United Nations is found in the proposed "Geneva Declaration on Terrorism," offered up in March 1987 by a grab bag of the globe's loony tunes, including Libya's Rajab Boudabbous, former IRA terrorist Sean MacBride (recently deceased), and former U.S. Attorney General Ramsey Clark:

> *Terrorism originates from the statist system of structural violence and domination that denies the right of self-determination to peoples* (e.g., in Namibia, Palestine, South Africa, the Western Sahara); *that inflicts a gross and consistent pattern of violations of fundamental human rights upon its own citizens* (e.g., in Chile, El Salvador, Guatemala, South Africa); *or that perpetrates military aggression and overt or covert intervention directed against the territorial integrity or political independence of other states* (e.g. Afghanistan, Angola, Grenada, Lebanon, Libya, Mozambique, Nicaragua).[28]

Not a word about bombings, hijackings, murders, or other attacks on civilians by vicious bands of terrorists sponsored by nations like Libya, Iran, Cuba, Syria, and North Korea. Not a word about Libya's direct and methodical support of international terrorism, which prompted the U.S. retaliation condemned in the definition as "military aggression" against various states. But, then, what should one expect from an institution that, in the words of Allan Gerson, indulges in the kind of doubletalk in which:

> Governments that are autocratic are called democratic, policies intended to incite to war are deemed peaceful, and that which is imposed by terror is termed "popular" and "progressive." Movements which are neither peaceful, popular nor democratic are associated with words like "peace" and "people's democ-

racy." And extremists and terrorists whose acts flout the letter and spirit of the U.N. Charter find justification in U.N. resolutions which endorse "the use of all necessary means at their disposal" where "self determination" and "national liberation" are deemed at stake.[29]

Indeed, the U.N. has become the institutional equivalent of Humpty Dumpty, who told Alice, "When I use a word, it means just what I choose it to mean—neither more or less." Alice, of course, had the right rejoinder: "The question is, whether you can make words mean so many different things?" Obviously not, if the words are to have any real meaning. Thus, what exactly is terrorism and how should it be defined?

During the struggle for Palestine, Gundar "Arieh" Yitzhaki, a member of the Zionist terrorist organization Irgun, was fabricating a homemade bomb, to be employed in a terrorist attack on the British, when it exploded, tearing him to pieces. When the British authorities arrived on the scene, the dying Yitzhaki was asked who he was. "My name," he gasped before succumbing to his injuries, "is death." In its most elemental sense, terrorism is death. But it is more than that, and can be defined as: *the calculated use of violence to attain political goals through the use of intimidation and fear.* But since its real audience extends far beyond its immediate victims, it is also a form of communication. Terrorists generally do not want a whole lot of dead bodies; rather, their goal is to intimidate and coerce, and murder and mayhem is the way they grab headlines and television time. As Sander Vanocur told an audience at the Fletcher School of Law and Diplomacy at Tufts University, "Today, power flows from the end of a cathode tube."[30] Prolonged hostage ordeals are often even better than murder, since murder is a transitory act, while hostage crises capture and sustain the public's interest over time, thereby ensuring continuous media attention until the incident is resolved. Terrorism is ideally suited to the electronics age. Unlike the nuclear arms race or the debt crisis in the developing world, a terrorist act is rarely complex and can be readily understood and assimilated by the viewer in a matter of seconds: innocent hostages being held at gunpoint by masked political outlaws or a street of shattered bodies in the aftermath of a terrorist bombing. Terrorism was made for "media bites," that is, tight, compact 90- or 120-second spots on the evening news, in which the essential elements of the story must be grasped instantly, without elaborate explanation or background information. Inasmuch as terrorism is a form of communication, it should be noted that terrorist attacks almost never occur in the boondocks, but almost always take place in the world's media capitals: New York, Paris, London, Rome, Vienna, Cairo, Tokyo, Athens. Guerrilla insurgencies, on the other hand, are essentially a rural phenomenon.

Insurgents have a defined organizational structure and territorial base, but terrorist groups need not have either. Unlike insurgents, terrorists operate covertly, without respect to the laws of war, and do not wear uniforms. Insurgents require a popular base of support, but terrorists do not. Terrorists often target civilians and innocent bystanders, whereas insurgents seek legitimate military objectives. Insurgents hope actually to seize political power instead of merely coercing the power structure to alter its behavior.[31]

Finally, terrorism is often confused with state terror, which is the oppression by the state of its own population. State terror is violence from the top down, in contrast to terrorism, which is violence from the bottom up. Terrorism is war by other means, used by the weak to prey upon the powerful. From the standpoint of the governments battling terrorism, however, it is constrained warfare. Western governments cannot use nuclear weapons or, except on rare occasions, tanks and planes to combat terrorists. In this sense it is generally referred to as low-intensity conflict, though there is nothing "low intensity" about it to those engaged in a firefight with terrorists.

The Terrorist Threat

By most yardsticks, terrorism pales in comparison to other weighty international problems such as the arms race, global hunger, government human rights abuses, and the declining scope of democracy and freedom in the world. A typhoon, for example, rakes the Philippines in November 1987, killing at least 228 people and destroying 14,000 homes, and it is reported on page A39 of the *Washington Post,* almost as a footnote. By contrast, the murder of a handful of people by terrorists in Europe produces screeching headlines and is the occasion for official statements by more than a score of governments.

From a purely statistical perspective, the number of people killed and injured in terrorist attacks is relatively insignificant. Since 1985, the average American's chances of being killed or injured in a terrorist attack has been negligible. In 1986, for example, 12 Americans were killed and 100 wounded by terrorists. In any given year, 200 Americans are killed by lightning, or more than sixteen times the death rate inflicted by terrorists. Thousands of Americans postponed or permanently canceled trips to Europe after terrorist incidents on two TWA flights in 1985 left six U.S. citizens dead, yet few of us live in mortal fear of being struck by lightning or alter our patterns of behavior to minimize this risk. Similarly, in 1987 more than 46,000 people died—though for the most part anonymously—in traffic accidents, without provoking a fraction of the outcry that terrorism does. Another 18,000 or so are murdered each year in this country. Most Americans would recoil in horror at the suggestion that they visit Belfast, Northern Ireland, a city generally viewed as gripped by pervasive political violence, but statistically it is far more dangerous to walk down a street in New York, Detroit, or Washington, D.C., than Belfast. Until recently, Detroit's murder rate was the highest in the nation, with 588 murders, or 59 homicides per 100,000 people, in 1986.[32]

In view of such figures, why then is there so much public outcry and trepidation over terrorism? Statistics alone obviously do not tell the whole story. Terrorism represents a real threat to our national interests and our democratic institutions. In recent years, it has brought the United States to the brink of war with Libya and Iran; others say a state of war, for all intents and purposes, actually exists. Terrorists have the ability to create crises that can escalate into major international confrontations. One has only to note the profound impact terrorism had on U.S. policy in the Middle East when the United States was forced to cut and run after the slaughter of 241 American military men by a Shiite suicide bomber who drove a Mercedes truck loaded with explosives into the U.S. Marine barracks at the Beirut airport. Terrorism complicates America's relations with its allies and trading partners, not to mention with its adversaries. It requires governments and private industry to spend billions of dollars in security enhancements, thus fueling one of the fastest growing businesses in the world. Finally, terrorism undermines what British historian Sir Harold Nicholson referred to as "the diplomatic method," by forcing diplomats to cower in bunker-like embassies and to curtail their contacts with those of opposing views out of fear for their own safety. In this sense, terrorism is a fundamental assault on Western values and institutions.

The Rise of the Counterterrorist

The eight black-clad figures, wearing flak vests, custom-made overalls and flash hoods, hip holsters, and gas masks (S6 respirators), H&K MP5 submachine guns slung over their backs, gathered on the roof of the Iranian embassy at number 16 Princes Gate in London. The year was 1980, and anti-Khomeini terrorists had seized the embassy and taken 26 hostages. As the world watched, SAS (Special Air Service) commandos began rappelling down ropes at the rear of the embassy toward second-floor balconies. Simultaneously, two other teams of commandos assaulted the embassy through a ground-floor window and from a first-floor terrace balcony. Thus began "Operation Nimrod," the only major counterterrorist operation to occur, at least in part, in front of television cameras.

Although one of the first two members of the assault group rappelling down from the roof became entangled in his rope, his companions reached a second-floor balcony, smashed the windows and screens with sledgehammers, tossed in stun grenades to clear the room, and entered the embassy, weapons at the ready. Six other SAS men stormed the embassy through a rear ground-floor window. A third team, meanwhile, blew a window at the front of the embassy with a frame charge and quickly swept into the building.

One terrorist opened fire on the hostages, killing one and wounding two, but was quickly overcome by a canister of tear gas (CS) fired through the window from the outside. A fierce firefight ensued in the following seconds, and four of the five terrorists were killed and one was captured. Meanwhile, the "flash bang" grenades had set the building ablaze, and dense smoke started to pour from the windows. The commandos formed a human chain and literally threw the hostages from man to man until the burning building was evacuated. The entire assault, from beginning to end, lasted only eleven minutes.

If the terrorist represents our darkest nightmares, the terrorist is not without his own nemesis: the counterterrorist. Indeed, one of the basic laws of Newtonian mechanics is that every action produces an equal and opposite reaction. This law finds its political corollary in the rise of the counterterrorist as a reaction to the violence perpetrated by terrorists and their state patrons. As a field of endeavor, counterterrorism (CT) is one of the fastest growing callings in the world today and, in its broadest sense, embraces many elements of the security industry, elite military special operations units, key sectors of the intelligence community, law enforcement, and a plethora of writers, commentators, and shadowy fringe operators to whom terrorism represents both a menace and an opportunity.

In 1983, President Reagan described Ian Fleming's great fictional hero James Bond as "the modern-day version of the great heroes who appeared from time to time throughout history. There were many like him in the past—pioneers, soldiers, lawmen, explorers, people who all went out and put their lives on the line for the cause of good."[33] Reagan went on to say that Bond was "a symbol of real value to the free world." In many respects, however, Reagan's assessment is a little dated: Bond is passé; he's been replaced by the counterterrorist. If the terrorist is the villain of our time, then the counterterrorist is the hero of our time. One suspects that if Fleming had been writing

his Bond novels today, he would have made 007 a counterterrorist rather than a spy.

Counterterrorists may be the heroes of our time in literature
and on the screen, but we are less sure what they are in reality.
They live in a world different from ours; perhaps that is why the
American public was so fascinated by the Iran/Contra hearings,
with its procession of men like Oliver North, Richard Secord,
Felix Rodriguez, and others, characters from Ludlum novels
come to life, veterans of years of nameless wars and secret operations against terrorists and other enemies, real and imagined, of
the United States. However, despite the public's fascination,
polls and interviews indicated that most Americans also had
trouble relating to the Iran/Contra figures, for they represented
the dark underside of the modern U.S. experience as a world
power, an experience that many citizens don't want to think
about or view as somehow inconsistent with and antithetical to
our national character and values.

A special mystique characterizes the world of counterterrorism. At its most dramatic, it's a world with its own taboos,
rituals, and folkways, many unrecognizable to outsiders, a
world with its own language and vernacular, of fetish tools like
K-bar knives, spike mikes, flash grenades, and silenced submachine guns. It is a convoluted twilight world of shadows, shif-
ting alliances, fleeting friendships, betrayal, and violence.

It's the world of an elderly man wearing a black monocle sitting in a Central American hideaway plotting the death of a terrorist, or Israeli hunter-killer teams known as the Wrath of God
tracking down and dealing out swift justice to the perpetrators
of the "Munich Massacre" of 1972, and of tough, athletic,
young U.S. counterterrorist commandos in an airport walking
around stiff-legged like they're looking for someone to piss on.
There is no other club like it, and a special bond exists between
the men of every nationality who "have seen the bear and heard
the hoot owl," who meet terrorists on their own terms in a high-
stakes contest where there is usually only one winner. They are
the special operators, "black workers" who are beckoned to the

shadows by something most can't even put their fingers on, something one counterterrorist commando called the "prospect of an exhilarating death." Others have described the lure of the "orgasmic rush" that comes from playing one of the toughest games to be found anywhere, against some of the most formidable adversaries to be found anywhere, and coming out alive. Like bullfighters, Grand Prix drivers, and devotees of other "blood sports," it is danger itself, what one CT commando called the "thirty seconds of stark terror" that every so often punctuate years of training and boredom, that is the real allure of the profession.

The very names of their terrorist opponents conjure up visions of the grave: Fang of the Earth, the Grey Wolves, Black June, the Party of God, M-19, the Autonomen, the Weather Underground, Direct Action, Black September, the Red Army Faction (Rote Armee Fraktion), Thunderbolt (Sa'aqa), the Machete Wielders (Macheteros), the Union of Fighting Communists, the Shining Path (Sendero Luminoso). Terrorists like Abu Nidal, Kozo Okamoto, and Carlos are the nightmares of our time, twisted and stunted killing machines who have been known to lap up the blood of their victims from the floor and speak of being the germs of a plague that will soon "infect the whole world."[34]

Welcome to the "weird world," the world of counterterrorist commandos and special operators, covert operations and hostage rescue units, writers cum operators and operators cum writers, the world inhabited by Oliver North and many of the Iran/Contra figures. At its best, the "weird world" consists of extraordinarily trained and motivated men and women who put everything on the line to protect our threatened societies from the depredations of terrorists and their state sponsors; at its worst, it is an aggregation of posturers, phonies, fear artists, bozos, hype, and hyperbole. In this connection, it is no coincidence that convicted Israeli spy Jonathan Pollard was a U.S. Navy terrorism analyst. Some observers see Pollard as a desperately insecure figure with thick glasses and an unimposing physique who viewed his work on terrorism and, later, his activities as a spy, as a way of affirming his manhood and as a means to live out his fantasies of being a man of action.

Finally, the world of counterterrorism, despite the secrecy that cloaks it, is also a "hot" field, very much in the public eye. It is a celebrity maker in academe and on the lecture circuit. What Washington dinner party would be complete without its counterterrorism doyen? Just as no candidate for president can afford to be without a policy on terrorism, no television network can afford not to have a "terrorism consultant" and no motion picture company can ignore terrorism as grist for films. The American public, after all, wants to see terrorists get what they deserve. As one high school student remarked in an interview: "Americans went through Vietnam and suffered terrorist attacks. People are sick of America always being wrong. Americans are sick of that. They want the movies to kick their butts around."[35] Americans also want to see terrorists get their butts kicked around in real life.

Anti-CT Paranoia

Not everyone is happy about the new emphasis on muscular counterterrorist skills and capabilities by some Western nations. The hunters are becoming the hunted, and terrorists, long accustomed to carrying out their operations with relative impunity, now often find themselves on the defensive. In addition to terrorists, state sponsors of terrorism like Libya, Iran, Syria, Cuba, the Soviet Union and the Eastern Bloc countries, along with their Third World toadies, regularly condemn the deployment of Western counterterrorist units against terrorist adversaries. But that is to be expected.

What is less well known is the alliance of left-wing journalists, lawyers, politicians, and other activists in Western countries who expend much of their time and resources opposing the efforts of their own governments to protect their fellow citizens from the ravages of terrorism. In the United States, the Washington-based Christic Institute and publications like

The Covert Action Information Bulletin are widely regarded, even within the liberal community, as paranoia mongers that view the counterterrorism community as a sinister aggregation of quick-on-the-trigger thugs and ideologues engaged in all manner of skullduggery from drug running to attempting to overthrow so-called progressive governments like Iran, Nicaragua, and Cuba.

The Christic Institute's founder, Danny Sheehan, maintains that a number of longtime CIA operatives, low-intensity warfare specialists, and Iran/Contra scandal figures are part of a so-called Secret Team that has for years manipulated events on a global scale by means of bribery, selling guns, the training of special counterterrorist and counterinsurgency units, and carrying the war to terrorists and other enemies of the United States by any means possible, including establishment of "an elite direct-action political assassination and terrorist 'interdiction' operation nicknamed 'The Fish Farm.'" In Sheehan's hallucinations, the "enterprise" first described by Richard Secord during the Iran/Contra hearings in 1987 is, in reality, at least a quarter-century old and functions like a secret government with enormous power and resources. Among those he has named as part of the "core group directing the operations of the enterprise" is this author. Despite the gravity of such charges, the Christic Institute has yet to produce any evidence supporting its contentions. In an attempt allegedly to "smoke out" the secret network, Sheehan and the Christics pressed a lawsuit by Martha Honey and Tony Avirgan seeking damages from twenty-nine purported members of the secret network stemming from a 1984 assassination attempt against Contra figure Eden Pastora. After two years of legal proceedings and more than a million dollars in expenses by the defendants, a U.S. District Court judge threw the case out of court. The judge later ordered the Christic Institute to reimburse the defendants for their legal expenses, saying that:

> after two years of protracted and extensive discovery and testimony from scores of witnesses across the United States, Costa Rica, and elsewhere, the plaintiffs were unable to produce a

single witness who could state the defendants exploded the bomb
or were responsible for the assassination attempt. . . . The
Christic Institute's allegations, essentially maintaining that the
plaintiffs were victims of a wide-ranging conspiracy spanning 30
years and involving the activities of former United States government officials, CIA operatives, Colombian druglords and arms
merchants in Cuba, Southeast Asia, the Middle East, and Central America, were based on unsubstantiated rumor and speculation from unidentified sources with no firsthand knowledge.

Some observers have suggested that the Christic Institute was
"fed" disinformation by hostile foreign intelligence services as
a way of attempting to discredit leading counterterrorist advocates both within and outside the U.S. government. Indeed,
long before the October 1986 revelations that led to the Iran/
Contra crisis, Lt. Colonel Oliver North worried aloud that
Sheehan was using the disclosure process, in conjunction with
various lawsuits his organization had filed, as a way of smoking
out the secret U.S. government efforts to support the Contras in
Nicaragua. Little did Sheehan realize that the whole Contra
resupply network, along with the shipment of arms to Iran,
would fall apart on its own.

Sheehan's reckless tactics and unsubstantiated accusations,
many of which smack of McCarthyism, have been pilloried by
thoughtful liberals like Jonathan Kwitny of the *New York Times*.
So low has Sheehan's credibility sunk that an article in *Mother
Jones* magazine described the Christic Institute as "beginning to
get a reputation for attracting the kind of fanatic camp followers
who have occasionally made the Left an embarrassing place to
be."[36]

The world of counterterrorist special operators and spooks is
extremely small and tight. Everyone, it seems, knows everyone
else, or at least someone who knows that person. Members of
the counterterrorist community are bound together by shared
experiences, common values, unusual skills, and what has been
described as the "love of the clandestine." Thus, it is not terribly difficult for the far left to construct real and fictitious link-

ages between different members of the CT community, and to divine monstrous conspiracies where only normal and logical relationships and common endeavors exist.

The Institute for Policy Studies (IPS) is also obsessed by the counterterrorist community and what its members see as a kind of malignant effort to "consolidate LIC (Low-Intensity Warfare) as a standard tool of U.S. intervention."[37] The glassy-eyed zealots at IPS are outraged by the Reagan administration's bombing raid on Libya and similar actions designed to remind terrorist-sponsoring states that there is a price to be paid for their support of international terrorism.

Various left-wing and civil liberties organizations, like the American Civil Liberties Union, have repeatedly attacked Justice Department and law enforcement efforts to monitor the activities of foreign terrorists, and suspected terrorists, operating in the United States. The FBI, for example, has come under fire for its surveillance of the Committee in Solidarity with the People of El Salvador (Cispes) as an antiterrorist investigation. The protests have arisen despite the fact that Cispes openly acknowledges its support of and links to Marxist FMLN rebels in El Salvador, who have committed numerous acts of terrorism, including the murder of four U.S. Marines and the assassination of a U.S. Navy SEAL involved in an undercover mission.

Perhaps most reprehensible are the radical chic attorneys, usually court-appointed, who spend endless hours and taxpayer dollars defending known or suspected terrorists in various courts of law, often completely disregarding considerations of national security or public safety. Many, like New York attorney William M. Kunstler, and organizations like the National Lawyers Guild, abuse their roles as defense lawyers and turn their activities into crusades and public courtrooms into platforms for trashing U.S. foreign policy and articulating their radical philosophies. Kunstler is currently defending a number of accused Puerto Rican terrorists, members of Los Macheteros ("The Machete Wielders"), who are being tried in Hartford, Connecticut, for a $7 million robbery at a Wells Fargo depot in 1983. The U.S. government contends that the money was to be used to support the revolutionary activities of the Macheteros, and that the ringleader, Victor M. Gerena, fled to Cuba after the robbery with the $7 million. According to prosecutors, several of the defendants are also connected to a 1979 attack on a U.S. Navy bus in Puerto Rico that resulted in two deaths.

At the time that Italy refused to hand over the *Achille Lauro* pirates, after the EgyptAir plane flying them to safety had been forced to land at Sigonella Air Base in Sicily by U.S. warplanes, some members of the National Security Council staff actually expressed relief. They had feared that hundreds of ambulance-chasing U.S. lawyers—all with private agendas or eager to garner the media attention surrounding the episode—would have stepped forward offering to represent the terrorists once they were extradited to the United States. Of course, every attorney, for the record, would have decried terrorism and argued that their representation was predicated solely on the desire to see justice done. In reality, the trial would have been a media circus.

2

The Fear Industry

It's a whole new profession in which things are moving so fast, because everything is in real time, that it is difficult to stay ahead of the bad guys.

—E.J. Criscuoli[1]

THE large desk, high-backed leather chair, comfortable sofa, the pictures of the wife and kids: from all outward appearances the office suite could belong to any high-level Washington executive or top-dollar attorney. Only it doesn't. The occupant is a short stocky man with cold grey eyes holding out a nineteen-inch-long German-made submachine gun to a potential customer for him examine.

"Would you like to see it in action?"

"Certainly," replies the prospective customer, examining what is generally regarded as the Cadillac of submachine guns. "I'll make arrangements to come out to your firing range sometime."

"Oh, that won't be necessary," says the weapons dealer off-handedly.

Without missing a beat, he walks over to a nearby closet and flings open the doors, revealing a fifty-five-gallon oil drum filled with sand.

Then, stepping back across the room, he levels the silenced submachine gun and empties a magazine of 9-mm parabellum cartridges into the oil drum, at the rate of twelve rounds a second. There is no real noise, only a faint "pffft" and the sound of bullets ripping into the metal skin of the oil drum. The pungent scent of cordite fills the room.

A scene from a James Bond thriller? Hardly. The incident just described was a routine demonstration of some of the world's deadliest CT small arms in a high-rise office building in the metropolitan Washington area. It is also evidence that one man's adversity is another man's opportunity. The growth of global terrorism has spawned a burgeoning new industry that one Wall Street investment banker has described as "the largest growth industry in the world."

Today, the sale of security services and related paraphernalia is probably a $20 billion a year business in the United States alone, although firm figures are hard to come by. Security school operator Dr. Richard W. Kobetz believes that the figure may be even greater, approaching $50 billion annually. It's hard to get an exact figure regarding the size of the security industry because not everyone defines it the same way or includes the same basket of products and services in assembling their data. While at least two private studies have attempted to reach some conclusions about the size and growth potential of the industry, the U.S. Commerce Department has not indicated any interest in doing a market survey of the industry or in funding a relevant research study.

One source of information about the industry is the American Society for Industrial Security (ASIS). The organization's Executive Vice President is Ernest J. Criscuoli, a short, stout man with powerful arms and shoulders. He wears a heavy linked gold bracelet, a steel-and-gold Rolex watch, and three rings. He is a chain smoker, and with his "tough guy" accent and tinted glasses, he looks like the kind of man who should be running the nation's top industry association for security professionals.

Criscuoli has a reputation as a blunt and effective spokesman for the security industry, and he has guided his organization through a period of rapid growth that reflects the changes taking place in the industry. According to Criscuoli, at the present time there are "probably in excess of one million people involved in the private security sector . . . all the way from the uniformed security officer up to the corporate director of security, and this includes suppliers of security equipment and products."[2] He also cited an estimate that by 1990, the American consumer will spend one percent of the gross national product (GNP) on home and industrial security, or nearly $50 billion.

Mirroring the growth of the security industry, the membership of ASIS has increased 150 percent during the past ten years, from approximately 10,000 members to a present organizational strength of 25,000. According to Criscuoli, over 80 percent of all ASIS members have joined in the past five years. This growth is also reflected in the number of exhibitors at the organization's annual meeting. In 1977, there were only 141 booths sold to exhibitors, involving fewer than 50 companies. A decade later, in 1987, there were 662 exhibit booths, of which 325 belonged to companies. Exhibition space was sold out four months in advance of the 1987 show, held in Las Vegas, and Criscuoli estimates ASIS could have sold booths to another 40 exhibitors if more space had been available.

In 1987, six of *Business Week*'s hundred "best small companies" in the United States were engaged in selling security-related products or services.[3] Today there are more than 5,000 companies engaged in the security business in the United States. They range in size from full-service giants like Pinkerton's, Burns International Security Services, Wells Fargo Guard Services, and Wackenhut, to one- and two-man shops offering only rudimentary flatfoot detective skills or room "sweeps" for electronic eavesdropping devices. In 1985, Wackenhut alone had revenues of more than $300 million, with operations in 28 countries. Founded in the 1950s by former FBI officer George Wackenhut, who presides over his security empire from a grotto-like office in Coral Gables, Florida, its board of directors has included such luminaries as former CIA Director William Raborn, Jr., and former Secretary of Defense Frank Carlucci.

If steel and autos represent industries in decline in this country, then security is one sure bet for lifetime employment without having to be totally retrained 2½ times, which some studies estimate will be the norm for anyone entering the work force today. More than 90 percent of the revenues in the security field are earned by firms that provide basic security services like industrial security programs, detective services, courier services, security guards, armored car deliveries, and the like, along with various hardware manufacturers of such products as security fencing, secure communications equipment, pop-up barriers, I.D. and recognition systems, body armor, and armored—or "hardened"—vehicles. Nevertheless, there is a growing demand for highly specialized counterterrorist and crisis management services geared to the international terrorist threat. As security specialist Richard Kobetz observes, "I recall vividly, ten years ago, when I talked about terrorism . . . . people thinking it was a big hustle." But no longer, says Kobetz, "Now those same people are terrorism consultants."[4] The demand for terrorism-related security services has been driven by a series of spectacular terrorist incidents. One need only consider the impact that skyjacker D.B. Cooper had on the airline industry, or the threat of vehicle bombs and their impact on the design and protection of government buildings and industry.

In addition to the more traditional services and equipment, the contemporary security industry embraces dozens of new skills and products. According to E.J. Criscuoli of ASIS, "security people are handling areas never thought of when I first entered the profession in 1956 such as substance abuse, bomb threats, executive protection, coupon fraud, computer security, product tampering and even AIDS."[5] According to Criscuoli, AIDS often becomes the security director's responsibility because he is charged with ensuring a "safe and secure" workplace. If an employee of the company contracts AIDS, the workplace may be disrupted by that individual's coworkers rebelling against the presence of an AIDS victim in their midst. To head off such a problem, Criscuoli says security officers may need to institute corporate educational programs.

The computer revolution has presented terrorists and criminals with dazzling new opportunities for mischief. As former Carter administration official R. James Woolsey has noted, much of our money and information have been "reduced to electrons."[6] Computers are vital to everything from our national defense to our transportation networks, food distribution systems, electrical grids, and nearly every other facet of our infrastructure, and one individual who knows how the system works can inflict tremendous damage on it, and potentially even dismantle our entire economy. The need for computer security has spawned dozens of new firms tailored to everything from preventing malicious mischief to computer theft, extortion, and sabotage. There is even one case of attempted murder by computer, which involved the 1980 attempt by an air traffic controller to create a mid-air collision involving an aircraft carrying former Soviet Ambassador to the United States, Anatoly Dobrynin. The controller apparently removed the Soviet plane from the master terminal to his own terminal, and then deleted it completely. The average computer security specialist has more in common with "Revenge of the Nerds" than James Bond, but in many respects computer counterterrorists are likely to be on the front lines of the war against terrorism in the not-too-distant future.

A closely related new security field involves efforts to prevent the pirating of computer software, videocassettes, and other so-called intellectual property, as well as the counterfeiting of designer goods like clothing and handbags. U.S. motion picture executives believe that the sale and exhibition of non-licensed videos costs them $1 billion a year.[7] Universal Studios' chief sleuth is a lawyer-turned-enforcer by the name of Charles Morgan, affectionately known to some of his adversaries as "Tombstone Face."

While the United States represents the single largest market for the sale of security products and services, the security industry is also booming overseas. The value of all products and services sold worldwide is estimated to exceed $150 billion. A recent Frost & Sullivan study on "Security & Intrusion Detection in Europe," for example, estimated that the $646 million in security and intrusion detection systems sold in 1987 would rise to almost $1 billion in 1991, measured in 1986 dollars.[8]

UXB International, Inc., which provides explosives training and bomb disposal services, sent out Christmas cards in 1987 wishing their friends and clients: "Have a *BLAST* during the Holidays!" Based in Washington, D.C., and headed by Philip G. Hough, a friend and U.S. Naval Academy classmate of Oliver North, UXB has rapidly established itself as a leader in the clearing of mine fields and artillery ranges, in the destruction of old ordnance and the handling of hazardous materials, and "combatting improvised explosive devices," meaning terrorist and criminal bombs. The firm takes its name from the World War II–era acronym for "unexploded bomb." All of UXB's personnel are former military EOD (explosives ordnance disposal) specialists.

The EOD community is a world unto itself. A former special operator attended a seminar on terrorist bombs for EOD specialists, and later reported that, "I've never been in a room with so many people missing parts of their bodies." Indeed, missing fingers are virtually a rite of passage. Because bombs are currently the terrorist weapon of choice, few specialties have as much relevance as military and law enforcement EOD teams and the private firms that work closely with them.

Bullshit Artists and Incompetents

The meeting was scheduled for midnight at the Crossways Motel near Miami International Airport. The motel was notorious for the frequent "floaters" in the swimming pool, and guests that failed—permanently—to answer their wake-up calls. On the positive side, the Crossways did have one of the best bars near the airport, with a nine-piece Latin brass band and good-looking Latin whores who sported only a limited number of tat-toos and gold teeth. It was one of those places where they were a little uncomfortable with credit cards since so many customers paid cash: crisp new hundred dollar bills peeled off thick rolls.

The security company chief was paranoid about his own security. The Colombian terrorist group M-19 was after him, he maintained over the telephone, because of the help his Bogota-based firm had given to the DAS, Colombia's dreaded secret police, in breaking open the case involving the theft of hundreds of weapons and thousands of rounds of ammunition from Colombia's national arsenal. It would be a low-profile meeting, he continued, and those he was meeting with should take pains to ensure that there was no surveillance.

The security man arrived at the Crossways at 12:05 A.M. His arrival on the scene, however, was far from being unnoticed—in fact, it was noted by virtually everyone within eyesight. He was 6 feet 6 inches tall, dressed from head-to-toe in white (white shoes, white socks, white pants, white belt, white shirt), and, as if that wasn't enough, he was an albino: pink eyes, bleached white skin, a white Afro. "This guy would have stood out in a convention of freaks," quipped one of those he met with, who immediately dubbed him "the White Knight." As every conversation stopped in mid-sentence and every eye turned toward him, he whispered conspiratorially that he was "the man from Bogota."

It later turned out that his security company was on the verge of bankruptcy and that most of the security systems he had installed were far inferior to those that his clients had paid for. He had siphoned off most of his company's profits into a foreign bank account; the only people after him were his creditors, not the M-19. He was the quintessential con man, and his unusual appearance and melodramatics, it was later discovered, had actually added to his credibility in the minds of many potential clients, especially business clients who should have known better. Victims of too many B-grade movies and cheap novels, they frankly expected that a counterterrorist security chieftain should look a little weird.

The chairman of a major motion picture studio fell into the same trap when he berated his bodyguard, an ex-Delta Force operator, for not standing next to him the way the bodyguards of one of his stars did. His security man patiently explained to him that wearing dark glasses, black shirts, and white ties, and bullying everyone that got in the way did not necessarily constitute good security. If he stuck to his client like glue, he continued, any assassin would be able to finger him as the security man and would take him out first, thus leaving the producer totally defenseless.

Security professionals, for the most part, provide their services quietly and competently, with a minimum of fanfare. For the security consumer, those who trade on mystique and flamboyance should be avoided, or at least examined very closely before any decision is made regarding their products or services.

The security industry presently is going through a major shakedown period, following its rapid growth during the 1970s. After the 1973 energy crisis, it sometimes seemed like every former service station operator hung out a shingle advertising himself as an "energy expert." Similarly, the security industry boom has witnessed literally thousands of retired law enforcement officers, ex-spooks, would-be soldiers of fortune, and a mixed bag of what can only be described as opportunists setting themselves up as security consultants, offering a wide variety of often inferior services and products to fill the market demand. "Everyone was purporting to be able to do a security survey," says Kobetz, "from former cops to schoolteachers." Horror stories abound. One security professional recounts stories of companies that sold elaborate security systems that failed to work at all and training programs with such poor-quality instructors that the entire class walked out by the second session. In Colombia, bullet-resistant glass installed in the windows of the presidential palace fell out because the security company was unaware that the window frames would have to be strengthened to accommodate the extra weight. A number of prominent individuals actually have even been victimized—usually robbed or blackmailed—by members of their security staff, the very people charged with their protection. Indeed, it is well to remember that Indian Prime Minister Indira Gandhi was assassinated by one of her own bodyguards.

The fly-by-night operators and incompetents are now being weeded out as customers become more sophisticated and discriminating. Some companies have failed as fast as their security systems, or at least as fast as they could cash the client's check. Others have failed because their products and services do not keep pace with technological developments or the changing threat landscape. Another problem is that many smaller security companies are simply poorly managed, since the skills needed to be a successful operator or security specialist do not necessarily translate to the executive suite.

Moreover, there has been too much crying "wolf" by some firms that employ fear as their chief marketing strategy. It has not taken long for most customers to catch on to the scam. "You don't find the fly-by-nights in the Yellow Pages a year later," says E.J. Criscuoli. Nor is it possible to simply trade on mystique, as many Israeli security firms have done. Indeed, dozens of former Israeli military men and Mossad operatives have attempted to supplement their modest pensions by going into the security business. The only thing many of these firms really have to sell is Israel's international reputation for conducting tough and effective counterterrorist operations. Nevertheless, there are still an estimated 200 Israeli security companies seeking to do business in the United States.

The turnover in the industry has been significant. One security company chief, whose firm provides extensive training programs, described how he sent out a mailing to 30,000 security specialists—firms, consultants, equipment suppliers—and had 3,000 returned to him with no forwarding address, representing a 10-percent attrition rate in only two years since his last mailing to purge his list of inactive customers. And this does not take into account marginal firms and retired half-timers still in the business.

It has been suggested in some quarters that greater government regulation of the security industry will be necessary to protect the public. ASIS's Criscuoli, however, believes that the marketplace will ultimately eliminate the incompetents and fast-buck artists, and that the industry does not need or require new regulations and licensing requirements. Word will get around about those who don't perform properly, he maintains.

Mission Impossible, Inc.

In chess, the term checkmate comes from the Persian word "shah-mat," which means that the shah is helpless. That was the case early one morning in 1980.

The man who summoned him was a partner in a leading Washington law firm. "The Shah is in trouble," explained the distinguished silver-haired attorney in the well-cut suit in a slow, modulated voice, hands folded together in front of him, as they sat in his glassed-in aerie in the nation's capital. "We don't know if the Panamanians will let him leave Contadora. In the event that he is placed under house arrest, can you mount a rescue mission to spirit him off the island?"

The counterterrorist specialist sat bolt-upright in his chair, nearly upsetting his coffee. It was too early in the morning for people to drop things like this on him.

He reflected for a moment, then spoke. "It can be done, but it would take a good deal of money."

"That, of course, is no problem," replied the attorney.

The security man agreed to stand by for further word. Ultimately, however, the operation was scrapped because the Shah, with the help of the CIA, managed to escape to Egypt before the Panamanian government could act to detain him.

To the uninitiated, such a request might seem bizarre, if not bordering on the fantastic. However, in our dangerous world it represents the daily stock and trade of a small handful of firms worldwide that undertake dangerous one-of-a-kind assignments. Many of the requests they receive read like scripts from "Mission Impossible." Most of the contracts are oral, and few of these operations ever appear in the media. Perhaps a majority of such firms operate in close cooperation with their national intelligence agencies, or at the very least their sufferance. A few may even be proprietary companies, set up and actually funded by intelligence services.

Secrecy and security are the hallmarks of such firms. As you approach the door of one company known for providing what can only be described as high-risk high-price services, one is immediately aware that your every movement is being scrutinized by a closed-circuit television camera. You ring the buzzer and a voice asks you to state your business. After a short delay the door buzzes open and you step inside, passing through a metal detector built into the frame of the door. Instead of a large reception room, however, you find yourself in a narrow booth of bullet-resistant laminated plastic. Only after a second perusal from inside does the door at the rear of the booth click open, allowing you into the actual reception area.

"We are a court of last resort," explains the managing director of the firm. "An option when all else fails. The gentle sheep that chases away nightmares."

One company, Oil Field Security Consultants, used to advise clients that it could have a team of commandos on location, anyplace in the world, within twenty-four hours to rescue hostage executives, captive oil rigs, or other company assets targeted by adversaries. Another firm, Corporate Training Unlimited (CTU), based in the Fayetteville, North Carolina, area and composed almost entirely of former Delta Force operators, will undertake dangerous one-of-a-kind missions so long as they do not violate U.S. law (see chapter 3). Defense Analysts, Ltd., a British firm, provides former British SAS and SBS (Special Boat Service) commandos and defensive technology to tanker firms transporting oil through the deadly waters of the Persian Gulf.

Two Texas men purportedly were paid $20,000 of a promised $2 million to secure the release of Soviet physicist Andrei Sakharov, but the attempt to trade Sakharov for allegedly highly sensitive intelligence information never materialized because of security leaks by the family, which jeopardized the mission. The two men claim that they later were approached by the U.S. government to conduct reconnaissance of secret terrorist training camps in Mexico, as well as to collect information on Libyan money laundering operations.

One of the most secretive and feared such firms is Keeny Meeny Services, Inc., or KMS, which is chartered in the Channel Islands and reputed to have "more badass soldiers than the 22nd SAS does." The term Keeny Meeny is Swahili for "slithering snake," and describes "the sinuous, unseen movement of a snake in the long grass."[9] Over the years it has come to mean, in SAS circles, a kind of quiet, lethal, high-risk, undercover work. Based in London and composed largely of former members of the twenty-second SAS commandos, KMS's founder, former SAS Major David Walker, apparently was in touch with Lt. Colonel Oliver North in 1984 about carrying out certain special operations in Nicaragua under contract to the FDN (Nicaraguan Democratic Force). Although details are sketchy, it appears that KMS supplied arms and contract pilots to the FDN, as well as conducted sabotage missions against the Sandinistas.

KMS reportedly has been involved in similar operations throughout the world, often carrying out "deniable" missions on behalf of the British government. According to newspaper reports, KMS men are known to have operated in Oman, Saudi Arabia, Kuwait, Lebanon, Pakistan, Bahrain, Sri Lanka, Northern Ireland, Uganda, Sudan, Argentina, the United States, and possibly in Angola, with Jonas Savimbi's UNITA rebels. One of the firm's biggest contracts in recent years has been with the Sri Lankan government which, until a settlement agreement was reached in 1987, was engaged in a protracted guerrilla war with Tamil separatists. The Keeny Meeny men provided training to elite Sinhalese counterterrorist forces and taught the Sri Lankans to fly U.S.-made helicopter gunships. KMS also works through an affiliated company known as Saladin, which currently has twelve men with diplomatic status in Washington, D.C., charged with protecting Saudi Arabian ambassador Prince Bandar.

Colonel David Sterling, founder of the British SAS (Special Air Service), recently founded a new London-based firm named KAS, offering a menu of highly specialized security services. Staffed with former SAS men, KAS reportedly is already thriving.

Many of the extraordinary-services companies are not companies at all, but loose aggregations of individuals with special backgrounds who come together to carry out high-risk, high-pay missions. Whatever their composition, however, during recent years there has been big money in hostage negotiation and, in special cases, retrieval. When a key corporate executive or loved one is kidnapped by terrorists or brigands, friends and relatives will often go to any lengths to secure their return.

It seems as though there is always someone in trouble in some distant land: a son jailed in a North African country for possession of drugs, the soles of whose feet are beaten once a week by a guard with a rubber truncheon in order to impede escape attempts; a businessman imprisoned in Iraq on trumped-up charges; a hostage in Lebanon held by the Hizballah. Although not a traditional hostage incident, there was the case of a private jet that disappeared with ten million dollars in industrial diamonds on board. Its last reported position was near Luxor, Egypt, and the owners want someone to go look for it.

Among the real-life rescue missions undertaken by individuals and firms in recent years have been the recovery of kidnapped children. Corporate Training Unlimited (CTU) has successfully mounted at least five real-life rescue missions since 1988. One episode involved the rescue of a child who had been kidnapped by her father and taken to Jordan, in violation of a U.S. court order (see chapter 3). Another was the rescue of an American mother and child from Tunisia, where they had been virtually held under lock-and-key by the father.

Yet another successful rescue mission in the Arab world (undertaken by a different firm) involved a U.S. businessman imprisoned in Saudi Arabia after a falling out with his Saudi business partners, in what has become an increasingly common tactic by the Saudis to extort money from foreigners. After nearly six months in prison, prison guards were bribed to permit the businessman to escape. Once on the outside, he took refuge in the U.S. embassy. For all intents and purposes, however, he was trapped there. Thus, a rescue operation was pulled together. After appropriate preparations, the man left the embassy, rendezvoused with the rescue team, and was placed behind a false wall in a cargo container and driven out of Saudi Arabia and over the border into Jordan, thereby eluding security at all Saudi ports and airports.

Sometimes the decision as to whether or not a rescue attempt is undertaken boils down to a matter of economics, as in the case of this 1979 memo to the operations chief of a counterterrorism/executive protection company:

I was talking to a man in Miami the other day who was on his way to El Salvador to help negotiate the release of a prisoner held by a terrorist group. This group allegedly had relations with the Sandinistas in Nicaragua. The victim, a wealthy Jewish businessman, was being held in [*sic*] $7,000,000 ransom. His family was reluctant to pay any ransom but had offered $2,000,000 to any group that could go in [and] snatch him back. They were going to pay my friend $25,000 just to go in for a look and maybe talk to one of the terrorists. He is an electronics technician and had little stomach for any violence which might be lurking in the city square.

The counterterrorism/executive protection firm expressed an interest in the $2 million, but the family delayed so long in making a decision that the patriarch was killed by the kidnappers, thus ensuring that his entire fortune would remain intact for them to inherit.

Another unusual request came from the legislative assistant to a powerful Democratic senator from a western state. "My boss," began the congressional aide, as the two men sat in the shadows in the back of the Monocle restaurant on Capitol Hill, "is deeply concerned about a friend and contributor who has been slapped into prison in Nigeria and is being held incommunicado. He has discussed the matter with both the U.S. embassy there and with the CIA, but since the man is neither a resident of this country nor an American citizen there's nothing really they can do for him. A lawyer from D.C. has been sent to Lagos with a suitcase of money in hopes of buying the man's freedom, but he was detained for not having a proper visa when he arrived." The aide paused for a moment to give his words added effect, then resumed speaking. "The man is extremely wealthy and will pay whatever it costs to get him out. What do you say?"

"Let me make a phone call."

Twenty minutes later they were joined by another man who, it turned out, had spent considerable time in Nigeria. They left the restaurant and walked through the tree-shaded park north of the U.S. capitol, dropping their voices whenever someone passed by. The most recent arrival knew the particular prison where the man was being held.

"The commandant can be bribed," he explained. "I suggest that we try to buy his way out, and only if that is impossible to hit the prison with a commando unit."

Ultimately, bribery worked and the rescue operation was never mounted.

Perhaps the most famous private sector rescue mission involving U.S. citizens was that orchestrated by Texas billionaire Ross Perot in 1979 during the turmoil that accompanied the fall of the Shah. Two executives of Perot's company, Electronic Data Systems Corporation (EDS), were imprisoned by corrupt Iranian officials and held for a $13 million ransom. Perot vowed to get the men back, whatever the cost. To this end, he contacted the legendary Special Forces officer Colonel Arthur "Bull" Simmons, who led the 1970 raid on the Son Tay prison camp in North Vietnam to rescue American POWs. Although the American commandos successfully reached Son Tay, the prison was empty, having been evacuated only days earlier. Before his retirement from active duty, Simmons had worked with Delta Force to improve the unit's sniping skills.

Simmons agreed to lead the effort to retrieve the EDS men, perhaps because of the heartbreaking failure of the Son Tay operation to free any American POWs, rejecting any notion of compensation from Perot. It was to be a fateful last hurrah for the old warrior.

From the executive ranks of EDS, Simmons recruited a team of men—all volunteers—to participate in the bold operation. He chose only combat veterans on the theory that they would not have any illusions about the hazards involved or false notions of glory. In fact, he wanted infantrymen, not pilots or naval officers, men who had not been detached from the grim reality of combat, who had actually seen others die at close range.

Simmons and his unit infiltrated into Tehran, which was chaotic and rife with civil strife. After deciding against a military attack on Ghasr Prison, where the EDS men were being held,

Simmons arranged for a mob to storm the prison, freeing the two jailed executives along with the other prisoners. From Tehran, they made their way overland to Turkey, but not before a series of narrow escapes.

The rescue operation cost Perot over $250,000, but the money was clearly immaterial to the risks involved. As Perot later told an interviewer Richard Shenkman:

> We were risking everything, facing the possibility of prison. Now you start thinking that all the way through. Put your lawyer hat on and say, What if this hadn't worked? What if some of the men or the rescue team had gotten killed? You see what I mean? The legal implications were a horror. Forget the imagery. The imagery would have been as bad as you could possibly make it. But the legal implications would have been terrible. EDS would have been blamed. I would have been blamed. And I would probably be in prison or on my way there right now, because we had the status of mercenaries. So we were betting the company name, its assets, our assets, everything we'd accumulated to get those two guys out. Thank God it worked.[10]

To the credit of Perot and his men, they succeeded. It was a classic American story of guts and derring-do. But more importantly, it is a clear indication of what can happen when governments fail to adequately protect their citizens from foreign despots and hostage-takers: it is an open invitation for the private sector to do the job. As Justice Benjamin N. Cardozo once observed: "Danger invites rescue."

Mission Mozambique

In recent years, one of television's most popular heroes has been the "Equalizer." Played by British actor Robert Woodward, the "Equalizer" is a man who runs an ad in the newspaper offering to "equalize the odds" for the downtrodden and the afflicted, especially when the authorities are blind or indifferent to their problems. According to producer Jim McAdams, "It's a nice thought that there's a number to call and a man who seems to have unlimited resources comes to your rescue if your cause is worthy."[11] Interestingly, during the late 1970s a Washington, D.C., security and crisis management firm ran ads in business and security magazines stating, "If you have only one call to make, call [firm's name]."

But are there real-life "Equalizers"? Men and women that will undertake, for a price, high-risk one-of-a-kind missions?

You better believe it.

One of those available to carry out unique and dangerous missions is Bob Jordan (not his real name).[12] Jordan is a 39-year-old Vietnam veteran who joined the Rhodesian SAS, and subsequently rose to become squadron commander. The SAS conducted a bitter counterinsurgency campaign against communist-backed guerrillas in Rhodesia, including bold cross-border raids into neighboring black-ruled nations that were providing aid and sanctuary to the guerrillas. Jordan was awarded both the Rhodesian silver and bronze crosses for gallantry, as well as other medals, making him one of the most decorated members of the Rhodesian Defense Forces. Following the fall of the white settler government, he served as commander of a South African reconnaissance unit, and later second-in-command of the Transkei Special Forces Regiment.

Today Jordan lives in Seattle, and divides his time between a foundation supporting "freedom fighters" and occasional special assignments that permit him to jump into the globe's "hot spots" to do what he calls "good deeds." A handsome, well-muscled man in a leather sport coat, boots, jeans, and dark glasses, he exudes quiet professionalism and none of the bravado so characteristic of frauds and phonies. Bob Jordan is a professional adventurer and soldier, and, in a world of posturers and con artists who wouldn't know an umbrella from an assault rifle, he's been at war for the past quarter-century, and is good at what he does. Some would call him a mercenary, but that would be unfair since he is motivated by a combination of strong principles and a lust for action. He is not unmindful of the money, since he has alimony payments and a son in military school, but the money is a secondary consideration.

His most recent mission began in the summer of 1987 when

he was contacted by the Washington office of RENAMO, the anti-communist Mozambican resistance movement. Six Western missionaries and a child, including a young woman from Texas, had been taken in tow by RENAMO guerrillas three months earlier, purportedly for their own safety. The guerrillas offered to turn over the missionaries to the International Red Cross, but Red Cross officials decided that it would be too dangerous. The State Department, for its part, was sitting on the sidelines, since the United States recognizes the Marxist regime in Maputo, and claimed to have no direct contact with RENAMO. The Texas woman's congressman, however, was calling for a helicopter carrier to be deployed in the Indian Ocean and for Delta Force to be sent in to get his constituent and her companions. Under pressure from the congressman and other lawmakers, Tom Schaaf, the head of the Mozambique Research Center, affiliated with RENAMO, agreed to help retrieve the missionaries. He called Jordan, knowing of his past experience in southern Africa and his ties to RENAMO.

Jordan met with Schaaf at the home of a well-known Washington banker. Also present was Larry Moffit, executive director of the World Media Association, an organization funded by the Unification Church. Moffit was about to embark on a three week fact-finding tour of southern Africa with a group of prominent Americans called "The Geopolitical Task Force on Southern Africa." From a public relations point of view, Moffit and the banker thought it would be just dandy if Jordan could locate the missionaries and bring them out of Mozambique in time to turn them over to the fact-finding group as it arrived in neighboring Malawi. Although skeptical of the timetable, Jordan agreed to undertake the mission for $1,000 a week, which would be paid by Youth With a Mission, a church group with whom the Texas woman was affiliated. The Geopolitical Task Force on Southern Africa would pick up the airline tickets, hotel bills, and car rentals. They also came up with funds for a high-frequency radio. Jordan still needed "walking around" money, so he called *Soldier of Fortune* publisher Bob Brown, who sent Jordan $1,500 by express mail for expenses. Brown later told Jordan that he was "crazy" for charging so little, that he "should have charged ten times as much," but Jordan felt that the retrieval fell into the category of "a good deed" and that he didn't have any interest "in ripping people off."[13]

Ultimately, Jordan traveled to Malawi, armed with a letter of safe passage from the RENAMO office and, since many of the guerrillas cannot read, photos of himself taken on an earlier trip with many top RENAMO leaders. He received some logistical assistance from a South African–based missionary, including use of a missionary "safe house" in Malawi and several dirt bikes. Using his contacts in the Malawi government, he arranged—or at least he thought he did—to transit the border on foot at a river crossing. Jordan passed through the Malawi checkpoint and crossed a narrow bridge. He rapidly made contact with a couple of young guerrillas, both around 14 years old and armed with AK-47s, on the other side of the river. Both were suspicious of him but agreed to take him to their local headquarters, about three kilometers distant.

As they walked down the rutted road, they were stopped by an older RENAMO guerrilla, apparently an NCO, who "was fucked out of his mind."[14] Not only was he drunk, but he took instant offense to the unarmed white man who had so brazenly entered RENAMO-controlled territory. Presumably illiterate, he waved off the letter of safe conduct and photos. He marched Jordan back to the bridge at gunpoint and ordered him to strip, confiscating anything he took a fancy to. By this time a small crowd of curious onlookers had gathered. Jordan knew he could "take out" the drunk NCO, but he didn't know how the other guerrillas would react. The incident began to get out of hand when the NCO tried to arrest the Malawi border guard for permitting Jordan to enter Mozambique.

Suddenly, a RENAMO officer appeared on a bicycle. Apparently one of the young guerrillas had gone to fetch him. Jordan assumed he was an officer because he was wearing a sidearm and a Sony Walkman, two ubiquitous hallmarks of RENAMO officers. Often there are no tapes or batteries in the Walkman; it's merely a sign of status. The officer realized the

NCO was drunk and he immediately took charge. After examining the documents and photos, he became very apologetic and dismissed the NCO harshly. "I'd like to think he was severely beaten later," says Jordan.[15]

The officer did not know anything about the missionaries nor had anyone told him that Jordan was coming. He said he would go back and make radio contact with his headquarters, and he and Jordan agreed to meet again 48 hours later. Jordan returned to Malawi, only to find that the incident at the border had "raised waves" back in Blantyre, the capital. Jordan was summoned back to Blantyre to meet with Malawi security officers, who were concerned that their apparent cooperation might offend the Mozambican government in Maputo. While affirming that they had given him permission to cross into Mozambique, they now contended that they meant at night, and not via the bridge.

Jordan readily acceded to their wishes, and the next night crossed the river on a flat-bottom punt with the dirt bikes and two companions. Once again, it did not take long to link up with RENAMO guerrillas. This time there was no problem in establishing his bona fides. After passing the night at a RENAMO base, they departed cross-country on the motor bikes for a larger base, which in turn sent them onto the provincial headquarters ("Zambezi Central") of RENAMO. All of this took the better part of a day, over extremely rugged terrain.

The headquarters was composed of two bases, each capable of holding in excess of a thousand troops. Most of the structures were grass-roofed huts, and there were parade grounds, soccer fields, ammo dumps, and even a reviewing stand. Although the bases were well camouflaged, they had been bombed on a number of occasions by Zimbabwean aircraft in support of their fraternal Marxist allies in Maputo. There were few anti-aircraft guns, bunkers, or gunputs, however, since RENAMO's general method of dealing with an air strike is simply to disperse into the bush until the attack is over.

Jordan met a number of old RENAMO acquaintances at the headquarters and relaxed in the mild upland climate while the

RENAMO leadership decided how a rendezvous would be arranged with the missionaries, who were two hundred kilometers to the south. In the meantime, the dirt bikes were requisitioned for a special mission by the headquarters commander, leaving Jordan without transportation. RENAMO's planes were grounded because of heavy enemy air activity between "Zambezi Central" and the region where the missionaries were, so Jordan could not be transported to the south. Thus, it was finally decided that the missionaries would move overland in a northerly direction and meet Jordan at a rendezvous point on the Zambezi River near the Malawi border.

Jordan was awakened in the middle of the night by guerrillas, who escorted him in a driving rain storm over the mountains and back down to the Zambezi, a distance of nearly one hundred kilometers. There, he waited at a platoon-sized RENAMO outpost, which he characterized as "a dump," for the missionaries to arrive. It was hot, humid, and the rations were poor. At one point, he received a message that the missionary party was being ordered to turn back because of fighting ahead of them. Jordan blew up, and demanded that they be ordered to press on. The whole world was watching, he told RENAMO leaders by radio, and if the missionaries didn't come out now it would be a major setback for RENAMO in the international media. After assessing the weight of Jordan's arguments, the RENAMO leadership relented and countermanded their earlier order. The missionary party was told to press onward.

Finally, after several more days passed, Jordan was breakfasting on yams in the sparse shade of a nearly leafless tree when he saw a weary-looking RENAMO guerrilla covered with dust stumble into camp. Seconds later, the post commander hopped on his motor bike and disappeared down the road, only to return a few minutes later with an elderly white woman and a small blond child on the back of the Honda. "Praise the Lord," she exclaimed when her eyes fell on Jordan, the first outsider she had seen in more than three months. The camp commander took off again, and soon all six missionaries and the child had been assembled at the outpost. Only one of the missionaries had walked the entire two hundred kilometers. The others, debilitated by malaria and poor diet, had been transported on stretcher-like litters. All had foot problems caused by parasites and were covered with mosquito bites.

Anticipating their condition, Jordan had brought with him clothing, medicine, sandals, soap, toothbrushes, sanitary napkins, and shaving material. After tending to their medical needs and hygiene, the missionaries were permitted to rest for the remainder of the day before departing for Malawi the following morning. It took about an hour-and-a-half on foot, and another hour-and-a-half by dugout canoe through a swampy area infested with hippos, to reach the Malawi border, where they were met by the U.S. chargé d'affaires and some missionary colleagues. They were taken to another missionary "safe house" until the next step could be sorted out between the various interested governments.

The Mozambique government wanted the missionaries flown to Maputo for an official "release" ceremony, so that the Marxist regime could take credit for their freedom. The missionaries, sick and exhausted from their ordeal, just wanted to return to their families and friends, and did not want to go back to Mozambique. Ultimately, it was decided they were to be flown to Harare, Zimbabwe, where there were some tense moments, requiring the intervention of the United States and other governments, before the missionaries were finally permitted to go on to wherever they wanted.

By this time, of course, Jordan had quietly slipped away to South Africa, in preparation for his anonymous return to the States. When asked later if, all things being equal, he would do it again, he responded, "Of course. I've got to do good deeds." The mission to Mozambique was not Jordan's first one-of-a-kind special assignment, nor will it probably be his last. After leaving military service in Transkei, Jordan, posing as a tourist, conducted a reconnaissance of the Seychelles in the aftermath of the failed coup led by "Mad Mike" Hoare. Jordan concluded that a second, better-planned and better-executed operation would probably be successful at overthrowing the existing regime and installing a new government, but nothing ever came of the plan. Jordan has also carried out a number of private intelligence assignments, served for several months in El Salvador as a recon instructor, and explored the possibilities of a coup in Suriname. He just returned from Mozambique after completing another mission. His work comes to him through word-of-mouth, and he performs his assignments quietly and efficiently, without notching his gun or advertising his successes. He's not in the Yellow Pages.

Caveat Emptor 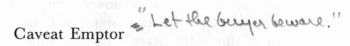 = "Let the buyer beware."

Unfortunately, some of those firms and individuals that offer to perform extraordinary services are, in reality, con artists and frauds. They generally take advantage of the grief and desperation of those in trouble, or their friends and relatives, in order to extract from them large sums of money for services they have no intention of performing or, even worse, for harebrained rescue schemes that could get them or the hostage(s) killed. A number of scams targeted at the families of those missing in action in Southeast Asia have been perpetrated in recent years. The pitch is always the same: the "rescuers" claim to have reports of fair-skinned men being held in a remote prison somewhere in Southeast Asia. They would be willing to mount an expedition to check out such reports, but they need someone to underwrite the cost. There is still hope, and, if the families would just dig into their pockets, who knows what miracles might be possible? Several of the families of hostages being held in Lebanon have also received unsolicited offers from various middlemen and private-sector commandos to rescue—for a price—their loved ones.

Then there are the would-be assassins who offer to kill terrorists or communists for a fee. "I don't do dogs or wogs, just terr's," offered one self-described "wet" operator of dubious credentials. Such men often pitch their services to governments and the exiled opponents of existing governments. "Hits are a big one," says one private operator, who knows of a number of plots to kill various African leaders. Most of the plots, he says, never had a chance of succeeding, because a majority of those offering to do the dirty work were frauds or incompetents. The Rev. Ndabaningi Sithole, who broke with his protégé Robert Mugabe and later tried to have him assassinated, was "taken" by con artists so many times that he once approached a man in an elevator to see if he would perform a hit for him.

Even individuals and organizations that should know better occasionally get taken by fast-talking con men who claim to be able to perform extraordinary services. The Seychelles Liberation Army (SLA), for example, a London-based group seeking to overthrow the Marxist regime in the Seychelles, lost $31,000 to a self-described purveyor of extraordinary services who promised to come up with a plan for a new coup attempt, after the failure of the one led by former Congo mercenary "Mad Mike" Hoare. Just before he was scheduled to deliver all of the plans and data, he staged a phony police raid and later told SLA leaders that all of his work had been confiscated. A number of U.S. police departments have also reportedly been victimized by bogus counterterrorism specialists. One California-based "operator" who solicited work on the East Coast even listed "wars, uprisings, revolutions, coups d'etat, and assassinations" on his business card. Subtle, eh? Another Rambo-for-hire ran the following advertisement: "FOR HIRE Short Term, High Risk preferred, have passport, will travel. No job too dangerous." Anyone interested should contact "Bob" at a post office box in Downey, California.

Central America has been overrun in recent years by "flakes" purporting to be assassins or counterterrorist specialists. The government of El Salvador, locked in a protracted struggle with Marxist guerrillas, has had dozens of offers from men with little or no military background or experience to "hit" enemy chieftains or to train Salvadoran troops in the finer points of counterinsurgency. In the early days of their struggle against the Sandinista government in Nicaragua, the American-backed Contras accepted offers of assistance from several American "soldiers of fortune," who later turned out to be frauds. After being rejected by the Contras, one of them became an outspoken foe of U.S. support to anti-Sandinista insurgents and an informant to a Senate committee investigating the Iran/Contra matter.

Another Contra washout is Sam Hall, who was captured by the Sandinistas in 1986 and subsequently released. Hall has recently collaborated on a book about his CT exploits entitled *Counter-Terrorist*.[16] One participant in the Contra war remembers first meeting Hall in a jungle camp near the Nicaraguan border. He was dressed in a white tee-shirt, olive drab shorts, combat boots, and utility cap, holding a branch tucked tightly beneath his arm like a swagger stick. He seemed to be relishing his self-asserted role as a white commandante to a group of Miskito Indian fighters. Contra leaders, however, distrusted Hall's abilities and worried about his mental soundness after he showed them photos of himself stitching up a bayonet wound in his side. Hall says that he received the bayonet wound "during a firefight in Nicaragua," but other sources say that it was inflicted during a training accident.

Lt. Colonel Oliver North's liaison to the Contras, Rob Owen, remembers being in a taxi in downtown Tegucigalpa (referred to in shorthand as "the Goose") with Hall when he looked over and said, "I'm forty-eight. By the time I'm fifty, I want to accomplish something really notable."[17] Two years later, in December 1986, in an incident that generated news accounts throughout the United States, Hall was arrested near a Sandinista air base as he was posing as a journalist but supposedly conducting a Contra reconnaissance mission. Recognizing Hall's sometimes tenuous hold on reality and the fact that his brother is a Democratic congressman from Ohio, the Sandinistas released Hall after a short incarceration.

Hall claims, during what his book jacket describes as "an action-filled, five-year career fighting terrorism," to have earlier headed an independent commando team called the Free Lancers in southern Africa, which carried out rescues and what he describes as "independent recon jobs." He also suggests that he once considered taking the Free Lancers "to the Middle East to hunt Carlos down if I could get a lead on him," a wholly preposterous suggestion.[18] Hall also apparently tried to interest the Israelis in his plan to create a so-called "Phoenix Battalion" of hired guns to "combat worldwide terrorism." On the proposed Phoenix Battalion organization chart, Hall lists himself as "Warrior Leader." Hall says he asked the Israelis for a training site in the Negev desert, weapons, transportation, Arabic-speaking commandos, and "a line on the people we wanted to put out of business."[19] One gets the feeling that Hall had read too many action-adventure novels like Gar Wilson's *Phoenix Force,* cited in chapter 1. Hall candidly describes his earlier problems with drugs, and one suspects that he is still suffering from flashbacks for imagining that the Israelis, who boast one of the best intelligence organizations in the world and a world-class counterterrorist commando capability, might have any interest in funding and supporting a group of American yahoos who want to kill commies and terrorists for Christ. Hall seems to have engaged in self-delusion for many years, and his book and purported adventures represent the kind of self-aggrandizement and posturing that gives the whole field a bad name. Nevertheless, one Contra war operative who knew him says, "Sam means well. I feel for the guy but I don't think he's playing with a full deck." Hall is a man, after all, who writes in his book about barrooms being places "electric with excitement because you never knew who you might meet or what they might be like. Who was the guy on the next barstool and what did he do for a living and what were his hobbies and did he have a family and what kind of car did he drive and did he know any good jokes?"[20] Now that's what I call exciting, all right.

Kidnap and Ransom

They arrived at the small French restaurant in the Belgravia section of London on motorcycles, two athletically built men in well-fitting jumpsuits, their identities obscured by helmets and visors. Once their motorcycles were secured, they stripped off their jumpsuits and helmets, revealing well-tailored suits underneath. They handed their motorcycle gear to the maître d' and were shown to a private table upstairs, where their guests were waiting.

They were Arish Turle and Simon Adams-Dale, the former managing director and the chief operations officer of Control Risks Ltd., two of the world's premiere hostage negotiators and crisis managers. Few business firms have inspired novels, but Control Risks is the exception. The reason has a lot to do with the personalities of Turle and Adams-Dale, as well as the nature of their business, and the secrecy in which it is cloaked.

The insurance industry was quick to seize the opportunities presented by the global epidemic of kidnapping that began in the late 1960s and extended through the 1970s. A variety of companies, most notably Lloyd's of London, began underwriting policies—known as kidnap and ransom policies, or K&R—insuring individuals against the possibility of being kidnapped. It is estimated that in 1985 Lloyd's received more than $50 million in premiums from such policies, thus making it a very lucrative enterprise. Individual premiums are quite reasonable in the United States and most parts of Western Europe, but rise dramatically in nations like Colombia, Lebanon, Guatemala, and El Salvador, where political violence is commonplace.

As Lloyd's business expanded, it was decided that there was a need for an "action arm" that could assess the potential risk to clients and their respective countries; assist clients in improving their security, thereby reducing their potential risk; and, in the event of an actual kidnapping, manage the crisis and handle the ransom payment, a risky proposition in and of itself. There was also the implied, if not fully stated, assurance that, if all else failed, a paramilitary hostage retrieval mission could be considered.

Control Risks Ltd., born in 1973, is composed largely of former distinguished SAS officers. One of its original directors was David Walker, who later formed KMS. Its present board includes a number of former high-ranking British military officers and law enforcement officials, and the firm reportedly has ready access to British political and intelligence leaders.

Since 1977 the real moving force in Control Risks has been former SAS officer Turle. No longer exclusively concerned with kidnappings and ransom demands, under Turle's leadership Control Risks became a far more diversified company, and today its services include security surveys, protection of installations, information security, crisis management, training, technical inspections, the recovery of materials stored on computers in the aftermath of disasters, investigations, and information services. Nevertheless, Lloyd's of London still guarantees Control Risks more than £1 million a year in fees, largely for managing security concerns related to its kidnap and ransom portfolio.

In 1986 London *Sunday Times* writer James Adams accused Control Risks of becoming too cozy with kidnappers, maintaining that a symbiotic relationship existed between the company and various terrorist kidnappers such as the IRA. Attorneys for Control Risks took exception to the article, of which they had received an advance copy, and threatened to obtain an injunction stopping distribution of the paper's magazine. The *Sunday Times* was forced to back down and print a public apology to Control Risks on the front page of the newspaper and in the Business News section, and to pay a reported £50 thousand in damages to a charity designated by the security company. According to the unprecedented apology, "TODAY's Magazine profile of Control Risks (on page 27) which forms part of James Adams' article on kidnapping contains statements which are untrue. Contrary to what is stated, at no time has CR paid, or been an agent for paying £2 million to the IRA, nor any sum to any terrorist organization; nor was CR involved in, or aware of, the alleged attempt to smuggle £300,000 into Ireland."[21]

Turle left CR in early 1988 after an internal dispute. Whether the company can continue to prosper without him is yet to be determined. During the past year and a half, however, the bottom has dropped out of the kidnap and ransom insurance market, and firms specializing in this part of the security industry have fallen on hard times or been forced to refocus their marketing efforts.

Private CIAs

This is called by many "the Information Age," and information represents one of the primary currencies of our time. Accordingly, a number of companies have emerged, often composed of former intelligence specialists, that collect and sell information to multinational companies and anyone else who can afford it. One French company even maintains a private "spy" satellite, called SPOT, which can be programmed to pass over nearly any part of the globe that a customer desires. While it is employed primarily for geologic, oceanographic, agricultural, and ecological studies, an American television network paid the company to photograph Iranian "Silkworm" missile sites and aired the resulting photographs on their evening news. The photographs from SPOT can distinguish objects on the ground as small as ten meters in length, and interpretation of the photos is enhanced with computers. The Pentagon has, on occasion, utilized SPOT photographs for intelligence purposes.

Ironically, some of the largest multinational companies in the world have made major corporate decisions regarding such things as expansion and investment without the benefit of timely and accurate information. In the late 1970s, for example, several officers of a U.S. security company met with top corporate officials, including the director of security and his deputy, of a major insurance company. Both the director and his deputy were accountants by training, not security specialists. The insurance executives described how their company had, until recently, been so sales oriented that little consideration had been given to the risk factors involved. As a result, an energetic salesman had sold nearly seventy kidnap and ransom insurance policies in El Salvador, which was beginning to unravel at the seams. Naturally the insurance had been very well received in El Salvador, but now corporate officials were worried about potentially having to pay off on a number of policies. The insurance company, moreover, had insured heavy industrial equipment and plants throughout the world with almost no consideration given to political risk and instability.

"There's a $5 million crane near Lake Maracaibo, Venezuela,'' continued one of the insurance executives, ''which we need to make a decision on today regarding insurance. And we haven't the slightest idea whether its a safe investment.''

''Well, surely you make some attempt to measure risk in various parts of the world?'' said one of the security men.

''No,'' came the embarrassed reply.

''Doesn't someone at least clip the newspaper?''

''No.''

''How do you decide, then, whether or not to proceed on a particular matter?'' asked the incredulous security man.

''We just ask around or kind of guess.''

As hard to believe as it sounds, many companies in this country and abroad simply plunge into the international arena with virtually no expertise, experience, or preparation. Although the Japanese are the most successful trading nation in the world, according to a recent private survey, only 20 percent of Japanese companies doing business overseas have a corporate security office. Only 51 percent have even ''considered'' developing a corporate security manual.

To redress this information deficiency, companies like Miami-based Ackerman & Palumbo and Business Risks International, located in a suburb of Washington, D.C., attempt to keep tabs on terrorist violence and general instability throughout the world. Ackerman & Palumbo claims that it provides such information to more than half of the 300 largest corporations in the United States for fees ranging from a few thousand dollars to as much as two hundred thousand dollars a year. Not only do such firms try to measure risk and make it intelligible to corporate strategic planners, but they seek to predict future events based on current indicators. This allows corporate officials to make informed judgments concerning where to invest or locate new subsidiaries, or perhaps from which country to purchase a particular strategic mineral or product to ensure an uninterrupted supply. They may also suggest to management the need to ''harden'' corporate facilities in a particular country or region to protect them from terrorist attack.

Corporate raiders also use such services to identify structural and personnel weaknesses in target companies that may affect value or performance. What is the health of top executives? Are any troubled by alcoholism or other problems? Is a forthcoming product behind schedule or plagued with cost overruns? Industrial espionage, moreover, is a pervasive feature of the U.S. business landscape, and most of those who engage in it are not Soviet or Eastern bloc spies, but rather corporate sleuths intent on stealing product secrets or investigating the competition. According to one survey, 80 percent of "Fortune 500" companies surveyed had increased their corporate intelligence budgets in the previous three years.[22]

Despite the increasing demand for corporate sleuths and intelligence, not every firm that tries to satisfy the market demand is successful. One of the most notable failures in recent years was International Reporting and Information Services, better known as IRIS. Started by Washington publisher Anthony C. Stout and located in luxurious quarters near the Pentagon, IRIS boasted state-of-the-art computers, nearly one hundred "correspondents," or intelligence collectors, around the world, and dozens of top-flight analysts. Stout's goal was to create a private intelligence network that would provide reliable forecasts and information to banks, insurance companies, and multinationals, including early warning of potential trouble.

More than $16 million was invested in the ill-fated effort to create a global corporate intelligence service before calling it quits in 1983. Most of the money was put up by a consortium of European investors. At the time it folded, IRIS was said to have received only one contract, and that for about $1,000. The chief problem, it turned out, was marketing, or the lack thereof.

The top management of IRIS was composed of men and women with distinguished public service careers, including a number of former CIA and State Department officials. In addition, IRIS hired former British Prime Minister Edward Heath, allegedly for a six-figure annual retainer and generous expense account, who was supposed to serve as part of an oversight board composed of prominent individuals to guarantee the integrity of IRIS's product. Heath's presence, however, was largely window dressing. Unfortunately, few, if any, of IRIS's top managers had any experience in the private sector; most had drawn government checks throughout their careers. Many were beginning second careers and lacked the entrepreneurial spirit and energy needed to make a new firm predicated on a novel concept successful. Worse, some of the so-called big names hired to ensure access to the U.S. government were ex-Carter administration appointees who were viewed with suspicion, if not outright hostility, by the recently arrived Reagan administration.

IRIS's failure was in its execution, not in the original concept. The demand for accurate and timely intelligence by companies has never been greater, and represents one of the most lucrative and growth-oriented sectors of the private security industry.

Executive Protection

The time: the early 1960s. The mission: to kill the man in the baseball cap on the deck of the rusty freighter in the Caribbean.

The operative and a confederate hail the aging freighter as they pull alongside in a cigarette-shaped swift boat. Three men—all wearing baseball caps—peer down at them from the deck. There is no time to reflect. The operative raises the assault rifle and cuts down all three men. Later he learns that none of the three was the intended target. Asked if it didn't bother him that he had killed three innocent men, he shrugs his shoulders: "They shouldn't have been wearing baseball caps."

His open and gregarious face belies his real occupation. A naturalized American citizen from Cuba, he served with the CIA in Southeast Asia, Latin America, and the Caribbean. Today, in addition to serving as a counterinsurgency advisor in the world's dirty little conflicts, he protects individuals of wealth and political position from terrorists. He is one of a handful of resourceful men and women who form an elite subculture of professionals capable of meeting terrorists on their own terms, striking back at them with the same ferocity they show their victims.

Such services are in high demand. One of the most dramatic

moments in the Iran/Contra hearings occurred when Lt. Colonel Oliver North was asked to explain why he accepted, as a government employee, a security system worth $13,900 from a former CIA employee by the name of Glenn Robinette. North told the hushed gathering in the Senate Caucus Room that he was informed by the FBI in April 1986 that he had been targeted for assassination by the Abu Nidal terrorist organization. Nidal, in North's words, is the "principal, foremost assassin in the world today. He is a brutal murderer."[23] Threats from Abu Nidal are never taken lightly, said North, citing U.S. State Department figures that Nidal and his organization had been responsible for murdering at least 181 people and wounding more than 200 in the previous two years. North explained that he had tried to get U.S. government protection, but was informed that no provision existed for protecting U.S. government officials at his level, despite the fact he was being singled out for harm as a result of his activities as the White House's top antiterrorist specialist.

"I'll be glad to meet Abu Nidal on equal terms anywhere in the world," North told the congressional panel, his voice filled with emotion. "Okay? There's an even deal for him. But I am not willing to have my wife and my four children meet Abu Nidal or his organization on his terms."[24] North admitted that it had been a gross error of judgment to accept something he hadn't paid for and then to attempt to paper over the gift with some back-dated correspondence. But that out of the way, he went on to publicly thank General Richard Secord for paying for the system and then to berate the Congress for allowing a situation to exist where public officials could be singled out for attack by terrorists without any recourse to federal protection.

North's predicament underscores the growing need many people feel for personal security in the modern world. An increasing number of prominent and wealthy people and their families are threatened by terrorists, kidnappers, disgruntled business associates, and those with disordered minds. Moreover, as one prominent Washington restauranteur, Victor Colucci, notes, bodyguards "are a mark of importance. When someone says to a maître d' that he or she needs an extra table for their security personnel, it is immediately assumed they are someone important."[25] Or, as a *Washington Post* list of "Ins" and "Outs" reported: "Bodyguards are deeply In." As a result, the bodyguard business is booming.

This is a relatively new phenomenon, however. As E.J. Criscuoli, Executive Vice President of the American Society for Industrial Security, has observed, executive protection used to be "something we never worried about." When Criscuoli got into the security business in the mid-1950s, "as far as most security personnel were concerned, the only person who got executive protection was the President of the United States. Well, there are some corporations today . . . that provide executive protection for their chief executive officer that ranks on a par with what is provided to the President of the United States."[26] It is a simple matter of economics, says Criscuoli: if anything happens to the CEO it may impact negatively on the company's performance and the value of its stock. He views executive protection as a kind of insurance policy.

As in the Oliver North case, the FBI and local authorities generally pass on to private citizens living in the United States intelligence that suggests they might be targeted by terrorists or hostile foreign governments. The FBI has, for example, advised certain Iranian exiles residing in this country to beware of attacks on their lives after their names were placed on "hit" lists broadcast over Iranian radio. Similarly, targets of possible Libyan violence have also been warned to take heed.

But as North discovered, beyond advising the threatened individual to take special precautions, there is little U.S. authorities can do to protect the terrorist target until an actual operation against them has been launched on U.S. territory and discovered by American intelligence. For the most part, the intended victim generally must provide for his or her own safety. For those with the wherewithal, often the only choice is to hire bodyguards. But when it comes to fighting terrorists, ordinary bodyguards will not suffice. There is now an increasing trend away from what one security professional calls "big Samoans with small minds and large bulges in their coat pockets." Observes the former chairman of a security firm: "No four-dollar-an-hour security guard is going to lay down his life to protect some fat-assed client. And even if he tried to save his client, more likely than not he'd just end up getting them both killed." According to former Delta operator and executive protection specialist Don Feeney of Corporate Training Unlimited, a bodyguard's job may be "to die in place," and that kind of professionalism and commitment to duty is not easy to find.

It requires men and women of uncommon ability and experience to match wits with terrorists, possessing what Tom Wolfe called "the right stuff." Some are freelancers, others work for firms. Most learned their trade in the military, the Secret Service, or by working in the intelligence community. What they all have in common is top pay: from thirty to sixty thousand dollars a year, plus generous living allowances and expense accounts.

King Abdullah, King Hussein of Jordan's grandfather, was often far too casual about his personal security and, if confronted with it, would quote an old Arabic proverb: "Until my day comes, no one can harm me. When my day comes, no one can protect me." Abdullah became a victim of his own fatalism, and was assassinated at the Jerusalem Mosque on July 20, 1951. Abdullah's case illustrates the degree to which any individual's personal security is a reflection of his or her own commitment to being protected and observing certain basic rules and procedures. A client who thinks it will "take a silver bullet to get him," in the words of one security man, is his own worst enemy. No amount of zeal and professionalism in his security detail will make it possible to protect him.

Similarly, the executive or government official who finds security procedures "a drag" or "too confining" may come to regret it. President John F. Kennedy, who died at the hands of an assassin, was well known for chafing at the restrictions imposed by the Secret Service, and loved to try to give his security detail the slip. One of his former "private" bodyguards, an Irish-American detective from New York, recalls Kennedy pacing the Oval Office at night like a caged animal, frustrated by his inability to live like a free man.

One former U.S. ambassador to Lebanon demonstrated the same callous disregard for good security in the most dangerous city in the world. The Ambassador ordered his security personnel to stop blocking the driveway after the visiting French ambassador complained about having to walk twenty yards. "The Ambassador chewed out my ass four or five times for it," recalls one of his security men, "telling me this is not an armed camp." The practice of blocking the driveway was discontinued, and a few years later a powerful car bomb destroyed the U.S. embassy, killing 63 people, including many members of the CIA's Beirut station and one of the Agency's top Middle East experts.

Aggressive/Evasive Driving

On May 26, 1987, a green Peugeot station wagon carrying several men tried to force a car from the U.S. embassy in Cairo over to the side of the road. Although the terrorists did not know it, their targets were the embassy's acting security chief, Dennis L. Williams, his deputy, and another embassy employee. Williams, who was at the wheel, had been trained in defensive driving techniques, and refused to let the terrorists push him off the road. At that point, they opened fire on the embassy car, and Williams made a U-turn on the eight-lane highway to escape the attackers. Williams and his deputy were slightly injured by flying glass, but thanks to his skill in defensive driving, they were able to avoid being kidnapped or killed.

Although the road conditions are rarely right, aggressive/evasive driving techniques have been used on occasion to outwit terrorists. Consequently, a number of schools have grown up dedicated to teaching such skills to government security specialists and private chauffeurs. One of the best-known schools is operated by Tony Scotti, who, to his credit, emphasizes avoiding vehicle attacks and spotting ambushes in time, rather than on dramatic driving maneuvers like J-turns and reverse 180s to escape would-be attackers. Indeed, many experts contend that such maneuvers, while exciting, are more applicable to Hollywood films than to the real world. The U.S. antiterrorist Delta Force, for example, rejects the value of the forward 180-degree turn, and instead teaches its men only to perform the reverse 180, on the theory that with a reverse 180 the car is withdrawing from the scene as quickly as possible rather than swinging into it. Moreover, the reverse 180 is normally done at a relatively slow speed, and is thus more applicable to the kind of roads and situations where terrorists are likely to strike. Unlike the incident in Egypt, terrorists generally are smart enough not to attempt an attack on a high-speed expressway with plenty of maneuvering room. Most often they will pick a narrow, crowded side street that can be blocked off with relative ease.

If trapped by terrorists on a narrow street, ramming is clearly an option. Schools like that run by Corporate Training Unlimited (CTU) in Fayetteville, North Carolina, teach students how to ram obstacles that are in the way, most often other vehicles. In contrast to Hollywood films, successful ramming is a matter of hitting the obstacle at the proper point of least resistance rather than high speed. Indeed, most ramming is done at relatively low speeds and represents more of a push than a dramatic impact. The instructors at CTU believe that ramming is, in some respects, more a question of confidence than anything else. Thus, they drill students on improving their overall driving technique, and on such things as cornering, how to do panic stops without losing control, and how to pick up vital seconds during a high-speed chase. Most students have never really pushed their vehicles to the limit, say instructors at CTU, and don't realize their own capabilities either. Once they have rammed another vehicle, and seen that it is neither a particularly complicated nor dangerous maneuver, their confidence level increases dramatically. After a student has experienced the jolt and witnessed, as sometimes happens, a car window explode on impact, he or she will be far less inhibited about ramming another car during a future attack.

As a confidence-building device and to increase the vehicle

handling skills of students, the CTU program also calls for students to drive on the high-speed NASCAR oval at Rockingham raceway. For most students, it is a first. Each student pilots an ordinary sedan with an instructor at his side. From a standing start, the student accelerates out onto the track and climbs up the five-story 28-degree banked oval, where both speed and keen reflexes are required to keep the car out of trouble. After completing about two-thirds of a lap, the driver slips down off the oval and onto a road-racing course, full of tight turns, laid out in the infield. Finally, tires burning, he or she exits the infield course and roars back up onto the oval, repeating the entire circuit.

A recent group of students at the driving course included a 60-year-old businessman from Washington, D.C., and a former Formula One Grand Prix driver. All found the course exhilarating and worthwhile.

Seminars, Schools, and Conferences

The number of seminars and conferences devoted to terrorism has proliferated all out of proportion to the threat in recent years. For the corporate executive or security professional seeking to overdose on the subject, a recent survey found that there were nearly four hundred conferences and seminars in the United States in 1986 focusing, at least in part, on the subject of terrorism, more than one for every day of the year.

A sampling of the many professional gatherings reveals conferences on subjects ranging from a three-day meeting on "The Use of Microcomputers in Counterterrorism Operations" to "Corporate Security for World Travelers," "Anti-Wiretapping and Anti-Bugging Workshop Seminar," "Terrorism and the Media," "Hostage Negotiations: Who Will Be Next?" "Designing Facilities to Survive Terrorist Attack," "The Hostages: Family, Media & Government," "Explosive Device Identification, Handling, and Disposal," and even a General Services Administration–sponsored conference on "Strategic Directions in Physical Security."

The number of schools and special training facilities addressing counterterrorism, executive protection, and other security issues is increasing rapidly to meet market demand. Some are excellent, but many are mediocre, and some are downright rip-offs.

Executive Security International Ltd. (ESI), based in Aspen, Colorado, offers regular training seminars on executive protection. A recent ESI newsletter described the firearms training that attendees were receiving ("Valerie, who has never fired a gun before in her life, is zinging those targets with great accuracy, but worried about her speed"), and then went on to note that "the coming week will bring the group back to the Aspen Club for Profiles of Terrorism and Observational Psychology, then return to the road track for Wally Dallenbach's Escape and Evasion Driving, First Respondent Medicine, scenarios, and final tests. By mid-afternoon of Saturday, May 9 we will be looking at a tired, tough, dirty bunch of students and instructors."[27]

One guest instructor calls ESI's proprietor, Bob Duggan, "the most deadly man with a knife I've ever met." Recalling a scene from the Inspector Clouseau movies, where the houseboy lies in wait for Clouseau to return and then jumps him, using a variety of Oriental weapons, Duggan and one of his instructors have an ongoing contest to determine who can get the drop on the other guy. The instructor describes returning to the Holiday Inn motel after a long day, only to have Duggan fall from the ceiling on top of him, knife drawn. He reacts quickly, unsheathing his own fighting knife, and the two men spill over the bed and crash into the TV set. As they parry knife thrusts, the instructor's blade misses and goes through the wall. And so it goes, until one of the combatants, usually Duggan, succeeds in overpowering his opponent.

Duggan is also a fourth-degree black belt in Haw Rang Do, one of the Korean martial arts. According to the editor of *Gung-Ho* magazine, "To screw with Duggan is to simply lose parts of your body—or your life."[28] Indeed, ESI actually began as a martial arts school and evolved into an instructional program for "protection specialists" because of market demand. In addition to being a lethal weapon, Duggan is a former Communist party official from California and Latin American guerrilla who discovered the error of his ways in the mid-1970s after reading about communist atrocities in Kampuchea and Vietnam.

In 1987, Duggan launched something called Life Force Technologies Ltd., a catalogue merchandising operation that falls someplace between CCS (Communication Control System) and The Sharper Image. In his slickly produced catalogue, Duggan offers consumers everything from a $6,100 single-seat hovercraft to wristwatch cameras, cameras built into cigarette lighters, telescopes, scrambler phones, passive infrared sensors, portable hot tubs, emergency food rations, "designer foods" for weight loss and muscle building, video cameras with night vision equipment, briefcases with built-in tape recorders, bullet-proof briefcases, mattress cushions and pillows, and, believe it or not, Protex Ultra-thin lubricated latex condoms ("In today's world, you need to carry the last word in protection").

Another firm that provides quality training programs and seminars is Richard W. Kobetz & Associates, Inc., located on the edge of Berryville, Virginia, near the West Virginia border. Kobetz is a husky former Chicago detective who originally came to Washington, D.C., on a one-year leave of absence to work at the International Association of Chiefs of Police (IACP) as director of a project on civil disorders. He never returned to the Chicago police department, and instead remained at IACP for eleven years, ultimately becoming Director of Training Programs and IACP's liaison with Interpol.

In 1979, in response to the growing market demand for security professionals, Kobetz left IACP and formed his own company, which is touted in one of his brochures as "the largest premier training group in the world on issues of security." His 1986–87 brochure offers dozens of seminars at locations around the country. His two-day "Contemporary Terrorism" seminar was held on eight different dates in cities ranging from Toronto to Las Vegas and New Orleans. Targeted at "those seeking information on organizations and operations of groups which threaten and attack government and industry throughout the world," the Contemporary Terrorism seminar includes topics such as "Understanding Terrorism," "Intelligence for Defensive Purposes," "Terrorist Goals and Operations," and "Target Hardening and Counter-Terrorism."[29] In addition to the seminar on terrorism, Kobetz also lists seminars on "Hostage Negotiations," "Corporate Aircraft Security," "Investigative Technology," and "Physical Security: Hotels, Motels, Offices." Kobetz says his philosophy is one of "rethinking the world of security"—instead of approaching security problems in a reactive manner, to "be proactive and start planning for the possibility, no matter how remote, that something could occur."[30]

In addition to his curriculum, Kobetz relies on a certain amount of mystique and the promise of a good time in order to draw students. He says he screens all potential students and that half of his attendees are interested chiefly in executive protection, 25 percent in counterterrorism, and the remainder in a combination of the two. According to Kobetz's published promotional literature, successful graduates of the seven-day $2,300 Protective Services Program "are certified by the Executive Protection Institute as a Personal Protection Specialist (P.P.S.), are nominated for membership in the exclusive fraternity of the NINE LIVES ASSOCIATES (N.L.A.) and are awarded their identification cards, suitable gift and highly coveted 'cat pin'," generally at a graduation banquet. Dining, in fact, is an important part of Kobetz's standard executive protection curriculum. In recognition of the fact that a large number of his trainees, many from blue-collar backgrounds, may be uncomfortable in top hotels and high-ticket restaurants favored by their clients, Kobetz has instituted lessons in table etiquette, protocol, and appropriate attire that, on the surface, seem more appropriate to a finishing school than to a tough training program for bodyguards capable of mixing it up with some of the world's most dangerous terrorists. It is important, Kobetz maintains, that a security detail fits into the client's surroundings with ease and without calling undue attention to their presence. Thus, along

with texts on assassination and terrorist mayhem, every executive protection seminar attendee is provided with a copy of *Amy
Vanderbilt's Everyday Etiquette* and handouts on dress and personal
grooming. Unlike most finishing schools, however, attendees
are advised to "cover tattoos" and, when unsure what to wear
in a small town, to "follow the lead of local bankers." As in the
military, umbrellas are frowned upon, and students are told that
"it's better to wear a raincoat and get soaked than look like 'a
Wally Cox pipsqueak figure, ineffective but nice.' "[31]

Kobetz takes his trainees through a number of simulated incidents and make-believe training scenarios where what they have
learned in the classroom is put to the test. "The eerie setting,
with the bound, explosive-laden victim illuminated by a powerful lantern, gave impressive seriousness to the proceedings,"
reads one handout for Advanced Counterterrorism Training.
"No less impressive was the well-planned and violently executed
escape of the kidnappers, who together with their victim drove
in pitch darkness across a seemingly impassable recently plowed
field to elude pursuit." Such hands-on training is popular with
the students and is designed to give them a feel for the "real
thing," although most are unlikely ever to encounter an actual
terrorist incident.

A 10- to 15-percent dropout rate is normal for his courses, explains Kobetz, who adds that despite his best efforts to weed out
those with unrealistic notions about the "glamorous" life of a
bodyguard, he always gets a few people unprepared for the
stress, physical challenges, and routine of executive protection.
About 15 percent of his students are women, and the number
is growing. Good judgment and the ability to attend to the
details is more important than strength, says Kobetz, who
believes that women are often superior to men as protection specialists. Indeed, Kobetz preaches "avoidance of the problem,
not confrontation," and contends that the need to use a firearm
to protect a client is an indication of failure, not success. He emphasizes the basics and is wary of courses that innovate too
much because, he maintains, terrorists are not very innovative.
"We know that they are predictably unpredictable."[32]

To date, more than 500 people have graduated from Kobetz's executive protection course, most of them seeking employment as personal bodyguards, with remuneration as high as $70,000 a year, although $25,000 to $30,000 is the norm. A small number are law enforcement officers sent by their departments to upgrade their executive protection skills, since local police and sheriff's departments increasingly find themselves called upon to protect visiting dignitaries.

But not all of those who attend such seminars and courses are intent on becoming serious security professionals. Some are bored housewives, yuppie attorneys, or assorted twinkies eager to live their fantasies, if only for a weekend or two. Such individuals approach counterterrorist training seminars as a kind of theme park or adult camp, where they can run around in their cammies and jump boots, fire submachine guns, and ram cars. By contrast to the reputable programs operated by ESI or Richard W. Kobetz, a number of fast-buck artists have moved quickly to capitalize on the public demand for security and counterterrorist training by offering seminars and retreats long on mystique and short on real skills. As part of their come-on, the fly-by-night operators tend to flog their own, generally unexceptional, exploits as military men or counterterrorists into tales of Ramboesque proportion.

The classified sections of many popular gun, adventure, and survivalist magazines are full of advertisements for such schools. "Tired of the Daily Routine? Need a change of pace and an entirely different form of personal challenge and knowledge?" reads one ad. If so, the Ranger Outreach Center of Pecos, New Mexico, will give you training in special operations and long-range reconnaissance patrolling. Fortune's Own, Inc., another New Mexico concern, promises "advanced commando, jungle, mountain, desert training." Yet another New Mexico institution of higher learning named the Action Commando School lists a lengthy menu of courses including "unconventional warfare ops; counterinsurgency; survival techniques; patrolling techniques; special assault weapons and tactics; electronic security measures; light and general purpose MG; exotic weapons;

adjustment procedures for artillery and TAC-AIR and much more.'' The Mecca Survival Center, located in Quebec, Canada, offers ''recon, ambush and more. Great discounts for 4 and up. Eat, sleep and train in the bush.'' Interestingly, none of the above schools gives an address: prospective students are asked to contact a post office box.

One school of dubious quality is Cobray International, Inc., in Powder Springs, Georgia, which was founded by the late spook and international gadfly Mitchell L. WerBell III. ''Our job,'' he was once quoted as saying from behind his thick handlebar moustache, explaining the school's philosophy, ''is not just to kill the crazies—you call them terrorists, I believe. Hell, anybody can do that with a screwdriver. What we want is to keep somebody from being killed. And that ain't easy.'' Eleven subjects are taught at Cobray over a six-day period, including fifty-and-a-half hours of classroom lectures, shooting, hand-to-hand combat, and two days of evasive driving. Three hours are devoted to killing with unconventional weapons such as the screwdriver, hatchet, and knife. Among the optional courses are Convoy Procedures, Shotgun Techniques, Crisis Intervention/Hostage Negotiation, Medical Trauma/First Aid, and Cardiopulmonary Resuscitation.

Many of WerBell's students were attracted by his reputation as a sometime soldier of fortune involved in plots to knock over various Caribbean governments in the 1960s, including the Dominican Republic in 1965 and the despotic regime of former Haitian strongman ''Papa Doc'' Duvalier. He also surfaced in Southeast Asia during the Vietnam conflict. Perhaps one of his best-known accomplishments is the development of an extremely effective ''silencer'' for the 9-inch-long Ingram submachine gun, a favorite weapon of Miami drug lords. ''Often, the loudest noise is when the bullet hits home,'' WerBell told Washington writer Rudy Maxa. ''If it hits a human, it makes a peculiar thunking sound, like hitting a watermelon.'' WerBell once demonstrated the silencer's effectiveness in a New York hotel room after ordering a round of drinks from room service. When the knock came on the door, WerBell whipped out the silenced submachine gun and emptied a whole magazine into the heavy Manhattan phone book. The room was thick with the acrid scent of cordite when they let the man from room service in. WerBell and his pals sat back, recalls one of those present, with "shit-eating grins on their faces, watching the guy from room service try to figure out what just happened." Mitch was that kind of guy.

Cobray came under criticism from many quarters for admitting just about anyone with the price of matriculation, including white supremacists and presidential fringe candidate Lyndon LaRouche's security contingent. Another "counterterrorist" training school that fell victim to indiscriminate admission practices was Vietnam veteran Frank Camper's Recondo School near Warrior, Alabama, that allegedly was used by four Sikh terrorists to acquire the skills they hoped could be used to assassinate Indian Prime Minister Rajiv Gandhi on a trip to the United States. Fortunately, the FBI got wind of the plot before it could be put into motion. There are also reports that one of the men trained by Camper was involved in the bombing of an Air India flight in June 1985. Responding to public criticism, Camper denied that he was operating a terrorist training camp and instead defended his school as "an asset to the state of Alabama as a private counterterrorist school."[33]

Most of Camper's students, it is true, were not terrorists. Indeed, they represented a grab bag of survivalists, fantasists, assorted yo-yos, and a number of would-be Rambos. One graduating class, for example, was composed of a lumberjack, a university library administrator, a railroad conductor, and a "demolition expert." One suspects that Camper's students were also either masochists or a little on the fruitcake side since, by all accounts, he put them through two weeks of absolute hell designed to demonstrate to them the hardships they would have to endure if they wanted to become real mercenaries. According to one dubious testimonial, "I respect Camper for his experience and service to Uncle Sam, however I did not care for his psycho executive officers." As such schools go, Camper's was a real bargain, costing only $350 for the entire two weeks. On the other hand, the graduation dinner was at Bob's Big Boy. So much for mystique.

Until recently, the chief magnet school for yahoos was G. Gordon Liddy's Academy of Corporate Security and Private Investigations, based in Miami. The school, in effect, licensed Liddy's name, and Liddy himself rarely appeared, preferring instead to spend most of his time on the lucrative college lecture circuit debating other ghosts from the past like the late Abbie Hoffman. In addition, Liddy concentrated on his acting career, doing guest appearances on shows like "Miami Vice," thereby confirming that he is far from a real operator any longer. A large proportion of the attendees at Liddy's school were journalists, drawn by the hype and Liddy's magnetic personality.

By early 1989, the phone number of G. Gordon Liddy's academy had been disconnected and a would-be student reported that the firm had closed its doors. Newspaper reports indicated that the firm had gone bankrupt.

Liddy also claimed to head a paramilitary unit called the "Hurricane Force," which purportedly undertook high-risk assignments for fees in excess of a half a million dollars. Liddy claimed that he was prepared to rescue hostages from any place in the world but Libya, China, and the Soviet Union. Although Liddy publicly stated that he had undertaken several high-risk operations, he refused to supply details, and most knowledgeable observers contend that the "Hurricane Force" was a publicity stunt rather than fact.

Perhaps the most absurd instructional program of all is something called "A Few Days in the Woods With Bo." It is billed as four days of "survivalist" training in the Pecos wilderness of New Mexico with sometime-Contra pinup girl Crissa Bozlee, otherwise known as "Bo," who posed bare-breasted in 1987 on a poster with an assault rifle. Bo also made a video called "The Last Drop," in which she field-strips, reassembles, and fires an M-60 machine gun in the desert while stark naked.

According to law enforcement officials, the number of paramilitary and "counterterrorist" training schools of dubious character in the United States is growing at a rapid pace and represents a potential threat to public safety and security.

Nearly anybody, it seems, can sell antiterrorist snake oil and get away with it. Many of the schools have a strong ideological content and are allied with extremist organizations, some of which subscribe to openly racist and anti-Semitic political orthodoxies. The questionable reputation of such schools is already having a negative impact on reputable schools like the one proposed for rural Culpeper County, Virginia, by Charles S. Vance, a former Secret Service agent and one of the top executive protection specialists in the country. After hearing about the proposed school, a dozen county residents appeared before the Culpeper County Planning Commission to question any effort to grant the school the necessary permits to go forward. Vance was forced to defend the school from charges that it might enroll potential paramilitary specialists and mercenaries.

"The New Feudalism"[34]

"It is very important for the American people to know that this is a dangerous world," Lt. Colonel Oliver North told the Joint House–Senate Select Committee investigating the Iran/Contra Affair,"that we live at risk and that this nation is at risk in a dangerous world."[35] Many observers, however, say that North overstates the case and that we may have as much to fear from men like North as from the terrorists and other enemies he opposed. In the view of critics, North too willingly went outside the law in the pursuit of what he considered to be his "higher" goals.

There is also criticism of the fact that North turned to the private security industry, and to individuals like retired Major General Richard Secord and his partner Albert Hakim, to operate the Contra resupply network and to serve as intermediaries in the so-called Iran initiative; that he, in effect, "privatized" American foreign policy. This, however, was hardly a new practice. Indeed, throughout the post-war period the United States has, at one time or another, found it convenient to use "private" firms in the pursuit of U.S. foreign policy objectives. Some of the firms were not really privately owned, and instead were proprietaries operated by the U.S. intelligence community as "fronts," either to shield the U.S. government's participation or to provide unofficial "cover" for U.S. intelligence operatives. Others were, in actuality, private firms that enjoyed a close symbiotic working relationship with the U.S. government. Such firms generally seek business on the open market, but they also receive clients that are discreetly referred to them by government agencies, notably the CIA. In some cases, the government may even contract with them directly, trusting that they will perform the required services with a maximum amount of discretion.

Contrary to the notion that the "privatization" of U.S. foreign policy is exclusively a phenomenon of the Reagan administration, the Carter administration also relied heavily on the private sector because it was publicly committed to various policies that ruled out the government-to-government transfer of antiterrorist hardware and services to certain nations. During the Carter years, for example, one Washington-based security company trained the praetorian guard forces in a number of developing countries, after having been recommended for the job by the CIA. Such a relationship can be of inestimable intelligence value, and if a U.S. firm does not do the job, the contract will surely be given to a company or government agency from some other nation. There are few better vantage points for intelligence collection than as a consultant to a nation's elite presidential guard. Indeed, such security consultants generally are given access to the presidential palace and other sensitive locations; they learn a great deal about the leader and his or her daily habits, not to mention strengths and weaknesses; and they often form close relationships with members of the presidential guard that can later prove to be useful.

Various writers worry that the new security and counterterrorist firms ultimately may represent a kind of monster that will devour the very societies they purport to protect. James A. Nathan, for example, maintains that they are engaged in usurping various police and other government powers, and that some of their activities amount to little more than a "return to the wild west." "If the international corporate sector seeks protection by private counter-terrorist security firms," writes Nathan, "a medieval situation may emerge in which the security function of the state is usurped by private contractors."[36] Similarly, James Hougan in his book, *Spooks,* contends that as more and more former intelligence agents enter the private sector, the U.S. is becoming " 'haunted' by its wandering spooks, much as Japan was formerly haunted by itinerant samurai cut loose from baronial service."[37] According to Hougan and others of similar persuasion, the creation of private intelligence networks, the widespread dissemination of eavesdropping and surveillance technology, and the emergence of paramilitary specialists not only willing to impart their skills to others for a price but also to carry out actual missions that were once the exclusive domain of governments, all represent a potentially grave threat to our democratic institutions. Companies like Intertel even advertise themselves as: "Your Solution to Terrorism."[38]

Modern surveillance technology, moreover, raises many questions relating to privacy. In 1987, nurses at Holy Cross Hospital in Silver Spring, Maryland, discovered that a surveillance camera had been installed in their locker room in an attempt to discover whether any of them was responsible for recent narcotics thefts at the institution. Whether unintentionally or by design, the camera transmitted scenes from the locker room to a television set in the doctor's lounge. Nurses were outraged, and their anger was not assuaged by hospital administrators who claimed that it was all a misunderstanding and that the locker room was supposed to be visible only on a private monitor manned by a member of the hospital's security staff. "That was supposed to make us feel better?" complained a nurse to the *Washington Post,* "That a man was going to be watching us without us knowing?"[39] Although the Maryland hospital incident clearly went beyond the bounds of propriety, surveillance in the workplace is becoming ever more prevalent as it becomes easier to implement.

Security industry advocates contend that such concerns are overstated and not supported by the evidence. There is room for abuse, they maintain, but it has only rarely occurred and on such occasions, appropriate steps have been taken to correct the situation. According to ASIS's E.J. Criscuoli, while a public perception of firms "providing an elite corps of Rambo-type individuals is not going to serve the profession very well," private security pre-dates public law enforcement by hundreds of years and has a legitimate role to play in modern society.[40] Governments have always failed to some degree to adequately protect their citizens. Even today, says Criscuoli, crime prevention is a low priority with most police departments; they are more concerned with response to crime. Thus, the private sector is, for the most part, primarily involved with the issue of prevention.

Governments have neither the resources nor the duty to protect every individual all the time: each individual has the responsibility to take appropriate steps to ensure his or her own safety. This is particularly true in the case of U.S. citizens and firms operating abroad in dangerous lands. It can be argued, for example, that, with the exception of the late CIA Chief-of-Station in Lebanon William Buckley; Lt. Colonel William Higgins, who was serving with the United Nations Truce Supervision Organization (UNTSO); and Associated Press reporter Terry Anderson, all of the current U.S. hostages in Lebanon demonstrated appalling bad judgment by remaining in Beirut, ignoring both considerations of common sense and their own government's pleas to leave that strife-torn country.[41]

In the final analysis, there are both practical and political limits to security. The Soviet Union and its East bloc satellites enjoy the lowest level of terrorism in the world, chiefly because totalitarian states so tightly control the activities and movements of their citizens that it is difficult, if not impossible, for terrorism to take root.[42] Indeed, there is no such thing as due process in such countries, and few restraints exist to curtail the pervasive police powers of the state. There is security from terrorism, but the average citizen pays an awful price for that security.

The real issue is what constitutes adequate and sufficient security. This question is currently under review by many American companies as well as government agencies. First, there is the matter of cost. But even more important are the constraints imposed by security. If we, as a nation, cower behind high walls and locked doors, if our embassies are constructed more like bunkers than inviting symbols of our preeminent role in the world, if our political leaders are cut off from us by phalanxes of guards, then the terrorists will have won.

3

Rescue American Style

"Rambo Raiders Save Tot"
—Headline, *New York Post,* March 14, 1988

"WE finally won one," Don Feeney announced excitedly over the telephone. He and two companions had just returned from the Middle East, where they had rescued a seven-year-old American girl and reunited her with her mother.

Their triumph was made especially poignant by the fact that Don and his colleague J.D. Roberts were former members of the super-secret U.S. counterterrorist Delta Force and survivors of the ill-fated attempt to rescue U.S. hostages from Iran in 1980. Both men had known their share of disappointment over the years in terms of failed missions and American hostages left behind.

In many respects, their whole lives were a preparation for the mission to Jordan in January 1988.

A Discreet Proposal

It all began in early December 1987. Feeney heads a three-year-old company called Corporate Training Unlimited (CTU) in

Portions of this article appeared in "Operation Lauren," by Neil C. Livingstone and David Halevy, *The Washingtonian* (September, 1988).

Fayetteville, North Carolina. Despite its innocuous name, CTU is no ordinary company. Made up largely of ex–Delta Force commandos, CTU provides specialized antiterrorist training and protective services to threatened individuals, industry, and U.S. government agencies. Its clients range from motion picture studios to foreign kidnap victims.

Feeney was sitting at his desk when a slight, well-built man in his late forties walked into his office. He had met Ev earlier that year and they had casually discussed common business interests. Ev was a highly decorated former navy pilot and prisoner of war in Vietnam who had served as a high-ranking political appointee in the Reagan administration.

After discussing CTU's capabilities and business operations, Ev asked Feeney if he and his company had ever given any thought to conducting rescue operations in foreign countries. Company executive Dave Chatellier, also one of the owners of CTU, recalls that "we told Ev that we were ready to consider the subject, but it would depend on a number of factors: the given country, the type of operation, who would be involved, and so on." Chatellier was wary of the proposal because "we did a lot of work overseas and had to make absolutely sure that there was nothing grey or black in what we agreed to carry out. It had to be just as white as the driven snow."[1]

The meeting was inconclusive, and Ev left Fayetteville and returned to Washington without really getting down to specifics. A short time later, Feeney received a call from a Texas executive, who was an acquaintance of Ev's. The executive said that he knew a woman who had a very serious problem and needed their help. Caution and discretion are virtually second nature to Feeney. He knew Ev, says Feeney, who "is well respected and well recognized. But we knew nothing about this guy." Feeney told him that he would get back to him, and placed a call to Ev to verify that the executive was who he said he was.

After Ev confirmed the executive's identity and bona fides, Feeney called him back. The executive told him that a seven-year-old child belonging to a Texas woman by the name of Cathy Mahone had been kidnapped by her ex-husband and taken back to Jordan, his country of origin. She was desperate to get the child back and wanted to talk to them about mounting a rescue.

Four days before Christmas, Feeney and Chatellier flew to Dallas for a meeting with the executive and Cathy Mahone, who were waiting for them at the airport when they arrived. There was instant rapport between the CTU men and the executive, a Special Forces veteran who headed an "A" team in Vietnam and still serves in the reserves, having attained the rank of full colonel.

Cathy Mahone, on the other hand, looked anything but the kind of person that would be hiring commandos for a risky foreign mission. The closest she had ever come to the world inhabited by the CTU men was Robert Ludlum novels and James Bond films. Vivacious yet vulnerable, Cathy was a blue-eyed beauty, with auburn hair, an animated personality, and a thick southern drawl that rolled off her tongue like molasses. She clearly was emotionally drained by the ordeal, but yet possessed an underlying toughness that impressed both Feeney and Chatellier.

In a motel room near the airport, Cathy briefed the CTU men. It was a quiet, competent, well-organized briefing complete with maps and photographs to help Feeney and Chatellier understand all of the relevant details.

Cathy's Story

Cathy was working her way through college as a waitress when she met a darkly attractive young man named Ali Bayan, who was working as a waiter and dishwasher at the same restaurant. A native of Jordan, he too was a college student. Despite their cultural differences, they seemed to share many common interests and soon began to date. It was an old-fashioned courtship, Cathy told the men from CTU, and he "swept her off her feet." Eight months later, they were married in a quiet Protestant ceremony.

Cathy's family "adored" Ali, and the young couple seemed

a perfect match. However, the marital bliss only lasted a few years. In 1979, Ali took Cathy to his hometown of Jarash, north of the Jordanian capital of Amman, to meet his properous and well-connected Sunni Moslem family. Cathy was impressed by the family's political pull, and recalled that Ali's brother Fwad had whisked them through customs without the usual formalities.

Fwad Bayan, Ali's older brother, is a wealthy pediatrician who works for the Jordanian government. His regional clinic is under the patronage and protection of the Jordanian royal family. Ali's father had two wives, who bore him twenty-four children. The two families reside in two large homes in Jarash, and both use the same last name.

While she was taken aback by the many cultural and actual physical differences between life in Jarash and her own small-town American upbringing, Cathy felt genuinely welcomed into the bosom of Ali's large, extended family. Although not a strident proponent of women's liberation, she was shocked by the subservient role women played in Arab society. In his native environment, Ali seemed to change, too. He was more demanding, less solicitous. He ignored her and spent most of his time with other men.

After returning to the United States, Cathy became pregnant. By contrast to the joy she felt, Ali blew up when she told him and left home, returning to Jarash for seven months. He came back six weeks prior to the birth of the baby. After the birth of the little girl, named Lauren, Ali hung Arabic medallions around her neck and informed Cathy that he wanted her raised in the Islamic faith. As a devout, born-again Christian, Cathy found this unacceptable, especially in light of Ali's strange absence during her pregnancy and the distance and aloofness he exhibited on returning. It was clear that the marriage was coming apart at the seams.

Six weeks after Lauren's birth, Cathy threw him out of the house and filed for divorce, which was later granted. The decree of divorce issued in the District Court of Dallas County, Texas (No. 80–17398–R–254), and dated December 30, 1980, appointed Catherine Phelps Bayan the "Managing Conservator of the child" and awarded to her "all the rights, privileges, duties, and powers of a parent, to the exclusion of the other parent, subject to the rights, privileges, duties, and powers granted to any possessory conservator named in this decree." Ali, by contrast, was "appointed Possessory Conservator of the child. It is Decreed that the Possessory Conservator shall have reasonable access to the child, but all such visitation periods shall be supervised by and in the presence of the Managing Conservator. The Possessory Conservator is hereby ORDERED to surrender the child to the Managing Conservator immediately at the end of each period of visitation." In addition, the decree also granted Cathy $175 a month in child support.

Ali didn't waste any time putting his life back together. A short time after his divorce from Cathy he remarried, this time an American woman of Jordanian descent named Maisha, who quickly bore him two children. He remained in the restaurant business, becoming part owner, with his brother Walid, of a Dallas restaurant called the Country Skillet. Cathy also remarried, to the scion of an old Texas family by the name of Lytt Mahone, who was old enough to be her father.

For the first few years after the divorce, Ali expressed little interest in his daughter, Lauren, and on two occasions Cathy had to take him to court when he failed to keep up with his child support payments. Gradually, however, he began to take his parental responsibilities more seriously, regularly visiting Lauren and taking her to movies and the circus. His restaurant was prosspering, and Cathy, too, was enjoying professional success after opening an employment agency.

When Lauren was four years old, Ali asked if he could take her to Jordan for a visit. Not wanting to alienate Ali or to discourage his interest in his daughter, Cathy agreed, although with some trepidation. Despite his promise not to stay for more than two weeks, Ali did not return as scheduled. Cathy panicked and called Ali and other family members repeatedly, until Lauren was returned to her after more than a month. Nevertheless, once Lauren was back home, Cathy began to think that she had overreacted. Ali, after all, had a thriving business in Dallas, along with a wife and two children. Why would he steal their daughter and remain in Jordan?

Things soon returned to normal, with Cathy permitting Ali to resume his visitation rights. Often he would pick up Lauren and take her to his house where she would play with his other two children. Ali's business, however, soon began to sour, a casualty of the worsening Texas economy.

Shortly before Halloween, 1987, recalled Cathy, Ali telephoned to ask if he could take Lauren to the State Fair in Houston the following weekend. He would pick her up on Saturday, he said, and have her back in time for school on Monday morning. Cathy demurred, saying that she and Lauren already had plans for Saturday. But Ali was persistent. He proposed instead that he pick Lauren up on Sunday morning, take her to the State Fair, and see that she got back in time for school on Monday. He would meet Lauren after school Monday so that she could spend the night at his home with his wife and children; Cathy could pick her up after school on Tuesday. Cathy saw no reason to be concerned, and readily agreed to the alternate plan. "That's fine," she remembered telling Ali. In actuality, Ali's request had come at just the right time since Cathy and her second husband, Lytt, were in the process of divorcing, and she thought that a few days of freedom would give her time to work out some of the details.

What Ali failed to tell Cathy was that he and his brother had sold the Country Skillet and divided the money between them. Nor did he mention that two weeks earlier he and his family had left Dallas and moved to New Jersey.

Ali came by early Sunday morning for Lauren, and Cathy spent the rest of the day and Monday morning attending to her personal matters. Finishing ahead of schedule, she decided to drive out to Lauren's school and have lunch with her, which she often did as part of a school program that encouraged parents to eat lunch with their children. But when she arrived at the school she found, to her horror, that Lauren had not attended class that day.

Cathy experienced a deep, sinking feeling. Something told her all was not as it should be. She left the school in a hurry, found the nearest pay phone, and tried to call Ali, but without success. Then she called Walid, Ali's brother. Where was Ali? she demanded to know. Walid pleaded ignorance, but added, almost as an afterthought, "He could have gone to New Jersey."

"What for?" pressed Cathy.

"Well, he was going to see his wife," answered Walid sheepishly.

"Since when does she live there?" Cathy exploded. "I didn't know that his wife was [in New Jersey]."

"He moved his wife to New Jersey two weeks ago," Walid told her.

Cathy hung up the phone and dialed Maisha's mother in New Jersey. She obtained the number from Walid, since his wife and Maisha were cousins. Maisha answered the phone. Cathy told her what had happened and demanded to know where Ali was. But Maisha explained that she thought he was still in Dallas. As they talked, Cathy could tell that Maisha was now growing alarmed.

After cutting short the conversation, Cathy placed a call to Alia, Jordan's national airline. They confirmed that Ali Bayan and Lauren Bayan had departed New York at 9:00 P.M. Sunday evening and had already landed in Amman. Now desperate, Cathy called Ali's house in Jarash, but no one would speak to her.

Cathy quickly pulled herself together and resolved that she was going to get her daughter back, whatever the risks or costs. She first turned to the Texas court system, which handed down an indictment for Ali's arrest on the grounds of second-degree kidnapping. In the event that Ali ever came back to the United States, he would be arrested on the spot.

A Dallas oil company lobbyist was foreman of the grand jury that indicted Ali, and he was deeply affected by Cathy's dilemma. He offered to be of help if he could and gave her his business card.

Shortly after the warrant was issued, Cathy began receiving phone calls from various creditors trying to track him down. During the twelve years Ali had resided in the United States, he had always had a spotless credit rating. However, it seems that prior to leaving for Jordan he had gone on a buying spree, maxing out all of his credit cards. He also had purchased a $23,000 Honda, putting a few hundred dollars down on it, and exporting it to Jordan along with the other goods when he skipped the country.

Armed with the arrest warrant for Ali, Cathy contacted the U.S. Department of State for help. According to the State Department officer who spoke with her, Cathy was informed that her problem was not unique: there were more than 500 active cases like hers on file. The State Department officer, however, could not offer Cathy a great deal of comfort or encouragement. If the child is an American citizen, the State Department can offer legal advice and attempt through diplomatic channels to secure the child's return. The local U.S. embassy is permitted to assist the parent in locating the child and to check to ensure that he or she is in good health. Despite the fact that the child has, in many cases, been kidnapped, the State Department maintains that the parents will have to be governed by the domestic law of the country where the child has been taken, even if the nation's judiciary is corrupt or unacceptably prejudiced. In the case of Jordan, it is the latter. As in other Moslem countries, Jordanian courts give custody to the father instead of the mother, regardless of the circumstances of the divorce or the father's character.

Cathy immediately perceived that the State Department was not going to be of much help since it appeared more interested in not disrupting relations with other countries than in assisting American citizens recover children abducted in custody disputes. This was confirmed by Holly Planells, with whom Cathy subsequently spoke. Planells, ironically, had also been married to a Jordanian. She had fallen in love with him while they were students at the University of Tennessee, but her prince charming turned into an Arab Archie Bunker when they returned to Amman together. He demanded that she be totally submissive to him, and even accused her of being a lesbian after she had lunch with a female friend. After the marriage failed, she was forced to return to the United States without her son. Today, the only way Planells can see her son is to travel to Jordan for short visits under her former husband's watchful eye. As a result, Planells formed a support group called "American Children Held Hostage" for other parents, nearly all of them mothers, in the same unhappy dilemma. She also told Cathy that she knew of only one successful attempt by an American mother to recover a child from a Middle Eastern country. In that case, the mother was living in Iran and fled over the border to Turkey with her child.

According to Planells, not only had the State Department been of little assistance, but a U.S. foreign service officer stationed at the embassy in Amman had actually warned her ex-husband to be careful since his former wife had organized a support group back in the States dedicated to securing the return of abducted children and was making "waves" in Congress and in the media.

Cathy was rapidly running out of options, but she was not about to give up. She turned to two former FBI officers for help, who asked her for $2,000 and told her to come back a week later. When she did, they informed her that the situation was hopeless and gave her a map of Jarash clipped from a magazine. She never heard from them again.

In the meantime, as she developed a plan of action, Cathy wanted to make certain that she didn't do anything that would spook Ali or tip him off that she would stop at nothing to get Lauren back. She knew he had relatives in Lebanon, and her worst nightmare was that he would flee there with their daughter. To make Ali think she was incapacitated by the trauma of losing Lauren, she called Jarash every day and talked to anyone who would listen: his brothers, his sisters, any member of the family. She wanted them to think she was incapable of action. Only once did Ali permit Lauren to speak to her mother for a few moments. During this period, Cathy was also communicating regularly with Maisha, Ali's wife in New Jersey.

Gradually she hatched a desperate plan to go over to Jordan and, in disguise, locate and rescue Lauren herself. It was at this point that she contacted the Dallas executive, who had served as foreman of the grand jury, and sought his advice. He urged her not to do anything rash and agreed to look into the problem. Shortly before Christmas he told her that he might have located some well-qualified people that would carry out a rescue operation.

Decision Time

Feeney and Chatellier knew that any successful military operation depended on accurate and timely intelligence. They were amazed when Cathy handed them a folder of well-organized information, including personal data and a full physical description of Ali, everything they could possibly need to know about Lauren, and three photos and a lengthy description of Jarash. She described the town, the roads leading in and out, the surrounding area, and the location—to the best of her recall—of the Bayan house. One of the photos, taken in 1979 during her trip to Jarash, showed Cathy and Ali sitting on the roof of what she believed was the Bayan house. In the background were Roman ruins that Feeney and Chatellier immediately realized would not be difficult to locate, and which could be used to zero in on the house. She described the house, noting that while it had indoor plumbing, which is unusual in Jarash, the lavatory consisted of holes in the ceramic floor. The kitchen was typically Arab and required the women of the Bayan family to cook over propane gas bottles. The folder also had the names of all of Ali's brothers and sisters and their spouses, their telephone numbers, approximate ages, physical descriptions, and a personality profile that made an effort to gauge whether they were "aggressive" or "non-aggressive."

For all of its status, Cathy explained to Feeney and Chatellier, the Bayan family made do without many things considered necessities in the West. "It was hard to believe that a powerful and prominent family like the Bayans of Jarash would just straddle a little four-inch hole in the floor to go to the bathroom,'' observes Chatellier. ''We're talking about a bath once a week on a Friday night. We're talking about a diet primarily of lamb, mutton, and rice . . . and a lot of beans.''

Cathy told the CTU men that while she was not completely familiar with Islamic customs, she knew that either Ali's mother or one of his sisters would have to be taking care of Lauren because it would be inappropriate for a father to look after the dressing, personal hygiene, and general upbringing of a daughter.

''Her story was a real heartbreaker,'' recalls Chatellier. Both he and Feeney were impressed with Cathy and touched by her dilemma. They wanted to help, but there was a question of money. Such operations, they knew, are terribly expensive. They huddled and made some quick calculations. Both the risk and the expenses would be high. They knew they should not consider it for anything less than $250,000, but both were family men who could relate to Cathy's personal anguish. Here was a woman in distress who needed their help. Equally important, though left unsaid, was the lure of such an operation. Feeney and Chatellier missed the excitement and purpose they had known during their military days. Unlike most of the services CTU performed, this was a *real mission,* and they wanted to do it.

''We told her . . . that we needed at least one night to think about it before we could give her a decision,'' remembers Chatellier. ''We also told her that we were looking, probably, for a sum in excess of $100,000 to do the job.'' Cathy, however, said that she could not scrape together more than $50,000, which represented the money she had left from the sale of her personnel agency.

It had been a long day. Feeney and Chatellier retired to talk the proposition over and to get some rest. They promised Cathy a decision in the morning. For the next several hours, the two CTU men debated the pros and cons of taking the job. It was clear that they would probably lose money on the deal, if not a whole lot more. On the other hand, they were intrigued by the wealth of intelligence data with which Cathy had provided them; it would save them a lot of time and effort. The more they talked about it, the more feasible the mission seemed.

Although Feeney once had been stationed in Beirut as part of a Delta contingent protecting the U.S. ambassador and had just returned from a job in Israel, neither he nor Chatellier was familiar with Jordan. Getting across the border from Israel into Jordan would be their first task. Then they would have to locate the girl, grab her, and spirit her back across the border.

According to Chatellier, they realized that Cathy was in a "real jam" and didn't have anyplace else to turn. "I just felt like this woman did not deserve to lose her daughter," says Chatellier.

> I also felt like the daughter did not deserve to be with a dirtbag like her Daddy. Now, we're talking about a car thief, a deceiver, a guy that stole money, plus a kidnapper. He had no use for that girl whatsoever. He knew he was taking her back to a life that she was totally unaccustomed to . . . to a world where she would no longer be an equal person, but a second-class citizen. Arabs treat their dogs better than they treat their women over there. I felt this little girl . . . did not deserve it. The mother did not deserve it. And you could feel the heart-felt emotion of this woman missing her child. I mean, the child was her whole life. She had no husband, no job, no income, no support from anyone, and had lost the one thing in her life that she loved.

There was also another reason. In Feeney's words: "This was an American child, no different than any of the other Americans that had been abducted in Beirut or Tehran. This was an American child being held against her will in an Arab nation."

They decided to undertake the mission. It was a "go"!

Operation Lauren

The following morning, Feeney and Chatellier reported to Cathy their decision. They told her that they would attempt to rescue her daughter and bring her home, but they didn't want Cathy to have any illusions about the mission. It would be dangerous and there were no guarantees of success. They would simply give it their best shot. Such operations, they told her, require careful planning and execution, as well as a large measure of luck.

She was ecstatic and agreed to do anything required of her, whatever the risks involved. They outlined certain operational guidelines regarding security and communications to which she readily acceded. Cathy, in turn, transferred $18,000 to CTU for expenses, the first of three payments that would total $50,000.

Feeney and Chatellier subsequently returned to Fayetteville, North Carolina, to begin the operational planning and to select the team that would go on the mission. Like so many times in the past when they were in uniform, Christmas would take a backseat to the requirements of the mission.

Their firm, CTU, occupies a yellow barn-like building on a busy thoroughfare not too far from Fort Bragg, the home of Delta Force, the Special Forces, and 82nd Airborne, and the U.S. Special Warfare School. For years, Fort Bragg has served as the organizational "hub" for U.S. special operations forces and activities. Despite the creation of the new Special Operations Command at McDill Air Force Base in Florida, few believe that Fort Bragg's importance with respect to special operations will be eclipsed. On any given day, there are a number of active-duty Green Berets, Delta men, or cops hanging around CTU's headquarters, having a cup of coffee and jawboning with CTU staffers.

CTU had eleven salaried employees, and another twenty or so on call, who were hired on a contract basis to perform specific kinds of work. All were experienced covert operators, most hailing from the Special Forces or Delta. All were former noncommissioned officers, and therefore not afraid to roll up their sleeves and do the dirty work themselves. There are no desk jobs at CTU.

The company owns—"together with the bank"—sixty acres of land outside of Fayetteville where it maintains a shooting range and training area. CTU instructors give courses in everything from pistol shooting to sniping and combat shotgun techniques. CTU also leases a nearby airstrip and the Rockingham NASCAR circuit when it is conducting defensive driving courses.

The first thing Feeney and Chatellier did was to begin the process of selecting who would go on the mission. Considerable thought was devoted to identifying the right mix of skills and backgrounds that would be needed. After that, it was a process of eliminating those in the firm who were already committed to other contracts or, for some other reason, couldn't go, and to judge each man left against the criteria that had been established. The team that was finally chosen was composed of four men:

DON FEENEY. Unlike most of his colleagues, Feeney is not a southerner. Small, wiry, a street-wise Irish-Italian kid from a broken family, Feeney dropped out of high school in Brooklyn to help support his family. At the age of seventeen, he enlisted in the Army and soon was hustling everything from pizzas to PX goods on the side. He admits that he was headed for trouble until he started raising his hand every time someone asked for volunteers. First he volunteered for corporal school, where he graduated near the top of his class. Next he volunteered to go to Ranger School, and subsequently volunteered for a three-year hitch in the 82nd Airborne. Finally, he joined the Special Forces and later volunteered for the ''new unit I heard they were starting,'' which turned out to be Delta. He was the sixth man in and stayed for eight years, until leaving the service in 1986.

During the 1980 mission to rescue U.S. hostages in Iran, Feeney intercepted the busload of Iranian civilians that unexpectedly came upon the Desert One refueling site. ''The situation was really comical,'' he recalls. ''We didn't know what to do with them. I screamed for a Farsi speaker. So here comes one of our guys from Georgia. I didn't know he spoke Farsi. He started screaming at the frightened passengers in German, like they were supposed to understand German with a southern accent.''

Feeney's biggest regret is that they abandoned the Sea Stallion helicopters at the site after a chopper hit one of the C-130s, which exploded, killing eight Americans and leaving a number badly burned. In addition to being serviceable, the choppers contained a bonanza of intelligence information for the Iranians. ''We were told that an air strike was coming in to blow them up,'' asserts Feeney. ''We should have never listened to the major who said it. In a moment like this, you don't trust anybody but yourself. We should have blown the birds.''

The debacle is never far from Feeney's thoughts, even today. After the failure at Desert One, Feeney spent time in Beirut guarding the U.S. ambassador and was involved in the American operation in Grenada. At the present time, he serves as the president of CTU and the driving force behind the company.

DAVE CHATELLIER. Over six feet tall and 230 pounds, Dave Chatellier is the kind of man ''you'd want as a back-up in a bar fight.'' The oldest man on the team, Chatellier, 48, is built like a tank, with wrists as thick as fence posts and the neck of an NFL lineman. Raised in Texas, his roots are part Cajun and part Cherokee. Soft-spoken and seemingly unflappable, Chatellier is a former military intelligence man who served with a variety of classified units conducting ''black'' operations in Vietnam, Europe, and elsewhere. So sensitive were most of his assignments that he still can't talk about them even today.

One of the original partners in CTU, Chatellier is responsible for intelligence and technical training programs. He is also the company ''worrier'' who, true to his training, analyzes every problem from every vantage point before deciding on a course of action. The classic ''intel'' operator, he is both coldly calculating and extremely methodical.

J.D. ROBERTS. By contrast to Chatellier, James Daniel

(better known as "J.D.") Roberts wears his emotions on his sleeve. By his own description, he's the kind of person that can be moved to tears "while watching the flag raised or a movie like Bambi." By the same token, he'll "smash your face if you try to make fun of me."

A natural combat leader, he was born in Memphis, Tennessee, forty-two years ago. Half American Indian and half Scottish, he is a James Garner look-alike, with curly hair, an easy wit, and a broad smile. The smile, however, hides lightning reflexes and an extraordinary capacity for controlled violence. He joined the U.S. Army the day his father, who had served with Patton during World War II, retired after twenty-two years of service. After boot camp, he was shipped to Vietnam and celebrated his nineteenth birthday in the Mekong Delta.

Although he was a qualified sniper, he was selected to become the assistant to the battalion's chaplain. J.D. was offended: he had come to Vietnam to fight and that's what he wanted to do. But after being assured he would see more combat as a chaplain's assistant than anything else (because the chaplain constantly moved from one scene of action to the next), J.D. capitulated. And sure enough, for the next twelve months, "I was in every battle the (first battalion) of the 12th Cavalry was in," he smiles, "as the chaplain's assistant." During his first tour he won a Bronze Star, a Purple Heart, and other medals and citations.

Back from Vietnam, he went to the 101st Airborne, was sent to Officer Candidate School (OCS), and graduated as a second lieutenant. However, someone read his orders wrong and instead of being shipped off to the 10th Special Forces Group, he was sent to Army Special Services where he "issued tennis shoes and basketballs for a year." Things finally were straightened out, and he joined the 10th Special Forces Group and was promoted to captain. He was sent back to Vietnam as a member of "Mike Force," but quickly ran afoul of an overbearing colonel who was poking him in the chest to make a point.

"I told him 'don't do that no more,' " says J.D.

But the Colonel continued to poke J.D., who responded by decking him. "I poked him back," he explains with a grin.

In view of the seriousness of his offense, another colonel suggested that J.D. get as far away from headquarters as possible. He could arrange for him to take over a Special Forces "A" team, he said, and J.D. readily agreed. He was flown out that night in a chopper to a fire base in the middle of the Delta. There were plenty of tracers and signs of combat everywhere.

As they approached the fire base, J.D. got out on one of the skids in preparation to jump off. But while they were still twelve or fourteen feet off the ground, he felt a powerful blow in the small of his back and the next thing he knew he was lying in the dirt, gasping for breath, in the middle of the fire base. The Colonel had booted him in the back. As his wind began to return, he looked up into the twin barrels of a 12-gauge shotgun.

"Who in the hell are you?" someone barked.

Before he could answer, an enemy attack on the fire base erupted. J.D. helped man a mortar, and when the attack was over he walked to the team house after introducing himself to one of the other men.

"What in the hell did they throw out of that chopper?" the team sergeant asked as they walked in the door.

"Our new commander," came the response.

J.D. stepped forward, and the sergeant shook his head. "I can't believe it."

"What do you mean?" questioned J.D.

"We never had a replacement this fast before."

"Huh?"

"Look behind the bar."

J.D. walked over and behind the makeshift bar was a captain lying dead. He had been killed earlier that day.

When he returned from Vietnam, reductions in force were under way. There was no place for him as an officer, so he accepted a demotion to sergeant and for five years served as a Ranger instructor. When Delta came along, he went through one of the early selection courses and joined the unit. "I loved

Delta," he reflects. "It was more than just a great unit: it was a family. Everybody had combat experience; all were Vietnam veterans. All of us were over thirty years old, all were married. In my squadron of 47 men, most of us were southerners or from the Midwest. One only guy smoked. That's how evenly matched we were."

When Delta went to Iran, J.D. carried an Indian tomahawk. To this day, he believes that the mission should have gone forward after the Desert One incident. After Iran and the retirement of the unit's commander "Chargin' Charlie" Beckwith, "The fun was over," says J.D. He went on one more secret mission, nearly got killed, and then retired to the family farm in Georgia on a $900-a-month military pension. Thus, when Don Feeney told him they were going to create CTU, J.D. asked to be counted in.

JIM HATFIELD. The fourth man on the mission, and the youngest, was Jim Hatfield. Raised in a small mining town in Arizona, Hatfield has a laconic smile and penetrating eyes. He doesn't speak unless spoken to. Unlike the other CTU men, "Nobody ever shot at me," he says. Discharged from the Rangers after being injured in 1974, he reenlisted and became an intelligence specialist with the Special Forces.

Despite their similar backgrounds and experience, there was a good deal of heated debate among the team members and some of their colleagues at CTU over the actual mission plan. Chatellier recalls the differences of opinion that emerged: "After Cathy left us that night, Donny [Feeney] said, 'This is a piece of cake. We just go inside, get the girl and take her home.' But it was not going to be that easy. If it was going to be a 'piece of cake,' it would be because we turned every stone over in advance and looked at every option."

"Donny wants to be told: this is the building, go kick in the door and kill everyone. That's the operation. Don't worry about anything else; just pack up and leave [when it's all over]." By contrast, says Chatellier, "I'm a very slow, methodical person. I want to know every detail, to know which way the door swings, to know how many people are in there, so that I don't have any surprises when I go in. Donny's virtue is that he is very spontaneous and that makes us work well together.''

By contrast to the unbridled enthusiasm of his colleagues, Chatellier knew that they might be gambling the very future of CTU on the success or failure of one operation. Indeed, thoughts of possible failure, and its repercussions, consumed him. While it would be planned and executed like a military mission, it clearly differed in one critical point: anyone captured would probably be tried as a criminal, or a mercenary, and sentenced to a long prison term. "We were concerned because of our military backgrounds," said Chatellier, "if anything went wrong in this operation it would turn into 'American terrorists invade Jordan.' We were genuinely concerned that we would be labeled CIA, or an undercover U.S. military operation. It would have given the Jordanians leverage against the United States, and it would probably have meant a longer jail term for us.'' It was unlikely, moreover, that the U.S. government would take any steps to intervene on behalf of the U.S. commandos in the event that something did go wrong.

Since Ali had Lauren's passport, they initially discarded any thought of escaping from Jordan via plane, car, or boat, since all would require them to pass through border control. They also rejected any method out of the country—such as ramming a Jordanian army checkpoint with a truck—that might result in gunfire or place Lauren in jeopardy. It had to be a covert operation, discreet and executed with precision. Thus, their original plan called for them to penetrate Jordan, grab little Lauren, and "rucksack" her, that is, carry her piggyback, about forty kilometers from Jarash to the Israeli border. It was open country, sparsely populated, with little vegetation or water. Once at the border, they would make arrangements for the Israelis to provide them with "safe conduct."

Finally, it came time to assign roles to the members of the team. It was decided that Dave Chatellier would go into Jordan ahead of everyone else and reconnoiter the situation. He would travel to Jarash undercover, locate the house and the girl, review the various escape routes, and collect as much intelligence vital to the mission as he could. Don Feeney and J.D. Roberts would carry out the actual "snatch" of Lauren and sprint her to safety. Jim Hatfield was to be the backup man, serving as a human message-relay station in either Cyprus or Israel.

Cathy was cautioned to keep her own counsel and not to speak with anyone but the executive in Dallas about the mission. She was told to maintain her routine and to continue calling Ali, so as not to tip him off that she was considering any kind of drastic action.

On December 27, only a week after first meeting Cathy, the CTU team departed North Carolina for Tel Aviv, where they were to be met by several Israeli contacts whose help they would require.

Back to the Drawing Board

To hide their real mission, the CTU men claimed to be Hollywood movie makers looking Israel and Jordan over as possible locations for a new motion picture. As they had recently provided security for a major motion picture filmed in Israel, Feeney was confident that no one was likely to question their activities.

Shortly after arriving, Feeney and his companions sat down with their Israeli contacts and described the real nature of their mission and their proposed plan of action. After listening to Feeney, the Israelis expressed a number of concerns. There was no way the rescue team could reach the Israeli border without being mistaken for a hostile force, they told the men from CTU. As to official Israeli cooperation, they were advised to "forget it." The Israeli government was not about to take sides in a complicated custody struggle, especially when it involved former U.S. Delta Force commandos carrying out an illegal paramilitary operation in neighboring Jordan.

After being taken for a tour of the Israeli border and observing firsthand the tank traps, gun emplacements, and concertina wire, it was clear to Feeney that another escape route was needed. "It was just impossible to cross the border between the two countries without being shot at by both sides," concluded

Feeney. "And to take a frightened little girl with you, on that path, would just be suicidal."

Although no alternative plan of escape had been agreed upon, it was decided that Chatellier should go ahead and do his reconnaissance of Jarash. He flew from Israel to Cyprus, and then on to Amman, where he booked a room at the Amman Holiday Inn and rented a car from Avis. He traveled under his own name on his own passport, and was given a two-week tourist visa. If anyone asked, he was scouting possible locations for the movie company, especially around the Roman ruins at Jarash. In view of the fact that tourism is one of Jordan's chief industries, no one bothered Chatellier or attempted to interfere with his activities.

In antiquity, the city of Jarash was known as Gerasa, and was a member city of the Decapolis, one of the ten cities that served as a buffer zone between the Roman province of Syria and the independent Nabataean Kingdom remembered for the cities of Petra and Ovdat. Located astride important trade routes, Jarash had prospered under Roman rule and been the site of an ambitious building program. Today, Jarash's Roman forum, theater, and Temple of Zeus are world famous and listed in most guides as outstanding monuments of Greco-Roman culture and civilization.

Chatellier's first task was to identify the Bayan house in Jarash. He couldn't risk asking anyone for the address of the Bayan family without possibly tipping them off that a stranger was in town asking questions. All he had to go on was the photo of Cathy and Ali on the rooftop, with the Roman ruins in the background, and her vague recollection of where the house was situated. "What I had to do was go to the Roman ruins and shoot an azimuth back to Jarash," says Chatellier, referring to a navigation technique for calculating another location from a fixed point. But he soon learned that Jarash had changed dramatically in the nearly ten years since the photo was taken: the town had quadrupled in size, new discoveries had also greatly increased the size of the Roman ruins, and a previously undeveloped area in front of the Bayan house was now covered with buildings.

To further complicate matters, the streets of Jarash are extremely narrow, permitting only one car to pass at a time. The streets have no names, and the houses are not numbered. The city has no hotels or motels, and only a few local restaurants. There are no taxicabs in Jarash, therefore Chatellier would have to drive himself around.

Tourists almost never ventured into Jarash itself. The road from Amman leads to a police station on the edge of town, and to a nearby parking lot from which tourists are taken to the Roman ruins. "Tourists never see Jarash," says Chatellier. "No tourists or foreigners drive or walk through the streets of modern Jarash. Not only could I not easily locate the house, but my very presence in the city of Jarash was very unusual." In order to be less conspicuous, Chatellier donned an Arab headdress and a goatee when he travelled around Jarash.

On his first trip to Jarash, Chatellier parked his car and paid a fee of one and a half dinars, which permitted him to spend the day at the ruins. He spent four hours taking pictures of the ruins and the city of Jarash from the Temple of Zeus. From the ruins he also surveyed the city as unobtrusively as possible, using an eight power moniker. Through the moniker, his eye fixed on a house that certainly appeared to be the Bayan residence. He couldn't believe his good fortune, especially since it was beginning to rain—a cold, freezing rain that chilled him to the bone. A short time later, as he drove around the city of Jarash trying to get close to the house, it began to snow. After some difficulty, he located the house he had spied through the moniker. He took pictures of the ruins from the vicinity of the house, and then familiarized himself with the city, its streets, buildings, and potential escape routes.

He nearly got stranded in Jarash as the snow began to pile up. There is no snow removal equipment, and the only effort local authorities make to keep the roads clear is to run army trucks up and down the highways. He managed to return to Amman, however, satisfied that he had accomplished a great deal.

The following day, he returned to Jarash to continue his reconnaissance, discovering to his dismay that there was a police station located almost directly behind the house he had identified. Even worse, there was an army post at the end of the street, a revelation that Chatellier admits "did not fill my heart with joy."

After watching the house he suspected belonged to the Bayan family for more than a day without seeing anyone who resembled Ali or Lauren, Chatellier began to have second thoughts. Maybe it wasn't the right house. As the hours passed, his doubts began to mount. To clear his head, he drove down to the city's central market and sat alone in his car pondering the situation and turning his options over in his mind. Then, suddenly, without warning, he glimpsed a group of children being led through the marketplace by a woman who resembled one of Ali's sisters. The woman was holding a young girl by the hand, a young girl with blue eyes and a pug nose! It was Lauren.

But before Chatellier could move, they disappeared into the crowd and were gone.

In the days that followed, Chatellier never saw Lauren again. He continued to maintain his surveillance of the suspected Bayan house without success, and soon began to monitor other houses as well. Gradually, he began to understand the routines and rhythms of Jarash. The rush hour began around 6 A.M., when hundreds of buses converged on the city to pick up people and transport them to work. Between 7:30 and 8:00 A.M., school buses appeared on the streets. All the children dressed in uniforms: blue for grade school students, green for middle school. Buses were segregated, with girls boarding one bus and boys another. Each bus appeared to have a chaperone. Chatellier never observed children alone or standing on the street. Generally, they waited until the school bus appeared and only then left the house or protected confines of a walled courtyard.

At least he didn't have to worry about dogs, thought Chatellier, which often are a real nuisance when conducting surveillance. There were no dogs in Jarash; the only dogs Chatellier ever saw roamed in packs in the countryside. There were, however, lots of rats and, as a result, literally thousands of cats in Jarash. "We saw some major rats [in Jarash]," recalls J.D. Roberts, "rats so big it would take four cats to whip one of 'em.''

Initially, he was greatly troubled by all of the stares he received from pedestrians as he drove around the city. Wherever he went, it seemed like people would turn and "look right at him." He soon figured out that they were afraid that he was going to splash them as he drove along the rutted streets full of potholes filled with water. Indeed, most people in Jarash walked in the middle of the street in order to force traffic to slow down so they wouldn't be splashed.

In order to keep a low profile, he tried to exchange his rental car every two or three days. This required Chatellier to come up with a variety of novel complaints and excuses to get Avis to take back his old car and give him a new one. But Avis was very accommodating, and in the space of two weeks he used six different cars. And to further minimize the risk that the car might attract suspicion, he generally parked it and prowled the city on foot.

Each day Chatellier drove to Jarash, he was stopped at police checkpoints along the road, sometimes as many as three times in 50 kilometers. The green tags on his rental car clearly indicated that he was not a local, and any time he pulled over to the side of the road, he attracted attention. Invariably someone—a soldier, a policeman, or just a local citizen—would come by and inquire if anything was wrong. At the checkpoints, generally he would hold up his American passport and start talking. If the policeman did not speak any English, he would normally wave Chatellier on through. If he spoke a little English, and attempted to ask him for his license, Chatellier would plead ignorance and finally the policeman would relent and let him continue on his way. The experience of dealing with Jordanian police at road checkpoints was invaluable to Chatellier in understanding the local mentality and in ascertaining how much he could get away with. He soon discovered that the Jordanian police never set up a checkpoint in Jarash; they were always placed outside of town on the highways and country roads.

The Search for Allies

Meanwhile, back in Israel, Feeney and his companions were exploring other options, short of an actual rescue, to secure Lauren's return to her mother. One of their contacts had put them in touch with an Israeli journalist known to maintain a close relationship with Jordan's former queen, Dina, King Hussein's first wife, who lived in London. The journalist, Aharon Barneha, was planning a trip to London in less than a week and he agreed to meet with Dina to see if she would take up Cathy Mahone's case with the Jordanian government.

Feeney also visited the U.S. embassy in Tel Aviv and met with one of the embassy officials to learn what, if anything, the American government could do to assist them. The embassy official provided Feeney with a number of documents, including the Hague Convention on the abduction of children. The Convention provides that an abducted child must be returned to the country where he or she was residing at the time of the abduction until the issues can be sorted out and a settlement effected. Feeney was also given the name of Donnie P. Minyard, a consular official at the U.S. embassy in Amman, who supposedly handled cases of abducted children in Jordan.

Feeney passed along Minyard's name to Chatellier, and Chatellier gave him a call at the embassy on January 14, saying that he wanted to discuss a child that had been abducted from the United States. Minyard told him to drop by the embassy, and a short time later Chatellier presented his passport at the consular affairs office. He was told to take a seat in the crowded waiting room; Minyard would see him in a moment. While in the military Chatellier had been stationed abroad for many years, and even when located stateside he often traveled to foreign countries and spent a good deal of time in U.S. embassies. He generally viewed foreign service officers as competent and helpful, and expected Mr. Minyard to be the same.

After waiting more than an hour, a tall, prissy man finally called Chatellier's name and he approached a bullet-proof glass window. "What's the nature of your business?" asked Minyard.

"I spoke to you on the phone," answered Chatellier, raising his voice in order to be heard over the din in the background.

Minyard didn't respond.

"Isn't there someplace we can speak privately about this?" asked Chatellier, not wanting to discuss a matter of such sensitivity in a room full of Jordanian citizens. "I've never been denied a private meeting with a U.S. consular official before."

Minyard responded that he was extremely busy: couldn't Chatellier see how many people were waiting to see him? If Chatellier wanted to talk, said Minyard, it would have to be in the waiting room.

Reluctantly, under the circumstances, Chatellier explained that he wanted some advice about an abducted U.S. citizen.

"Is this a child you are talking about?"

"Yes," said Chatellier.

"Well, I'll read this to you," Minyard said, fumbling for a piece of paper. "I wrote it down somewhere. I think I've still got it." His prepared statement informed Chatellier that the U.S. embassy could not get involved in matters relating to the abduction of children, even if tne child was a U.S. citizen. He stated that if the child was with a Jordanian, the Jordanian had all legal rights to it and that he would not support the mother's claim because she did not live in Jordan.

"We're talking about an American citizen," Chatellier shot back, incredulously. "Are you telling me that you will not help an American citizen?"

"No," Minyard corrected him. "That's not what I am saying. What I am saying is that I cannot and will not help the mother. Regardless of where the child was born, and regardless of how it got here, if the child's in Jordan, it is considered a Jordanian resident.'' He then gave Chatellier a form letter pertaining to child custody disputes and said that if he was formally requested to do so by the Department of State he would inquire as to whether the child was being abused. But he would not do anything else. As a final rejoinder, he recommended that the mother retain a Jordanian attorney and take the father to court.

Chatellier thanked Minyard for his time and left.

The next day he drove back to Jarash convinced, now more than ever, that the only way Lauren would ever be reunited with her mother would be if they mounted a successful rescue operation. His next goal was to find an acceptable overland escape route. He ruled out any attempt to exfiltrate the rescue party through either Saudi Arabia or Iraq, since both borders were too far away. Jarash, however, was situated close to both Israel and Syria.

Chatellier decided to check out the southern Jordanian port city of Aqaba, which lies just two kilometers from the Israeli port of Eilat. The rescue team could easily reach the Israeli coast from Jordan with a small boat or Zodiac raft. It took eight hours to reach Aqaba from Jarash, and when he got there he discovered that a brigade-sized military force was stationed in the city. Shtire armored vehicles, with fifty-caliber machine guns mounted on the turrets, seemed to be everywhere. The streets were full of soldiers, and every major intersection had five or six policemen in it.

Given the time it would take to reach Aqaba, it was clear that the military and the police would be on the lookout for Lauren and the rescue party. It was very unlikely that they could get through the city unobserved. Although he could see Eilat from the shore, and was so close he could swim to Israel with Lauren on his back, prudence dictated that he abandon Eilat as a possible escape route.

He returned to Jarash and decided to investigate the Syrian border. He drove northward toward Syria, but the closer he came to the border, the more the road deteriorated. At times he slowed to a crawl. He knew the Jordanians would not expect the rescue team to escape via Syria because of its tight border controls and pervasive police state apparatus, but these same factors made such an escape problematic and very risky. Thus, by process of elimination he knew that they would have to escape from Jordan by crossing into Israel at some point other than Aqaba. The only real option left was the Allenby Bridge, linking Jordan and Israel. He would have to find the fastest route to the bridge from Jarash and then worry about how to get Lauren across without a passport.

Reinforcements

On Friday, January 15, Israeli journalist Aharon Barneha returned from London to Tel Aviv with the news that former Queen Dina had flatly refused to get involved in the matter. It turned out that she had tried to help in an earlier case and had gotten burned, and therefore was reluctant to do anything to assist Cathy Mahone. It was evident that nothing short of a rescue operation was likely to produce results. As a result of Barneha's report, Feeney and Roberts immediately left Israel for Cyprus. They reached Amman on the 18th, and went directly to the Holiday Inn to meet Chatellier.

According to Chatellier, "Donny felt that since I had seen Lauren, we ought to just go take care of it. I felt, however, there was a lot more to do before we could go and get her." Chatellier convinced his companions that their operational intelligence still was incomplete and that more time was needed in Jarash. While three people would certainly increase the risk of unwanted attention, the extra manpower would mean that they could do the kind of surveillance required to produce results.

By now Dave Chatellier was a familiar figure around Jarash. "Dave tried to be covert and sneaky," recalls J.D. Roberts. "But when you are six-foot-three and built like a small mountain, it's rather hard to do when everyone else hits you chest high." Feeney was having his problems too. Despite his best efforts to blend in with the locals, upon seeing him kids would approach him with a big smile and try out their English on him.

Roberts, who has a dark complexion and black moustache, was faring only a little better.

Time was running out. They could not count on their luck holding forever; soon someone was bound to get suspicious about the foreigners in Jarash and mention something to the police or military.

It was now more vital than ever that they locate the Bayan household. They continued to maintain surveillance on the house that had been identified by Chatellier. They also went back to the ruins and, now that there were three of them, attempted to identify the right house by means of triangulation. Their results, however, were still inconclusive. Their frustration was mounting.

Roberts decided to risk a close-up look at the house that Chatellier had been watching, and under the cover of darkness he approached the house from the rear. It was late, and everything was still. Suddenly, he heard voices behind him. Thinking quickly, he slipped into a crack in a crumbling wall that bordered the alley. As he flattened himself against the wall in the shadows, two local men stopped just a few feet away and lit up cigarettes and talked animatedly. Finally, they ground out their cigarettes on the ground and proceeded on their way. Roberts moved closer to the house, but there was no visible activity; nothing to indicate who lived inside. He rejoined his companions empty-handed.

It was now obvious that they were going to need Cathy Mahone's help. Not only could she probably identify the Bayan house, but the more they thought about it, she could provide other valuable assistance. Her presence would be needed to calm and reassure Lauren during the actual rescue. Although they had planned on showing Lauren photographs of themselves with her mother, they could not count on her reaction. Even if no alarm had yet gone out, two or three American men traveling with a terrified, or possibly even hysterical, young girl was bound to raise suspicions at the various checkpoints they would have to transit.

After spending so much time in Jarash, moreover, Chatellier had concluded that the best place to grab the girl was on her way to or from school. From watching the school buses leave Jarash in the morning, he was convinced that she was not attending school in Amman, as Cathy had earlier been led to believe. But if not in Amman, where was her school?

It was time to call Cathy.

On their way to Jordan, Feeney and Roberts had met in Cyprus with Cathy, whom they had summoned a few days earlier. She brought with her Lauren's American passport, which was in the name of Lauren Bayan. Cathy, it turned out, had continued to call Ali, but a few days before arriving in Cyprus had finally lost her temper, screaming that he was "no good," a "rotten wimp," and "a thief," and so on, until he hung up on her. She had remained in Cyprus with Jim Hatfield in case she was needed in Jordan.

Feeney called her from Amman, and in guarded language told her that it was vital for her to reestablish contact with Ali and to attempt, if at all possible, to learn where Lauren was going to school. "I don't care what you do," he explained. "Promise him anything. Grovel, beg, cry, anything. Just find out where Lauren is going to school."

Accordingly, Cathy placed a call to Ali and apologized for her earlier outburst. Without telling him where she was calling from, she pleaded with him for news of her daughter. He told her that Lauren was all right. "What do you mean, 'all right'?" she demanded. "She doesn't even speak Arabic."

"I've got her in a new private school here in Jarash," he responded. "She is learning Arabic and doing just fine." Then Ali put Lauren on the phone, and she told her mother that she was the biggest child in the school.

Cathy quickly passed the information on to the CTU team, and after a few inquiries, Chatellier learned the location of the new private school in Jarash. He also found out from one of the local citizens that the school's pupils rode to and from school in a little orange school bus.

The following day, while Feeney stayed in Amman to handle

other details, Chatellier and Roberts returned to Jarash. Both
men are born-again Christians, and en route they decided to
pray for God's help in achieving their objective. According to
Roberts, the prayer went something like, "Lord, we have been
doing this for almost three weeks and have got no results. We
need your help. It will not happen without your help. So please,
if you want this thing to work, help us."

Shortly thereafter, while parked along a narrow street in
Jarash, a little orange school bus passed by and there, in the
front seat of the bus, remembers Roberts, was Lauren, "looking
at me through the window. All I saw were these two big blue
eyes and that pushed up nose. But I had no doubt in my mind
[who it was]." Chatellier was driving, and he took off in pursuit
of the bus. "Dave is used to covert stuff in Europe, spy versus
spy," says Roberts. "So he's trying to follow this bus, staying
back two city blocks. That doesn't work well in Jarash. We lost
the bus in five minutes." However, a few minutes later they
spotted the bus again and continued their surveillance until it
reached the school. Roberts, however, worried that their car was
too visible and that the driver would pick up on the surveillance.
"We're in a red Nissan. I mean fire-engine red," he says,
laughing at the memory. "It stands out like a maraschino cherry
in a snowbank." But, fortunately, nothing happened. The bus
driver surely noticed them, but it didn't seem to register that he
was being followed.

Over the next several days, they continued to follow the bus
on its daily rounds. The bus took a highly circuitous route,
sometimes doubling back on the same street twice to pick up
children. Chatellier and Roberts were mystified, and only later
realized that the children were never permitted to cross a street
to board the bus; indeed, every child climbed on the bus on the
left side, after being handed over to the chaperone on board by
a family member. No child was ever allowed to be in the open
for more than a second or two. The practice had evolved not
only for safety reasons, but also due to the legacy of blood feuds
in the Arab world. Vengeance is sometimes visited on a family's
children for alleged sins committed by parents or even grand-

parents. Thus, children are closely protected and never left out of sight.

While Chatellier and Roberts continued to search for the Bayan house in Jarash, Don Feeney was in Amman making arrangements to get across the Allenby Bridge when the moment came for them to escape. One of those he turned to for advice was the Assistant Regional Security Officer (ARSO) of the U.S. embassy, Frank Baker. As a former Delta Force member and embassy protection specialist, Feeney is part of the "old boy" network and, when he travels abroad, often stops by to get acquainted with the RSO or ARSO. Baker, a quiet and effective Marine veteran who had previously served in Beirut, had never met Feeney before but welcomed him and extended to him the kind of professional courtesy he would to anyone with Feeney's background.

Feeney never told Baker his real mission in Jordan, but instead inquired about Jordanian security procedures and border controls. He asked Baker for the name of a trusted Jordanian citizen who might serve as a guide, and Baker introduced him to Adil Abdilhafiz Abdilrahman Abbadi, a part-time employee of the embassy who occasionally served as a guide and expeditor for visiting Americans. The thirty-four-year-old Abbadi is a former Jordanian military officer and father of three children. Feeney hired him to assist in the rescue.

Abbadi's reach into the government was evident when he took Feeney, Chatellier, and Roberts to the Ministry of Interior to secure passes for the Allenby Bridge. He seemed to know everyone, and quickly obtained passes for the three CTU men. However, the ministry official would not issue passes for Cathy and Lauren until Cathy appeared in person at the ministry.

Now was the moment for Cathy to come to Amman. Feeney called her in Cyprus and she took the first available flight to Jordan. They met her at the airport and drove straight to Jarash in a newly rented car. To avoid anyone recognizing them, the CTU men all wore Arab headdresses and Cathy donned a veil. They arrived in Jarash just before nightfall and told Cathy that they were not going to tell her anything. She was to take them through the city, relying on her memory. Initially, everything was strange and different to her. It had, after all, been almost a decade since she had been in Jarash.

On a second swing through the city, Cathy remembered the location of the home of Ali's aunt. It turned out to be the house that Chatellier and his companions had been surveilling for days. Then it came back to her: the pictures had been taken on the roof of the aunt's home, not on the roof of the Bayan family home. They had spent days looking for the wrong house.

Now that Cathy had recognized the aunt's house, other sites and locations began to come back to her in a flood of memories. The Bayan house was near a drugstore, she remembered. Just around the corner from a drugstore owned by his uncle. She had walked there once.

From the days he had spent in Jarash, Chatellier knew that all of the drugstores and doctors' offices were located near the central business district, in a quarter that was a little off the beaten track. He drove her to the district and found a drugstore that looked familiar to her. They proceeded past the drugstore at a crawl until Cathy indicated a dark side street a short distance away.

"Are you sure?" Chatellier pressed her.

"When I looked down the street I got a cold chill," she responded.

Tension was mixed with relief as they turned up the street and spotted, among the Mercedes sedans owned by the doctors in the neighborhood, a white Honda Accord with Texas tags.

Cathy began to tremble. "It's him," she said, indicating two men near the Honda. One of them was handing the other a transistor radio. "It's Ali."

They continued on by, trying to make themselves invisible by scrunching down in the seats. Fortunately, it was dark and he was engrossed in conversation. Cathy pointed out the Bayan family house. Unbelievably, the house was only a few hundred feet from the school, which was located on the other side of the street. Although she easily could have walked to school, Lauren was subjected to a lengthy bus ride every day because of the local preoccupation with security and the fact that it simply wasn't local practice for children to walk to school.

After days of fruitless searching and endless hours of surveillance, they had finally reached their objective. All that remained was to learn where and when Lauren boarded the bus.

Final Preparations

The following morning, Adil Abbadi took Cathy to the Interior Ministry to get passes entitling her and Lauren to cross the Allenby Bridge. It had been decided that once they had Lauren, Cathy, Feeney and Roberts would head for the Allenby Bridge. Since Lauren had entered Jordan on her Jordanian passport, and was going to leave using her U.S. passport, she would be missing a vital entry stamp. Abbadi assured them that for a little money the officials at the bridge would overlook the matter of the entry stamp. They agreed that Chatellier would remain behind to pay off Jordanian officials at the bridge, to return the cars, and to run interference in the event that there was hot pursuit by the Jordanian police or military. He would fly or walk out later, depending on the circumstances.

In order to locate the quickest route from Jarash to the Allenby Bridge, Chatellier and Roberts combed the highways and back roads throughout the area. Because of the poor condition of most of the roads, they concluded that they would have to stay on the primary road leading to the bridge. There were only two checkpoints on the road, but occasionally random police checkpoints—which they could not anticipate—were also thrown up.

If everything went without a hitch, it would take them approximately an hour and a quarter to reach the Allenby Bridge from the city limits of Jarash. Chatellier and Roberts stopped at the bridge and checked the hours that it was open for crossing. That accomplished, they returned to Amman to get some sleep. They would have to be up bright and early the next morning, for they still lacked one last vital piece of information: did Lauren actually live in the Bayan house?

They were waiting for the bus when it appeared at the Bayan

house the following morning. Chatellier and Cathy were in the car, its engine idling. Feeney and Roberts were loitering in an alleyway across the street. A minute or two before the bus chugged into view, the front door of the house opened and one of the aunts walked Lauren to the edge of the street and stood with her hand on the girl's shoulder. When the bus pulled up in front of the house, the aunt physically turned her over to the chaperone and Lauren boarded the bus. The bus continued on its rounds, traveling to the outskirts of the city and then back again until it reached the school, a ride of about twenty minutes.

Without waiting around any longer, the CTU men left Jarash and headed for Amman. They had spent too much time in Jarash already and had been lucky that no one had grown suspicious of them. Now they had all of the "intel" necessary to do the job. The only real decision that remained was where to grab the girl.

On the way back to Amman they weighed the various options. They could grab Lauren from her aunt as they waited for the school bus in the morning, but the alarm would go out so quickly that they would probably be apprehended before they even got out of Jarash. They could blow up Ali's car in downtown Jarash as a diversion, and simultaneously stop the bus and grab Lauren. But such an operation, even if well planned and executed, ran the risk of innocent casualties. The CTU men did not want to be branded as mercenaries or terrorists, and thus ruled out any thought of using violence to effect the rescue. Indeed, they even decided not to carry firearms on the mission.

The decision was made to take Lauren from the bus as it made its morning rounds. Initially, they thought about hijacking the bus, taking it to a remote location, taping the driver and the chaperone like mummies, and making a run for the border with Lauren. However, such a plan might result in some harm to the other children, and would certainly traumatize them. Other parents would be outraged, and the Jordanian authorities would certainly view it as kidnapping. Finally, there really wasn't anyplace to hide the bus near Jarash where it wouldn't be readily discovered.

The best plan of action, they finally concluded, would simply be to grab Lauren when the bus stopped on the outskirts of Jarash to pick up the two children that lived furthest from the school. Lauren would already be on the bus and they could leave directly for the Allenby Bridge without having to fight the traffic in Jarash.

Now, at last, all was in readiness for the final act. In twenty-four hours a young girl would either be reunited with her mother or they would all be in a Jordanian prison.

When they reached Amman, Cathy was informed: "We're going to do it the following morning." Then Feeney made reservations for her and Lauren on Alia, the Royal Jordanian Airline, departing Amman at 10:45 A.M. for New York the next day. Two Nissans—one red and one white—were rented for the operation, and Adil Abbadi was advised to be ready. He would meet Cathy, Lauren, Feeney, and Roberts at the Allenby Bridge and accompany them through passport control, where his brother-in-law was scheduled to be on duty. Once they were safely in Israel, Chatellier would pay Abbadi and give him the keys to one of the rented cars. Then he would take the remaining car back to Amman and leave the country by the best available method.

Feeney prepared a thick envelope loaded with cut-up newspapers in the size of U.S. currency. On the outside of the envelope, they instructed Abbadi to write in Arabic, "Take this directly to Mr. Ali Bayan. Give it only to him." A note was placed inside the envelope along with the bogus money. It read: "You took my daughter. Now I have her back. Your brother and your wife are safe in the United States, for now. Don't come after us and don't give me any trouble. Remember, the eyes of Texas are upon you." It was signed Cathy Mahone.

D Day

They checked out of the Amman Holiday Inn early in the morning, and told the desk clerk that they were going to the ancient Nabatean city of Petra and then onto Aqaba. Feeney then gathered the little band together in the parking lot. "I have never done anything without a pre-mission prayer in my life and I ain't starting now. Grandpa," he said, fixing his gaze on Chatellier, the oldest member of the group, "make it short and sweet."

Chatellier said a short prayer and they departed for Jarash without further ceremony. Everyone knew what he or she was to do. It was January 28, 1988.

Feeney drove the white Nissan to the Bayan house to make certain Lauren got on the bus as scheduled. Cathy, Chatellier, and Roberts went directly to the house on the outskirts of Jarash where the actual "snatch" would be made.

The site was a farm overlooking Jarash. There were two houses on the property made of earth-colored stone and brick, which blended into the barren rocky hillside. At the top of the hill, parallel to the asphalt road that passed by the farm, was a stone wall, a clump of olive trees, and some old barns. A dirt road nearly a half-mile long led to the houses, and the orange school bus normally pulled off the main road and stopped a short distance away to pick up the children. Once the children were aboard, the driver backed the bus out onto the asphalt road, since there was no place wide enough to turn around on the access road.

Chatellier parked the red Nissan at the top of the hill on the right side of the road near the turnoff to the farm and he, Roberts, and Cathy waited for the bus. The cold, grey, overcast sky added to the somberness of their moods. No one spoke. Cathy, sitting in the backseat, moved her lips from time to time as if saying a silent prayer. The tension was thick enough to cut with a knife.

As the minutes ticked by it soon became evident that the bus was late. Ordinarily the little orange bus runs like clockwork. During the surveillance of the bus, it had never been late before. Chatellier had a sinking feeling in the pit of his stomach: perhaps something had happened? Maybe Feeney had been arrested, and the authorities were on their way to the farm to apprehend the rest of them?

They continued to wait, growing increasingly nervous. Then they heard a straining engine and saw Feeney's white Nissan speeding toward them. He screeched to a halt in front of them, and Cathy and Roberts jumped into his car and they sped away, leaving Chatellier by himself. Chatellier wheeled his car around and headed back toward Jarash, passing the little orange school bus seconds later as it chugged up the hill toward the turnoff to the farm. Once the bus had gone by, Chatellier cranked the wheel of the red Nissan and followed the bus at a safe distance.

The bus made a left turn by the wall and stopped to take on the two schoolchildren who lived at the farm. But before the bus could back out, the white Nissan with Feeney at the wheel came back down the road and blocked the access road so that the bus could not back up. Feeney, Roberts, and Cathy jumped from the car and converged on the bus.

Feeney approached the bus on the driver's side and tried to grab the driver through the window. Roberts, meanwhile, shouted to the driver to open the door, which was operated by air pressure, but the driver was distracted by Feeney. So Roberts kicked the door open, bounded up the two steps, and grabbed the driver. He stuffed the envelope addressed to Ali Bayan into the driver's hands and said, "Can you read this? Take it to Ali Bayan." He also thrust about $20 in Jordanian currency at the driver, and told him, in English, that it was for him. Roberts then pulled the bus keys out of the ignition, showed them to the driver, then flipped them over the stone wall into a patch of grass.

Cathy, who was only one step behind Roberts, ran down the aisle toward Lauren. All of the children were sitting in stunned silence, eyes as big as saucers, not comprehending what was happening. Cathy gave Lauren a quick embrace and told the frightened girl to come with her. As they left the bus, they were followed by the nineteen-year-old female chaperone who, by this time, had recovered her wits and was not going to let Lauren go.

Cathy hustled Lauren into the backseat of the white Nissan, but before Cathy could get in herself the chaperone grabbed her sweater and they struggled. As Roberts stepped in to break it up, he saw a white taxi packed with men coming up the road, and two of the men were hanging out the window to see what was going on. "I said to myself," he remembered, "that we are in for a fight." He leaned heavily on the chaperone's shoulder and pinned her against the car, speaking all the while in a soft, soothing voice, telling her to hush. She wanted to scream and Roberts told her that "this is Mama. She is taking her baby home."

"Mama?" said the chaperone, beginning to calm down.

"Yes, Mama," reaffirmed Roberts.

As the chaperone conceded defeat, the taxi passed by and disappeared over the hill. Roberts pushed the chaperone back toward the bus, then yelled, "Let's gooooooo!"

The chaperone, stunned and forlorn, stood next to the bus, tears streaming down her cheeks, as the white Nissan pulled away. The bus driver rummaged through the grass on the other side of the wall for the keys. But as the white car accelerated, the driver looked up, and he and the chaperone seemed to be making a mental note of the license plate.

Chatellier was waiting in the red Nissan only a short distance away. The white car screeched to a halt and Cathy, Lauren, Feeney, and Roberts all piled into the red car. Once the switch was made, they immediately started for the Allenby Bridge, which lay nearly an hour away. Lauren was stretched out on the backseat under a blanket, and Cathy and the commandos once again donned their disguises. Lauren was whimpering softly beneath the blanket and muttering, "Mummy, Mummy." Later, as they passed through the Jordan Valley, Cathy dressed Lauren in different clothing.

Chatellier, meanwhile, drove the white car down to Jarash. He needed gasoline, so he pulled into a service station, topped off the tank, and waited for the bus. Seven minutes later, the bus came roaring down the road, and Chatellier honked at the driver, pulled out in front of the bus, and raced away. Seconds later he doubled back and began his own run toward the Allenby

Bridge. He was about fifteen minutes behind the red car, but unlike Feeney, he did not speed. Instead, he plodded toward the bridge at about twenty-five miles an hour.

As he entered the Jordan Valley on the two-lane road with no shoulders, he encountered some of the thickest fog he had ever seen. "I mean, it was thick, thick, thick," said Chatellier. "The road is real narrow and I'm praying to myself that I don't hit any roadblocks."

There were no roadblocks, but his rear-view mirror was suddenly filled with flashing red lights as a police car loomed through the fog behind him. The Jordanian police were hanging out of the windows and trying to wave him over. He pretended, however, that he did not notice them and moved to the center of the road so they could not pass. The police then used a loudspeaker to order him over. He continued to ignore them, poking along as though on a Sunday drive without a care in the world.

As the police begin screaming in the loudspeaker, he finally "noticed" them and eased his car over slightly and rolled to a halt, still blocking the right lane. The police roared by on the left and stopped in front of him. Six officers jumped from the car and surrounded the white Nissan.

Chatellier was munching on a Baby Ruth candy bar, seemingly oblivious to the commotion. They shouted at him in Arabic, since none of them spoke English. Chattelier knew they wanted his passport, but he stalled for time, explaining that he was a tourist and was going to the Dead Sea.

"No! No! No!" screamed the police commander. "Passeport! Passeport!"

Chatellier played dumb. "I'm a tourist going to the Dead Sea."

"Passeport! Passeport!"

At last, Chatellier indicated that he understood and fished his passport from his jacket.

Two more carloads of police roared up, one boxing in his car from behind, the other alongside. There were over two dozen policemen, and they had also brought the bus driver. He gazed at Chatellier and shook his head, since Dave does not look anything like either Feeney or Roberts. They went through his rucksack, which was in the backseat, and which contained only a pair of jeans, a souvenir plate from Jarash, and some dirty clothes.

"License! License!" one of them shouted at him.

Chatellier handed over his driver's license and the rental car agreement, which was in Abbadi's name, and grinned at them. Now they were totally confused.

It was like the keystone cops. Traffic was backing up behind them, with people honking their horns. The policemen were arguing over whether they had the right car. One of the officers, from the first car on the scene, held a piece of paper with two Arabic numbers on it that Chatellier could see: they were the first two numbers on his license plate. The officer knew he had the right car, but the others weren't convinced, especially when they looked at Chatellier sitting like a fool, grinning at them and chomping on another candy bar.

Finally, they ordered him out of the car and pointed at the trunk. Chatellier unlocked the trunk, which was completely empty and did not even contain a spare. More than twenty minutes had gone by since he was pulled over, and Chatellier could see that the cops were becoming more and more agitated and confused. Then, in the background, the police radio in one of the cars crackled with the excited voice of the dispatcher. Chatellier could not make out what the dispatcher was saying, but the word "Alia," the name of the national airline, was repeated twice. They're talking about the airport, he realized. Evidently they'd found out about the phony reservations.

The officer holding Chatellier's documents threw them at him, and all of the policemen piled into their cars, did U-turns, and raced back up the road toward Amman, leaving Chatellier sitting beside the road with a long line of traffic behind him.

Chatellier proceeded on his way, a short time later picking up two Jordanian policemen who were hitchhiking alongside the road. He passed through a half-dozen roadblocks, which apparently had been set up within minutes of the red car's passing over the same stretch of road. Every time he saw a tall antenna, indicating a police or army post, Chatellier craned his neck look-́ing for the red Nissan, in case Feeney and the others had been apprehended.

The Allenby Bridge

It took Feeney and his passengers seventy-six minutes to reach the Allenby Bridge over the Jordanian River. By the time they neared the bridge, named after the World War I British field marshal, most of the fog had burned away, leaving stark blue sky overhead. A light breeze was blowing toward them from the west.

The landscape near the bridge was far different than the bar-ren hills of Jarash. The area is intensely cultivated, with banana plantations and truck farms that produce an amazing array of fruits and vegetables, including cucumbers, strawberries, and tomatoes. The village of Karameh, once the "capital" of the Palestine Liberation Organization, lies twelve kilometers north-east of the bridge. As they passed through the dusty main square, Roberts whistled to a group of children playing beside the road. When they looked up, he tossed a bundle of clothing out the window of the car. It was the clothing they had worn ear-lier, along with the red-and-white headdresses and the veil Cathy had used to hide her features. As the car sped away toward the bridge, the kids converged on the bundle and began tearing at the contents.

Eight minutes later, the car pulled up at the Allenby Bridge bus terminal, a small, dusty, nondescript building that was once part of a British military camp. A few dust-laden banana and eucalyptus trees surrounded the terminal and the sun-baked parking area. A short distance beyond the building, armed Jor-danian soldiers blocked the road. The Allenby Bridge serves as the main crossing point between Jordan and Israel, and as the principal transit point for goods—chiefly agricultural produce—from Israel and the West Bank being shipped to the Arab world. Hundreds of people, mostly Arabs, transit the bridge every day. Prior to the recent disturbances on the West Bank and the Gaza, the number was in the thousands.

Feeney parked the car in a large lot next to the terminal building, and he and his passengers climbed out, stretched their legs, and retrieved their luggage from the trunk. Moments later they were joined by Abbadi.

"Mr. Abbadi, it is so good to see you," said Feeney, stretching his hand out in greeting. "Is everything in order?"

Calm to the point of being laid back, Abbadi shook hands with everyone, including Lauren, and assured them that all was well.

Feeney handed the keys to the rented car to Abbadi and told him that, "Mr. Chatellier will be coming very soon. He will take care of you and pay you." Then he injected a note of urgency, realizing that every moment they wasted placed them in greater danger. "We want to be on our way as soon as possible."

Abbadi nodded, took their passports and bridge passes, and disappeared into the shade of the terminal building. Cathy and Lauren, flanked by Feeney and Roberts, walked over to an ancient bus parked next to the terminal building and climbed aboard. There were three other passengers on board. Roberts positioned himself near the door and Feeney guided Cathy and Lauren to seats in the rear of the bus. No one said a word. Minutes seemed like hours as they waited for Abbadi to return, the heat adding to their discomfort.

Finally, Abbadi emerged from the terminal and sauntered over to the bus. It was like we were in a slow-motion picture, thought Feeney, who was trying to mentally will Abbadi to move more quickly. Abbadi walked down the aisle and handed Feeney their documents with a nod and a smile, "See, I told you. Everything OK."

"Where is the bus driver?" Feeney wanted to know.

"Everything is OK," Abbadi assured him.

But Feeney was insistent. "Where is the bus driver?"

"Nothing to worry. He is having lunch."

"Lunch!" cried Roberts, raising his voice. "Lunch! At ten-thirty in the morning?"

"J.D.," said Feeney calmly, turning to his partner. "It seems that we will have to get the bus driver."

Abbadi got the message, and disappeared once again inside the terminal. A few seconds later he reappeared with an elderly man carrying a glass of tea in his hand. He quickly finished his tea in one gulp and took his position behind the wheel. The bus cranked slowly to a start. Abbadi waved at them as they departed and yelled once again, "Everything is OK." The driver pulled out of the parking lot and they rattled down the road toward the bridge, which was obscured by eucalyptus trees, pulling along a great cloud of dust behind them. Lauren was sobbing again and crying, "Mummy, Mummy." Cathy was trying to calm her.

They passed the shattered ruins of a number of buildings destroyed in one of the Arab-Israeli wars, and soon an enormous blue-and-white flag emblazoned with a Star of David came into view about three hundred yards ahead. There is no Jordanian flag at the bridge. The bus shuddered to a stop next to what appeared to be an office building of some sort. A Jordanian officer came aboard and collected all of the bridge passes.

To the left of the bus was a two-story bunker with heavy caliber machine guns aimed at the Israeli side of the river. Three soldiers loitered nearby, but Roberts could see that they did not have magazines in their assault rifles. Should everything come apart at the last minute, Roberts calculated how they would fight their way across the bridge. He caught Feeney's attention with his eyes and flicked his head in the direction of the bunker, indicating that he would jump off the bus, overpower the soldiers, and seize the bunker if necessary. Feeney, he knew, would spring forward, throw the driver off, and drive the bus across the bridge.

Roberts' contingency planning, however, wasn't needed. The Jordanian officer returned, handed the bus driver the bridge passes, and waved them on toward the bridge. The bus crossed the narrow Bailey bridge and halted on the Israeli side. Everyone breathed a sigh of relief as an Israeli officer with a cockney accent boarded the bus and welcomed them to Israel.

"I'm really happy to be here," Roberts exclaimed, his body losing some of its rigidity for the first time that day. The Israeli officer, not used to such enthusiasm, studied him with a puzzled look, but did not say anything.

The bus continued onward until it reached another terminal, and the passengers disembarked. Feeney and his companions were waved to a different line from the other passengers, and there, with a big smile on his face, was their Israeli contact. After greetings were exchanged, Feeney noticed that Cathy looked absolutely drained, almost on the verge of collapse. "Sit down and relax," he told her. "The worst is over." He took Cathy and Lauren over to a bench where mother and daughter could finally succumb to their emotions. Cathy no longer had to be strong, and, once seated, she burst into tears and smothered Lauren with hugs and kisses.

The emotion of the moment was sensed by others in the terminal, including a group of black pilgrims on their way to the holy places. Roberts was approached by a woman from the group, who inquired as to what had happened and asked whether or not she could be of help. Normally tight-lipped, Roberts was positively bursting with pride over the happy scene in the terminal, and he told the black woman that, "This little girl was kidnapped from America. That's the girl's mother. They were just reunited. We're taking the little girl back to the United States to live with her mother."

Fascinated by the story, the black woman returned to her companions. A few moments later, they surrounded Cathy and Lauren, lifted their hands high in the air, and began singing "Hallelujah." Roberts, the hardened combat veteran, was overcome by the scene and began sobbing like a baby.

A Narrow Escape

Dave Chatellier pulled into the parking lot next to the terminal on the Jordanian side about forty-five minutes after his companions reached Israeli soil. He was met by Abbadi, who informed him that everything had gone smoothly.

"Where have you been?" inquired Abbadi.

"Oh, I got tied up down the road for a while," responded Chatellier with typical understatement. He paid Abbadi and then told him that he wanted to go to Amman to catch a plane out of the country as soon as possible.

Moving with uncharacteristic speed, Abbadi got into the red Nissan, pulled out of the parking lot, and headed for Amman at more than 110 kilometers an hour. Chatellier was forced to flag Abbadi down and order him to slow down because they were likely to get pulled over by the police for speeding. "Stay within the speed limit," Chatellier demanded.

Halfway to Amman, Abbadi pulled off the main road in a small village and stopped next to a police station. Chatellier did not know what was going on. Fearful that he was being double-crossed, he stopped his car about forty yards behind Abbadi and waited for an explanation.

Abbadi walked back to Chatellier's car and told him that, "In all of Jordan, this is the best place to buy chicken. It is also the cheapest price. I'm going to get my wife some chicken."

Chatellier couldn't believe it. "You've got to be kidding?" he told Abbadi.

"No, no, I'm not kidding. This is the best place for chicken."

For all Chatellier knew, every cop and soldier in Jordan was hunting them and Abbadi wanted to stop and buy chicken. Before he could respond, Abbadi crossed the road and purchased some live chickens and put them in his car.

Once they were under way again, Abbadi stopped his car and picked up a hitchhiker, an old man with a walking stick. Chatellier was beside himself with anxiety. He couldn't figure out what was going on. Surely Abbadi appreciated the serious nature of what they had just done?

But his troubles with Abbadi were not over. Abbadi took Chatellier home and invited him to have lunch. It was at this moment that Chatellier put his foot down and told Abbadi, in no uncertain terms, that he wanted to go to the airport without further delay. Not later, but at that very moment! Without lunch!

Abbadi finally got the message and proceeded to Amman International Airport, which was surrounded by so many police and troops that it looked like it was under siege. Abbadi flashed his credentials at two checkpoints on the way into the airport, and they were permitted to pass on through. But once inside the terminal, Chatellier found that all passengers waiting to depart had been rounded up by armed military guards and taken to a cordoned-off area at one end of the airport. All flights out of Amman were canceled. All, that is, but one. There was a special Alia flight leaving within minutes for Paris.

Abbadi said that he didn't understand what was going on and walked away to see what he could learn.

While Abbadi chatted with some guards, Chatellier strolled over to the ticket counter and, thinking quickly, said, "I hope I haven't missed that Paris flight. I need to get to Paris."

"Do you have a reservation?"

"No, I don't."

The woman at the ticket counter looked at her computer screen. "We only have one seat left on the flight, and it's first class."

"I'll take it," said Chatellier, unable to believe his good fortune.

"Have you got any luggage?"

"No, just this rucksack."

"The security officer will have to look through it, and you'll have to pay your airport tax."

Chatellier asked to whom he should pay the airport tax.

"The security officer can take it for you," she answered.

Chatellier had 40 Jordanian dinars left in his pocket, worth approximately $130. Although the airport tax was only two dinars, he handed the Jordanian security officer all 40.

"Will this cover the airport tax?" Chatellier asked, with a wink.

"Oh, yes. That's just right." The security man smiled, stuffing the bills in his pocket. He spoke rapidly into his walkie-talkie to the plane, and then started to lead Chatellier to the gate, without inspecting the rucksack.

At this moment, Abbadi returned.

"This guy is holding the flight for me," Chatellier told him. "I've got to run and get on it. It's been nice knowing you. I've really enjoyed it."

He pumped Abbadi's hand and hurried down the jetway to the plane.

The flight to Paris was uneventful, but when he landed at Orly, he was detained for not having a French visa or a ticket on a connecting flight. He was questioned by three different French security officials, and became alarmed when they threatened to put him on a flight back to Jordan. Ultimately, he was able to strike a compromise with the French, whereby they allowed him to sleep overnight in the airport, and the following morning he purchased a ticket on the next flight to the United States from an American Airlines agent who came to the place where he was being held to sell him the ticket. "I was never so relieved in all my life," said Chatellier, recalling the departure of the American Airlines flight for the United States.

Aftermath

It was only later that Chatellier learned how narrow his escape from Jordan actually was. It turned out that the Jordanians had sealed the nation's borders and actually shut down Amman International Airport in a futile attempt to interdict Lauren and her rescuers. Within days of the incident, Abbadi was arrested; he was indicted a short time later and remains in a Jordanian jail. The Assistant Regional Security Officer at the U.S. embassy in Jordan, Frank Baker, was removed from his position and is being terminated from the Foreign Service. State Department investigators allege that he knowingly "assisted directly or indirectly in the abduction of an American citizen child" and "illegally aided and abetted the efforts of American citizens in their attempts to violate host-government law." Although

Feeney and Chatellier offered to submit written statements, on the penalty of perjury, that Baker had no knowledge of their real mission in Jordan, the State Department never contacted them. Baker, moreover, agreed to take a polygraph examination regarding his knowledge of the abduction, but one was never administered to him. The U.S government expressed regret to the Jordanian government over the incident, without making mention of the fact that Ali Bayan is currently a fugitive wanted in Texas or that he had illegally abducted his daughter from the United States to Jordan. Ali Bayan has even asked the U.S. embassy in Jordan for help in getting his daughter back. Some observers believe that Baker is being made a scapegoat for the failure of U.S. policy to adequately come to grips with the problem of international child abduction.

While incidents such as the rescue of Lauren Bayan certainly complicate the conduct of U.S. foreign policy, a desperate mother would not have felt the necessity to hire commandos and carry out a risky paramilitary operation on foreign soil if the U.S. State Department had been more effective in assisting parents to recover their kidnapped children.

4

High-Tech Counterterrorism

There is no such thing as a fair fight.
—Counterterrorism Specialist

H E is reflecting on a dirty little war in Latin America over a bottle of sweating beer. Sitting in the cheerful surroundings of a Georgetown bar, he seems curiously out of place, eyes hidden behind dark glasses, hair trimmed close to his head, hinge tattoos in the crook of each arm. He belongs in a steamy fleshpot in Colón or Bangkok with whirling fans overhead and an out-of-tune piano playing in the background.

He is describing a tactical bombing raid. They came in low over the treetops, he explains, his voice rising with excitement, in an old prop-driven fighter with so many holes in it it looked like a Georgia stop sign. They no longer had any bombs, so he was dropping hand grenades in peanut-butter jars on the airfield below, trying to hit parked aircraft and drums of fuel. The hand grenades didn't explode until the jar struck the ground and shattered, releasing the spring handle.

The story is finished. He says he is waiting for a contract, one last contract to cash in on so that he can retire with a little dignity. The colonial wars that once provided him with a livelihood are finished, but with the rise of international terrorism he senses new opportunities.

"Can you get me one of those contracts to kill Qaddafi?" he asks with all the emotion of a man buying fish at the market.

"Or maybe something down in Salvador or 'the Goose.' They need bodyguards, don't they?''

While such men exist, they are dinosaurs. Men whose time has come and gone. There is little work for them in the modern high-tech, highly skilled and disciplined world of counterterrorism. From the "wires and pliers" technical specialists to bodyguards and elite counterterrorist commandos, the watchword is professionalism. "There is no room for error," comments former SEAL Team 6 member Neil Smit. While there are "some interesting characters" in the SEALs, says Smit, they "are all mentally disciplined. They know themselves and what they are capable of." There is no place in the SEALs or anywhere else in the counterterrorist community for grandstanders and the long-on-bravado-short-on-skills types of the past, Smit believes.[1]

His view is seconded by E.J. Criscuoli, who contends that the security and counterterrorist field has become a "science." Some of the equipment being displayed at the annual ASIS meeting in Las Vegas, says Criscuoli, "is truly exotic, twenty-first century state-of-the art, computer operated. You can't put someone behind such equipment who lacks sophistication."[2] Indeed, much of the technology being displayed at the Covert Operations Procurement Exhibitions in London, or its counterparts in the United States, would have been regarded as something from science fiction only a few years ago.

Until the last decade or two the security and antiterrorist field was dominated by "fence putter-uppers, door strikers, and goons," observes one security specialist. Recalling his introduction to the security industry in the mid-1950s, Criscuoli maintains that security specialists thirty years ago were "primarily concerned with government classified information in private industry. We wore badges. We didn't know it, but those were the good old days. The threats today are far more sophisticated."[3]

On March 12, 1985, Armenian terrorists seized the Turkish embassy in Ottawa, using all of the same tactics normally employed by law enforcement units: explosive entry, room-clearing operations, automatic weapons.[4] Not only are terrorists adopting law-enforcement and military tactics, but most terrorist groups have access to the same portable and highly reliable weapons and explosives used by their adversaries. Perhaps a dozen terrorist groups even boast surface-to-air missiles. In November 1987, for example, French authorities seized a rusty freighter off France containing 150 tons of arms, including 20 Soviet-made SAM-7 surface-to-air missiles, being shipped from Libya to the outlawed Irish Republican Army.[5] Although this shipment was denied the IRA, another four shipments of weapons and explosives—containing perhaps a dozen SAM-7s—are believed to have reached the Irish terrorists.

Sony and Radio Shack have provided terrorists with portable communications centers that not so long ago would have been the envy of any police department. Indeed, a terrorist can stay in constant touch with the rest of the world, even in the midst of a hostage takeover, with a briefcase communications center containing a Sony "Walkman," a Sony "Watchman," a two-way radio, a cellular telephone, and a world-band radio. Some terrorist groups are even using computers to plot their outrages and to store material about their potential targets, and the day may not be far away when technoterrorists follow the lead of renegade hackers and use personal computers to disrupt vital nodes and networks. Terrorists may also choose to attack the computer systems by planting malicious logic "bugs," resembling programming errors, in computer software, thereby making computers malfunction. "Like mines in naval warfare, all software warfare bugs are carefully designed to be small and hidden and to leave few telltale traces," write Scott A. Boorman and Paul R. Levitt, "even after being activated with devastating effects, such as causing repeated crashes of a major computer system."[6] Even more devastating are software "viruses" that replicate themselves and spread to other computer systems. At the rate things are going today, the "Carlos" of the future more likely will be armed with an IBM PC than a Czech-made VZ61 machine pistol.

As terrorism and crime become even more sophisticated, so

must the governments and private sector firms that protect the public. "In combat there is no such thing as a fair fight," observes one counterterrorism specialist. Anything short of draconian methods that will give the West an edge in its struggle against terrorism, therefore, "should be encouraged." In this connection, the war against terrorism has gone high-tech and, in the final analysis, it may well be that technological superiority will be the most important factor in the West's ability to withstand the terrorist challenge. The terrorist, after all, can choose the time, place, target, and method of attack, whereas those on the defensive must maintain a constant state of readiness, anticipating every conceivable threat, 24 hours a day, 365 days a year. If they let down their guard even for a moment, an alert terrorist group will choose that moment to strike.

"If you ignore technology," maintains security specialist Richard Kobetz, "like history, it's going to come around and hit you in the back of the head."[7] Today modern technology makes it possible to eavesdrop on a hostage plane from across a tarmac, or to follow the movement of every armed terrorist aboard a hostage aircraft or train simply by tracking the metal in their guns. It is possible to peer into a totally dark room from more than a mile away, and sophisticated spike and tube microphones the size of a needle and cameras with pinhole lenses permit a degree of electronic surveillance unknown even a decade ago. During the April 1984 siege of the Libyan People's Bureau (embassy) in London, for example, the Chief of Scotland Yard's technical support branch, C7, had a nearby room with:

> a battery of monitors where he could keep an eye on pictures from tiny visual probes planted into the inside of the [Libyan Peoples] bureau. Officers had planted auditory bugs in all outside walls of the bureau. For the first time it [C7] was using infrared detectors which pinpointed where everyone in the bureau was—from his bodyheat. Among the many other gadgets used by C7 was a television aerial which was attached to the bureau's own aerial and allowed Scotland Yard, if it wanted, to pipe in false television programmes.[8]

The technological revolution in the security industry reaches down to every level. Burglar alarm sales are soaring, and security systems are now a common feature in homes and businesses. Residential security companies, for example, are putting systems in some homes that only five or ten years ago only could be seen at industrial locations. There are Beverly Hills homes that boast more elaborate security systems than some U.S. embassies. Secure communications systems, with scrambler telephones and burst transmissions, are increasingly commonplace in American industry. "Secure transmission is a business we once thought was reserved to certain government agencies whose initials were top secret," notes Criscuoli. "And today you have people providing industry with cryptographic devices that at one time were reserved only for intelligence areas of the government."[9]

Long before Fawn Hall, firms producing document shredders were having trouble keeping up with demand. Not only is document retention costly, involving extensive handling and storage costs, but destroying documents also makes good sense from a security point of view. Hall and her boss, Lt. Colonel Oliver North, used an Intimus shredder, aptly designated the Model 007-S, which costs the U.S. government around $4,400 and can shred 75 pounds of paper per hour. On a larger scale, Document Destructors Inc., located in the Washington, D.C., suburbs, shreds more than a million pounds of government and private paperwork every year, turning the most sensitive material into powder. Shredding technology was substantially improved in the wake of the seizure of the U.S. embassy in Tehran in 1979, and the meticulous reconstruction of thousands of supposedly shredded documents, including extremely sensitive CIA materials, found in the embassy by Iranian fanatics. Then again, it should have come as no surprise to U.S. authorities that people capable of the exacting and painstaking work of producing such exquisite carpets would be able to piece together the long strips of paper left by the embassy's shredders. Today, as a result, most high-quality shredding machines turn paper into confetti or strips too narrow to be pieced together. As another solution to the proliferation of sensitive documents, consider the recent development of paper that cannot be photocopied. According to the *Wall Street Journal,* sales of the magenta-colored paper, which is produced by a Canadian company, "are sky-rocketing."[10]

The increasingly omnipresent surveillance camera is another hot item. Frost and Sullivan report that closed-circuit television (CCTV) is the most popular security measure in Europe today, with $186 million worth of equipment sold in 1986.[11] Today closed-circuit cameras are becoming ever more miniaturized, and can be hidden almost anywhere. Several companies offer cameras that can be activated from anywhere in the world simply by placing a telephone call to the phone number where the camera is located; it rings silently, and the camera transmits images to a monitor that the caller carries in a briefcase and hooks up to the phone he is calling from. A Virginia firm hopes to develop a similar system that could be installed on airplanes. A camera in the cabin of the aircraft would transmit the image of every passenger via microwave or satellite to a central computer where every face would be matched against the images of known terrorists.

In an effort to catch illegal exports of U.S. high-tech equipment and other smuggled goods, Customs agents X-ray all of the luggage being loaded aboard random flights. A suitcase containing state-of-the-art night-vision equipment was recently intercepted in Miami. It belonged to an American, whose final destination was Managua, Nicaragua, and underscores the value attached in some quarters to the latest developments in night-vision equipment used for surveillance and sniping. Night-vision technology is also finding increasing favor with TV news reporters, who use it to film stories where there is insufficient light. As the promotional literature for one unit marketed in the United States states, "The DARK INVADER model 3010 with its infrared spot illuminator specializes in viewing into darkened windows, or reading a license plate of a vehicle tucked away within a darkened building, or clearly define and photograph (if necessary) facial characteristics of a person hidden deep in the shadows." There are even night-vision goggles that can be used by counterterrorist commandos in night operations and by chauffeurs so they can drive without lights, thereby assisting them in escaping from terrorist ambushes. Night-vision technology generally falls into two categories: infrared, described above, and passive, in which existing light from stars or general background "scatter," no matter how weak, is used to enhance an image. Passive systems have the advantage of being undetectable to countersnipers and therefore do not give away the user's position.

A British firm, UTILEX Limited, constructs what are called "live fire, advanced, stress related, urban warfare and antiterrorist training facilities." An expansion on the old "shooting room" concept, one of UTILEX's creations in Hong Kong is a several-square-block training area designed to look like an ordinary city, but which, in many respects, has more in common with an elaborate Hollywood set. Constructed with bullet- and rocket-resistant materials, the facility permits police and military units, using live ammo, to be trained in an authentic urban environment. Its facilities can also "take the form of an ordinary suburban house or office, a section of the bridge of a ship or oil rig, an aircraft fuselage or part of an embassy or palace." The UTILEX facilities are a vast improvement over shooting rooms made by stacking car and truck tires on top of each other, which still suffice for many U.S. law enforcement and even government agencies.

Another British company, using portable frames, will mock-up any known room or structure within twenty-four hours so that antiterrorist commandos can practice assaulting it.

For those without the luxury of such elaborate training facilities, a wide variety of realistic simulation equipment is available, designed along the same lines as flight simulators where pilots are trained. Today it is possible for police or antiterrorist units to put a whole firing range in an ordinary room or office using state-of-the-art simulation equipment. Each soldier lies on a mat and aims a rifle at a television screen. Various targets are simulated on the screen, and the shooter's "hits" register on the screen as well. Another simulation format, designed for police and antiterrorist units, involves the participant standing in front of a large screen on which a wide variety of simulated incidents are portrayed, such as a man and a woman struggling in a car, the car door flying open, and the man pushing the woman out onto the ground as he aims a weapon at the participant. The participant, in each case, must size up the incident, decide whether to use force, and in the event he does, hit the target on the screen without harming any innocent bystanders.

During "Security Awareness Day" at the U.S. Department of State in January 1988, a similar system developed by the Firearms Training Systems Center was on display. Designed to test both reflexes and judgment, participants play the role of bodyguards and are confronted on a large video screen with a number of potential, though often ambiguous, threats known as "shoot/no shoot" situations. If participants make the wrong judgment or hesitate too long, the "ambassador" being protected or the participants themselves may be "shot." If they overreact, they may "shoot" an innocent bystander. If the threat is an actual terrorist, they may be forced to shoot it out with him or her, and the system measures the accuracy of their shots.

Similar simulation exercises are run at Brookhaven National Laboratory near Boston. Department of Energy security teams engage in mock gun battles with "terrorists" utilizing weapons that fire laser beams and trigger sensors on vests and caps worn by participants.

Antiterrorist simulation exercises have resulted in a whole new series of products and services. The "pop-up" and turning targets used in shooting houses and on shooting ranges are more lifelike and realistic than ever before. Gone are the old bull's-eye targets. In their place are targets that represent a series of both hostile figures and ordinary bystanders, some with guns in their hands and others with ordinary household objects. The shooter must make an instantaneous decision whether to shoot or not. One British company located near the Scottish border that produces such targets attributes its recent growth, in part, to its obsession with realism. By contrast to single-color targets that are virtually terrorist caricatures—portraying swarthy men dressed in black with heavy beards, tattoos, and evil expressions on their faces—McQueens of Galashiels turns out some 13 to 15 million targets a year, most life-sized and in full color, which feature male and female "hostiles" and "friendlies" in ordinary clothing and a variety of poses. The SAS and some other elite counterterrorist units reportedly are experimenting with systems where the targets are three-dimensional holograms projected into the shooting house.

Even something as ordinary as paint may have a security dimension. In El Salvador, for example, troops are dispatched every day at dawn to spray olive drab paint over the antigovernment graffiti that has appeared during the night. As a result of the demand, several companies are experimenting with a new kind of paint that graffiti does not adhere to, which could be used on public buildings and other frequent targets of the antigovernment sloganeers. Another paint product, already on the market, explodes when struck with a sharp object. It is being used as a deterrent to safe-cracking, since any effort to knock off the tumbler with a chisel will likely cause the material to detonate and give the criminal flash burns. Consideration is being given to using such paint on doors and other thresholds to make it more difficult for terrorists or saboteurs to gain access to certain rooms or buildings.

Bomb Detection

Today, the chief aviation-related security deficiency is the inability to reliably detect sophisticated bombs, such as the one that brought down Pan Am flight 103 in December 1988. Bombs have become the terrorist's weapon of choice, and the development of equipment that can identify the presence of explosives—especially small amounts and thin sheets—in luggage or on a passenger's person is vital to ensuring public confidence in the safety and integrity of the international civil aviation system. In this connection, a number of promising technologies have emerged, none of which is fully operational today. According to terrorism expert Brian Jenkins of the Rand Corporation, we are "several years away from a reliable, practical bomb detection capability."[12]

Presently, the most advanced technology utilizes what is known as thermal-neutron activation. The passenger's suitcase is put on a conveyor belt and travels into a closed chamber where chemical analysis is used to determine gamma-ray emissions from the contents. Prototype machines have demonstrated a success rate of more than 90 percent in revealing the presence of explosives. In the wake of the Pan Am 103 disaster, the FAA ordered six of the machines; the order was increased in April 1989 to as many as a hundred machines by the Secretary of Transportation.

Other technologies are also being explored, including so-called "sniffers" designed to detect explosives hidden in baggage or on an individual's body. A walk-through screening system based on light-emitting detection is presently being tested at Boston's Logan Airport and at several U.S. embassies. The problem with all such technologies, including thermal-neutron activation, is that they are still experimental. No one knows for certain how well they will work. Not only are there many "bugs" to work out, but most of the prototype units are slow and cumbersome, unable to process the volume of luggage required. At its present level of performance, the prototype thermal-neutron activation unit would require almost six hours to process the average number of checked bags (700) on one 747. Even if it meets the FAA's target of ten bags per minute, the unit will still take more than an hour to process the baggage on a 747.

Work is also under way to develop better and more efficient X-ray screening systems. Many airport X-ray systems provide a poor image of a bag's contents on a low-resolution screen, thus requiring an extremely alert and well-trained operator. In recent years, however, a new generation of X-ray scanning machines has appeared that make weapons and explosives far more identifiable. One system, the E-Scan device, developed by Astrophysics Research, even displays objects too dense to penetrate in a bright shade of green, a signal to the operator that the bag should be opened and the object more closely scrutinized. The E-Scan system separates organic materials from inorganic materials, classifying materials according to their composition on the basis of their atomic number.

Such sophistication is necessary because terrorists have found a variety of methods to "beat" X-ray machines. Indeed, in a series of recent tests conducted by the federal government, security personnel failed to detect 20 percent of the weapons that FAA inspectors tried to smuggle through security checkpoints. Conducted at 28 major U.S. airports, the survey saw 496 weapons, out of a total of 2,410 guns and other weapons, pass through security checkpoints undetected.

Hijackers are becoming far more ingenious in hiding or disguising their weapons. It is believed that the hijackers of one flight were able to pass through the X-ray scanner by shielding small grenades and a gun in the base of a lead crystal vase, the lead in the crystal being sufficient to make the image appear "muddy" on the operator's screen. Passengers heard the vase shattered by one of the terrorists in a rest room immediately before the plane was commandeered.

In another incident, authorities discovered a suitcase on Cyprus full of plastic explosive that had been camouflaged as marzipan candy. Each lump of explosive was individually wrapped like a piece of candy, and almonds had even been added to some of the pieces. Had it not been for the fact that the explosives "sweated" through the leather suitcase, the shipment probably would have gone undetected.

One of the most insidious, yet imaginative, explosive devices is the so-called "baby bomb." A woman wears a dome-shaped device strapped to her stomach that makes her appear pregnant but which, in reality, contains a bomb. When she arrives at the target destination, she goes to a rest room and removes the bomb, and then straps the dome-shaped device back on. She leaves the bomb in the rest room, generally in a trash can or toilet-tissue dispenser, and a short time later it goes off.

Terrorist groups like the Palestinian May 15 Movement, which has largely been subsumed into the Colonel Hawari organization, pioneered the development of highly sophisticated and almost undetectable aviation bombs. Indeed, it could be said that they turned bomb-making into an art. Their specialty was suitcase bombs, such as the one that nearly made it onto a flight departing from Athens in 1983. This bomb was almost invisible to the naked eye. The plastic explosive had been rolled out in flat sheets and hidden in the lining of the bag, and the detonator, batteries, and timing device were secreted in various innocent-looking consumer electronic items packed in the bag. Had not British and American intelligence gotten wind of the planned bombing and intercepted the bag, it would most probably have resulted in an airline tragedy. The May 15 group is also believed to have been responsible for constructing the bomb, under contract to other extremists, that blew a hole in TWA flight 840, killing five Americans.

Characteristic of the sophisticated bombs that are turning up with increasing frequency was the device hidden in the luggage of the unsuspecting pregnant Irish girlfriend of Jordanian-born Nizar Hindawi in 1987. Ann Murphy was intercepted as she was preparing to board an El Al jumbo jet in London, which was en route to Tel Aviv. In her carry-on bag was a bomb manufactured with three pounds of dense sheet explosive secreted in the lining. It was triggered by punching in the time of the explosion (2:04 P.M.) on a hand calculator, which contained the detonator and was packed inside the bag. The bomb had been crafted by Syrian intelligence operatives and passed to Hindawi by his Syrian handlers.

A number of firms manufacture desk-top bomb detectors that screen incoming mail for letter and parcel bombs, and such devices are taking their place right alongside the Xerox machine and the telecopier as an indispensable element of the workplace.

Access Control

Great strides have been made in physical security hardware during the past decade. Access control is one of the most important elements of physical security. How does a firm or government agency distinguish between authorized and unauthorized people seeking admission to a particular facility? The access-control system selected must be effective without being overly complicated or time-consuming. Obviously, guard stations are often erected at doors and other access points, but such stations can be seized or defeated with false identification badges and cards. For example, an American serviceman in West Germany was murdered by terrorists in order to obtain his I.D. card, giving them access to an American military base so they could plant a bomb.

Among the new developments in this area are systems that are virtually tamper-proof and guarantee positive identification of the individual seeking admission to the facility or building. The old fingerprint identification system—which is susceptible to forgery—is being replaced by twenty-first century equipment that measures hand geometry or scans the blood vessel pattern in an individual's eyes. The person being scrutinized is required to either place his or her hand on an imaging device or to peer into the viewfinder of a machine that performs a retinal scan. Since no two individuals have the same hand geometry or retinal patterns, their patterns are then compared to file material, and must match perfectly before they are admitted to the facility. Many highly sensitive facilities are using multiple levels of verification today before clearing an individual—for example, an identification card, a personal code number, and a retinal-scanning or hand geometry system.

Credit card companies are currently experimenting with retinal scanning devices to prevent credit card fraud. An individual's retinal pattern would be stored on the credit card in digital form on a band of magnetic tape. To verify that the customer is the actual owner of the credit card, the store would have a device into which the credit card would be inserted. Then the customer would peer into the device and it would compare the information on the card with the individual's retinal pattern. If they matched exactly, the transaction would be approved.

At the White House, so-called "fence jumpers" are immediately detected by sensors on the grounds, which alert security personnel, who normally intercept the unauthorized individual long before he or she reaches the presidential residence. In addition to other deterrents, Israel's borders are protected by a security fence employing mechanical sensors. Other sensors alert the Israelis of possible infiltrators even before they actually reach the fence. Intrusion detection sensors are a major element of any physical security system today, and come in many different forms, including mechanical/vibration, photoelectric, microwave, and pressure-sensitive sensors.

Designing Terror-Proof Buildings

Shortly after 6:22 A.M. on October 23, 1983, a Mercedes truck loaded with 12,000 pounds of explosives drove through the perimeter of the U.S. Marine compound at Beirut International Airport and into the lobby of the headquarters building, where it exploded with such violence that the entire structure pancaked. Two hundred forty-one Americans died in the attack, a number equivalent to two-thirds of the combat deaths suffered by the United States in the entire Spanish-American War. The bomb, which was gas-enhanced and probably constructed with Syrian assistance, was one of the most powerful conventional explosive devices ever built. According to the report of the so-called Long Commission, which was set up to investigate the bombing, the explosive device was so powerful that "major damage to the Battalion Landing Team Headquarters building and significant casualties would probably have resulted even if the terrorist truck had not penetrated the USMNF defensive perimeter but had detonated in the roadway some 330 feet from the building."[13]

The attack on the U.S. Marine headquarters underscores the vulnerability of modern structures not only to vehicle bomb attacks but to the new generation of weapons available to terrorists around the world. Prior to the advent of modern terrorism, most buildings and structures were sited and constructed with little or no regard to security considerations. If any attention was paid to security by architects and engineers, it was to incorporate design features to prevent unauthorized entry, to maintain inventory control, and to secure classified data and equipment. Even security considerations of this kind, however, were generally afterthoughts that were not accorded priority over other design criteria. Moreover, there was little common consensus as to what constituted good security. At one time, good security at the Foreign Ministry in Colombia, for example, involved the guard checking an individual's bag or briefcase *on the way out* of the building rather than on the way in because the problem they were most concerned about was the theft of equipment and office supplies.

All of this has changed in recent years. Architects and engineers are being required to give high priority, and in some cases top priority, to security considerations. The U.S. State Department has adopted a $4.4 billion, five-year security enhancement program intended to upgrade security at U.S. diplomatic and related facilities around the world. As a part of the program, security at some U.S. embassies will be substantially increased, and in other instances new embassies will be constructed from the ground up. Similar reviews and security enhancement programs are currently under way throughout the federal government, especially at military bases and other key federal installations.

Initially, some architects and engineers sought to address the security problem by turning buildings into what amounted to bunkers, with thick walls and narrow slit-like windows. In recent years, however, more attention is being paid to designing defensive characteristics into structures to counter specific terrorist threats without sacrificing aesthetic or functional considerations. By calculating the blast effects of various terrorist explosives and munitions in various combinations and configurations, for example, architects and engineers now believe that they can design buildings that will better dissipate the force of terrorist

bombs and not lose their structural integrity. More consideration also is being given to using features of the natural landscape
to shield and protect buildings.

One of the tools design personnel are using in this effort is
CAD, or computer-aided design. By simulating various attacks
on a particular building, designers can identify specific vulnerabilities and use that knowledge to redesign and reinforce the
structure to minimize the impact of a wide range of attacks.
Everett I. Brown and Company—a family-owned and -operated
architectural and engineering firm located in Indianapolis, Indiana—is perhaps the leader in applying CAD techniques to security problems. Not only do CAD techniques permit decision
makers to scientifically weigh competing design solutions to a
particular problem—taking into account security, aesthetic,
functional, and budgetary considerations—but computerized
3-D visual modeling can be used to defeat specific threats like
sniper attacks. "In order to anticipate a possible sniper attack,"
says Wally Howard, an Everett I. Brown executive formerly
with the U.S. Army Corps of Engineers, "we can depict a particular U.S. embassy building on a computer screen. By rotating
the building in conjunction with its surroundings, we can become
completely aware of every accessible interior and exterior vantage
point. Once that is known we can suggest appropriate remedial
measures. Nothing need be left to chance."

A great deal of work is also being done to devise methods of
preventing hostile vehicles from getting too close to potential
high-consequence targets like embassies and military installations. In this connection, at a number of new federal installations security designers have recently unveiled a variety of
innovations intended to identify and deter car bombers. They
are also engaged in retrofitting many existing installations with
new roads and countermeasures that permit controlled access to
a facility but interdict and defeat approaching threats. Sensors,
for example, are used to identify vehicles traveling at excessive
speed, and pop-up barriers, tire-puncturing devices, rising bollards, nets, and crash beams can be used to block their approach.
Modeled on tank traps, pits that open up in the road offer
another alternative for stopping hostile vehicles.

Access roads can be straddled by low bridges that permit a car to pass underneath but block larger vehicles. Speed bumps, friction devices, and chicanes can be utilized to slow down an approaching vehicle and allow guards more time to react. A winding road designed like a "slalom course" or a road with sharp right- and left-angle turns will also impede oncoming vehicles and force them to reduce their speed. Chicanes and slalom-like roads may have the added advantage of breaking the hostile driver's concentration, which, according to some recent studies, is likely to undermine his or her resolution to carry out an attack.

Nozzles can be mounted near the road that spray a slippery substance that reduces tire adhesion, a chemical vapor to overpower the driver of the vehicle, or even a smoke cloud that obscures the road. Windshield-level sprayers could even "shoot" white paint at the oncoming vehicle to "blind" the driver.

Military designers are also considering various ways of killing or disabling the driver of a hostile vehicle. For example, photoflash bombs of several million candlepower and laser projectors could be utilized to actually blind the driver, or automatic shotguns and pyrotechnic fireball projectors can be deployed at windshield level and engaged by remote control. In particularly dangerous regions of the world, antipersonnel devices like Claymore mines and mines buried in the road could be deployed and detonated in the event of an emergency.[14] If the hostile vehicle is stopped some distance from the target structure, barricades and walls can be utilized to shield the structure and personnel at the location from blast effects. All of these examples illustrate the great progress that is being made in devising new methods to deny terrorists one of their current weapons of choice: the vehicle bomb.

Counterterrorist Chic

Clothes may not make the man, but today they can clearly save his life. In recent years bulletproof clothing, or body armor as it is known in the trade, has become a big-time business, with dozens of firms here and abroad competing to meet the growing demand for protective clothing. Only two decades ago, body armor was bulky, uncomfortable, and had all of the fashion appeal of the suits that used to be worn by Soviet Politburo members. But with DuPont's development in 1972 of Kevlar, a puncture-resistant, 1,000-denier fiber, the whole industry was revolutionized.

Kevlar was originally developed as a light-weight armor for helicopters in Vietnam, but it was quickly found to be perfect for dozens of other applications, including protective clothing. Kevlar works by dissipating the force of a bullet as the fabric gives without permitting penetration. It has a remarkable tensile strength of 400,000 pounds per square inch, by comparison to 250,000 pounds per square inch for stainless steel.[15]

The National Institute of Justice has developed a standard-ized rating system for body armor, indicating various material weights required to effectively stop different rounds. Type 1, for example, weighing 9 ounces per square foot, will stop a variety of different .22, .25, and .38 slugs, along with 12-gauge #4 lead shot. By contrast, Type 4, which weighs 20.5 ounces per square foot of fabric, will defeat a .44 magnum 240 grain SWC slug and a number of high-velocity 9-mm rounds. It goes without saying that anyone wearing body armor who is shot in the chest at close range is likely to remember the impact of the slug for a long time. While the body armor may prevent the slug from penetrat-ing, it will generally leave a severe bruise and may even break a rib or two. However, given the alternatives, no one is likely to complain.

To defeat high-powered rifles, metal or ceramic plates, or so-called "shock plates," can be inserted in many bullet-resistant vests in the "kill zone." While such apparel may be satisfactory for SWAT teams and certain military units, it will likely be too bulky and uncomfortable for most government officials or other threatened individuals. Moreover, if it is too obvious that the potential target is wearing body armor, the would-be assassin is likely to try a "head shot."

Today's soft armor fashions range from lingerie to designer dresses and suits, and are sold in some of the most chic boutiques in the United States. Former President Reagan has, among other garments, a bulletproof raincoat, and Mrs. Reagan often wears a bulletproof lace-trimmed slip. There are no restrictions on who can purchase or own bullet-resistant clothing, and many ordinary citizens are snapping up items like bulletproof black Israeli utility vests and Kevlar jockstraps for their mystique value. While body armor has saved the lives of more than 700 police officers in the United States alone, criminals and terrorists are increasingly armoring themselves with protective apparel in order to reduce their vulnerability. In order to counter the possibility that their terrorist adversaries might be wearing body armor, U.S. Delta Force commandos live by the motto: "Two to the body, one to the head, makes you good and dead." The Delta operator is taught to squeeze off two quick rounds to the adversary's body and, in a single fluid motion, raise the pistol sights slightly and aim for the head, all three shots taking less than two seconds.

It should be noted that while body armor may protect the wearer from gunshots, it may not defeat a knife-wielding attacker. It is possible to drive a sharply-pointed fighting knife through many protective vests. In 1982, for example, the owner of a security firm in Oklahoma City was killed while demonstrating a bulletproof vest. He urged a friend, who reluctantly complied, to stab him with a two-and-a-half-inch paring knife. The knife penetrated the vest and entered the man's chest.

A similar tragedy was narrowly averted when a potential customer refused to lunge at a salesman wearing soft body armor in the offices of a suburban Washington firm. The salesman thereupon took the vest off and placed it over the back of a leather chair. "See," he said, drawing a long-bladed knife from a sheath, "I would have been perfectly safe." He rammed the knife into the vest and, instead of bouncing off, drove the blade all the way through the back of the chair. Although taken aback, he barely missed a beat as he put on a new riot helmet and asked the same individual, "Hit me over the head as hard as you can with the butt of this assault rifle." The customer, needless to say, demurred and left as soon as he could without buying anything.

It is not uncommon for body armor salesmen to demonstrate their faith in their products by wearing them during actual tests with live ammunition. One producer of body armor shows a videotape at military and law enforcement trade shows where he shoots himself in the stomach with a .38 Special. While the vest does not permit the bullet to penetrate, the impact knocks the man backward, but he recovers instantaneously, spins, and fires at a pop-up target. The whole sequence is filmed in slow-motion and looks more like the climactic scene from a Peckinpah movie than a sales film. Afterward, while the camera is still rolling, the man strips off the vest and raises his shirt to reveal a bloody welt on his sternum. It goes without saying that selling body armor this way may not be everyone's cup of tea.

Although it was announced in 1987 that free protective clothing would be made available to U.S. general officers stationed in Europe as well as to their aides, security personnel, and drivers, at last count fewer than one percent of those eligible had taken advantage of the offer.[16] Such apathy is indicative of the "it won't happen to me" syndrome that retired Major General James Dozier admits characterized him before his abduction by Red Brigades terrorists in Italy in 1981. However, as the number of attacks against NATO personnel increase, top-ranking military men and women may want to reconsider their decisions and opt for new wardrobes.

Counterterrorist Driving Machines

On June 26, 1979, General Alexander Haig's limousine was speeding toward NATO headquarters in Mons, Belgium, taking a route that had been selected only at the last minute, randomly, from among several alternatives. The limousine was accompanied by a "chase" car with three security men. Passing over a culvert near Oubourg, Haig noticed two motorcycle riders speeding away from an overpass. At the same moment, a loud explosion rent the air and the roadway disintegrated. Miraculously, the explosion detonated between the two cars, sparing Haig's life by a fraction of a second, but destroying the chase car and inflicting minor injuries on those inside. The explosives buried in the road left a crater five feet deep and twelve feet wide. German Red Army Faction (RAF) terrorists were suspected in the attack.

Two years later, the RAF made an attempt to kill another top American officer—General Frederick J. Kroesen, U.S. Commander in Europe. Using a Soviet-made RPG-7, RAF terrorists fired a rocket-propelled grenade at the general's limousine. The fin-stabilized HEAT round embedded in the vehicle's rear fender, but did not fully detonate. Moreover, the limo's armor-plating shielded the general and his wife from the most serious effects of the blast. The gas tank was also protected and did not explode.

The assassination attempts on Haig and Kroesen illustrate one of the hazards of automobile travel that even Ralph Nader has overlooked. As a general rule, at no time is an individual more vulnerable to terrorists than when traveling by automobile. Today, makers of custom-built "terror proof" vehicles are finding a ready market for their products, even at a price tag of $60,000 to $100,000 and more per vehicle. CCS Communication Control even goes so far as to call the hardened Cadillac featured in its catalogue "SuperCar," which it notes is a registered trademark. "SuperCar" boasts more than 25 safety and security systems, which CCS offers to install in any vehicle. While nearly every car can be "hardened," that is, made bulletproof, some of the more popular models include Mercedes-Benz sedans, the Jeep Wagoneer, the Chevy Blazer, and standard Ford or Chevrolet sedans. There is a trend toward more modest, less ostentatious cars that do not call attention to their owners.

In contrast to years past when hardening took the form of heavy iron and steel plating, today's armoring consists of space-age materials based often on fiberglass and resin compounds, such as Kevlar. The level of hardening depends on the anticipated threat and the size of the client's wallet. It must be remembered that any armoring, even using the most modern materials, increases the weight of the vehicle and reduces its handling capabilities.

In addition to armoring the vehicle and installing bullet-resistant glass, dual reinforced bumpers suitable for ramming are a must. To prevent the tires from being punctured by bullets, compartmentalized "run flat" tires are a necessity. Anti-hijack bolts and special locks will make it more difficult to pry the car doors open. To discourage pursuers, blinding high-intensity lights can be mounted on the rear of the car, along with devices that will lay down an oil slick or spit out tacks and heavy clouds of smoke. The lower edges of the car can be made razor-sharp so that hostile mobs will cut off their fingers if they try to pick up the car and tip it over. Some custom vehicles even have nozzles mounted around the car, often in each fender well behind reflectors, that can release tear gas, acids, chemicals, or poisons if the car is surrounded. Those inside the vehicle are protected by a special ventilation system that recirculates the air already inside.

Other accessories include a remote control ignition so that the car can be started from a distance, tampering alarm systems, bomb-scanning devices, ear-splitting sirens, fire suppressant systems, dual batteries, and a loudspeaker/microphone system that permits those inside the car to communicate with those outside.

Gun ports allow the occupants of the vehicle to return hostile fire without risk to themselves. A whole variety of custom weapons—shotguns, submachine guns, grenade launchers—mounted in hidden gun racks can be used to repel attacks. One Florida security man owns a Cadillac with two machine guns built into the front grille; when he throws the car into a spin, he can "take out" everything in a 360-degree arc. Four shotguns loaded with Double O buckshot are secreted behind the rear tail-light assembly, and are used to broadside pursuing vehicles as they turn corners.

The late Shah of Iran ordered a custom-built limousine from a Texas company in 1979. He told designers that he wanted a system that would neutralize an intruder or would-be assassin even if he got inside the car. They came up with an ejection seat and a reinforced roof. That's right: press the button and the adversary is catapulted into the ceiling, squish! The idea, however, was rejected. Instead, an alternative system was adopted which consisted of three shotgun tubes built into the seat. Messy, but effective. Events overtook the Shah, however, before he was able to take delivery on the quarter-of-a-million-dollar rolling fortress. Indeed, because their clients tend to be threatened people with questionable life expectancies, Cincinnati-based Hess & Eisenhardt International, the oldest producer of hardened vehicles in the United States and perhaps the finest manufacturer of security vehicles in the world, requires "not less than 50% of the contract price to be paid in United States dollars upon signing of the contract of purchase."

The "Brave New World" of Security

The future holds many new and exciting innovations in antiterrorism and security technology. "Robocop," one of the hit movies of 1987, will soon be Robo-Security Guard, as mobile robots take their place as guardians of the American workplace. Several companies are already experimenting with R2D2 lookalikes that prowl plants and businesses at night, ever on the alert for intruders, fires, and other hazards. While it will still be a while before robots replace the average security guard, especially in terms of the cost factors involved, recent technical advances in robotics make it clear that security robots are far more than just a curiosity.

Unbeatable identification and recognition systems, new bomb-resistant building materials, and explosives "sniffers" are all rapidly making their way into the marketplace. For more than a decade, the French gendarmerie have had computer terminals in many of their police vehicles tying them into a national information network designed not only to facilitate the exchange of operational messages but also to make identification of vehicles and suspected criminals/terrorists easier. The French hope to upgrade the system sometime in 1988 so that photographs and other visual material can be transmitted through the system. A number of U.S. law enforcement agencies and police departments are experimenting with similar systems.

Nevertheless, some advances in security technology also raise many new and disturbing questions concerning the right to privacy and the ease with which a police state can be imposed on modern societies. A recent article in the British science journal *Nature* went so far as to suggest that surveillance technology had progressed to the point that every man, woman, and child in Northern Ireland could be fitted with a personal radio transmitter that would permit authorities to track their every movement.[17] While admitting that it smacks of ''Big Brotherism'' and conceding that citizens would be up in arms over any effort to seriously implement such a proposal, the article went on to recommend that ''all vehicles in Ireland should be fitted with a radio-transmitter merely announcing their true identity to a cellular radio network,'' thereby making it ''much easier than now to tell which vehicles have been stolen and which have carried people to places where terrorists have been at work.''[18] Welcome to the ''Brave New World'' of modern security.

The misuse of security technology is also a growing problem. On a benign level, it includes a number of wealthy Arabs buying sophisticated micro homing devices to keep track of their falcons. But far more serious are corporations that illegally eavesdrop on competitors and detective firms that use state-of-the-art surveillance technology to gather information on individuals involved in divorce suits and custody battles. In Latin America and some parts of the developing world, moreover, security firms operate almost as private vigilante organizations, meting out punishment to lawbreakers in any fashion they desire. One company in Colombia, for example, put up electrified fences that could kill, rather than just stun, intruders. Technicians from another company were fond of packing more explosive than would be permitted in the United States into devices designed to discourage bank robberies and the theft of briefcases. One executive briefcase was nicknamed the ''three fingered briefcase'' because ''that's all the fingers a thief would have left on his hand'' if he tried to snatch it away from its rightful owner. The explosive was packed in the handle of the briefcase and was automatically triggered after being separated from a band worn on the owner's wrist for more than ten seconds.

This same firm also distributed so-called ''dye-packs'' to banks. Dye-packs are hollowed out stacks of phony currency, with real bills on the top and bottom, normally containing a small amount of explosive and an impermeable red dye that spews all over bank robbers as they flee the scene of the crime, marking both them and the money. Dye-packs are generally triggered by the bank teller or by devices placed in the door frame of the bank's entrance. In one case, the thief left the bank and casually sauntered over to a nearby stand-up coffee bar, stuffing the money down the front of his pants. As he stood at the bar, one of the dye-packs went off, blowing the man's pants open, burning his private parts, and covering him with red dye. Needless to say, he was rapidly apprehended.

5

Writing Terrorism to Death

Every new writer ought to be required to bring along two
terrorists just to keep the field going.

—J. Bowyer Bell

"AFTER Munich, terror became trendy," writes J. Bowyer Bell. "And those in the know (or on the make)
have hurried to their typewriters—the most effective weapon of
the weak."[1] The rise of global terrorism has spawned an enormous subculture composed of writers, researchers, publishers,
and commentators who feed off the public's fascination with the
subject as well as attempt to satisfy the need for instant information about various terrorist groups, tactics, and sponsors every
time an incident occurs someplace in the world. Most leading terrorism "experts" appear more often on television in an average
year than many cabinet members or prominent congressional
lawmakers. It would be a rare television producer, indeed, that
did not have the names of several articulate terrorism specialists
in his or her Rolodex. Similarly, every major publisher has at
least one or two terrorism books on its current list of publications.

Terrorism as Meal Ticket

One of the consequences of the extraordinary public attention
focused on terrorism is that it is rapidly becoming one of the
most overwritten fields of inquiry in the modern world. Some
writers are climbing on the bandwagon for money, others for

celebrity. Scholars, by contrast, have discovered that it is often easier to find publishers for tomes on terrorism, no matter how pedestrian, than on many other weightier subjects, which is extremely important in the "publish or perish" environment of academe. As J. Bowyer Bell has quipped, "Every new writer ought to be required to bring along two terrorists just to keep the field going."[2] The avalanche of books and publications on terrorism has resulted in many volumes that are highly derivative or of suspect authenticity. One of the worst is by a writer who calls himself Gayle Rivers, who has authored a number of books, including *The Specialist* and *The War Against the Terrorists.* In *The Specialist* ("Does the United States Hire Assassins? This book is by one") Rivers claims to be a counterterrorist assassin employed by Western governments to carry out retributive actions against various terrorist groups and their state sponsors. *The Specialist* opens with a scene straight out of a James Bond movie, in which Rivers claims to be cruising along the shores of Lake Geneva in his "Pacific blue Porsche Targa, with the local VD license plates of the canton of Vuad," when he gets a call from Lebanon. " 'Hello, this is Tom,' " the caller tells him. "I knew the voice well; it was the only identification he would give," writes Rivers with an air of mystery. " 'Gayle, there's a matter we'd like your help with again, concerning our blue guests. Could you manage a quick trip?' "[3]

So begins another preposterous adventure by Rivers, who explains that the caller, an American, "was calling me in as a mercenary but money was not mentioned on the phone."[4] How's that for knowledge of tradecraft? "For this kind of mission," Rivers continues:

> I charge the Americans a basic retainer of $75,000 plus expenses, which is paid by direct transfer from an American or Swiss-owned private company into one of my offshore holding companies and is described usually as a consultancy or survey fee. That figure gets me to Beirut for a briefing. At the briefing I will decide whether to accept the final mission and a full fee is agreed. Even assuming it was a solo mission, Tom the caller had probably committed at least $120,000 by picking up the phone to me.[5]

Rivers allegedly traveled to Lebanon, where he was told by a U.S. Special Forces representative that "the target was a Syrian major, a senior intelligence officer who had been flown from Damascus specially . . . to stiffen the Druze efforts in his sector. He was operating from a four-story building that had been set up as a Druze command post. The mission profile was to infiltrate the command post, capture the major, kill as many others as possible, then lay explosive charges on exfiltration and do as much damage as possible to the building after we had left it."[6] We are expected to believe 1) that U.S. special operations units are so bereft of talent that they must go to outside contractors to lead their operations, and 2) that Rivers was also hired in order to give the operation deniability (which explains, of course, why all of the other participants are regular members of the U.S. Special Forces). Rivers offers up an extraordinary menu of platitudes that pass for tradecraft, such as, "It is always a sound move for a mercenary to get right away from the scene of a mission, just in case there is a security leak."[7] This guy has been watching too much TV. He is also a cereal box philosopher: "I know that nothing in life is permanent, including life itself, yet I remain an optimist,"[8] or "In my experience, terrorists generally are people who serve their own self-interest under a phony banner of idealism and in the process contribute nothing to the improvement of anything."[9]

Gayle Rivers is, in the opinion of many observers, the Clifford Irving of international terrorism, that is to say, a fraud. During meetings with members of the Irish Republican Army in early 1988, J. Bowyer Bell asked them if they had read Rivers's allegations regarding the IRA in *The War Against the Terrorists.* They responded: "Nothing in it is true," and Bell concluded from his own research that as Rivers's work "relates to the IRA, it is a work of fiction" and "belongs to the Sam Hall school of fiction."[10] Rivers refuses to appear on television except in silhouette, ostensibly for security reasons, but in actuality to prevent anyone from exposing him. He cloaks himself in the secrecy that characterizes covert antiterrorist operations and uses it both to enhance his mystique and to prevent his real identity from being revealed. He is confident that no reputable government or Western intelligence agency will dignify his fiction by publicly attacking it, and even if they did, he would simply say, "See, that's all part of the plan. They always refuse to acknowledge my actions in order to preserve the deniability of what I have done " Rivers is reportedly a former warrant officer in the New Zealand Air Force who once tried to get into the SAS reserves in Great Britain, but was rejected. He is said to get most of his information about special operations from other books and from hanging out in pubs frequented by the SAS. The United States, however, is not his only target—he also claims to have hunted down and executed Basque terrorist leaders for the Spanish, carried out operations against the IRA for the British, and even led commando raids against Iranian targets for the Iraqis. I bet this would come as a surprise to Saddam Hussein.

It is often suggested that we should just ignore Rivers's books because they don't really do any harm. But that is not true. His invented assassinations and counterterrorist operations play into the hands of foreign propagandists and disinformation specialists and lend credibility to conspiracy theories and outlandish charges that hold the United States and its allies responsible for accidental and unrelated fatalities and events throughout the world. Recent Soviet disinformation efforts, for example, have attempted to link Mehmet Ali Agca, the man who shot Pope John Paul II, with the CIA; to suggest that the assassins of Indira Gandhi "received their ideological inspiration" from the CIA; and even to blame the CIA for assassination attempts on Philippine president Corazon Aquino.[11] In this way, Moscow hopes to "neutralize accusations that the USSR and its proxies support terrorism and engage in political murder"[12] and to demonstrate that "murder is a routine instrument of American foreign policy."[13] Although the evidence suggests to many experts that he is simply a fraud and a profiteer, Rivers—for all the strident anticommunism he expresses in his books—could not be a more effective agent of Soviet disinformation if he were on the KGB payroll.

Terrorism is also a rich vein of inspiration for the writers of formula thrillers and pulp novels, although most works of this genre betray considerable ignorance of the subject matter.[14] Writers like Robert Ludlum (*The Bourne Identity*), Larry Collins and Dominique Lapierre (*The Fifth Horseman*), Frederick Forsyth (*The Devil's Alternative* and *Day of the Jackal*), Tom Clancy (*Patriot Games*), and John le Carré (*The Little Drummer Girl*), to cite only a few examples, have all discovered the profit in terrorism during the past decade or two, but only Forsyth, in *Day of the Jackal*, has come close to achieving a purity of expression and realism that transcends the realm of the ordinary. Unfortunately, very few really serious or insightful works of fiction focusing on the subject of terrorism have appeared in recent years, and none on a par with classics like Dostoyevski's *The Possessed* (Besy), Malraux's *Man's Fate* (*Condition Humaine*), O'Flaherty's *The Informer*, Conrad's *Secret Agent*, or Greene's *The Honorary Consul*.

Scholars and Nonfiction Writers

Perhaps the best-known writer on terrorism in the world is expatriate journalist Claire Sterling, whose 1981 book, *The Terror Network*, created a sensation by describing the extensive ties between terrorist groups and the growing support they receive from governments, especially the Soviet Union and its allies. Sterling, a former left-of-center journalist living in Italy who wrote for the *New Republic* in the mid-1970s, is described by a close colleague as ''an extremely spirited and lively person, full of curiosity.''[15] In the course of reporting on the Italian Red Brigades and other European terrorist organizations, Sterling began to see overwhelming evidence of the existence of a ''terrorist international,'' in direct contradiction to the situation painted by Soviet apologists and those attempting to describe terrorism as largely a spontaneous, isolated, and unconnected phenomenon. The fact that she was not a right-wing ideologue gave added import and currency to her study, and perhaps accounts for the bitterness and vituperation that characterized the attacks on her by her former liberal colleagues. Almost overnight, she became a pariah to the left and a folk hero to the right, but she never quite seemed comfortable with the adulation showered upon her by conservatives.

She was also roundly criticized by traditional writers and researchers on the subject who faulted her sometimes sloppy research and her prose, which some maintained was more befitting a novel than a work of serious scholarship. In retrospect, however, many of the negative critiques and much of the grousing can be attributed to "sour grapes" on the part of Sterling's detractors, who may have resented her success and her ability to write for a mass audience that they, themselves, were unable to reach.

Sterling's thesis was immediately embraced by the Reagan administration, which had just come to power, and especially by Secretary of State Alexander Haig and CIA Director William Casey. However, many in the media, the Congress, and the Washington foreign policy community took issue with her study. Casey tasked the CIA to check it out, and they came back with a negative verdict. This outraged the director of central intelligence, and he purportedly upbraided CIA staffers, telling them to "read Claire Sterling's book and forget this mush."[16] Although she may have overstated her conclusions, over time Sterling's thesis has won wide acceptance, and she has clearly had an enormous impact on how the subject is viewed today. Whatever the shortcomings of her work, she has contributed significantly to public awareness and debate on the subject of terrorism. In 1983, she wrote a book on the assassination attempt on Pope John Paul II, and today she commutes between her homes in Rome and Tuscany completing a new book on the Mafia.

There are very few liberal writers on terrorism. Some would say that the field has largely been co-opted by centrists and conservatives. This may reflect, to some extent, the cynical nature of the subject matter, and the fact that some liberals—especially during the Carter administration—have a tendency to view counterterrorism as somehow antithetical to the promotion of human rights. Terrorism, moreover, has been employed as a tactic by antigovernment forces opposed to reactionary and authoritarian regimes, and many liberals have difficulty in deciding which side they are on. While a number of liberal professors have found terrorism academically erogenous, their writings on the subject are usually rather weak due to their lack of hands-on experience and their general distaste for the covert world.

One of the few prominent nonconservative writers on terrorism is fifty-six-year-old J. Bowyer Bell, whose work in the field is universally well regarded. "Bow," as he is known to friends, is a large man with a ready wit and a healthy skepticism about what often passes for "conventional knowledge" in the field. He wears something like a dozen elephant-hair bracelets on his thick left wrist, purportedly one for every close brush with death he's had in more than twenty years of researching and writing on the subject of terrorism. With thick dark hair licking his collar, a greatcoat thrown over his shoulders, and a long scarf like the one that strangled Isadora Duncan draped around his neck, both ends nearly dragging on the floor, Bell affects a studied casualness that gives him something of a romantic and bohemian air. He more closely resembles a poet than a terrorism expert, by contrast to the comment of a CNN television producer who once observed that "terrorism experts all tend to look more like terrorists than the terrorists themselves."

With nearly a dozen major books to his credit, including one of the finest studies on the Zionist terrorist organizations that fought for the creation of the state of Israel, he is perhaps best known for his classic work *The Secret Army: The I.R.A., 1916–1974.* Bell spent more than five years researching the work, much of it with the IRA, observing their operations, talking to their rank-and-file members, and even watching in fear and fascination as they constructed their bombs. His puckish sense of humor surfaces when he travels to Ireland and sends IRA postcards ("Printed and published by the Republican Movement") back to his colleagues in the United States. On the front, the postcards have featured everything from Christ-like portraits of the late IRA hunger-striker Bobby Sands, superimposed on a photo of Maze prison, to pictures of British troops in riot gear above the caption, "The British Way of Life in Ireland." On the back, however, they always contain the same message from Bell: no words, only a drawing of a round black bomb with the fuse burning and the signature "Bow."

According to Bell, he spends his time "talking to gunmen, and the rest of the time running around trying to find money so that I can continue to talk to gunmen." Bell has just returned from six months in Ireland, working on an updated version of his study on the IRA, but complains that "I'm getting too old to talk to old gunmen, because all of the old gunmen are younger than I am."

Mainstream writers in the field tend to be employed by the large think tanks, institutes, and so-called "Beltway Bandits" that survive on federal grants and contracts. Brian Jenkins of the Rand Corporation is probably the most respected professional authority on terrorism in the United States and is responsible for developing much of the typology and intellectual framework used by contemporary scholars in researching and writing about terrorism. He also reportedly has the largest data base on terrorism in the country. Other prominent writers include Bob Kupperman of the Center for Strategic and International Studies, former Deputy Director of the State Department's Office for Counterterrorism Terrell E. Arnold, former deputy director of the CIA Ray S. Cline, historian Walter Lacqueur of Georgetown University, *Terrorism* editor Yonah Alexander, retired British general Richard Clutterbuck, journalist Jillian Becker, British scholar Paul Wilkinson, Israeli expert Ariel Merari, terrorism columnist John B. Wolf, security specialists H.H.A. Cooper, Philip A. Karber, Jay Mallin, and the writing teams of Charles A. Russell and Bowman H. Miller, and Christopher Dobson and Ronald Payne. Among the writers that are less well-known and prolific, but no less important, are the late Roberta Goren, Israel's Ambassador to the United Nations Benjamin Netanyahu (whose brother Jonathan led the Sayaret Matkal force at Entebbe, where he was killed), U.S. Naval War College professor William Regis Farrell, Robert A. Friedlander,

Albert Parry, psychiatrist Dr. Frederick J. Hacker, former chief hostage negotiator for the New York City Police Department Frank Bolz, and airline consultant Dr. David Hubbard. Both CIA intelligence analyst Edward F. Mickolus and librarian Amos Lakos have published excellent bibliographies on the literature of terrorism, although Lakos's is more up-to-date. Mickolus has also done a fine chronology of terrorist events. There is also a substantial body of writing by former hostages, including former U.S. Ambassador Diego Asencio (Colombia), Moorhead Kennedy (Iran), Kurt Carlson (TWA 847), and British Ambassador Geoffrey Jackson (Uruguay).

The Writer as Counterterrorist Operator

Perhaps one of the most unique writers on the subject, and certainly one of the most controversial, is Washington-based Michael Ledeen, a central figure in the Iran/Contra scandal. He has been accused by his detractors of working for at least three intelligence agencies: the CIA, Israel's Mossad, and the Italians. The left-wing *Covert Action Information Bulletin* (CAIB) is obsessed with Ledeen, and has portrayed him as a leading "disinformation agent," an Israeli "mole," and a behind-the-scenes manipulator of international events. "If Contragate is the new Watergate," wrote Fred Landis in CAIB, "then Lt. Colonel Oliver North is G. Gordon Liddy and Michael Ledeen is E. Howard Hunt. One thing that unites these two characters is an almost infantile fascination with psychological propaganda operations—'psyops.' "[17] Ledeen has been accused, for example, of masterminding the theory of the Bulgarian connection in conjunction with the assassination attempt on Pope John Paul II in Vatican Square.

Ledeen is the classic writer cum operator who, like the moth that flits before the flame, sometimes gets burned, as he did in the Iran/Contra affair. Ledeen, however, maintains that he is "an intellectual" and that he has "no operational involvements of that sort." "I've never received anything, or any money in any form, from the Israeli government," he contends. "I've never done any work for them or any Israeli entity of any sort. As for the Italian government, my company did a risk assessment for them. We were then asked to do a crisis management game for which we were then issued a contract and we did about half the work on the contract before the Italian government fell."[18] He has yet to be paid by the Italians, he claims. Even if one accepts his denials at face value, it is clear that Michael Ledeen is no cloistered academic immersed in stacks of dusty books.

This bearded terrorism specialist with a weakness for thick, premium Honduran cigars could be glimpsed in early 1985 in a military hotel in Istanbul, high above the Bosporus, at a conference on the Rehabilitation of Terrorists. The hotel was one of the last projects of the Turkish military before voluntarily relinquishing power back to civilian government in the early 1980s, and although it had the outward appearance of a hotel, it was, in reality, just a glorified barracks. On each hall a young conscript dressed in white server's garb replied dutifully in English to any request, "Yes, my commander," even if he could not understand a word that was being said. The conference ultimately concluded that trying to rehabilitate terrorists was about as productive as trying to rehabilitate horses with broken legs. But for Leeden it was just another stop in his peripatetic travels throughout Europe and the Middle East, meeting, lecturing, and conferring, always on the go.

The forty-seven-year-old Los Angeles native is a former professional bridge player who once coached the Israeli national team and for two years toured Europe and the United States as a member of the Omar Sharif Bridge Circus. A historian by training, after the birth of his first child in 1975, Ledeen gave up the life of a journeyman bridge player and settled down in Rome as a correspondent for the *New Republic*. There he became fascinated by the Red Brigades terrorist group, and for the next several years reported on the political violence rocking Italy and on the European infatuation with Eurocommunism. It was during 1975 that he met another expatriate American journalist, Claire Sterling, who was to have a profound influence on him.

"I learned a great deal from her about journalism and journalistic ethics," he observes. "How to check out leads, stuff like that. She is a first-class journalist. Very careful."[19] Like Sterling, Ledeen has always regarded himself as left-of-center, in contrast to how he is generally perceived today. It was in Italy, he says, that he came to realize that the Communist party was a reactionary force, opposed to human rights, pluralism, and Western values.

In 1977, based on the recommendation of Georgetown University historian and writer on terrorism Walter Lacqueur, Ledeen was hired by David Abshire, who headed the Center for Strategic and International Studies (CSIS), a center-right Washington think tank then affiliated with Georgetown. Ledeen returned to the United States and became the founding editor of *The Washington Quarterly,* which was to become a prestigious forum for articles on public and international policy, at a time when CSIS served as something of a government-in-exile during the Carter administration.

Based on his work at CSIS and an acquaintanceship with incoming Secretary of State Alexander Haig that dated back to Haig's tenure as NATO commander, Ledeen joined the Reagan administration in the spring of 1981 as Special Assistant to Haig at the State Department. His initial duties were to serve as a contact point with the Socialist International, as well as monitor various issues concerning Western Europe, Poland, and Central America. He subsequently came to have the terrorism portfolio as well. According to Ledeen, he reported directly to Haig and, when he traveled, he did so as the personal emissary of the Secretary of State. "It was basically the equivalent of an Assistant Secretary position," says Ledeen.[20]

When Haig resigned in 1983, Ledeen also left the State Department, although he continued to maintain close ties with many of those with whom he had worked, including Noel Koch, the Defense Department's terrorism/special operations czar; Under Secretary of State and Kissinger protégé Larry Eagleburger; and Robert C. "Bud" McFarlane, who would become the President's National Security Advisor in October 1983. In

December 1984, at McFarlane's behest, Ledeen became a consultant to the National Security Council (NSC).

According to Ledeen, it was while working as a consultant to the National Security Council that he was tasked by McFarlane with doing a research report on Iran, paying particular attention to Iran's support of international terrorism. Ledeen was a logical choice for the assignment inasmuch as he had published a book on Iran and was generally deemed knowledgeable on the subject. During the preparation of the research report on Iran he met with a Western European intelligence specialist in March 1985, who advised him that the United States "really ought to get interested in Iran again." There were opportunities that could be seized if the United States would only recognize them, said Ledeen's contact. Ledeen replied: "We really don't know anything about Iran," and his contact advised him to "go talk to the Israelis. They know everything."[21]

Ledeen came back from his trip and described to McFarlane the meeting with the European intelligence contact and his advice regarding Iran. McFarlane was intrigued. "Bud said, 'You know [Shimon] Peres, go talk to him,'" recalls Ledeen, who indicated that McFarlane gave him very specific instructions regarding any discussions with the Israeli Prime Minister, including the precise questions that needed to be asked. "'Do not be aggressive on the subject,'" Ledeen says McFarlane told him. "'Simply say Iran is something we're trying to understand. We feel our information is unsatisfactory. Do you people think you have satisfactory information about it? Do you understand what's going on there, and if so would you be willing to share it with us?'" According the Ledeen, "That was the essence of this discussion, and there was no policy content to the discussion at all."[22]

When he got to Israel, he met with Prime Minister Peres. As Ledeen recalls this meeting, "We did not talk about weapons, and we did not talk about hostages, and we did not talk about contacts. The only subject we discussed was what do you know about Iran." According to Ledeen, Peres told him, "'We don't know much about Iran either. We probably know more than you do. There are a lot of Jews coming out and we're talking to them, but it's not what it used to be. But we'll be glad to work with you to get a better picture.' ''[23]

Ledeen says he dutifully reported his findings in Israel to McFarlane and others at the NSC. All, especially senior NSC staff members Donald Fortier and Howard Teicher, felt that Iran deserved a careful and comprehensive assessment, and, according to Ledeen, this was the genesis of the so-called Iran Initiative. It was never intended as an arms-for-hostages swap, Ledeen maintains, but rather "a proposal for a reciprocal set of gestures by two countries hopefully moving in the direction of better relations, provided one country—Iran—showed itself capable of changing and reforming itself and bringing into play new policies."[24]

Ledeen says he continued to work with McFarlane and others at the NSC on the Iran assessment until November 1985, when the United States became operationally involved with Iran. "Up until then," says Ledeen, "in terms of anything operational going on, it was Israeli. And my role was simply to attend meetings and report back to McFarlane on what had happened. But there was nothing operational,"[25] he emphasizes, although he notes that he volunteered his judgments concerning the course of the U.S. initiative to Iran. In December 1985, for example, Ledeen says he told CIA Director Bill Casey about the interest some Iranian officials had in normalizing relations with the United States, and expressed his misgivings that the Iran Initiative was degenerating into an arms-for-hostages deal.[26] According to Ledeen, he also warned McFarlane that the original initiative was becoming untracked, but McFarlane was preoccupied with other matters and resigned on December 5, 1985, at a crucial moment in the whole process.

"My role in the government," says Ledeen, "whether it was for Haig, for McFarlane, or Noel Koch, was always the same: there would be a certain body of intelligence material—cables, etc.—that I would be asked to read regularly on subjects that I would follow. And then I would be asked to travel and talk to people and see if I could develop a better understanding of what was happening.''[27] This description of Ledeen's role is supported by DOD official Noel Koch and Oliver North's former secretary, Fawn Hall, who said that Ledeen reviewed DIA (Defense Intelligence Agency) assessments on terrorism and other related reports. Hall testified: ''I think that Mr. Ledeen mostly came to the office to read . . . . The phone calls that came in, basically, were to say, 'Hey, I'm going to stop by today and read.' ''[28] If not an operator in the classic sense of the term, then, Ledeen was clearly a player: a mover and shaper of events. That remains one of his strengths. Unlike many academics who posture as operators, Ledeen is an operator who postures, when it serves his purpose, as an academic.

Lt. Colonel Oliver North testified that he believed Ledeen was profiting from the arms sales to Iran. Ledeen, however, is offended by reports that he received $50 for every missile sold or transferred to Iran, a charge he adamantly denies. If he had accepted money for the missile transactions, says Ledeen, it would have been substantially more than $50 per missile. Ledeen also denies North's contention that he actually negotiated prices for at least one missile shipment.[29]

One of the most curious aspects of Ledeen's involvement in the Iran/Contra affair concerns his relationship with Iranian arms dealer and middleman Manucher Ghorbanifar, who allegedly was the NSC's principal contact with Iran in late 1985 and early 1986. Although Ghorbanifar flunked every polygraph test administered to him by the CIA and was generally regarded as ''untrustworthy,'' Ledeen continues to stand by him, maintaining that the ''hijacking of the TWA plane in June 1985 could not have been resolved so happily without Mr. Ghorbanifar.''[30] Ghorbanifar's contacts with the Iranians were real, says Ledeen, and without his help ''the Rev. Benjamin Weir, the Rev. Lawrence Jenco and David Jacobsen would still be hostages today.''[31]

Despite Ledeen's instrumental role in the Iran Initiative, he was never called to testify by the Congressional committees investigating the Iran/Contra affair. Nevertheless, he reportedly cooperated with Independent Counsel Lawrence Walsh's investigation, and recently completed a book on the Iran/Contra crisis entitled *Perilous Statecraft: An Insider's Account of the Iran-Contra Affair*. [32] When asked about his future plans, Ledeen expresses an interest in finishing a study of the Socialist government of Felipe Gonzales in Spain. As to another book on terrorism, he contends that terrorism is "not an intellectually interesting subject" because it is "no longer mysterious."[33] It is difficult, moreover, to do research on terrorism as a private citizen, he says, because a real understanding of the subject and what is going on requires intelligence material. On the other hand, "counterterrorism is interesting," he believes, because too little attention has been devoted to it as a separate field of inquiry. Today we understand the problem, he concludes; it is what we do about the problem that is still a matter of debate and contention.

Unlike many other writers and commentators in the field, Michael Ledeen is concerned chiefly with values; that is, the preservation and advancement of Western concepts of democracy, humanism, law, and religious tolerance, which are under assault as never before by Soviet bloc and Third World despotisms extolling totalitarianism, violence, and either religious extremism or an outright denial of man's inherent spiritualism. In this connection, he remains convinced that while terrorism remains an egregious affront to all of the values the West holds dear, it will "never threaten Western democracy." Only we can do that, says Ledeen, by overreacting to the threat it poses.

The Ten Worst Books on Terrorism

It seems as though there is a "top ten" list for everything today, and terrorism should be no exception. In this case, what follows is my list of the ten worst books this author could locate on the subject of terrorism. Included are the worst achievements in both fiction and non-fiction categories:

1. Gayle Rivers, *The Specialist*. Rivers has the distinction of being the only author with two books on the ten worst list, for

reasons already set forth. Pure fiction disguised as reality; a disservice to all who serve in the war against terrorism.

2. Robin Morgan, *The Demon Lover*. Described as "the first feminist analysis of the phenomenon of terrorism," the dust jacket says it all: "Lucidly, eloquently, she [Morgan] shows us that the terrorist has been the ultimate male sexual idol of a male-centered cultural tradition from pre-Biblical times to the present. The terrorist *is* the Demon Lover—sexy because he is deadly, he excites with the thrill of fear. He is both a hero of risk and an anti-hero of death. We have invoked him for centuries. Now, he is becoming Everyman."

3. Sam Hall, *Counter Terrorist*. Unbelievably self-parodying, yet you get the feeling that Hall doesn't have a clue about how stupid he sounds. Sam Hall is no more a counterterrorist than my dog is a brain surgeon.

4. Gayle Rivers, *The War Against the Terrorists*. See number 1 above. Pseudo-theory by a pseudo-theorist.

5. Bob Woodward, *Veil*. Another work of fiction disguised as fact, which does great violence to U.S. antiterrorism efforts. Following surgery on December 18, 1986, the late CIA Director William Casey suffered from a condition known as expressive aphasia, which is the inability to express oneself. Speech comes out garbled, gibberish, or slurred; one physician likened it to a computer without a printer. Casey only spoke eleven words (repeating some of them more than once) from the date of the surgery until his death in May 1987. He was totally incapable of stringing words together in sentences or of engaging in normal conversation. Thus, there is no way he could have had the nineteen-word conversation with Bob Woodward of the *Washington Post* described in *Veil*, even if one suspends credulity and accepts Woodward's word that he somehow got past family members and CIA security into the gravely ill old spook's hospital room.[34]

6. Alan Hart, *Arafat: Terrorist or Peacemaker?* The banner on the cover says it all: "Written in co-operation with Yasser Arafat and the top leadership of the PLO." If you believe Hart's

account, Arafat has always been morally repelled by terrorism, and only "join[ed] the terrorists in order to beat them."[35] As a PR exercise, Hart's book ranks with Palestinian hijacker Leila Khaled's *My People Shall Live: The Autobiography of a Revolutionary,* which is so polemical that, as one expert has stated, "The rhetoric at times becomes unintentionally humorous."[36]

7. Tom Clancy, *Patriot Games.* The silliest premise for a novel in recent years, by one of the finest living fiction writers. In the book, our hero, Jack Ryan, while vacationing in London, saves the lives of the Prince and Princess of Wales when they are attacked by Irish terrorists. Eternally grateful, Charles and Di accept Jack's invitation to a barbecue at his house on Maryland's eastern shore, where they are attacked by hordes of Ninji-like terrorists. Not anticipating such a calamity, the G-men are quickly overwhelmed, and only Jack's resourcefulness once again saves the day. Sure.

8. Michael T. Klare and Peter Kornbluh, Editors, *Low Intensity Warfare.* Disguised to look like a legitimate inquiry into "counterinsurgency, proinsurgency, and antiterrorism in the eighties," the publisher probably hoped that thousands of well-meaning readers, interested in expanding their knowledge of this very important subject, would unwittingly purchase the book without realizing that it is leftist tripe aimed at discrediting U.S. low-intensity warfare capabilities. Full of conspiratorial references, it describes how "a small contingent of officers, analysts, and political operators inside the national security establishment, supported by a growing neoconservative movement, committed themselves to restoring the United States as the 'guardian at the gate' of a global hegemonic order."[37]

9. Senators William S. Cohen and George J. Mitchell, *Men of Zeal.* Although purported to be the inside story of the Iran/Contra affair by two of the members of the congressional investigating committee, this is really the story of how Cohen and Mitchell have met the enemy, and it is Oliver North and a cabal of like-minded fellow travelers. In view of more recent

revelations suggesting that, far from being a rogue operation involving a cabal of zealots, the Iran/Contra affair involved the highest levels of U.S. government, the senators' account increasingly appears to be wide off the mark. The book is both self-righteous and petty, and reads more like an effort to justify the congressional inquiry than to get at the truth. Indeed, Congress has been a broken reed when it comes to doing anything meaningful about terrorism, and the failure of the authors to address the real issues that gave rise to the Iran/Contra affair—such as congressional inaction—undermines the very validity of the book.

10. Richard Falk, *Revolutionaries and Functionaries*. "Over the past decades," claims the dust jacket, " 'counterterrorism' has become a rallying cry to justify the use of state-sponsored violence." Falk, the liberal international law professor from Princeton, has once again offered up an apples-and-oranges analysis, wherein he maintains that "we cannot stop violence from below while we continue it from above." Like other ivory-tower theorists with little understanding of the real world, Falk equates terrorism and counterterrorism as two sides of the same coin, each with roughly the same moral authority, and suggests instead that we adopt a strategy of "progressive counterterrorism" whereby we seek to "inhibit recourse to terrorism by peaceful means." Sounds great in theory, but Falk once again sounds like he just fell off the academic equivalent of the turnip wagon.

Obviously, not everyone will agree with the choices listed above. The compilation of any such list is highly subjective; however, the author believes that the books named above cry out for special recognition, and that even a cursory reading by an unbiased party would confirm most of my conclusions.

Mayhem Manuals

Ironically, many publications ostensibly written to help protect society from the depredations of terrorists have been turned into instructional handbooks for terrorists. They are called mayhem manuals, and the United States has the only publishing industry dedicated to the manufacture and distribution of such materials in the world. They are basically "how to" books: how to torture, how to make bombs, and how to kill. The late Arleigh McCree, head of the Los Angeles Police Department's bomb squad, who was killed by a bomb in 1986, told the Senate Judiciary Committee's Subcommittee on Terrorism and Security in 1982 that the Federal Freedom of Information Act was responsible for the declassification and release of dozens of military handbooks providing detailed instructions on bomb making, sabotage, and booby traps.

This writer has identified some 1,600 titles available on the open market. For those interested in murder, there is John Minnery's six-volume *How to Kill* series, and titles like *The Hit Parade* ("a welcome supplement to our best-selling *How to Kill* series"); *The Death Dealer's Manual; Hit Man: A Technical Manual for Independent Contractors; Deadly Substances; Assassination: Theory and Practice; Deal the First Deadly Blow; Ambush and Counter Ambush; Training the Gunfighter; Mantrapping; Principles of Quick Kill;* and a reprint of the U.S. Marine Corps *Sniping* manual. Rex Feral, author of *Hit Man*, tries to justify his literary pretensions by suggesting: "It is my opinion that the professional hit man fills a need in society, and is, at times, the only alternative for 'personal justice.'"

If bombs and explosives are more to your taste, there are literally hundreds of titles to choose from: *Improvised Munitions Black Book; CIA Explosives for Sabotage Manual; Kitchen Improvised Plastic Explosives* (vols. 1 & 2); *Kitchen Improvised Blasting Caps; Kitchen Improvised Fertilizer Explosives; Improvised Shaped Charges; SECRET!! Two Component High Explosive Mixtures; Expedient Hand Grenades; Explosives and Propellants from Commonly Available Materials; Improvised Munitions Systems; Elements of Explosives Production; Special Forces Demolition Techniques; Hi-Low Booms;* and that all-time favorite of the radical right and left alike, *The Anarchist's Cookbook*. Described in the foreword as "a brutal book—sensual, rude, coarse, and cruel," *The Anarchist's Cookbook* is perhaps the all-time best seller in the mayhem field.[38] Law enforcement officials say it turns up more often than any other similar publication in the safe houses and car trunks of criminals, terrorists, and political radicals. In the chapter on "Explosives and Booby Traps," author William Powell writes that:

> I have a friend who worked with demolitions in the Middle East, and he has told me on several occasions that an explosion for him was an experience very similar to a sexual orgasm. This may seem strange to anyone who has no experience with explosives, but in many regards it is absolutely true. An explosion is an amazing phenomenon. Coupled with the destruction of an object of popular hatred, it can become more than just a chemical reaction. It can take the shape of hope for a nation of oppressed people.[39]

Powell goes on to describe how to make nitroglycerin, blasting gelatin, dynamite, TNT, and other explosives. That accomplished, he then describes how to drop bridges with explosives, how to rig up explosives under the driver's seat in a car, and the construction of booby traps. A recent advertisement for the book called it "The best 'How-To' book on improvised weapons in years!" The ad goes on to say, "Everything is completely explained in simple, everyday language everyone can understand, and profusely illustrated. The use of inexpensive and accessible materials is emphasized throughout the text, making this a 'must' book for serious weapons enthusiasts."[40]

The literature on torture is also extensive, and probably would be instructive even to an Argentine colonel. *Physical Interrogation Techniques* may be one of the most depraved books ever published. The abuses it describes are so vile that they should place this book well beyond any standard of First Amendment protection. The book covers such "techniques" as the use of sandpaper and wire brushes on the skin; the application of razors, whips, dental instruments, electricity, and caustic chemicals to the victim; sexual abuse; sewing a subject's hands or lips together; mutilation; castration; humiliation; bone scraping; fingernail pulling; burial alive; skinning alive; drugs; and burning subjects with propane torches. "A small propane torch can provide stripe after stripe of searing agony as it is passed again and again across his [the victim's] chest or back," writes author Richard W. Krousher. In the back of *Physical Interrogation Techniques* is the reassuring suggestion that "you will also want to read" *Disruptive Terrorism* ("how a handful of terrorists can bring America . . . to its knees by systematic disruption of centralized power, communications, and food distribution facilities"), *Manuals on Mayhem* ("a must for all professionals"), and *Exotic Weapons: An Access Book* ("Need a blackjack, or some brass knuckles? How about electrical weapons, or a blowgun?").

Perhaps the largest single category of mayhem literature concerns firearms and other weapons. The casual reader can choose from hundreds of titles like *Workshop Silencers I; Bloody Iron; Improvised Weapons of the American Underground; Selective Fire Uzi: Semi-Auto Modification Manual; Cold Steel; Slash and Thrust; Home Workshop Guns for Defense and Resistance: The Submachine Gun; Automatic & Concealable Firearms Design Book* (vols. 1 & 2); *The Crossbow as a Modern Weapon; Improvised Weapons in American Prisons; Flexible Weapons; Prison's Bloody Iron; Pananandata Knife Fighting; Close Shaves: The Complete Book of Razor Fighting; The Quiet Killers I and II; Knife Throwing: A Practical Guide;* and *Ninja Shuriken Throwing.*

There are books on how to beat a lie detector, how to open a Swiss bank account, how to commit crimes (*The Perfect Crime and How to Commit It, Involuntary Repossession or In the Steal of the Night, How to Rip Off a Drug Dealer*); how to get a machine gun license; smuggling (*Sneak it Through, Duty Free, The Complete Book of International Smuggling*); false I.D.'s (*Mail Order I.D., How to Get I.D. in Canada, New I.D. in America, Paper Tripping Overseas: New I.D. in England, Australia and New Zealand*); electronic eavesdropping (*Wiretapping and Electronic Surveillance, Covert Surveillance and Electronic Penetration, Bugs and Electronic Surveillance*); lock picking (*Surreptitious Entry, Lock Picking Simplified*); revenge (*The Revenge Book, Consumer Revenge, I Hate You!, Techniques of Revenge, Techniques of Harassment, Get Even*); and gunrunning (*Gunrunning for Fun and Profit*). Under the heading of "Terrorism" in one mayhem catalogue is a listing for *The Turner Diaries,* which is the "bible" of the Aryan Nations movement. It is not a book about terrorism, but rather *for* terrorists. The listing actually quotes the FBI, which has called *The Turner Diaries* a "manual of hatred," as a way of promoting its sale. "If the government had the power to ban books," it goes on to say, "The Turner Diaries would be at the top of their list. Order your copy today!"

The largest publisher of mayhem literature in the country is Paladin Press in Boulder, Colorado, which reportedly published more than 300,000 copies of such books last year. A recent Paladin Press catalogue listed 279 titles presently in print. Other publishers include Delta Press Ltd., Alpha, Desert Publications, and Loompanics Unlimited, whose motto is "No More Secrets, No More Excuses, No More Limits." A number of mayhem and survivalist newsletters are also published, such as Kurt Saxon's "The Gun Runner."

Paladin's owner, Peder Lund, is a smart, affable, streetwise Vietnam veteran who is happy to show off his clean, modern, efficient facility to visitors. It is an extremely cheerful environment for someone engaged in such a dark enterprise, and has a laid-back counterculture feel more suggestive of a purveyor of drug paraphernalia and books on bionic gardening. There are lots of potted plants and Levi-clad, healthy looking women with long hair and easy smiles.

Lund, for his part, attired in a tweed coat and open collar, looks more like a local college professor than the "mayhem king" as he leans back in his chair and places his cowboy boots on top of the desk. "We disseminate information," he says, dismissing more negative characterizations of the material he publishes. The irony, however, is that Lund himself refers to his publications as "burn and blow" books, in other words "how to burn things down and blow things up." Lund readily admits that his publications could be going to terrorists, or even children, but he asserts, "We don't make a moral judgment" about the material. "We don't make value judgments. We don't tell people how to use the information." Readers can take comfort that "We don't encourage . . . any felonies. We don't encourage crimes." When asked if Paladin Press isn't providing textbooks for terrorists, Lund tries to deflect the question by focusing on the Carter administration: "I think the Carter administration, through their ties with Libya, provided far more problems for the U.S. and other . . . nations than Paladin Press will ever provide."[41]

Pornographers of Violence

Kurt Saxon is the kind of person, one suspects, that would stand up and yell "encore" in a burning theater. He lives on the outskirts of reality. A self-described member of the Posse Commitatus, the Minutemen, the Ku Klux Klan, the American Nazi Party, the Aryan Nations movement and, by his own admission, "eight satanic cults," Saxon ricochets off the walls while standing still. Yet the resident of Harrison, Arkansas, doesn't look like the kind of man who has belonged to every loony-toon organization in the country and who writes and publishes "how to" books on murder and mayhem for a living. Of medium height, with long sideburns and a moustache, and dressed in a white turtleneck, corduroy jacket, and double-knit trousers, his appearance suggests the kind of a man who, if hit by a car, would probably welcome the interruption. The only clue to his unusual livelihood is a disfigured hand.

Saxon is the author of *The Poor Man's James Bond,* which is "Affectionately Dedicated to Dee Hoffgott" of the Coalition for Handgun Control, "whose campaign for civilian disarmament has done more to encourage the interest in improvised weaponry than even dingbats like Ted Kennedy and Birch Bayh."[42] Earlier editions were "affectionately dedicated to Lee Harvey Oswald, James Earl Ray, Sirhan Bishara Sirhan, and Senator Ted Kennedy," but apparently someone decided that that was in bad taste.[43] One catalogue hawking *The Poor Man's James Bond* declares: "It's all here! How to make explosives, booby traps, tear gas, fireworks, bombs and electric arson devices. Also covers Army and Marine hand-to-hand combat. All the chemical formulas, illustrations and instructions needed for combat either one-on-one or a major war!"[44] Now there's a comforting thought. In addition to the weapons and devices described in the ad, *The Poor Man's James Bond* instructs readers on how to manufacture homemade incendiaries, gas tank bombs, pipe bombs, flame throwers, napalm, firearm silencers, and eleven-shot shotguns, as well as sections entitled ''how to beat a metal detector,'' ''blowing up a car,'' ''poisons,'' ''counterfeiting,'' and ''people's grenades.'' The book also contains a reprint of something called ''Arson by Electronics,'' a handbook for torching buildings. ''There are many books for bomb buffs on the market,'' modestly admits Saxon. ''I'm happy to admit that mine is by far the best.''[45]

But he really likes poisons. Saxon is particularly fond of the poison ricin, a derivative of the lowly castor bean, that is thousands of times more potent than many nerve agents. He sells the formula for making ricin through the mail. It was ricin that was suspected in the death of Georgi Markov, a Bulgarian dissident attacked in London in 1978 by a man with an umbrella. The umbrella apparently was a compressed gas-powered gun that fired a tiny pellet (1.52mm in diameter), made of platinum and iridium and containing ricin, into Markov's thigh. The assassin was most likely an East-bloc intelligence operative.

Saxon showed up in Boulder, Colorado, for an interview, arranged by this author, with ABC correspondent Tom Jarriel, carrying a battered bag. Although he had not alerted or forewarned the author or ''20/20'' producer Martin Clancy, Saxon reached into the bag in the glassed-in dining room of a local hotel to find the vial of ricin he claimed to have brought with him. Much to his chagrin, he couldn't locate it. ''Maybe it fell out on the plane,'' he offered as he rummaged through the bag. Finally, much to the relief of all present, he discovered it in a seam in the bag. If it *was* the real thing, there was enough in the vial to wipe out hundreds, if not thousands, of people—and he was afraid he'd lost it on the plane![46]

His ''favorite'' poison, says Saxon, is nicotine sulfate. ''A fine way to use nicotine sulfate,'' he contends, ''is to carry it in a soft drink cup and act like you accidentally spilled it on the victim. If he doesn't wash it off in a matter of seconds, he will be dead in a matter of minutes.''[47] Such suggestions, however, make it abundantly clear that his book is not, as he claims, about self-defense, but rather about murder, since few of us carry around cups of nicotine sulfate in order to defend ourselves from muggers, rapists, and terrorists.

Saxon does not deny that he actually sells ricin and the other poisons he writes about, although he says he never uses the U.S. Mail out of fear of prosecution. Gun shows are a great place to market such substances, he maintains, and if someone in another state desires to buy a particular poison, he can always make arrangements to have it delivered.

In *The Poor Man's James Bond,* Saxon recommends testing poisons on the homeless, whom he refers to as ''winos'':

> In every city there are hundreds of winos sleeping out in nests in vacant lots, abandoned houses, under bridges, etc. It's very easy to find such nests. They are usually made up of flattened cardboard boxes and newspapers and littered with wine bottles.
>
> Put the dose you want to test in a half full fifth bottle of sweet wine. Then tuck it in the nest where the wino will be sure to find it. He will just think another wino hid it there.
>
> If the nest has a dead wino in it the next morning you've figured out the right dose. If both the nest and the bottle is empty, it's back to the old drawing board. Try increasing the dosage.[48]

Saxon concludes his section on poisons by advising the reader: ''Another good thing to know about the poison of your choice is its legitimate use. If a druggist or someone else asks you what you want with it, it's embarrassing to have to admit you want to kill someone. A cover story is always good.''[49]

Saxon is quite candid when asked how he got into the business of writing such books. ''I needed the money,'' he explains. ''I realized there was a market for it then I started selling it purely for profit and also maybe to use against communists and so on, if there should be an invasion or whatever might happen.''[50] In a recent interview, however, he maintains that one purpose of *The Poor Man's James Bond* is to wipe out the subhuman population of cities. ''Urbanites are all subhuman,'' he told a reporter.

"No one in their right mind would live in the city. I'm a hill person myself."[51] He claims that *The Poor Man's James Bond* has sold more than 55,000 copies to date, and describes it as "my best seller," a "classic in the field," and his "bread and butter."[52] He offers no apologies for the broad dissemination of his books, and even derides rival authors for saying that their books are restricted to police, firemen, and military personnel. "This is a paranoid cop-out," maintains Saxon. "They will sell you any book even if you write your order on a paper sack with a crayon."[53] Evidence suggests that he's right.

It doesn't particularly bother Saxon that his books may be used to commit all sorts of crimes against society. That is society's problem, Saxon says, without the slightest trace of remorse. In fact, he writes proudly of how *The Poor Man's James Bond* can "transform" the ordinary terrorist or militant:

> To others he may seem a shabby, nondescript, run-of-the-mill loser. But to himself he is a one man army with the power to destroy any individual or hundreds of any group. This poor man's James Bond not only has the power to destroy but to disrupt and terrorize with relative impunity.
>
> A militant with an eighth grade reading level can fix up a mad scientist's laboratory out of odds and ends and with easily purchased chemicals become more dangerous than a foreign saboteur.[54]

That's a reassuring thought, isn't it? Saxon takes issue, however, with evidence that terrorists use his publications. He claims that terrorists are "supplied basically by the Russians. They don't use improvised weaponry. They don't need my book. My book is for individuals who feel insecure in whatever area they're living in or who anticipate an invasion from Russia or Mars or wherever."[55]

Saxon says he does not know of an instance in which his book has been used in the commission of any crime. Nevertheless, he indicated that he was pleased when a copy of *The Poor Man's James Bond* was discovered in 1982 in the apartment of a Chicago man arrested for having five unregistered guns, ammunition, cyanide, and mayhem manuals. The individual, Roger Arnold, worked for the Jewel grocery store chain, owners of two of the stores where four of the seven people bought the cyanide-laced Tylenol that later killed them. There is a disclaimer of sorts on the back cover of *The Poor Man's James Bond,* just in case someone should misuse the information contained inside: "It is bad to poison your fellow man, blow him up or even shoot him or otherwise disturb his tranquility," the disclaimer reads. "It is also uncouth to counterfeit your nation's currency and it is tacky to destroy property as instructed in Arson by Electronics."[56]

Saxon won't talk very much about himself. A few details of his life slip out in his conversation, but it is hard to assemble them in any coherent form. He says he studied journalism, took dramatic lessons, once worked as an attendant in a mental institution, and dabbled in radical politics. He met his wife after she saw him on a television program and wrote him a letter. His writings are sprinkled with allusions to drug usage, and Saxon admits to using drugs, but never—he declares—while building explosives. When questioned about his mental stability, Saxon complains: "I'm not a nut. I used to be a nut. But now I'm successful. So now I'm eccentric."[57]

The Locksmith from Brantford, Ontario

He lives in a narrow, dark little house in Brantford, Ontario, with a Filipino wife who waits on him hand and foot. John Minnery is, in every respect, "king of his castle," and woe to anyone who would try to violate his castle, as he is armed to the teeth with every conceivable killing instrument known to man. The rear door of the house and several of the internal doors are steel, and permit him to turn the place into a bunker at the first sign of trouble. Although he is by trade a local locksmith, John Minnery is known to thousands of readers in the United States and elsewhere as the author of the six-volume set of books entitled *How to Kill,* which he hopes ultimately to expand to ten volumes. He also wrote another old favorite, the *Trapping and Destruction of Executive Armored Cars.*

Minnery, like Saxon, is an inherently benign-looking man: short, overweight, baby-faced, with a perpetual wide-eyed expression suggestive of a young boy lost in the lingerie department at J.C. Penney's. Minnery, in fact, looks like the classic nebbish as he sits in his den in a saucer chair covered with fake leopard fabric, wearing a white shirt, sweater vest, thick-soled oxfords, white socks, and baggy trousers. The only thing he is missing is a milk ring around his mouth. The walls, however, are covered with guns, assassination devices, and instruments of torture: a Venus machine gun, a miniature gun built into a cigarette lighter, tiny hand grenades, a North African sword with grooves designed to hold poison, a silenced DeLyle carbine, Russian submachine guns, an AK-47 assault rifle, a crossbow and steel darts, an M-1 carbine with an infrared scope, throwing crescents, war quoits, even a short gun with a bent barrel allegedly capable of shooting around corners.

Minnery says he began the *How to Kill* series simply as part of his personal research; he was not even aware that there was a market for his writings until an acquaintance shared a copy of one of his manuscripts with Peder Lund of Paladin Press, who offered to publish his research in book form. While admitting that his books are primers on how to commit murder, Minnery claims that he originally hoped that his research would be useful to criminal investigators, counterterrorists, and members of the military. In his opening paragraph in volume one, Minnery states that "the object of this study is to instruct the reader in the techniques of taking another human life, up close, and doing it very well. You may well find this booklet offensive, repulsive, brutal and vicious. It is meant to be. It is completely contemptuous of human life and my only admonition to the would-be assassin is: Kill without joy."[58] As if he has not made his point already, he repeats his assertion: "The will to kill, the complete lack of sympathy and compassion, and no hesitation in killing the subject is paramount. You must take his life as detachedly as you might swat a fly or crush an ant."[59]

It is his contention that virtually any practical joke can be turned into a "killing technique" or "terror device," such as the "barrel of laughs." This involves stuffing the victim in a 55-gallon oil drum where "he can not extricate himself . . . and will expire from constricture and muscle exhaustion."[60]

To Minnery, killing is a science worthy of study like any other science, and in his cosmology it is a value-free science. He vows to leave questions regarding who is killed and for what reasons to others. Using his twisted logic, however, even the victim benefits "because he is dispatched with as little pain as possible and his suffering and misery need not be great."[61] What a humanitarian. In keeping with his pseudoscientific efforts, Minnery has a section entitled, "A Good Day to Die," which claims to be "bio-climatology applied to necrotechnics." Warm sunny days, he postulates, are best for shooting or stabbing the victim because "a man's blood flows freely through his veins; his saliva protects his breath and keeps his breathing light and swift. There is no obstruction to blood or breath circulation." On cold blustery days, by contrast, "the blood flows thickly and the breath is denied protection and keeps ebbing. Studies have shown that most coronary occlusions occur during such periods. Best time for strangulation, choking, and some poisonings."[62] He even takes the would-be murderer by the hand and leads him or her through "your first kill." "Unless you're a fool you're going to be scared," he writes sympathetically. "Your hands are going to sweat—dry them. Your knees are going to knock—brace them. Your stomach is going to be queasy—this is caused by your diaphragm falling on it making you want to vomit and have butterflies."[63] Well, you get the point. And if you want to make a murder look like a suicide, Minnery offers a "faked suicide checklist" full of helpful tidbits like "bullets fired into mouth must miss tongue to tend to be a suicide indicator."[64]

Minnery provides an extensive section on assassinating political leaders, or those he refers to as "VIP's." In one volume he addresses hitting executive convoys, and in another how to rig up a gun disguised as a microphone.[65] Indeed, Minnery says that he can analyze most failed assassination attempts and come up with suggestions for guaranteeing success the next time around.[66]

Minnery says that he believes his books have received a bad "rap" and that he would have thought that law enforcement agencies would be more grateful to him for pointing out such deficiencies as the vulnerabilities of armored cars. Like Saxon, he dismisses notions that terrorists would find his books of value. They are, after all, "minions of foreign governments," he maintains, and despite evidence to the contrary, he contends that they are all suicidal. On the other hand, "the weapons that I point out are ones for killing and getting away with it," by which he means that he counsels people on how to commit quiet murders rather than noisy headline-grabbing events.

In 1982, William Chanslor, a Houston attorney, contacted Minnery about obtaining an effective poison with which to murder his wife. Apparently Chanslor knew of Minnery through his books, and initially asked him if he would be willing to give a lecture in Texas on poisons. Minnery ultimately contacted Canadian authorities who, in turn, worked with their counterparts in the United States to mount a "sting" operation against Chanslor. A Canadian agent posing as Minnery flew to Houston and delivered a package purportedly containing the poison ricin to Chanslor, who paid him $2,500. The whole transaction was videotaped, and Chanslor was arrested. He later pleaded no contest to the charge of solicitation to commit murder.

In another case, an ex-marine bought some of Minnery's books, studied them, and offered his services as a professional killer. Apparently he was hired by a Chicago dentist to kill a local druggist, but he then murdered the wrong man. When he finally got the right victim, an eyewitness spotted the license number on his car, and he was apprehended a short time later. Minnery denies that he bears any moral responsibility for what happened, maintaining that the killer used "a .38 and a shotgun which is not stressed at all in my book." The only contribution his *How to Kill* books might have made is to have "aided him [the killer] in narrowing down what devices he was going to use to commit this murder." Indeed, Minnery claims that if the killer had read his books more closely he probably would not have been caught: "If my techniques were used, you would not know that there was a murder committed in the first place. Most deaths would appear natural or accidental. And so, the murders, the successes you will never hear about.'' How's that for a comforting thought?

Minnery acknowledges that his books are banned in Canada, where they are regarded as a form of pornography and as seditious literature. He says he fully agrees with the ban. When asked whether it doesn't trouble him that they are sold in the United States, he shrugs: ''You are willing to . . . pay for them and I'm willing to send them to you.''

Lower the Decibels

There is a real need today to lower the decibels and reduce the level of hysterics that characterizes a good deal of writing and reportage on terrorism. Morever, there are too many purely descriptive works on the subject and not enough constructive efforts designed to offer up practical suggestions and solutions to policymakers and others engaged in the ongoing struggle against terrorism.

Publishers also have a public responsibility not to add to the problem by publishing books of dubious authenticity, such as those that purport to be factual accounts of U.S. or Israeli ''hit teams.'' Such books may actually jeopardize the lives of innocent Americans abroad. By the same token, mayhem manuals, such as those written by Saxon or Minnery, are patently offensive and serve no useful purpose to society. In view of the fact that they give practical support to terrorists of every persuasion, consideration should be given to banning their publication and sale, as is done in Canada and Great Britain. Freedom of speech is not an unlimited right, as Mr. Justice Holmes observed: ''The most stringent protection of free speech would not protect a man falsely shouting fire in a theater and causing a panic.'' Thus, if society deems it illegal to shout ''fire'' in a crowded theater, then surely by the same reasoning it should be illegal to teach someone how to actually set the theater on fire, or how to bomb the theater and murder the audience.

Finally, in the wake of the recent Iran/Contra scandal there is a flood of books, such as Bob Woodward's *Veil,* James Adams's *Secret Armies,* and Steve Emerson's *Secret Warriors,* to name only a few, designed to expose the covert U.S. war against terrorism and the units set up to conduct that war. While any abuses of public money or the public trust cannot be condoned and are fair game for enterprising writers and journalists, care must be taken that such books do not lead to a public "feeding frenzy" in which U.S. antiterrorism policies and capabilities suffer long-term, or even permanent, damage as a result of unsubstantiated charges and accusations. Terrorism remains a serious threat to individual Americans and the security of this nation, and it will be necessary for the United States to combat terrorists and their state sponsors aggressively and effectively in the future.

6

Soldier of Fortune and the Armchair Counterterrorist

Our readers get a megadose of realism.
—SOF's Statement of Principles

"ALL of the spooks and gooks are here," announced the man standing by the door cradling a beer in one hand.

He was right. There was Bob Brown, the publisher of *Soldier of Fortune* magazine, and several of his colleagues. Off in one corner was former CIA explosives specialist and one-time employee of Edwin P. Wilson, "I.W." Harper, who runs a bait and tackle shop in the Washington suburbs and has a reputation for making the best explosive devices money can buy. After the botched bombing attack on Contra leader Eden Pastora, the former Commander Zero, in his jungle headquarters, it was rumored in some circles that I.W. had built the device. But, as I.W.'s associates quickly pointed out, "If I.W. had built the goddamn thing, everyone would have been killed."

Jim Morris, author of *War Story,* one of the finest books on Vietnam, was sitting on the couch in animated discussion with another bearded man. Behind him was the Russian pilot who defected with a MiG-25 and the Afghan pilot who flew a

MiG-21 to Pakistan in 1986. The Russian was describing his exploits to former CIA officer Larry Sulc, now the head of the Nathan Hale Foundation.

There were a number of former members of SEAL Team 6 and more ex–Special Forces men than you could shake a stick at. A former member of the Phoenix program chatted quietly in the kitchen with the South African military attaché and the Washington representative of RENAMO, the anticommunist Mozambique guerrilla group. The legendary Air Commando commander from Southeast Asia, Brig. General Heinie Aderholt, wearing a red stocking cap, was telling "war stories" to a rapt circle of listeners, including David Isby, the leading expert in the West on Soviet- and East-bloc weapons, a marine aviator, a French intelligence officer, and an officer from the Defense Intelligence Agency (DIA).

There were only a few women present, and all but one seemed to be Oriental.

Welcome to *Soldier of Fortune* magazine.

"A Market That Needed Filling"[1]

"Boom! I opened one eye from my siesta and groggily speculated on what foolishness the guerrillas were up to now. Another boom . . . and a third. No commie aircraft overheard, so it had to be the Gs. The hell with it. Back to sleepy bye."[2] So begins another often breathless report from the field in the ongoing saga of "dirty little wars" and antiterrorist engagements that are the monthly meat and potatoes of *Soldier of Fortune* (SOF) magazine and its colorful publisher, Robert K. Brown.

Few magazines in America spark the controversy and, in some circles, the enmity that *Soldier of Fortune* does. Published in the "New Age" city of Boulder, Colorado, and described by one former employee in an article as the personal "sand box" of its unreconstructed and sometimes outrageous publisher, Robert K. Brown, perhaps no other magazine mirrors the societal changes that have occurred in this country in recent years. Unreservedly anticommunist in orientation, SOF serves up a monthly menu of features on antiterrorist operations, small arms, Vietnam, and combat reporting from places like Angola, Nicaragua, and Afghanistan.

Few publishers in the United States are as well known, or perhaps even better known, than their publications. Like Henry Luce in an earlier era, and Malcolm Forbes and Hugh Hefner today, Bob Brown is the living embodiment of his magazine. So intertwined are their identities and, possibly, destinies, that it is hard to tell where one ends and the other begins. So great is Brown's mystique that when his picture appears on the cover of SOF the magazine generally records larger than normal newsstand sales. For all of the armchair warriors, Brown—like *Playboy*'s Hugh Hefner—has created a lifestyle which his readers can glimpse, if only vicariously, through the pages of his magazine.

Interesting enough, there is almost no sex in SOF, and Brown and the editors intend to keep it that way. It isn't that they have anything against sex, it's just that Brown does not feel that they can compete with *Playboy, Penthouse,* and the other "skin" magazines for that audience. The only story anyone can recall with a "sex angle" had to do with sex and psywar.

Brown sees SOF as the successor to traditional men's magazines like *True, Stag,* and *Argosy,* which went out of business in the 1960s. Brown, for his part, believes they tried too hard to compete with magazines like *Playboy.* "I felt they had lost their market trying to cover too much of the men's leisure spectrum," comments Brown. "There were articles on sports figures, rock stars. They tried to adjust to what they perceived as changing times and didn't make it."[3] Brown wanted to create a traditional "hard-core, no-nonsense" men's magazine, focusing chiefly on adventure, with tough editorial positions on issues of concern to diehard anticommunists like himself, but paying particular attention to Vietnam and Southeast Asia. "I felt there were a lot of Vietnam veterans that had come back to the United States that believed in what we were doing over there, that were not being heard from, that resented the fact they'd received no recognition," says Brown, who vowed to "do what the rest of the media was not doing and still doesn't do":

that is, tell the Vietnam story, as well as cover the fight against
terrorism and the dirty little wars of the contemporary world,
where the same issues are on the line.[4]

Brown was born in 1932 in Monroe, Michigan, the birthplace
of another famous lieutenant colonel: George Armstrong
Custer. He grew up in Indiana and attended Michigan State until being thrown out for selling condoms and running a roulette
wheel, as he tells the story. He moved with his mother, a
schoolteacher, to Boulder, and enrolled at the University of Colorado. Instead of returning to teaching, his mother went into the
real estate business and, by all reports, made a good living,
amassing a tidy sum of money. Brown, meanwhile, was involved in pro-Castro activities at the university, and went to
Cuba in the late 1950s to do a thesis on Cuban labor unions. In
reality, he was violently anti-Batista and swollen with idealism.
He picked up a job stringing for a U.S. newspaper and attempted to get involved with Fidel Castro. He never met Fidel but,
in what was to be a fateful meeting, he did stumble across an
American adventurer by the name of William Morgan, who was
the only American commandante of the Cuban revolution that
brought Castro to power in 1959. Morgan ultimately opposed
Castro's effort to turn Cuba into a communist state, was accused of plotting against the government, and was executed by a firing squad in 1960. As Brown describes the scene in the book he
coauthored with Jay Mallin, *Merc: American Soldiers of Fortune,*
Morgan was ordered to kneel and beg for his life. When he
refused, he was shot in both knees, then in each shoulder, and
finally dispatched with a burst from a Tommygun.[5]

Castro's "betrayal" of the Cuban revolution and the Morgan
episode were to have a profound impact on Brown. Up to that
time his political leanings were decidedly left-of-center, but in
the aftermath of his experiences in Cuba and his disillusionment
with Castro, he became a rabid right-winger. By his account, he
passed the early 1960s in Miami, involved in efforts to overthrow both Castro and the Haitian dictator "Papa Doc" Duvalier. Despite the fact that he has often been accused by the media
in this country and abroad of being a CIA operative—a charge

repeated most recently by the leftist *Covert Action Bulletin*—ever since his Miami days Brown has regarded the CIA with disdain. He reportedly became so exasperated with what he perceived to be CIA incompetence in its efforts to overthrow Castro that he spent months trying to expose the Agency's south Florida proprietaries, mail drops, and activities, as a way of demonstrating its incompetence. Because of his propensity for raiding trash bins and dumpsters in his quest for information, Brown is said to have been described by the late CIA official David Atlee Phillips as "one of the first garbologists." Brown still claims to have serious reservations about the competence and capabilities of the CIA. Indeed, he says that the only people who stayed in the Agency after Stansfield Turner became Director of Central Intelligence under President Jimmy Carter were "the has beens and never weres." Brown is convinced that the CIA has become overly bureaucratized and top-heavy, full of paper shufflers and deadwood.

As the conflict in Southeast Asia began heating up in the early 1960s, Brown, who was a member of an army reserve unit in Boulder, tried to join the fray. However, none of the services would have him. He even enlisted the help of his legendary friend, Lt. Colonel John Paul Vann, U.S. advisor to the 7th ARVAN Division in the northern part of the Delta, but to no avail. Just when he was despairing that the conflict would pass him by, his reserve unit was activated and he was shipped off to Vietnam. He ended up spending eighteen months in Vietnam, mostly along the Cambodian border, commanding a U.S. Special Forces "A" team at Tong Le Chon.

When Brown returned from Vietnam, he resuscitated a business he had started in 1963 while living in a $15-a-month log cabin in a Colorado ghost town named Wall Street. He and a partner had started a publishing company called Panther Press, which was later renamed Paladin Press after they were subpoenaed by a congressional committee that thought they had some connection to the Black Panthers. His original motivation for entering the publishing field stemmed from his unsuccessful attempt to interest a conventional publisher in *150 Questions for the Guerrilla,* a manuscript by General Alberto Bayo, the "man who trained Che and Castro." Brown published Bayo's manuscript himself, and today Paladin Press is the largest publisher of mayhem literature in the United States, and possibly the world. During the early years, however, most of its publications were reprints of declassified military manuals.

In 1970, Brown bought out his partner and subsequently sold one-half interest in Paladin to another Vietnam veteran, Peder Lund. The partnership lasted for four years, until 1974, when they concluded that they had incompatible management styles. They tossed a coin to see who would buy the other out; Bob lost and Peder gave him $15,000 for his interest in the publishing company.

Once again out of work, Brown tried to find a newspaper that would hire him as a journalist, but the closest he got was the sale of a few free-lance articles, his most notable success being a piece to the *National Enquirer.* He was forty-two years old, with a master's degree in political science, a rapidly declining balance in his bank account, and few prospects. "I was essentially unemployable," recalls Brown. "I could have tricked out a job working security, Pinkerton's or something, wearing white socks and black shoes. I could not get a job in journalism, and had I been able to get one I doubt I could have lasted long. I was not of the mood and mindset to cover city council meetings and PTA meetings. So what the fuck was I going to do?"[6]

The Birth of SOF

As desperation set in, he gave serious consideration to going to work as a mercenary for the government of Oman, which was engaged in a protracted guerrilla war with communist-backed insurgents. He wrote the Omani Defense Minister asking for information and received a thick packet of materials. Reasoning that the Vietnam War had left the United States with the largest body of unemployed combat veterans in the world, Brown decided that there might be others out there who would be interested in plying their skills in Oman. Accordingly, he ran an ad in *Shotgun News* under the caption, "Do You Want to be a Merc in Oman?", offering an information kit for $5 that was little more than a reproduction of the material he had received from the embassy. He netted nearly $5,000 from the ad.

Although he was investigated by the FBI after the State Department requested that Justice look into Brown's distribution of Omani materials to ascertain whether he was violating the Foreign Agent's Registration Act, the public response he got to the ad was so overwhelming that he was encouraged to pursue an idea that had been jelling in his mind for some time: the creation of a new adventure magazine devoted to Vietnam retrospectives and current features on fighting terrorism and communist-backed insurgencies in other parts of the world. He launched *Soldier of Fortune* on his kitchen table in 1975 with $8,500, $4,000 of which was borrowed from his mother. He calculated that he needed $36,000 to operate for one year, not counting any compensation to himself. Brown decided that he needed to sell 4,500 annual subscriptions to the magazine at $8 each to break even, reasoning that "if I don't sell that many subscriptions I ain't gonna publish the fucking magazine."[7] So, armed with several mailing lists he had purchased, Brown sent out a promotional piece offering introductory subscriptions to *Soldier of Fortune,* which was still merely a concept.

The response generated by the mailing was phenomenal, representing an extremely high rate of return for the number of names solicited, and "we went to press." The inaugural issue was, by all accounts, "a mess." But what it lacked in sophistication and printing quality, it more than made up for in terms of shock value and controversiality. While the cover was fairly tame, inside was a close-up shot of the fly-covered head of a black Rhodesian with a bullet-hole between the eyes, another nameless casualty in the bitter war waged by black insurgents to overthrow the white settler government that had seized power in 1965 and declared its unilateral independence from Great Britain. Dozens of newspapers and other publications carried stories, many of them dripping with outrage, about the new magazine, which only served to provide *Soldier of Fortune* with free

publicity and to broaden its subscription base. Indeed, it was
evident to Brown from the first issue that he would never have
to pay for advertising so long as he could generate enough controversy to stay in the spotlight; in this way, the liberal publications and television news reporters that Brown so often editori-
ally condemned played a large role in his success.

Despite the initial enthusiasm that greeted SOF, however,
Brown was still so uncertain he had a hit that he did not cash
the subscription checks until after the second issue was out.
Even today, Brown seems a little in awe of his success. "I didn't
know if it was gonna fuckin' fly or not," he observes, adding
that he "was so fucking ignorant" he didn't know that you
couldn't start a magazine with $8,500. In retrospect, he claims
to be glad he was forced to begin on a shoestring because, "Had
I had a million dollars I might not be where I am today. I had
so little money I couldn't make big mistakes money-wise."[8]
The magazine was a learn-as-you-go proposition, or what one
former employee called the "feel good" school of journalism, as
in "We just did what 'felt good' each day." To this day there
is no formal business plan, and things are still so loose that staffer Gary Crouse claims that "Stephen King should write the
business profile of *Soldier of Fortune*."[9] Despite its initial success
and steady growth, it took several years for the company to
make serious money. For some time, Brown published the magazine out of a one-room office and carried the company receipts
around in a cigar box in his car.

Phenomenal Growth

The magazine started out as a quarterly, quickly graduated to
bi-monthly status, and became a monthly in January 1979.
When Brown was attempting to get the money to become a
monthly publication, he went to his local bank and met the president for the first time to talk about a loan. Brown, contrary to
habit, wore a coat and tie and was, at least initially, on best behavior. He carefully detailed for the bank president SOF's
steady growth and market potential, and described the reason he

needed the loan, but he could tell that the man was not relating to what he was saying. Finally, in exasperation, he demanded of the bank president: "Have you ever seen my magazine?" The man folded his hands fastidiously and asked, "Does it have a bridge column? I only read magazines with bridge columns." Brown reflected for a moment then, without missing a beat, responded: "Sure, we have a bridge column. How to blow them up." Needless to say, he didn't get the loan, and instead took out a second mortgage on his house.

By the first nine months of 1979, SOF was selling on the newsstand at the rate of 70,000 copies per issue. In November, the magazine registered its first newsstand sale in excess of 100,000 copies (106,596 copies, to be precise), featuring a pugil stick fight at Parris Island on the cover. Newsstand sales are SOF's bread and butter, since the magazine only has around 37,000 paid subscribers (at last count). It is no surprise that 99.4 percent of SOF's readers are male, but would you believe that more than half have attended college? Fifty-seven percent of the readers have incomes of $25,000 or more, and 36 percent earn in excess of $40,000. According to surveys conducted by the magazine, 34.7 percent of SOF's readership are Vietnam veterans, and another 13 percent are involved with law enforcement. Ironically, it is also popular reading with convicted felons, and a number of prisons have prohibited the magazine because it has articles on improvised weapons. This generated a recent letter to SOF from a prisoner enclosing the wrap-around cover from a copy of *Sports Afield,* along with the request that the editors insert the current issue of SOF in the phony cover and mail it to him. "It would mean a lot to me," pleaded the prisoner. "Every fruit loop in the world writes *Soldier of Fortune,*" says Gary Crouse. The most outrageous letters are posted on the refrigerator near the coffee pot for the entire staff's enjoyment. One of the all-time favorites was signed, "No one you ever met."

Aside from convicted felons, SOF appeals, in many respects, to the target audience most eagerly sought by magazine advertisers in terms of sex, age group, education, income, and demographics. Yet it has never been able to draw big-time cigarette,

auto, and electronic products advertising. This is attributable to
a number of factors. First, SOF has only a two-person advertising department, and does not put much effort into soliciting
advertising. Secondly, most ad agencies and corporate advertising units are dominated by young, politically liberal, urban,
professional women who, as a group, recoil at the hard-right,
macho, unapologetic image and editorial policy of *Soldier of Fortune*. Finally, SOF still lacks mainstream respectability. It remains the political equivalent of an outlaw bikers' magazine,
and most corporations are reluctant to place their advertising in
such a controversial publication. As one of the magazine's pieces
of promotional literature states, perhaps not reassuringly:
"After years of success, we continue to fight against the
'magazine for mercenaries' label that would have all of us dragging our hairy knuckles on the ground and foaming at the
mouth."[10] As a consequence, most of the advertising in
SOF—and there is a lot of it—is confined to knives, jump boots,
cammies, holsters, adventure books, wolf pups, slingshots,
blowguns, pistols, posters, and invitations to learn gun repair at
home. And, of course, there is the infamous classified ad section
in the back of the magazine, although the ads for mercenaries
and those of the "I'll go anywhere and do anything" persuasion
are gone, having fallen victim to a number of lawsuits and
criminal investigations. One of the most memorable classified
ads submitted to the magazine was from a man who offered to
give one year of his life doing anything in exchange for a BSA
motorcycle. Today, in place of the mercenary ads, is a
disclaimer: "Soldier of Fortune does not intend for any product
or service advertised to be used in any illegal manner."

The elimination of the classified ads for mercenaries has
meant that some would-be "mercs" have taken to contacting
the magazine directly, as though it were an employment agency.
The staff pinned the following letter up on the refrigerator:

> Dear Sir,
> I first thought I would write and ask you if you could help me.
> I am a mercenary and it has lasted about 1 1/2 years now I havn't
> [*sic*] found any employment at all.

I was wondering if you could help me. I would really like to find some work. Please help me. I have always dreamed of working with some freedom fighters, or help with the cease fire manuevers [sic] in the phillipines [sic]. I would never ask for help unless it is necessary. So I came to you the editor. Please help.

There's a man who needs help, all right. Another letter was from a man who offered to sell "the Dragon/Snake Ring," whatever that is, "at a reduction of $15,000 cash. If you are interested please mail cash to above address specified by registered mail; I plan to use the funds to establish myself and family here in the Philippines and develop [sic] programs contrary to communism." Then there are the letters that raise more questions than they answer. Not long ago the magazine received a letter, addressed to *Soldier of Future* [sic], from a Brooklyn scoutmaster: "This letter is being written to you to inform you of letter [sic] that was mailed to you by a Mr. J. Cavalari [not actual name] regarding a Boy Scout Troop whom call themself's [sic] "F" Troop 750. We hope you will disregard the letter sent to you by Mr. Cavalari, since he has no involvement in this troop." At the bottom of the letter it indicated that copies were also sent to two other magazines: *New Breed* and *Outlaw Bikers*. A check through the files could not find Mr. Cavalari's mysterious letter, and the staff of SOF is still waiting for it to arrive.

And then there was the letter from the man who had the answer to protecting U.S. embassies in the Middle East:

Quite possibly, I think, hostility in that region [Middle East] could be halted with a weapon that has to this point gone completely undiscovered, *PORK*.

There is literally nothing that can keep a Moslem contaminated with Pork from going to where Allah isn't and the ramifications bear consideration.

Terrorist repercusions? [sic] What kind of Moslem truck bomber would drive through lard to commit suicide? Surround our embassies and military installations with tank traps full of it.

Oil embargoes? Hardly likely as both Iran & Iraq need customers to keep their war going. And if they do anyway? Lard them until they give oil away.

I know this sounds simplistic but it is a weapon that was used by the British in India. At that time there were Moslems who would lay on the railroad tracks & let trains run over them in protest but not after the Brits spread lard on the rails. Perhaps its [sic] to use lard as an offensive weapon.

Silkworm missiles? No problem. Gunboats firing rockets? Same thing. Equip tankers with pork belly cannons. Nobody that I've talked to with any experience in that region can find any loophole in this + most seem rather amused at a solution that is so low tech + so effective.

Perhaps the only drawback might be to raise the price of breakfast meat, but then it sure could help the pig farmers of America.

What a guy. All of the time the solution to vehicle bombers was right under our noses, on the breakfast table.

The last issue of SOF that sold under 100,000 copies on the newsstand was January 1980 (95,000 copies). The following month, according to managing editor Jim Graves, a beefy ex-Marine and former sports writer from Jonesboro, Arkansas, "we went over a 100,000 and stayed there; we never went back."[11] Throughout the rest of 1980, the magazine sold between 106,000 and 119,000 (average 108,000) copies on the newsstand. Ironically, SOF became the largest single customer of the bank that had previously turned Bob Brown down for the loan.

The following year, however, was when sales really took off. Newsstand sales for 1981 ranged from between 121,860 and 155,813 (average 139,985) copies per month. The average newsstand sale in 1982 climbed to 141,495 copies, and SOF chalked up its second best-selling issue (168,000) in January, featuring Bob Brown on location with Laotian resistance fighters on the cover. From its 1982 peak, average newsstand sales declined to 134,910 in 1983, 134,078 in 1984, 145,145 in 1985, and 126,855 in 1986. The magazine's all-time best-selling issue (180,700 plus) appeared in 1985, with Sylvester Stallone as "Rambo" on the cover. Today *Soldier of Fortune* and all of its related opera-

Paramilitary training in rural America.

The kind of firepower available at most gun shows.

Weekend counterterrorist.

The new genre of men's adventure magazines focusing on antiterrorism and counterinsurgency.

Just what you need if you meet a terrorist on the freeway.

SEALS. Some say they're the "best".

Olliemania.

J.D. Roberts, one of the ex-Delta men that rescued little Lauren.

The firepower demonstration at the 1988 *Soldier of Fortune* convention. *Courtesy of Omega Group.*

Soldier of Fortune's outrageous publisher Robert K. Brown, on location in Surinam. *Courtesy of Omega Group.*

Soldier of Fortune reward poster for former Ugandan dictator Idi Amin. Amin cooperated with terrorists that hijacked an Air France jetliner to Entebbe in 1976. *Courtesy of Omega Group.*

Gotcha! The rigors of becoming a counterterrorist.

Anti-terrorist training at CTU.

French GIGN sniper.

GIGN counterterrorist fast-roping from a chopper.

Stand by! Stand by! GIGN commandos prepare to clear a room.

Chargin' Charlie Beckwith, first commander of the U.S. Delta Force. *Courtesy of Tom Freeman, Wide World Photos.*

Edwin P. Wilson, who was ''seduced by the dark side'' and went to work for Libya, leaves federal court accompanied by U.S. marshals. *Courtesy of Tom Freeman, Wide World Photos.*

Lt. Colonel Oliver North arrives in Cyprus on a secret mission to rescue U.S. hostages held in Lebanon. *Courtesy of Tom Freeman, Wide World Photos.*

Writer-cum-operator Michael Ledeen. *Courtesy of Tom Freeman, Wide World Photos.*

Master spook Bill Casey, who conducted a relentless war against international terrorists. *Courtesy of Tom Freeman, Wide World Photos.*

Self-proclaimed counterterrorist, Sam Hall, meets with Mike Wallace of "60 Minutes" in Nicaragua. *Courtesy of Tom Freeman, Wide World Photos.*

Doer of "good deeds" Bob Jordan during his mission to Mozambique. *Courtesy of Tom Freeman, Wide World Photos.*

tions, which have been consolidated as the Omega Group, are estimated to have gross annual sales of around $5 million, showing a 1987 net profit in excess of $700,000. In addition to *Soldier of Fortune* magazine, the Omega Group publishes various special topic publications and books, and markets a host of other products from tee-shirts (700 a month) to commemorative knives.

If imitation is the highest form of flattery, then *Soldier of Fortune* must be doing a good deal that is right, because it has spawned a host of imitators such as *Gung Ho, Eagle,* and *New Breed. Gung Ho,* started in 1982 by a former SOF employee, was the first "clone." Although the employee had been fired, Brown had given him a generous severance, and he used the money to underwrite publication of an earthier, less self-conscious version of SOF. Some have compared *Gung Ho* to *Playboy* imitator *Penthouse,* but in actuality it is more the *Hustler* of adventure magazines. *Gung Ho*'s sales are currently about a quarter of SOF's. "Terrorism is on the Rise," trumpets the bold lettering on *New Breed*'s August 1983 cover, as if it has a "stop-the-presses" scoop worthy of a Pulitzer. Indeed, virtually all of SOF's rivals are shallow imitators at best, lacking solid reportage and technical reports.

The SOF Convention

There is even an annual *Soldier of Fortune* convention. Speakers for the 1987 convention, held in Las Vegas, included Ambassador Lewis Tambs of Iran/Contra fame, the former U.S. ambassador to Costa Rica, and General John Singlaub, who assisted Lt. Colonel Oliver North's private Contra resupply effort. Previous years' speakers included G. Gordon Liddy and Contra leader Enrique Bermudez. The eight hundred or so attendees have been described, perhaps uncharitably, by a former employee in a *Playboy* article as "the biggest collection of hopeless dingdongs to trouble this weary earth—twerps, grocery clerks with weak egos, various human hamsters come to look deadly in jump books, remember wars they weren't in and, for a weekend, be of one blood with Sergeant Rock and his Merry

Psychos.''[12] Brown shrugs off such criticism of the convention, accusing the author of the *Playboy* article of deliberately focusing on the yahoos. ''I mean, in any convention I'll find the fat man unless it's a convention of iron man athletes,'' says Brown. ''At any convention you're gonna find a guy that looks a little weird or strange, even a convention of Baptist ministers.'' He admits that ''sure, you've got some freaks (at the convention). Sure, you've got some knuckle-draggers. Sure, you've got some people with potbellies and tattoos on their arms.'' But, contends Brown, it is easier to spot the goofballs than the ''low profile real operators'' who are also in attendance.[13] Derry Gallagher, who served until recently as Brown's right-hand man and bodyguard and who spends his free hours during the summer team-roping at local rodeos, concedes that a majority of the convention attendees are armchair warriors and posturers, but maintains that there are about sixty or seventy serious people at the convention.[15] However, a definition of what constitutes ''serious'' remains elusive. One story that circulated about the SOF convention relates that when a 1987 convention attendee was asked by a London reporter if he had served in Vietnam, he replied, ''No, I was in prison then for dealing drugs.''

In 1986, author Hunter Thompson attended the convention, and despite the fact that he never completed a thought or a sentence, most of the other attendees seemed to have had no trouble communicating with him. Thompson was drunk the entire time, and when one of the SOF staffers visited Thompson in his hotel suite he found that the gonzo journalist had tacked a number of posters to the walls with some of the more than a dozen fighting knives he had purchased. Later, Thompson wanted to go to the shooting range, and he and his attractive female companion assured the range instructors that the journalist had done ''lots of shooting.'' After watching Thompson pop away at a target for several minutes with little success, one of the SOF staffers inquired of Thompson's companion: ''I thought you said he did a lot of shooting?'' ''He does,'' she replied. ''But mostly it's at night.''

Brown and the SOF staff do their part to add to the convention mayhem. After several smoke grenades went off in Brown's room, filling the hall with green smoke, two elderly women with canes were observed making their way down to the lobby. "These *Soldier of Fortune* people may think this is funny," groused one of the women to her companion, "but I was in the MGM Grand fire and don't think it's funny at all." Later, the magazine had to pay the hotel for stress cracks and other damages inflicted on the swimming pool by Brown and his buddies after they fired a silenced .45 pistol both into and under the water.

The first year the convention was held in Las Vegas, the management of the Sahara complained to Derry Gallagher, who was acting as chief of security, that someone had stolen the helmet from a suit of armor that stood at the entrance to the casino. Gallagher, who rarely says anything at all, startled other SOF staffers by rising at the banquet, which Gary Crouse charitably describes as a "real goat fuck," and offering a reward for the return of the helmet. Afterward, one of the conventioneers approached an SOF staffer and inquired about how to return the helmet. He was directed to Gallagher's room. Later he was observed with a bruised and puffy face; he not only had not received a reward, but when he complained about the fact, he was given a bum's rush out the door. To add insult to injury, he was also forced to make an involuntary contribution to the Afghan freedom fighter's fund. Despite the harsh treatment from the magazine's staff, he attended the convention again the following year.

Despite all of the carousing and hijinks at the convention, the Sahara Hotel is actively soliciting SOF's business again this year, maintaining that they don't cause any more damage than conventions of Shriners or car salespeople.

SOF's Outrageous Side

At times the magazine can be just as outrageous as the convention. During the flap over the infamous CIA manual prepared for the Contras, the magazine reprinted it in its entirety. What other magazine, moreover, provides its readers with pull-out targets of the Ayatollah Khomeini or Nicaraguan President Daniel Ortega? In 1979, SOF issued a wanted poster of fugitive Ugandan dictator Idi Amin, offering a $10,000 reward, payable in gold, for information leading to his capture alive and delivery to the government of Uganda to stand trial. Other rewards advertised by the magazine included $100,000 for the delivery of a communist aircraft armed with biological weapons, $1 million for the first Nicaraguan pilot to defect with a Mi-24 (HIND) helicopter gunship, and most recently, $28,000 in gold to the first verified Cuban or Nicaraguan intelligence officer to defect during the 1987 Pan American Games held in Indianapolis. While such grandstanding garners the free publicity on which the magazine has been built, it has been reported that the $1 million reward for the first Nicaraguan pilot to deliver his HIND into friendly hands was a very effective piece of psychological warfare, and prompted the Sandinistas to ground their fleet of Mi-24s for at least two weeks. They were allowed to fly again only after a political officer had been placed on board each chopper.

Perhaps the most outrageous idea editors of the magazine ever came up with was the "Adopt a Dead Russian Soldier" program. Afghan rebels had provided SOF with dozens of pay books and other personal effects from Soviet soldiers killed in combat in Afghanistan. Former editor in chief Bill Gutherie, a bearded and erudite Ph.D. whose academic specialty was medieval languages, including early Norse, and assistant editor Gary Crouse thought it would be great to solicit $1,000 contributions on behalf of the Afghan resistance, in consideration of which contributors would be given an "official" certificate of adoption bearing the name of a dead Soviet soldier, the soldier's pay book, and any other personal effects, along with a letter of condolence in Russian that could be sent to his next of kin. The magazine's Boulder attorney, an engaging rugby player in his late thirties named Bob Miller who says that Bob Brown has been his client since "before Brown could afford to pay me," was outraged, and threatened to quit if the program went forward. "It was the most tasteless thing they ever tried to do," says Miller.[14]

On a more sedate note, the editors of SOF set up the "Bull Simmons Scholarship Fund" for the children of the Americans killed trying to free the U.S. hostages in Iran. Brown's next project, he says, will be to offer $100,000, payable over twenty years, and a job at *Soldier of Fortune* to the first Soviet *spetsnaz* (special operations) officer to defect.

Reporting on the Globe's "Hot" Wars

Because of the convention, the classified ads, and Bob Brown's own penchant for flamboyance, it is easy to criticize *Soldier of Fortune.* Yet, the fact remains that SOF does some things as well, if not better, than any other magazine in the country. Combat reporting, for example. Brown's ragtag collection of reporters and free-lancers are not afraid to travel to the globe's toughest hot spots and bring back solid, well-researched, well-written accounts of the fighting. According to an article in *Newsweek,* "The CIA and the Pentagon rely on *Soldier of Fortune* for some of their best information on Soviet military operations in Afghanistan." Indeed, there may be no magazine in the world with better access to the U.S.-backed rebels in Afghanistan, Angola, and Nicaragua.

Critics say Brown and SOF get too involved; that they lose their objectivity and become part of the story instead of simply covering it. Even their own readers occasionally write that they are trying too hard "to sell Central America." The editors of SOF, however, are unrepentant about their lack of detachment. "When the *New York Times* sends a guy into Afghanistan, he doesn't go in with a group of Mujahadeen [. . . and] deliberately pick on a Russian base and shoot at it," says Managing Editor Jim Graves, adding, with characteristic understatement, "The *New York Times* would get very upset if he did that."[15] To get the real story, maintains Brown, you must get down and dirty with the Mujahadeen and win their trust. "We pick sides," he continues, and only in this way can SOF give its readers "a grunt-level view of the world.'' Sure, he and his reporters carry guns on assignment, says Brown, but so did a number of top press reporters and network journalists in Vietnam, even though they knew the practice was frowned upon by their editors.

Soldier of Fortune's lack of detachment extends to providing military advisors to local troops in El Salvador, assisting with the resupply of the U.S.-backed Contras in Nicaragua, and a heavily bankrolled effort to find rumored U.S. POWs in Laos. While much of the operational side of the magazine is pure nonsense and showboating, with an eye toward raising SOF's circulation figures, some of the activities cut deeper, and represent the deeply held convictions of its publisher and staff. Brown is not grandstanding when he says, ''I want the magazine to support changes, the things we believe in.''[16] This is reinforced in a statement of principles included as part of the pitch to potential advertisers:

> *Soldier of Fortune* focuses on news and adventure based on first-hand reports. Our readers do not have to read between esoteric lines because we tell it as we see it. Since we actually go to the hot spots to get the true story, our readers get a megadose of realism; *not* the watered-down media press releases so necessary to appease all the complexities of high-level diplomacy.
>
> By opposing tyranny of all kinds, we support the basic freedom of mankind. We feel that people have to fight to preserve freedom. To take up the sword to create or maintain freedom is honorable and necessary. It is our opinion that ultimately the way to prevent violence is to make people aware of the horror it engenders.
>
> As you read *Soldier of Fortune* you will understand that our editorial policy is anti-communist, pro-military, pro-strong U.S. defense, pro-law enforcement and pro-veteran, particularly the Vietnam veteran. We strongly support the right of the individual to keep and bear arms.[17]

Some may see such pronouncements as self-serving, but few other magazines trot out their editorial and corporate philosophy in such plain view. Other criticisms leveled at the magazine include the charge that ''SOF's message is all hate'' and that a subscription represents an ideal ''gift for sadists.'' On a more serious level is the suggestion that SOF is far too uncritical about Vietnam and many of the contemporary conflicts that it covers. While Brown retorts that the magazine's articles on Vietnam ''have not all been hero pieces,'' there is no denying that most of the articles published in SOF smack of boosterism and reflect a decidedly uncritical view of the subject matter. This is ironic, since Brown and his colleagues are certainly not without criticism of the way either the Vietnam War or the war in Central America has been conducted.

There remain some moral dilemmas that SOF has yet to resolve as well. A few years ago, an article appeared in the magazine about an assassination carried out in Spain by the Basque terrorist group known as the ETA. The reporter had apparently been invited to witness and actually photograph the killing. SOF published the piece, along with the photographs. When asked if this did not make the magazine an accomplice to murder, Jim Graves replied that the incident had occurred prior to SOF's purchase of the story. ''If I had known about an assassination before it had taken place,'' said Graves, ''yeah, that would give me some problems.''[18] Nevertheless, SOF's emphasis on participatory and first-person stories is a double-edged sword: while it clearly enhances the authenticity and quality of the reportage, the closeness to the subject matter sometimes compromises objectivity and common sense.

Perhaps there is no better example of *Soldier of Fortune* attempting to put its money where its mouth is than Brown's ill-fated effort to investigate long-standing reports of American POWs in Laos and to bring them out alive.[19] Although it was a fiasco that ultimately cost the magazine as much as a quarter of a million dollars, it is representative of both Brown's gullibility and his practice of translating his philosophy into action. The scam revolved around a former CIA officer named William Young, who had been born into a missionary family and raised in the ''Golden Triangle'' region of southeast Asia, source of much of the world's heroin. Young had, by all accounts, an extraordinary penchant for local languages and dialects that had made him indispensable to the CIA during the 1960s. "He's Caucasian physically, but not mentally, baby," recalls Brown, who hired Young as his man-on-the-spot after he "ran into some guys" who claimed to have actual knowledge of America POWs still imprisoned in Laos. As Brown relates the incident, he and his associates interrogated the sources at great length and "their stories kinda matched." At that point he went to the Defense Intelligence Agency (DIA) with the information, but DIA refused to do more than provide SOF with a list of potential captives and certain questions to establish their bona fides.

Brown, working through Young, hit on a plan to buy freedom for the allegedly captive Americans, agreeing to pay $20,000 per man for an estimated twenty prisoners to a local governor eager to defect to the West. "That's $400,000 in a country where you can get someone greased for five bucks," observes Brown. Accordingly, Young and a half-dozen other SOF retainees set up and paid for an armed camp inside Laos for more than a hundred Laotian mercenaries, or "freedom fighters," as Brown prefers to call them. "We went in and built an 'A' camp," effuses Brown even today. "I mean with slit trenches, bunkers, and all that shit. We'd support them (the Laotians) and then when we needed them, they'd provide us security when the transfer was made." According to Brown, they paid Young $8,000 a month for the resistance base and other expenses. They first became suspicious of him when it was learned that he was also funding Burmese insurgents, in addition to the Laotians. Brown said that he told Young: "Look, let's be realistic, we can only support one revolution at a time."

In retrospect, Brown concedes, "We got fucked over. At one time we thought we were supporting the whole Laotian resistance. The way we were scammed was wonderful. I mean this guy [Young] came up with reports, documents, progress reports. We got the staff here, we got the headquarters here, we're moving people here, and we've got people going out. He was just buying more young Thai wives." Brown finally pulled the plug on the operation after almost two-and-a-half years of effort, without ever so much as glimpsing a real POW, much less rescuing one. The whole thing had been a sham from the start. But Brown contends that it was still worth it, even if the odds had been a hundred-to-one that they would succeed. "We don't want 250 or 300 grand in the bank or to drive fancy cars, have plush offices, or whatever," he muses philosophically. Jim Graves adds that, like much else connected with the magazine, it was a learning experience and that they were able to expose a lot of the charlatans ripping off the American public on the POW and MIA issue as a result of what they learned in Laos. In keeping with their knack for finding the bright side to any disaster, SOF published a lengthy exposé on how they were taken by Young and his cohorts.

Mission Control

Today the Omega Group is headquartered in an industrial park on the edge of Boulder in a building owned by Brown and the bank and leased back to the company. The building and the main computer inside are Brown's retirement nest egg. The decor is early utilitarian and eclectic in the extreme. The reception area, for example, features a mélange of anti-Qaddafi posters and a small Van Gogh print. There is a large sign-in-and-out board on the wall that strives, one suspects in vain, to keep track of the peripatetic 28-member staff with notations like "got lost," "got away," and so on. By contrast to its public image, there are no racks of small arms, instruments of torture, or cammie-clad staffers at SOF's headquarters. Even the glass case with the rattlesnake inside, labeled "complaint department," no longer exists. Indeed, the whole place looks, well, almost respectable. With the exception of Bob's office, that is. Brown's second-floor office is a monument to chaos, full of piles of paper and files, animal heads, maps of the world, and general clutter. A zebra hide graces one wall above a camouflaged rifle case and a spittoon, for it seems like virtually everyone at the magazine chews tobacco. The top of his desk is covered with mounds of paper, a large hunting knife, a tin of chewing tobacco, and a windup walking plastic penis. There is a pile of dirty tee-shirts in the middle of the room. The tee-shirts are on the floor because the nearby closet is full of utilities in a dozen or more different camouflage patterns; no matter where the war is, Brown already has the uniform. Brown is also partial, it seems, to footgear; there are jump boots, cowboy boots, and running shoes strewn about the room.

In the bookshelf behind Brown's desk is a photograph of someone holding a .45 to the head of a Santa Claus sprawled on the ground. Brown, it turns out, hates Christmas. He hates it with a passion. He and his brother once decorated the front yard of their Boulder home at Christmas time with an elaborate sign trimmed in Christmas lights that read, "Santa is Dead." The neighbors were outraged, and the police arrived a short time later. Brown claims that every year he watches "The Grinch Who Stole Christmas" on TV, "up to the point that the Grinch starts losing."[20] Despite Brown's aversion to Christmas, the magazine holds an annual Christmas party, perhaps more accurately described as a blowout. "I usually wear my raincoat and rubber boots to the Christmas party," says Gary Crouse, "because of the food fights and the people vomiting on your feet."[21]

The magazine's staff is laid back, and, as Crouse has quipped, "If it weren't for the last minute, nothing would ever get done around here."[22] Brown is notorious for arriving at around 10:30 A.M. and calling the staff together because he has just learned that the Sandinistas are illegally importing 6,000 pounds of lobster a week into Miami, or Soviet *spetsnaz* frogmen have been seen in the St. Lawrence Seaway, or the Salvadorans need mine-detecting equipment. Everything else screeches to a halt, including work on the next issue of the magazine, while the editorial staff is sent off to investigate the current "bee in Bob's bonnet."

There is a great deal of good-natured horsing around at the magazine as well. Several years ago, when they decided to find a new distributor for SOF, SOF's business manager made an appointment in Los Angeles with Warner, the magazine's present distribution company. He took along five copies of *Soldier of Fortune* to show to company executives. However, unbeknownst to him, SOF's art director had bought five of the vilest, sleaziest, filthiest pornographic magazines he could find, all of them emphasizing various forms of deviant behavior, including what was euphemistically labeled "water sports" by one magazine. He had carefully removed the cover of each magazine and substituted *Soldier of Fortune* covers, then replaced them in the business manager's briefcase.

While en route to Los Angeles, the business manager struck up a conversation with a nice old lady sitting next to him. She had never heard of *Soldier of Fortune,* so he pulled a copy from his briefcase and handed it to her. He saw her blanch as she flipped it open to a scene that could only be described as a graphic portrayal of an "unnatural sexual act." Outraged, the business manager cursed and grabbed the magazine from the old lady, tearing it into little pieces on the spot. He assumed, however, that it was the only copy of SOF tampered with, and didn't bother to check the others. This was a big mistake.

When he arrived for his meeting with Warner, he found a group of serious-looking executives gathered around a long conference table. Whipping the other four copies of SOF out of his briefcase, he threw them on the table and announced: "Gentlemen, this is what we do." It was a total gross out, and the business manager left *Soldier of Fortune* a short time later.

Another recent victim of SOF madness was the magazine's technical editor, a man of serious and sober demeanor. Staff members once again purchased the worst collection of pornographic rags they could find and cut out all of the close-ups of various unmentionable parts of the human anatomy. They then stuck the pictures randomly in all of the clothes the technical editor had packed for a SOF trip to China. He did not run across any of the pictures until the SOF staff had its first face-to-face meeting with a delegation of grim-faced Chinese military and political officials. As the meeting began, the technical editor felt a strange piece of paper in one of his suit pockets. He pulled it out and unfolded it on the table as his Chinese hosts looked on.

Suddenly he realized that he was staring at a close-up of a very private part of the female anatomy, at which point he hurriedly crumpled it up, but not before the Chinese got a look at it. They were not amused. The technical editor, meanwhile, nearly collapsed of embarrassment.

Later he went through all of his clothes, removing the offensive pictures. But he forgot his trench coat, and several months later, when he was at home visiting his family, he attended a Chicago Bears football game with his parents and sister. Once again, he felt a strange piece of paper in his pocket and, well, you know the rest.

The shipping room is run by Giang Bang La, affectionately known as "Gangbang Lee," Bob's former Vietnamese interpreter. He escaped from Vietnam in October 1981. Told in the refugee camp that he needed a sponsor to come to the United States, Giang still had one of Bob's old business cards from Panther Press, which dated back to the mid-1960s. He called Brown collect in the middle of the night, and Bob agreed to sponsor Giang and his wife. Giang, of course, had no idea that the former Green Beret officer he served had become a well-known public figure.

There is also the "house liberal," a young woman with long, dark hair that cascades down her back, who has worked for the magazine off and on for nearly ten years. When asked why she stays on at SOF if she disagrees politically with most of its public positions, she responds: "Well, there are interesting people in and out. You learn something new every day." One suspects, however, that her real reason for staying on is that any other job would be dull by comparison. The staff is small, and most of the articles are done by free-lancers. Some writers come to the magazine, others the magazine locates through word-of-mouth or by means of referrals from other correspondents. Many of the best combat reporters are hard to locate; they're always off in the bush somewhere. It once took Jim Graves a year and a half to track down one combat reporter he wanted for a particular story. Occasionally a reporter who runs with the Left will turn down an opportunity to write for SOF, but most agree to do so, even if it means using a nom de plume. SOF got its technical editor when he wrote a letter to the magazine criticizing a particular article. If you think you can do better, they responded, why don't you go to work for us. He did.

On the Road with Bob Brown

If Brown has a passion, it is travel. He is a restless man, rarely content to spend more than a few weeks in Boulder before the itch returns to leave for some distant unpronounceable locale that may or may not be on anyone's map. He logs tens of thousands of miles each year in pursuit of stories on combat, coups, and hairy chested adventure; although getting him to actually commit the stories to paper is a real chore. By the time he returns from one trip, he is already plotting his next one, and has all but forgotten why he just went someplace and what he saw there. As anyone who has ever traveled with Brown is quick to observe, his madcap trips are often experiences never to be forgotten. A good example is the trip he took to Guyana after being tipped off that a pro-Western coup was about to occur.

"If you are Bob Brown," recalls Gary Crouse, "the only way into Guyana is through French Guiana."[23] Brown rendezvoused with his three traveling companions at the Miami Airport, which Crouse describes as "a minor miracle," and they flew on together to San Juan, Puerto Rico, where they had booked passage on a plane scheduled to depart for French Guiana. Unbeknownst to the little party, the flight to San Juan was the last occasion that anything would go according to plan on the entire trip.

They arrived in San Juan several hours before their next flight, so Brown—who has little patience for sitting—decided to find a barber and get a haircut and a shave to pass the time. That done, he poked around the airport shops, and stopped to peruse the magazines and books at one store. When he finally returned to the waiting area by the gate, he found Derry Gallagher in a highly agitated state. The plane, it turned out, had already taken off: Brown had forgotten to reset his watch to accommodate the time change. The next plane was not for several days, but Brown refused to wait; they might miss the coup. Besides, the other members of the party had gone ahead on the flight in order to keep track of their luggage, which had already been checked. The only problem was that they didn't have any money, since Brown had been carrying their bankroll.

Brown read in a schedule that there was a flight departing from Caracas to French Guiana, so he and Gallagher booked seats on the next available plane to Venezuela. When they reached Caracas, however, they learned that Brown had misread the schedule and that the flight had already departed to French Guiana. They subsequently learned of a flight to French Guiana from Rio de Janeiro, and, after verifying that it was still operating, Brown and Gallagher flew to Brazil. But when they arrived at the airport in Rio, the authorities refused to let them into the country since they didn't have visas.

To make matters worse, they were ordered to leave Brazil (including its airspace) within twenty-four hours, despite the fact that the flight to French Guiana did not depart until the following day. The authorities were adamant in their refusal to let them wait for the flight. A helpful airline employee discovered a flight to French Guiana from Quito, Ecuador, but since there were no connections to Quito during the allotted time period, they had to fly to Lima, Peru, and then to Quito. Finally, they reached French Guiana, but on the same day they would have arrived if they had waited in San Juan for the next flight. It had only cost them another $30,000 and four days of aggravation. What's more, the coup in Guyana never came off.

The People's Republic of Boulder

Brown and the magazine have reached a kind of "live and let live" modus vivendi with the city of Boulder, often referred to by some SOF staffers as "the People's Republic of Boulder." But it was not always that way. In 1979, a group seeking to "eradicate all mercenary activities in Colorado" took its case to the Boulder City Council, describing *Soldier of Fortune* as a "serious threat to international race relations and to Afro-American relations.'' They apparently hoped to have the city council rule that SOF was an illegal or disorderly business enterprise. The chief instigators of the movement were a local left-wing professor and Colorado congresswoman Patricia Schroeder. Schroeder also contacted the Justice Department, requesting a probe to determine whether any of SOF's activities were in violation of the Neutrality Act.

The movement against the magazine ran into problems almost immediately. First, it turned out that SOF's offices were located outside the city limits, beyond the jurisdiction of the city council. Second, the head of the city council was one of the magazine's free-lance writers. Finally, a bit of research turned up the fact that the professor's father was one of the few Americans ever convicted of violating the Neutrality Act, as a supporter of the Loyalists during the Spanish Civil War. The campaign against *Soldier of Fortune* quickly collapsed, and today Brown and the magazine keep a low profile around the city so as not to antagonize the locals. Nevertheless, there are occasional demonstrations against the magazine by leftist students from the University of Colorado, but none have represented a serious threat to the publication or its staff. According to Jim Graves, the biggest problem is keeping Brown from overreacting to the demonstrations and ''breaking out the ax handles.''[24]

Before an upcoming demonstration organized against the magazine, one member of the SOF staff proposed to Brown, in all seriousness, that they blow up the magazine's building and blame it on the demonstrators. Brown, however, had other ideas. He knew that the protest would be a media event, and he decided that once the demonstration began he would lock all of the doors and then he and the rest of the staff, all dressed in dark pin-striped suits, would make their way to the roof, where they would be evacuated by a helicopter hovering over the building; shades of Vietnam.

The magazine's attorney, Bob Miller, was hard at work when he got a call from Brown explaining his latest inspiration. He urged Brown to wait until he could check out local statutes governing choppers hovering over commercial establishments next to busy thoroughfares. After a little research, Miller advised Brown in the strongest possible terms not to do it, since it would probably result in the arrest of the magazine's staff and the grounding of the chopper pilot.

On the day of the demonstration, Brown was still stewing over the fact that Miller had thrown cold water on his idea to evacuate the magazine by chopper when he was jolted from his thoughts by the raucous scream of machinery from up on the roof. Climbing up to investigate, he found a crew hard at work replacing part of the roof. Suddenly he had another inspiration. "Would you like to earn a little extra money?" inquired Brown. "Doing what?" came the answer. Brown told them about the demonstration and asked that when the speeches started they move over to the front of the roof and turn on all of their ear-splitting machinery. They readily agreed, and the rest is history. When the first speaker began to address the assemblage, he was drowned out by the sound of roofing equipment, and spent the rest of the demonstration shouting at the workmen instead of haranguing the magazine and the crowd. The demonstration rapidly petered out.

Despite all of the admonitions about how unpopular the magazine is in Boulder, when the author went to dinner with Brown and some other staffers at a local hotel, the maître d' sent a complimentary bottle of wine to the table, and later came over to express his admiration for Brown and the magazine. "There are some good people in this town," Brown later admitted.

Publishing's Huck Finn

Success has not changed Bob Brown, as anyone who knows him will tell you. Despite all of the bravado and tough talk, he remains the Huck Finn of the publishing world: at once a free spirit, sometimes incorrigible, always unconventional, a romantic with an easy wit and a heart of gold. "Bob's got this magnetism for little kids, old ladies, and dogs," says Derry Gallagher.

Stories of Brown's generosity are legion; he reportedly is an "easy touch" who loans out or just gives away thousands of dollars to anyone with a hard-luck story or a lost cause. In fact, he appears to have little regard for money except as a means of buying airline tickets and supporting causes that are near and dear to his heart. "Bucks are important," says Brown, "because I can cause more trouble with more bucks. More trouble for the bad guys. If I had the money, I'd run a fucking operation to help the Contras. I'd go take Bluefields. I know the arms dealers. I know where I can get the boats."[25]

"He's not into possessions," observes Jim Graves. "If he has $20,000 in this pocket, he's liable to charge off to Afghanistan for two months."[26] Brown occasionally talks about buying something outlandish like a train or a motorcycle, but never does. "We had some bikers over at a party the other night," he explains, "and this one guy had a $12,000 Harley. 'What are you, fucking crazy?' I tell him. 'No, no, man, it's a good bike,' he says. 'I'm sure it is,'" responds Brown, shaking his head incredulously, as if he still finds it hard to believe that anyone could spend so much money on something like a motorcycle.

Brown reportedly plows most of his profits back into the magazine, with the exception of a reported $100,000-a-year salary. But associates note that he spends little of the salary on himself, and is always generous to his daughter, who lives in Boulder. For the most part, Brown has rather unassuming tastes and few of the trappings of a successful publisher. He drives an old Chevrolet Blazer, lives in a modest house, and owns two cheap suits and a lot of blue jeans. To say that Brown is not into clothes is an understatement. On a recent visit by this author to his office, Brown was seated with his cowboy boots on his desk, clad in Levis, a Denver Broncos baseball cap, and no shirt. "One of the good things about owning your own company," he explained, "is being able to set the dress code." When it was time to go to lunch, Brown rummaged through a pile of tee-shirts on the floor before sniffing one and then slipping it on.

Brown once appeared on the Phil Donahue show wearing two different colored cowboy boots: one brown and one black. No one could understand why Donahue kept staring at Brown's feet, which were off camera, with a quizzical look on his face. Later, when Brown removed his boots, one of his traveling companions noticed that his socks also did not match: one was a white athletic sock and the other an army-issue drab green sock. Since Brown had an important meeting in another city following his appearance on the Donahue show, he decided to see if he couldn't do something about his mismatched boots while waiting to board his next flight. He stopped at an automatic shoe-polishing machine and stuck his brown boot under the black polisher in hopes that it could be darkened up enough not to be so obvious. No such luck, however. In the end it looked even worse.

Perhaps Brown's most notable expenditure is a $2 million underground bunker outside of Boulder, which someone convinced him to build a few years ago as a place to sit out Armageddon. Like so many things, Brown lost interest in the project, and it sits neglected today beneath a house that Brown rents out. There are still 50,000 rounds of ammunition stored in the bunker, but Brown rarely visits it, and it is only used now and then as a place for staff parties.

Brown's tastes are decidedly lowbrow. "He buys art by the inch," chuckles Jim Graves, referring to a massive painting that hangs in the office above the stairway. It was sold to Brown during one of his journeys to Africa by an artist who paints his customers into the picture, in this case Bob and a colleague stalking wild game on the African veld.

Brown is virtually deaf in one ear, and the hearing in the other ear is also open to question. "He's the world's only deaf commando," says Crouse. "And on top of that he can't remember anything." In 1986, Brown was in Washington on business and staying at a hotel in a recently revitalized area of the city near 14th Street, known for its streetwalkers and sleaze joints. Late one evening, he decided he needed a hamburger, and with a small retinue in tow he headed down 14th Street to the nearest McDonald's. On the way they passed a long line of prostitutes wearing hot pants, leather microskirts, and other revealing clothing. More than two dozen women solicited Brown, offering every kind of sex act imaginable, as he strolled by, without so much as turning his head. However, when Brown and the others reached the McDonald's, he looked over at his companions and shook his head. "You know, I thought those girls were hookers," he observed in a deadpan voice, "but not a one gave me a come-on." No one could believe it—Brown is so deaf that he hadn't heard a word! Brown directed journalist Robin Wright, when she first met him in Rhodesia during the early 1970s, to speak into his good ear. "I'm a little deaf," he told her. "I don't know if it was from the sound of guns or the screams of my victims."[27]

For relaxation Brown likes to ski, deer hunt, fish, and read. He also likes a good party. As Derry Gallagher explains, "Going into a hotel after Bob Brown is a little like going in after a rock group has just been there. You tell them you're a musician and they slam the door."[28] One never knows who will turn up at Brown's bashes: mercs and would-be mercs, military types, movie stars, bikers, rodeo riders, journalists, cops, spooks, Vietnam veterans, and the IBM salesman Brown just met in a bar somewhere, his philosophy being the more the merrier. If Brown has one material weakness, it is knives. He owns an enormous knife collection, numbering in the hundreds, described as "a real primo thing" by one of his cohorts. Most are custommade fighting knives. Every knife bears the serial number 007, and some are valued in the thousands of dollars. He also has a collection of contemporary pistols with the 007 serial number. When asked if Agent 007, James Bond, holds some unique attraction to Brown, Graves responds, "Nope, but he says one of these days some idiot collector is going to pay him a lot of money for his 007 knife and gun collection."[29] Of course, the question remains: what would Brown do with the money? Probably buy more knives, someone answers.

Today, both Brown and the magazine are going through midlife crisis. "It would definitely improve our sales if we elected a Democrat [in 1988]," offers SOF's house liberal, when asked about the current malaise that has set in. "Reagan agrees with most everything the magazine believes. I mean, we're no longer rebels any more.'' She is not alone in her assessment that another Jimmy Carter would breathe new life and vigor into the magazine and the staff. ''I'm bored,'' complains Brown. ''I'm bored, but I got something I'm working on now. Otherwise I'm fucking bored.''[30] Circulation figures have dipped in recent months, necessitating some layoffs, although by most accounts the staff had gotten flabby and top-heavy and needed some paring down.

There are two mutually contradictory schools of thought at SOF on how to increase readership. One group holds the view that the magazine has striven too hard for respectability and, as a consequence, has gotten away from the things it traditionally did best. This, in turn, resulted in defections among some of SOF's readers, who sought out the magazine's grittier imitators. The other group believes that SOF is still in transition, and needs to continue upgrading its writing, photos, covers, and combat reporting. When that process is complete, the advocates of the ''quality'' approach contend, the magazine will have broadened its appeal considerably and will finally be able to tap into the mainstream marketplace.

It is hard to say which approach is correct. One thing, however, is clear, and that is that Brown wants to have political influence in Washington. ''I don't know if that is possible for us,'' Graves reflects. Nevertheless, political influence means that SOF will have to transcend its past and maintain the commitment to improving the magazine and its content. In order to be closer to the ''action,'' Brown has even considered moving the publication to Washington.

Brown reportedly also would like to see the magazine win the recognition he believes it deserves. To date, the only awards SOF has ever won are for design and layout, not for content. Brown and his editors contend that *Soldier of Fortune* has scored a number of major journalistic coups relating to Soviet chemical warfare in Laos, U.S. government ineptitude in identifying MIA remains, the appearance of new Soviet weapons in Afghanistan, and secret links maintained by the now-deposed

Marxist government of Maurice Bishop in Grenada to members
of the U.S. Congress and the *Washington Post,* to cite but a few
examples. The magazine's biggest scoop, however, was knowledge that the United States was preparing a second rescue mission for the American hostages in Iran, after the Desert One debacle. SOF voluntarily refrained from publishing the story, but
Brown believes that such security breaches contributed to the
decision by the White House and the Joint Chiefs not to go forward with the mission.

Brown was amused to find that he was described as a secret
agent of the *New York Times* by *Spotlight,* the publication of the
anti-semitic organization Liberty Lobby, something that is sure
to come as a shock to the editors and reporters of the *Times.*
"Brown, who affects the editorial posture of a 'conservative'
patriot in public," reads the *Spotlight* article, " . . . has, for
many years, been performing covert services for the New York
'Times'."[31] *Spotlight* goes on to say that, as a result, Brown gets
preferential treatment by the media so as not to jeopardize "the
covert interests of Israel."

In the final analysis, *Soldier of Fortune* is still very much Bob
Brown, his broad range of contacts and acquaintances, and his
penchant for the outrageous. Critics within the company say
that he travels too much and doesn't find time to write as much
as he did in the past. They worry that the magazine would not
survive without Brown, and for that reason doubt that it will
ever be purchased by one of the big mass-market periodical publishers. The Omega Group took out a "key man" insurance policy on Brown in the early 1980s when he "was screwing around
in Laos." Jim Graves says he once told Bob's daughter, Jan,
that if "Bob should get killed, my advice to you is to sell the
magazine fast, before they figure out that his Rolodex, his memory, and his promotion are what really drive it."[32]

Despite the current "flat" circulation figures, and if SOF is
not killed by a $9.4 million judgment levied against the com-
pany, SOF probably will remain a money machine for Bob
Brown, who—in the words of one associate—won't be able to
"piss it away as fast as he earns it." On the other hand, Brown

is very good at "pissing it away." In 1986, for example, he bought a California-based travel magazine, which ultimately cost him somewhere in the neighborhood of $150,000.

There will probably be more coverage of terrorism in SOF in the future, given the keen public interest in the subject and the mystique associated with counterterrorist commandos. Moreover, issues with terrorist-related themes on the cover have generally sold exceptionally well. Jim Graves, for one, would like to do more off-beat stories, like one on Iranian postage stamps, which are being used as propaganda tools, including special stamps issued during the 1979–1981 hostage crisis.

Brown recently appeared in a low-budget commando movie, along with SOF Explosives/Demolitions editor John Donovan, whose shaved head and massive frame make him the prototypical movie merc. Now Brown is talking about a proposed $5 to $6 million TV movie pilot based on the magazine and its zany cast of characters. The producers envision a 26-episode series which, in Brown's words, will be "about these guys going out and doing all sorts of weird things." One of the producers sent Brown a note saying, "Our mission is one of greed, so long as what we do is real." "I like that," says Brown, savoring the image. " 'Our mission is one of greed.' You bet your fuckin' ass."[33]

7

Oliver North's Passionate War against Terrorism

Ollieluja. Keep North, Fire the Congress.

—Bumper sticker

O N January 19, 1981, the day before Ronald Reagan was inaugurated, President Carter announced that an agreement finally had been reached for the release of the 52 Americans held hostage for 444 days by the Iranian government. It had been a humiliating and frustrating period for the United States, and the Carter administration's inability to bring about a satisfactory and speedy resolution of the hostage crisis had, more than any other single issue, doomed Carter at the polls the previous November. Thus, almost from the outset the incoming Reagan administration adopted a strategy of tough rhetoric regarding terrorism.

While welcoming home the recently freed hostages barely a week into his administration, President Reagan set a markedly different tone from his predecessor: "Let terrorists be aware that when the rules of international behavior are violated, our policy will be one of swift and effective retribution."[1] Reagan's militant rhetoric was quickly reinforced by Secretary of State Alexander Haig, who said that antiterrorism would, in effect, replace the Carter administration's emphasis on human rights as the administration's chief priority, because terrorism "is the ultimate abuse of human rights."[2] Haig also attacked the Soviet

Union as a leading state sponsor of terrorism, but when pressed by the media for substantiation of his claim, he was unable to provide the kind of unimpeachable evidence needed to build public support for the administration's war against terrorism.

In a surprising 1987 admission, Deputy CIA Director Robert Gates told a Princeton University audience that CIA analysts had been overzealous in attempting to disprove Haig's assertions. According to Gates, "agency analysts initially set out not to address the issue in all of its aspects but rather to prove the secretary wrong. But in so doing, they went too far themselves and failed in the early drafts to describe extensive support for terrorist groups and their sponsors."[3]

During the weeks and months that followed, the administration's rhetoric against terrorism and its state sponsors continued to escalate, but there was little evidence that new policies or capabilities had been adopted or put into operation to address the problem of terrorism. In reality, no consensus existed within the Reagan administration as to what form U.S. opposition to terrorism should take. Some in the State Department saw it as an issue that provoked needless confrontation with America's adversaries. They also maintained that public efforts to chastise U.S. allies for the chronic weakness they demonstrated in the face of terrorist attacks would be counterproductive.

Another problem concerned the fact that the U.S. was woefully ill-prepared, from both a military and an intelligence perspective, to effectively address the issue of terrorism. The CIA's human intelligence, or HUMINT, capabilities had suffered tremendously in the wake of Vietnam, Watergate, and congressional investigations into alleged CIA wrongdoing during the mid-1970s. Thus, not only was there a need to retarget certain intelligence assets at terrorism, and to provide for better and more timely analysis of intelligence data, but the Agency's covert capability had to be rebuilt. The CIA that the Reagan administration inherited in 1981 was, according to one former CIA man, like "a thin, emaciated man who's had nothing to eat or drink in six months, lying naked in the snow, who is ordered to pick up a sledgehammer and go to work."[4]

In addition to the need to revitalize the intelligence community, U.S. military capabilities for addressing terrorism and other threats on the "low frontier" of warfare left much to be desired. Although the Carter administration had created a military unit—what ultimately became known as Delta Force—specifically tasked with engaging terrorists and rescuing hostages, much more remained to be done. The disastrous Iranian rescue mission in 1980, in which eight men were killed and four seriously injured, had underscored many organizational, training, equipment, and leadership deficiencies. Since Vietnam, U.S. special operations units had represented a military backwater in terms of promotions, priority for equipment, and funding. As late as 1984, only .26 percent, or twenty-six cents out of every hundred dollars, of the Pentagon's total budget was being allocated to U.S. antiterrorism and unconventional warfighting capabilities, for fighting the war that was already here as opposed to the war that might not ever come.

During the first two years of the Reagan administration, antiterrorism remained a constant theme of the administration's verbal offensive against the Soviet Union and its satellites, but no major initiatives were offered up to improve U.S. capabilities for dealing with the problem. The only exception was at the CIA, where William Casey had taken over from Admiral Stansfield Turner as the thirteenth DCI, or Director of Central Intelligence. Casey was hard at work revitalizing the U.S. intelligence community, reshaping and expanding its capabilities to better anticipate and respond to such challenges as terrorism. As a part of this process, he mandated the creation of a new counterterrorist unit at the CIA, which former NSC consultant Michael Ledeen called "a qualitative improvement over what existed before. For the first time since we started taking the subject seriously, we had good coverage of international terrorism." While its chief function was analytical, Ledeen continued, the new unit was "also capable of taking action to foil terrorist deeds before they are under way." Casey had no illusions about fighting terrorism: it was a dirty business, but it had to be done. Too many in the administration and Congress, he knew, found it easier to deplore terrorism than to take meaningful action against it. What the U.S. needed was unconventional responses to unconventional threats. Above all, he maintained, terrorists must not feel that we are inhibited from responding with force, either overt or covert.

Initially there was little sympathy for Casey's views within the Reagan administration. Even at the National Security Council, terrorism was accorded such a low priority that Oliver North, at that time an obscure marine major, was given the responsibility for "coordinating the policy and plans of the U.S. Government for low-intensity conflict and counter-terrorism."[5]

Facing Up to the Threat

It was not until the multiple traumas of 1983 in the Middle East that the Reagan administration finally was galvanized into action regarding the terrorist threat. Iranian-backed Shiite terrorists bombed the U.S. embassy in Beirut in April, the headquarters of the U.S. Marine peacekeeping force at the Beirut airport in October, and the U.S. embassy in Kuwait in December. The April bombing was to have particularly far-reaching consequences, since it wiped out most of the CIA station in Lebanon along with the Agency's top Middle East expert Robert Ames, thus "blinding" the United States at a critical moment. The CIA contingent had been the real target of the terrorists, who were tipped off about the meeting of senior spooks by a female accomplice who was employed in the embassy's kitchen.

As the administration debated endlessly about how to respond to the Beirut bombings, the United States was victimized by a new round of aircraft hijackings, bombings, and hostage incidents. The media and the Congress demanded: where was the administration's much-vaunted war against terrorism? From all outward appearances, the Reagan administration seemed to be no more capable than the Carter administration of effectively fighting terrorism. It was into this breach that Oliver North stepped. As the problem of international terrorism assumed ever larger proportions in the Reagan administration, North's power grew accordingly. His rapid rise at the NSC was assisted by his warm relationship with CIA director Casey, who early in the administration had taken a shine to the bright and aggressive young marine officer with the piercing blue eyes. North started at the NSC as an "easel carrier" and soon became, in the words of one observer, "the world's most powerful lieutenant colonel."

North threw himself into the vacuum that existed within the government regarding U.S. counterterrorism policy with élan and an almost fanatical dedication to hard work. Other administration officials, for the most part, took the position: "Let Ollie do it," rather than stick their own necks out. Secretary of Defense Caspar Weinberger, for example, had little stomach for antiterrorist operations, believing that they were both risky and highly politically charged, and that one false step could jeopardize the progress made since the 1970s in restoring the prestige and power of the military, as well as the massive defense buildup to which he was so committed. In addition, Weinberger was something of an "Arabist," and worried constantly about the possible disruption of U.S. relations with the Arab world in the event the U.S. took military action against Arab terrorists.

Secretary of State George Shultz, for his part, expressed little interest in the subject of terrorism until the bombing of the Marine headquarters, with its loss of 241 Americans. As a former Marine, Shultz was very conscious that the tragedy had happened on "his watch," as a result of a U.S. presence in Lebanon that he had helped to engineer. Those closest to Shultz believe that prior to the bombing he was considering leaving the administration after the 1984 election, but that the Beirut tragedy gave him a renewed sense of purpose and "a fire in his gut to do something about terrorism." In this connection, he convened a unique all-day meeting of senior officials from the Reagan administration on March 24, 1984, and invited five outside terrorism "experts." In addition to Shultz, who looked very professorial in a tweed coat and red sweater vest, those present included Defense Secretary Caspar Weinberger, FBI Director William Webster, CIA Deputy Director for Intelligence Robert Gates, and Presidential Counselor Edwin Meese.[6]

Throughout the day, the remarkable gathering engaged in a no-holds-barred discussion of the options available to the United States to deal with the looming threat of international terrorism. The Pentagon's top counterterrorism official during the Reagan administration, Noel Koch, later described this as a watershed meeting, after which the whole tensor and tone of the administration's antiterrorism policy shifted substantially. It represented, in his view, the "greening" of George Shultz: his formal introduction to the challenge of terrorism and the various options for dealing with it.

A week later, on April 3, 1984, the President signed National Security Decision Directive 138 (NSDD 138) which, in effect, amounted to a declaration of war against international terrorism. In the preamble to the still-classified document, the United States announced that "states that use or support terrorism cannot be allowed to do so without consequences," and went on to enunciate that when all other efforts to dissuade states from supporting terrorism fail, "the United States has a right to defend itself." Oliver North was one of the chief architects of NSDD 138.

Shultz soon became one of the most outspoken advocates in the administration of using force to combat terrorism. He called for a bold new policy to fight terrorism, including retaliatory and preemptive actions, and on October 25, 1984, at the Park Avenue Synagogue in New York gave the strongest public speech to date on the subject of terrorism. "We cannot allow ourselves to become the Hamlet of nations," he told the assembled audience, "worrying endlessly over whether and how to respond. A great nation with global responsibilities cannot afford to be hamstrung by confusion and indecisiveness. Fighting terrorism will not be a clean or pleasant contest, but we have no choice but to play it."[7] He even went so far as to suggest that the United States should be ready to accept the loss of some innocent lives as a collateral result of its retaliation.

In many respects, Shultz's situation was analogous to that of the Pope, of whom Stalin once said: "The Pope! How many divisions has he got?" While ostensibly the lead agency in combating international terrorism, the State Department had few actual resources to bring to bear against international terrorism; they all belonged to the Defense Department, where a reluctant Caspar Weinberger jealously guarded them and found every conceivable excuse to avoid using them. Weinberger even promulgated his now-famous "six tests for using force," which one critic described as "six tests for never using force." Shultz could jawbone American allies and adversaries alike in an effort to convince them about the error of their ways, but without Weinberger's cooperation, U.S. policy lacked teeth. Indeed, without the threat of judicious application of force, there is little incentive for other countries to embrace or be influenced by peaceful options for combating terrorism like political, economic, and diplomatic sanctions.

The NSC Becomes Operational

As a result of the Shultz-Weinberger feud, the National Security Council—not by design but by default—became the command center of the administration's antiterrorism efforts. According to Noel Koch, the Defense Department's top official for terrorism and low-intensity warfare, "Without any goddamn leadership from this administration, you knew . . . that this empty talk about terrorism was going to come back and bite you in the ass and that someone was going to have to put something behind it; it was all going to devolve on one or two guys that were willing to do what the President wanted done."[8] As it turned out, Oliver North was that man.

There is a tendency to portray Oliver North, at the time of his dismissal, as standing two feet deep in grenade rings, with bodies strewn all around him. By contrast to such images, however, it was North's agility and brilliance as a bureaucrat, not as the warrior he had been in Vietnam, that was the source of his power. When he came to Washington, he traded his M-16 for telephones and computer terminals, and, working out of his cramped office in the Old Executive Office Building next to the White House, number 392 for most of the time he was at the NSC, he conducted a fierce and unrelenting war against the enemies of the United States.

From the moment he arrived in Washington, North grasped the power of information; he knew that the person with the best information usually prevailed in the decision-making process. He was, moreover, endowed with brilliant communications skills, which were clearly showcased during his rout of the Congress in July 1987. Finally, he was an absolutely indefatigable worker. There are countless stories of North waking senior CIA and Defense Department officials in the dead of night and ordering them to meet at his office for a 2:30 A.M. meeting, armed with charts and reams of statistics. It was not unusual, moreover, for North to put in a full day at the office and then fly to Central America or some other trouble spot for a meeting and then be back at his desk the following morning, having caught only cat naps on the plane. At one point, he told friends that he and his wife Betsy had struck a deal, whereby he agreed to come home at least once a week. North seemed to live on adrenaline, subsisting on coffee and hamburgers eaten at his desk or on the run at the McDonald's on 17th Street, just a half-block from his office. The coffeemaker in the narrow corridor that one passed through on the way to North's office disgorged quarts of the black liquid every day to North and the constant stream of visitors who came to see him. Later, it would become clear that North's chief failing was that he never caught his breath, if only for a moment, and engaged in serious reflection about the larger implications of the operations and initiatives he was undertaking. He was a man who lived perpetually in the present and, despite a keen appreciation for history, he never had time to view things with historical detachment or to look down the road at the projected impact his decisions would have on the future.

Uninterested in the prerogatives and trappings of power, North's office was cramped and stuffy, filled with stacks of paperwork and reports such as the daily CIA intelligence digest. In many respects, it more nearly conformed to the general public's perception of a command center than the actual Situation Room in the basement of the White House which, by comparison, is rather spartan and looks more like a board room. If one wanted to know what was really going on, they had only to glance at the

walls of North's office, which were covered with aerial reconnaissance photos and maps of Libya, Lebanon's Bekaa Valley,
Beirut, El Salvador, and Nicaragua. The only incongruous
touch consisted of drawings and fingerpaintings by North's children, taped to the wall behind his desk. Behind the leather sofa,
where a painting on loan from the National Gallery of Art had
once graced the wall, were a number of framed pictures, including the famous photo of the medical student kissing the ground
as he deplaned in the United States after being rescued in Grenada, and the front page from the *New York Daily News* proclaim-
ing "We Bag the Bums" following the interception of the *Achille
Lauro* pirates.

On the coffee table in front of the couch were copies of the
report of the Vice President's Task Force for Combatting Terrorism and the book *Fighting Back: Winning the War against Terrorism,*
which had a foreword by his boss, Bud McFarlane.[9] A Chinese
fur military hat emblazoned with a red star sat on the window-
sill. The window looked out on 17th Street and, when talking
with visitors, North would often sit in an overstuffed chair in
front of the window with his feet up on the coffee table. Since
the window faced west, late in the afternoon bright, butter-rich
sun would sometimes stream through the window, making it
impossible to look directly at North during a conversation.

North's desk almost touched the coffee table, but it was so
cluttered with equipment and stacks of paper that former *Time*
reporter David Halevy called it "absolutely unbelievable" and
a "scene of complete disorder."[10] There were three computer
terminals, one on the desk and two on a table to the side, which
also held one of the secure telephones. Two more telephones
were buried beneath the paper on the desk, and another was
kept in one of the desk drawers. The safe behind the desk, underneath still more paper, was the one in which North had discovered the watches and cash given to former National Security
Advisor Richard Allen by the Japanese.

During most of the time he worked for the National Security
Council, North had no personal staff other than his devoted
secretary, Fawn Hall. Later, Robert L. Earl, a Marine officer,

and CIA man Vince Cannistaro, the NSC's Senior Director for Intelligence, who oversaw covert activities, were able to take some of the load off North. As a result, North built a private network of advisors, spooks and retired spooks, military men, conservative activists, and amateur "operators" in a futile effort to hold the line in Nicaragua, advance a new opening to Iran, secure the release of American hostages in Lebanon, and conduct a relentless campaign against international terrorists and their state sponsors.

If, to many, Oliver North represented the ideal son, then his liaison to the Contras, Rob Owen, known as "T.C." or "the Courier," was everyone's kid brother. The fresh-faced Stanford graduate idolized North and, next to his mentor, gave the most moving testimony during the hearings. The rest of the cast included retired Air Force Major General Richard "the fat man" Secord; his business partner, the slippery Iranian arms merchant Albert Hakim; conservative activist Andy "Mad Dog" Messing; the outspoken former commander of U.S. forces in Korea, John Singlaub; the leather-clad blonde Contra arms supplier Barbara Studley; the hunter of Che Guevara, who still wears his watch, Felix "Max Gomez" Rodriguez; and Costa Rican rancher John Hull. Conservative fund-raisers Carl "Spitz" Channel, Dan Conrad, and Richard Miller provided North with the unappropriated cash he needed to operate.

From within the U.S. government, North worked closely with the combative Assistant Secretary of State, Elliot Abrams, and the U.S. Ambassador to Costa Rica, Lewis Tambs. From the CIA there was the flamboyant Dewey Clarridge, who later headed the Agency's antiterrorism unit, and Costa Rican station chief, Joe Funandey. There was also six-foot-five Alan Fiers, who once snarled at a woman from the State Department's human rights office, "I'm paid to defend my country. I'll lie, manipulate and deceive to do my job."

Field Marshal North

Lost in all of the clamor over the Iran/Contra crisis is Oliver North's remarkable role in the U.S. efforts to combat terrorism during the Reagan administration.[11] After nearly two decades of suffering terrorist outrages without visible response, during the early 1980s the United States struck back at terrorists and their state sponsors both publicly and covertly, and Oliver North was never far from the action. "Ollie North's biggest contribution to Western society," observed a top Israeli intelligence official, "was his ability to persuade American decision makers to take active measures against international terrorism." Indeed, North had many admirers within the Israeli defense and intelligence establishments, who saw in him the virtues of toughness, courage, and self-reliance that they so often extolled. North, in return, forged extremely close ties to the Israelis, whose tough stance on terrorism he greatly admired. The benefits of this relationship could be glimpsed during the TWA 847 hostage drama.

At 9:10 A.M. on June 14, 1985, a TWA jetliner bound from Athens to Rome was hijacked by Shiite gunmen and forced to fly to Beirut, and then on to Algiers. After being refueled, the plane returned to Beirut, then back again to Algiers, where U.S. Delta Force commandos were waiting. They had been given permission by the Algerians to land, but not to operate on Algerian soil. The U.S. Ambassador to Algeria and the White House (NSC) had asked the Algerians for permission to let Delta "take the plane down," but it never was given. Ultimately, the plane flew to Beirut for a third time.

On the second day of the crisis a young U.S. Navy diver, Robert Stethem, was murdered in cold blood by the terrorists. Although some passengers were released in both Algiers and Beirut, the terrorists broke up the remaining 39 passengers and crew into smaller groups that were dispersed throughout Beirut to make any rescue attempt by the U.S. more difficult.

From the moment Washington had been notified of the skyjacking a little after 4:00 A.M. on the first day, top administration antiterrorism officials, including Oliver North, went into action. The United States quietly conveyed to the Syrians and Iranians, as well as to Shiite Amal leader Nabih Berri, whose gunmen controlled the fate of most of the hostages, that the United States wanted a speedy resolution of the problem, and that if any harm befell the remaining captives, U.S. military action was sure to follow. President Reagan said publicly that the United States would continue to show restraint for the time being, but warned the terrorists and their state sponsors that U.S. restraint had its limits. To give added impetus to his words, U.S. military forces including the aircraft carrier Nimitz and a U.S. Marine amphibious force, were massed in the Eastern Mediterranean. In addition, elements of the U.S. Delta Force were deployed on Cyprus; an advance party had already infiltrated Beirut. Still other U.S. military assets were waiting in Israel for the word to move. The administration's resolve was further toughened when four U.S. Marines were gunned down in a cafe in San Salvador during the middle of the hijacking drama.

As an indication of the minutiae that North sometimes became involved in, during the TWA 847 hijacking he was overheard on the phone trying to get the flags lowered to half-mast for Robert Stethem. Similarly, after the four marines were killed in El Salvador, he took time from the hostage crisis to assist in making arrangements for the transport of the bodies back to the United States. Not only was North never good at delegating responsibility, but the fact remains that he was, for the most part, a lone operator without immediate staff or resources; hence, there was no one to whom he could really delegate. To get things done he had to beg, borrow, cajole, inspire, and intimidate those with the necessary resources, something at which he became very adept. He occasionally joked that his only tangible resources were White House stationery and the White House switchboard.

Finally, with the threat of U.S. military intervention looming over the region, negotiations secured the release of the 39 remaining hostages, but not before some very tense moments. According to the final agreement that was reached, Israel released—in what was purported to be an unconnected action—more than 700 Shiite prisoners to pave the way for the freedom of the hostages from TWA 847. According to North, however, the agreement broke down late on June 29 when Hizballah terrorists, holding the four Jewish passengers, refused to go along with the deal. The administration, however, was adamant: it wanted *all* of the hostages back or the agreement was off. North, who was already deeply involved in secret diplomacy with Speaker of the Iranian Parliament Ali Akbar Hashemi Rafsanjani, said that he contacted Rafsanjani by means of a pre-arranged channel to elicit his help. North says that Rafsanjani personally intervened to secure the release of the Jewish hostages, thereby permitting the deal to go forward.[12] Ultimately, all of the hostages were transported to Damascus in a Red Cross convoy.

During the TWA hijacking crisis the United States and Israel reached a new level of antiterrorist cooperation. In order to facilitate this cooperation, a secret channel of communication was established between the two nations, and Oliver North was designated as the U.S. point man. The decision to name North as the American liaison, ratified by top Pentagon and intelligence officials, was known to only a very small group at the National Security Council. Key players on the U.S. side were Secretary of Defense Caspar Weinberger, Assistant Secretary of Defense for International Security Policy Richard Armitage, Joint Chiefs of Staff Chairman John Vessey, CIA Director Bill Casey and his deputy Robert Gates, and a handful of others. The Israelis most actively involved were Defense Minister Yitzhak Rabin, the Prime Minister's counterterrorism advisor Amiram Nir, former Mossad official David Kimche, Israeli Chief of Staff Lt. General Moshe Levy, Military Intelligence chief Major General Ehud Barak, and Israel's chief Defense Attaché in Washington, Major General Uri Simhoni. Together, the NSC staff and their Israeli counterparts examined the military and other options for securing the release of the TWA passengers, and coordinated all actions that were taken.

It was during the TWA 847 hijacking that the role of the Iranians as leading sponsors of Middle East terrorism became firmly established to everyone's satisfaction. Earlier in the year, CIA Director Casey had said that ''more blood has been shed by Iranian-sponsored terrorists than any other,'' but there were still those in the U.S. government who maintained that the connection was tenuous and difficult, if not impossible, to prove.

No more. If there had been any doubts about the 1983 bombings in Beirut and the 1984 aircraft hijackings, Western intelligence firmly established Iran's links to the TWA 847 hijacking. In retrospect, it appears that Nabih Berri's Amal, acting on orders from Tehran, carried out the initial hijacking and then turned it over to the "more radical" Hizballah. Subsequently, Berri stepped back into the picture at the end to play peacemaker and resolve the crisis, although certain recalcitrant elements in Hizballah nearly scuttled the whole plan.

The Hunt for Immad Mughniye

North's first major operation was an effort to apprehend Immad Mughniye, the operational chief of the radical Hizballah Shiite terrorist organization in Lebanon. Mughniye is perhaps one of the most cunning and ruthless terrorists in the world today and is responsible for the 1983 bombing of the U.S. embassy in West Beirut that wiped out most of the CIA station in Lebanon. He was also behind the bombing of the U.S. Marine barracks, as well as the attack on the French peacekeeping force. Another Mughniye operation nearly wiped out Israel's counterterrorist network in southern Lebanon, and it is generally believed that he orchestrated the March 16, 1984, kidnapping of the new CIA Chief of Station in Lebanon, William Buckley, who later died after prolonged torture by his captors, as well as numerous other kidnappings.

It is doubtful that Buckley ever should have been sent to the Middle East again. His "cover" had been blown in at least two countries, one of which was Syria; therefore, it must be assumed that his captors knew exactly who he was. Buckley was reportedly one of approximately eight candidates for the position of Beirut station chief, and he was reluctant to go. But he confided to friends that it was likely he would be selected for Beirut because, unlike the other candidates, he was not married and did not have a family, although he did have a close girlfriend.

By 1985, Mughniye, along with Abu Nidal, was perhaps the most wanted terrorist in the world. Within the Reagan administration, Mughniye's capture or murder was almost an obsession. CIA Director Casey wanted him because of the loss of the CIA station and the abduction of Buckley, a personal friend. Shultz and McFarlane were both ex-Marines, and had been traumatized by the bombing of the Marine headquarters; North was an active-duty Marine who had vowed to do everything in his power to bring Mughniye to justice and thereby avenge the 241 American servicemen who had perished in the attack at the Beirut airport. "Ollie," said a close friend and colleague at the NSC, "took an oath to hunt and bring to trial the Shiite terrorist who was responsible for the bombing of the Marine headquarters."

A remarkable set of events was almost to fulfill North's wish. While Mughniye was in France, Hizballah had kidnapped four Russian diplomats from the Soviet embassy in West Beirut. When their demands were not met, the Hizballah terrorists executed one of the diplomats. Unlike the United States, the Soviets did not procrastinate or worry about legalisms; instead, they assigned their proxies, the Druze Progressive Socialist Party, under the leadership of the warlord Walid Jumblatt, to get their diplomats back and to teach Hizballah a lesson.

The Druze fighters did not waste any time. They quickly picked up one of Mughniye's deputies, since Mughniye was abroad, and brought him to the basement of the Soviet embassy in West Beirut. They permitted him to make several phone calls only after dispatching a special courier to his confederates with one or more of his fingers to demonstrate their seriousness. In view of the emergency, Mughniye was contacted in France by his headquarters in Beirut. At the time, Mughniye was on the south coast of France, traveling under an assumed name and using a false passport. In response to the urgent message, Mughniye ordered the release of the three surviving Soviet diplomats and the return of the body of their murdered colleague in order to secure the freedom of his deputy. The Israelis, however, were monitoring the communications, and were therefore able to pinpoint Mughniye's location.

Upon learning of Mughniye's whereabouts, North went into

action at once. He requested that the Israelis maintain close surveillance of Mughniye and not let him slip away. At the same time, he informed the CIA and his superiors at the NSC of the exciting development, and a task force composed of CIA operators and DOD special operations representatives was set up to monitor developments. In order to secure French cooperation, he traveled to France to hammer out the necessary details. While the French initially promised full cooperation and assumed the task of maintaining prime surveillance of Mughniye, the United States could not get French assurances that Mughniye would be extradited once he was apprehended. Indeed, it appeared that the French wanted to try him themselves since, after all, Mughniye had also been responsible for an attack on French forces in Lebanon. The French position was strengthened by new intelligence that Mughniye had come to France not only for rest and relaxation, but also in order to plan a series of terrorist operations on French soil designed to win freedom for the notorious terrorist Georges Ibrahim Abdallah. Abdallah was implicated in the murders of U.S. Deputy Military Attaché Charles Ray and Israeli diplomat Yacov Barsimantov, in reality chief of the Israeli Mossad in France.

As North worked to hammer out an agreement with the French, he got word from the Israelis, who had maintained their surveillance of the terrorist, that French police had arrested Mughniye and bundled him off to the airport and put him on the first flight to the Middle East. North was outraged, but there was nothing he could do. Later, the French claimed that they had saved the United States and Israel a major embarrassment, since the man was not really Mughniye, but the victim of mistaken identification.

The failure to apprehend Mughniye was North's first major disappointment in his long and unrelenting struggle against terrorism, and one that he would not soon forget. It also served to underscore the difficulties involved in securing allied cooperation in combating terrorism. The Mughniye incident, moreover, convinced him that the United States would have to go it alone in fighting terrorism, at least until the Europeans could be convinced that cooperation was preferable to the unilateral use of military force by the United States. Thus, he began the process of seeking an appropriate opportunity to strike a decisive military blow against terrorism, which would shake the Europeans out of their indifference and lethargy. In addition, the Mughniye failure reinforced his efforts to undertake extensive covert measures against terrorists and their state sponsors.

In retrospect, the fact that Mughniye, the murderer of so many of his fellow Marines, slipped through his fingers produced great frustration and resentment on North's part, and played a major role in his later willingness to consider any means, however unique or outlandish, to deal with the problem of terrorism. As he saw it, U.S. policy with respect to international terrorism was not working, therefore, it was time to try something new—the worst that could happen was that it would not work either. He railed against naysayers from other government agencies who could find a dozen reasons why something was either ill-considered or impossible instead of looking for ways to surmount problems and handicaps. North rapidly developed a reputation for "walking over" those he considered obstacles to making things happen, especially when he believed he was acting to give substance to the President's words and policies. Later, he would be criticized for being too "task oriented" and "tunnel visioned," but he viewed himself as the President's instrument, and he was not about to let anything deter him.

In many respects, North's ascension at the NSC represented the "Israelization" of U.S. antiterrorism policy under the Reagan administration: the willingness to consider, if not use, any means available to combat terrorism. In this connection, he was a strong proponent of covert action against terrorists and their state sponsors, and what he generally referred to as "special activities," that is, activities conducted in support of U.S. policy objectives abroad, without attribution, such as disinformation. Bogus stories were fed to the media about Qaddafi and various terrorist leaders, designed to humiliate them and undermine their authority. False rumors were planted claiming that certain terrorists were "agents of Israel or the United

States," thus sowing suspicion within their own ranks. A phony assassination of a Qaddafi foe in Cairo was orchestrated to embarrass the Libyan leader. Qaddafi fell for the ruse, and publicly claimed credit for the attack. The CIA reportedly encouraged and supported the anti-Qaddafi opposition group that launched the unsuccessful May 1984 attack on Azzizia Barracks, where Qaddafi lived, near Tripoli.

There is no hard evidence, however, to support the claim that the United States attempted to assassinate Shiite religious leader Sheikh Mohammed Hussein Fadlallah, as satisfying as his death would have been to North, Casey, and others in the government. Fadlallah was the spiritual leader of Hizballah and, according to journalist Amir Taheri, "the idol of the radicals" in the Lebanese Shiite movement.[13] Fadlallah reportedly had been involved in the selection of targets and in planning the three vehicle bomb attacks on the United States in Beirut, and had personally blessed the young Shiite suicide bomber before he drove a truckload of explosives into the Marine barracks at the Beirut airport. Bob Woodward, however, relates in his book *Veil* that CIA Director Bill Casey had hatched a plot with Saudi Ambassador to the United States Prince Bandar bin Sultan to strike back at Fadlallah, and on March 8, 1985, a car loaded with explosives detonated about fifty yards from Fadlallah's Beirut residence, killing approximately 80 people and injuring more than 200.[14] The Saudis were given control over the operation, maintains Woodward, and they contracted with a former English SAS commando, who hired a number of Lebanese to carry out the actual attack. After the operation failed to kill Fadlallah, it was decided to bribe him instead, says Woodward, after which "There were no more Fadlallah-supported terrorist attacks against Americans."[15] There is no evidence to support Woodward's claim; however, a month after the assassination attempt against Fadlallah, Casey told a restricted audience that anti-American terrorist "attacks have not passed without significant response," although he did not go into any detail.[16]

During the mid-1980s, moreover, an effort was made to undermine the infrastructure and logistics apparatus of a number of terrorist organizations. Electronic fund transfers and travel arrangements disappeared, communications went astray, terrorist safe houses and other cover operations were disrupted or shut down, and defective weapons were sold to terrorist groups. In one instance, according to North, ultrasensitive bomb detonators were sold to Hizballah terrorists in Lebanon. As the terrorists were loading a bomb into a vehicle in the basement of a high-rise building, it detonated, bringing down the apartment house on top of them. It was not something that the United States could openly take credit for, said North, since civilians had died in the mishap, but the terrorists "got the message."

Mr. Ice and Mr. Wood

One example of the extraordinary lengths North and others in the administration were prepared to go to combat terrorism concerned an effort to trade three convicted Mexican drug dealers for the notorious Puerto Rican terrorist William Morales, also known as "Three Fingered Willie" in some police circles, since his features and hands had been maimed when a bomb he was putting together blew up in his face. Morales, a fanatic FALN (Fuerzas Armadas de Liberacion Nacional/Armed Forces of National Liberation) terrorist, had been convicted of a series of deadly bombings in New York City during the 1970s and sentenced to 99 years in prison. Unfortunately, Morales had escaped from a prison hospital, and had made his way to Mexico where, four years later, he was apprehended following a shootout 65 miles southeast of Mexico City. Two of Morales's female companions and a Mexican police officer were killed in the incident. It was believed that Morales intended to bomb a meeting of U.S. and Mexican parliamentarians scheduled to be held in the city of Puebla.

A U.S. extradition request was ignored by Mexican authorities, and instead Morales was tried and sentenced to a long prison term in Mexico, consistent with Mexican law, which requires that Mexican prison sentences be served before any extradition requests are considered. Both the Cuban and Nicaraguan governments, however, began exerting enormous pressure on the Mexican government to release Morales, whom they regarded not as a terrorist but as a hero. In view of the "porous" reputation of Mexican prisons, Reagan administration officials, especially then Presidential Counselor Edwin Meese, were extremely worried that Morales would be permitted to escape, either by corrupt prison officials susceptible to bribes or by the Mexican government, which might just decide to look the other way.

Against this backdrop, two men from Missouri with names that sounded too contrived to be real, Mr. Ice and Mr. Wood, came to Washington in 1984 to make a trade: one of the most notorious terrorists in the nation's history for three drug dealers, a mad dog for three scumbags. On first impression, Randall Wood and Cody Ice looked like a couple of Midwestern rubes: both were large men, overweight, dressed in light suits, brown shoes, and wide ties. But once they opened their mouths, any doubts about their competence vanished immediately. They were all business.

Wood is a prominent Springfield attorney who has represented a number of convicted drug dealers, and Ice is one of the largest bail bondsmen in the Midwest. They had come to Washington to propose that three Mexican drug dealers incarcerated at the federal correctional facility in Leavenworth, Kansas, be transferred back to Mexico under the provisions of an agreement between the United States and Mexico that allows nationals of each country to serve their time, for crimes committed in the other nation, in their native country. Originally designed as a way of ensuring that Americans would not have to suffer the depredations of Mexican prisons, the three Mexican drug dealers knew that, by contrast to the "hard time" they were serving at Leavenworth, their money would buy them a relatively luxurious existence in a corrupt Mexican prison. Moreover, there was every reason to believe that they could bribe their way to freedom at some point down the road.

The Mexican drug dealers were aware that the United States was unlikely to send them back to Mexico unless there was someone in a Mexican prison whom the Justice Department wanted even more than them. It did not take them long to find out about the intense U.S. interest in Morales, and they soon hit upon a plan to structure an exchange between the two countries: themselves for Morales. To ensure that Morales did not escape in the meantime, they hired extra guards for his prison cell and paid off the warden. Agents for the drug dealers reportedly also bribed a number of high Mexican government officials, not only to prevent Morales from being extradited to the United States prior to an agreement being struck or expelled to Cuba or Nicaragua, but so that when the time came the officials would secretly hand Morales over to the United States and accept the drug dealers in return. It was proposed that the exchange of Morales for the drug dealers occur at night on the Rio Grande. The Mexican authorities were even prepared to see that Morales did not make it across the river alive, if that was more convenient to the United States. In other words, he could "drown" crossing the Rio Grande.

Ice and Wood, as representatives for the imprisoned Mexican drug dealers, made every effort to reach an agreement with U.S. authorities. They met with North on at least two occasions, and received encouragement in their efforts. Senator Strom Thurmond, then chairman of the Senate Judiciary Committee, and Attorney General Edwin Meese also reportedly favored an exchange. Despite the desire to see Morales back in U.S. custody, however, the Drug Enforcement Administration (DEA) understandably opposed the exchange, since DEA agents had risked life and limb to bring the Mexican drug dealers to justice and felt it would set a bad precedent. In the end, it was impossible to reach a consensus within the U.S. government regarding the proposed exchange, and the three drug dealers remain in U.S. custody. Morales, however, was released by Mexico and is presently thought to be in Cuba.

"We Bag the Bums"

On June 19, 1985, CIA Director Casey told a closed-door session of the Senate Intelligence Committee that "the United States is at war" with international terrorism and that "the TWA hijacking is just the beginning.'' His words soon proved to be prophetic. While North had little room to operate during the TWA 847 crisis, perhaps his finest hour would come three-and-a-half months later in the wake of the seajacking of the Italian cruise ship *Achille Lauro*. On October 7, 1985, Palestinian terrorists, members of the radical splinter faction known as the Palestine Liberation Front (PLF), seized control of the ship and its 507 passengers and crew, including a number of Americans, off the coast of Egypt. Fortunately, many of the passengers had disembarked on a side trip to see the Pyramids.

The four pirates were dark, sullen young men whose behavior and appearance were in stark contrast to the rest of the passengers, mostly middle-aged and elderly tourists. Despite the fact that they kept to themselves and did not participate in shipboard activities, no one found their presence disconcerting enough to make an issue of it. Perhaps this was not unusual, considering that the last major cruise ship hijacking had occurred a quarter century earlier when the Portuguese cruise liner *Santa Maria* had been taken over by opponents of the Salazar dictatorship.

At 8:45 A.M. on October 7, the seajackers burst into the ship's dining room with weapons blazing, wounding two passengers. Once in control of the ship, they demanded the release of 50 Palestinians being held in Israel. When negotiations began to falter the following day, the terrorists brutally murdered wheelchair-bound Leon Klinghoffer of New York, dumping his body over the side of the ship. Reportedly, they had shuffled the passports of the Americans to see who would die, and Klinghoffer's had come up on top.

From the outset, the Reagan administration, its patience already worn thin by the TWA 847 incident, began planning the possible rescue of the ship in the event that the situation began to deteriorate precipitously. The Navy SEALs—commando frogmen capable of operating in water, in the air, and on land—were chosen for the mission. Perhaps the finest special-operations unit in the U.S. military inventory, SEALs undergo two years of basic training before they are entitled to wear the ''Budweiser'' flash on their uniforms. SEAL units operate under the command of the various theater commanders-in-chief, with the exception of SEAL Team 6, which is attached to the Joint Special Operations Command. The SEALs are probably the U.S. combat unit most frequently involved in deep penetration operations on unfriendly territory.

One senior U.S. Defense Department official recalls meeting with members of SEAL Team 6 at Fort Bragg one day. "They looked like a band of pirates. One guy was wearing a loud sport coat and others were dressed in jeans. None of them stood up when we entered the room and they would only speak if spoken to, although their answers were very direct and forthright when asked a question." In order for them to blend in with the local population anywhere in the world, some members of the SEAL unit have long scraggly hair and beards, and more than one sports an earring or two. For those who remember "high and tight" military haircuts, from an appearance point of view some SEALs are downright unmilitary. But there is nothing unmilitary about their combat skills, which are honed to perfection.

Thirty hours after the seizure of the *Achille Lauro,* U.S. antiterrorist forces arrived at the British Royal Air Force Base at Akrotiri, on the southern tip of Cyprus. It was at Akrotiri, with the full cooperation of the British government and the RAF base commander, that the Americans established their operational base. While the U.S. commandos were preparing their operation, heavy USAF transporters brought other elements of the U.S. counterterrorist force to Akrotiri. As it began to take shape, the plan they devised called for the SEALs to take off under the cover of darkness in a high-flying aircraft, from which they would execute a precision high-altitude parachute drop over the Mediterranean. Using specially devised parachutes, they would glide down on the captive ship and—dressed in black battle gear and equipped with silenced guns and shock weapons—take the vessel back from the terrorists.

The operation was scheduled for the night of Wednesday, October 9, and it was at this point that highly accurate and detailed intelligence information became critical. North, who was coordinating the operation as head of a special White House counterterrorist task force, was flabbergasted to learn that U.S. intelligence had lost track of the ship on Tuesday, despite all of the sophisticated satellite and communications monitoring equipment possessed by the United States. Without knowing the exact location of the ship, the rescue operation was obviously out of the question.

In defense of the intelligence community, ship detection in mid-ocean is not all that easy. There are a number of ways of locating a ship, including through the signals emitted by its radar, its radio communications, and by means of aerial reconnaissance and photos. The U.S. intelligence community is configured to track the Soviet navy, not commercial vessels. The inability to locate the *Achille Lauro* was a major embarrassment to the Navy, nevertheless, and at least one high-ranking admiral was overheard to remark that the whole NSG (Naval Security Group) should be shut down because ''it's not worth anything when we need it.'' The Israelis, by contrast, had suffered a number of terrorist penetrations involving ''mother'' ships off the coast, and possessed sophisticated monitoring devices capable of locating and tracking potentially threatening vessels.

Using the channel established during the TWA 847 crisis, North turned to the Israelis for help. He called Major General Simhoni at the Israeli embassy in Washington and explained the situation to him. Simhoni, in turn, immediately contacted Israel and was able to report back in minutes with the information North had requested. Apparently the Israelis, fearful that the terrorists on board the *Achille Lauro* might try to carry out their original plan of attacking the Israeli port of Ashdod, had kept the ship under close surveillance.

The *Achille Lauro* was, at this time, steaming along the Syrian coast, since the terrorists hoped that the Syrians would give them safe haven at the military and oil terminus of Tartus. North passed along the information he had received from the Israelis to the National Security Agency (NSA) which, in the interlude, had managed to locate the elusive ship. North, however, had asked Simhoni to keep him posted on the ship's movements. On Wednesday, the day of the planned operation, NSA, like the Navy on the previous day, could not locate the hostage cruise liner, and an embarrassed North was forced to turn to the Israelis yet another time. As before, Simhoni was able to supply North with the ship's exact coordinates. According to Simhoni, from that moment onward, "We kept a secure line open between military intelligence headquarters in Israel and my office at the embassy." Because of Israeli assistance, preparation for the nighttime assault went forward unimpeded, but ultimately the operation was never launched.

After the Syrians refused to let the ship dock at Tartus, the *Achille Lauro* sailed back to Port Said, where it was met by a senior PLO official and Mohammed Abbas, leader of the PLF. They conferred with the terrorists, and it was agreed that they would surrender to Egyptian authorities, who subsequently took control of the ship and its passengers. North soon learned, however, that a secret deal between the Egyptian and Italian governments, and the PLO, was in the works. According to North, "The first deal was made between Hosni Mubarak, the Egyptian president, Italian Prime Minister Craxi, and the Chairman of the PLO, Yasir Arafat. It called for freeing the ship and hostages, and the safe return of the terrorists to their base in Tunisia, and would have turned Yasir Arafat into the hero of the day."[17]

Since the incident seemed to have been resolved, the American commandos waiting at Akrotiri, Cyprus, under the command of Major General Carl Stiner, were ordered home. Meanwhile, intense diplomatic efforts to convince the Egyptians to turn the terrorists over to Italy or to the United States were making little progress.

The regular NSC staff meeting was interrupted the following morning with a message from Mubarak informing National Security Advisor Bud McFarlane that the terrorists had already left Egypt. Mubarak had given the same information to U.S. Ambassador to Egypt Nicholas Veliotes, and even repeated it publicly. McFarlane was not convinced. He turned to North and asked where the U.S. commandos were.

"On their way home," replied North, cognizant that some members of SEAL Team 6 were already on Gibraltar en route back to the United States.

"Check where the terrorists are," McFarlane ordered, unwilling to trust the Egyptians.

"Will do," said North, who immediately began polling U.S. intelligence sources. Failing to get definitive information, he called General Simhoni again.

"Uri," North inquired, "where are the four thugs?"

"Give me thirty minutes and I'll get back to you," Simhoni answered.

The main intercept of Egyptian telecommunications comes from Israeli installations in the Negev, which are shared with the United States as part of Israel's equipment-leasing agreement with NSA. The Israelis, it turned out, had intercepted a number of communications, not only from Mubarak to other members of his government, but subsequently a telephone conversation between the Egyptian chief of internal security to the captain of the EgyptAir plane that was to carry the terrorists out of the country. The flight plan and time of departure were discussed, along with the fact that there would be Egyptian commandos on board. Ironically, Secretary of Defense Caspar Weinberger had ordered both DIA (Defense Intelligence Agency) and the NIO (Naval Intelligence Organization) not to talk to the Israelis, presumably because they might learn something that would precipitate U.S. action.

By 8:45 A.M., Simhoni was able to get back to North and report: "The four are still in Egypt."

"Are you sure?" North demanded, his voice rising with excitement.

"Absolutely."

North went back to U.S. intelligence with the information provided by the Israelis, and was soon able to obtain a second confirmation.

Armed with the startling information he had obtained, North rushed upstairs from the Situation Room to McFarlane's office. There he found McFarlane, who was just preparing to board the Marine One helicopter in order to accompany the President on a campaign swing to Chicago; McFarlane's deputy, Vice Admiral John Poindexter; NSC spokesperson Karna Small; Middle East specialist Jock Covey; and McFarlane's secretary.

North immediately launched into a crisp report of the facts in hand. "The friends," he began, using the common euphemism of the U.S. intelligence community (until the arrest of Israeli spy Jonathan J. Pollard), when referring to the Israelis "have the four in Egypt. We have confirmation." Then he spoke for everyone in the room: "We have to do something about it."

"What can be done?" inquired Poindexter.

"Do you remember Yamamoto?" North asked, recalling the Japanese admiral who had led the attack on Pearl Harbor. In 1943 U.S. codebreakers learned that Yamamoto was going to conduct an inspection visit of Japanese forces in the Northern Solomons, and they laid a trap for him. His aircraft was intercepted and shot down by American P-38 fighters, with the loss of all aboard.

"You don't want to shoot it down?" ventured Poindexter uneasily, referring to the EgyptAir plane.

"No," replied North. "Just force it to land at Sigonella, Sicily."

McFarlane had already made up his mind. "Get moving," he ordered North, before rushing out the door to the waiting helicopter.

In view of the imminent departure of the EgyptAir jetliner with the terrorists on board, every second counted, and North went to work like a man possessed to pull the necessary operation together. A short time later, he presented an outline of his plan to Poindexter, who signed off on it at once, and then contacted McFarlane on a secure communications link. McFarlane consulted briefly with the President and came back to ask for more details. North and his team immediately set about assembling the information requested, including the proposed rules of engagement governing the operation.

By 2:00 P.M. Washington time, the President had given the order to proceed, but not before encountering strong opposition from Secretary of Defense Weinberger and his deputy, William Howard Taft IV. Weinberger was concerned about the impact the interception would have on U.S. relations with Egypt and the rest of the Arab world. In addition, he raised questions about the procedures that would be used to force the EgyptAir jetliner down and, in general, did everything possible to dissuade the President from giving the mission a green light. Indeed, at one point the security of the mission was compromised by a conversation over an open line between Reagan, on board Air Force One, and Weinberger, en route to his summer home in Maine, which was monitored by a ham radio enthusiast.

Following Reagan's approval, the Sixth Fleet was given new orders and the aircraft carrier *Saratoga* directed to sail in the vicinity of Crete at full speed. Accurate real-time intelligence, however, was still a problem. Although U.S. intelligence was doing a good job of keeping the NSC continuously advised as to the whereabouts of the terrorists, the tail number and departure time of the EgyptAir flight still were in question. North once again placed a call to General Simhoni, who had an open line to the office of Major General Ehud Barak, the chief of Israel's military intelligence branch known as AMAN. Simhoni passed along North's request to AMAN and established an open line to the White House Situation Room, from which North was monitoring the operations of the Sixth Fleet.

Minutes later, Barak came back on the line with the needed information, but Simhoni interrupted him and asked him to hold for a moment while he got the White House Situation Room on the line for a three-way conversation. North was later to remark, "The Israelis had it all." They provided the United States with the plane's identification numbers and call sign seconds after it was in the air. North, from his desk in the Situation Room, transmitted the crucial information to the *Saratoga* over a secure open line. While the *Saratoga* was launching its F-14 fighters to carry out the interception and takedown, North watched the U.S. commandos, now over the Atlantic, turn around and make for the NATO air base at Sigonella.

For the *Saratoga's* fighters, finding the EgyptAir jetliner at night in the busy international air corridor along the coast of North Africa promised to be no easy task. Indeed, at the time that it was intercepted, there were 67 other civilian/commercial jetliners flying in the same vicinity.

In view of the difficulties, McFarlane had raised with North the need for some kind of backup plan. North shared McFarlane's concerns with General Simhoni, and work began on an alternative plan to force the Egyptian jet down at an Israeli military base.

"Will you be able to move in time?" North pressed Simhoni.

"We will give you all the assistance we are able to provide." responded Simhoni.

Presaging concerns that were already troubling administration planners about Sigonella, North wanted to know, "Will you hand the terrorists over to us or bring them to justice yourselves?"

"Whatever suits you better," responded Simhoni.

Soon the Israelis were back on the line with even more stunning news: PLF leader Mohammed Abbas was on board the Egyptian jetliner. Although he knew that it might get a bit dicey in the end, North was ecstatic, for it was becoming clear that Abbas probably had masterminded the seajacking. The chance to bring a top terrorist leader to justice for his crimes was too good to be true.

The key was now to buy more time for the Tomcats so that they could locate the EgyptAir jetliner and force it to Sigonella. To accomplish this, North reached deep into his bag of tricks. He asked the Israelis if they could isolate the jetliner by jamming all of its communications, except those they wanted to get through, and at the same time so intimidate their air traffic controller at Tunis that permission for the EgyptAir flight to land would be denied.

At that moment, the Israelis had one of their homemade RC-135 intelligence-gathering clones, built from a Boeing 707, airborne in the Mediterranean. The Israeli Boeing was capable of monitoring an entire conflict theater, interpreting the data, and serving as a flying command post. In one compartment on board, Arabic-speaking Israelis were tuned to every military and civilian radio frequency in the region.

The deception the Israelis were about to engage in was not without precedent. During the Israeli raid on the Iraqi nuclear reactor on June 7, 1981, the Israeli version of the RC-135 picked up an urgent attempt by a pilot to get in touch with the Jordanian Air Force command post. The intelligence officers on board the 707 quickly identified the caller: Jordan's King Hussein, who happened to be enjoying a pleasant afternoon of recreational flying over Jordanian territory in his personal plane. Hussein, it turned out, had just seen the Israeli raiding party, made up of F-15s and F-16s, on its way to Baghdad. Without missing a beat, an Israeli officer in the 707, some 250 miles to the west, acknowledged the King's call and identified himself as the duty officer in the Jordanian Air Force situation room.

"Your majesty," said the Israeli captain in fluent Arabic, "this is Colonel Hisham. How can I be at your service?"

The King, himself a fighter pilot, was direct and to the point as he spoke with the man he assumed was the chief duty officer of his air force. "Eight F-16s and a number of F-15s just flew over the area," he reported crisply. "They penetrated into Saudi territory. Inform our brothers in Saudi Arabia and Iraq that the Israelis are on their way. They are up to something special."

"Will inform the Saudis and the Iraqis right away, sir," came the response from the Israeli 707.

Satisfied that he had, by sheer coincidence, been able to warn the Saudis and Iraqis of some extraordinary Israeli operation, Hussein swung his plane around and made a direct line for the Jordanian capital. Needless to say, Hussein's message never reached the Saudis or Iraqis. The entire conversation remains on tape within the archives of the Israeli monitoring and listening unit as a classic example of creativity under pressure. Hussein learned only two days later, after a thorough investigation, that he had actually been speaking to an Israeli military officer, who not only spoke Arabic with the proper Jordanian-bedouin accent, but also used proper Jordanian call signs and designators to remove any suspicion from the King's mind.

In a rerun of this incident, four years later, when the pilot of the EgyptAir jetliner bearing Mohammed Abbas and his gunmen to safety sought permission to land from what he thought was the Tunis air traffic controller, his request was denied. As before, the hapless pilot was really communicating with an Arabic-speaking Israeli military officer in the flying intelligence center.

Shortly thereafter the Tomcats, flying with darkened cockpits and without lights, intercepted the jetliner near the island of Crete. The pilot of the jetliner urgently tried to contact Cairo for new orders, but was prevented from doing so by a U.S. EA-6B, which was jamming his radio communications. Just in case the pilot decided to try to make a run for Athens, Beirut, or some other "friendly" city in the region, the U.S. government sent a strong warning to those governments not the let the aircraft land.

Finally, the desperate EgyptAir pilot capitulated and agreed to follow the warplanes surrounding his aircraft. Meanwhile, the Italians were in the process of cutting a new deal with the Egyptians. According to North, "The Italians promised the Egyptians that Abu Abbas [Mohammed Abbas] would be saved, as he was the only link between the terrorist attack and the PLO chairman [Yasir Arafat]." The Italians would keep the four seajackers, they promised, but permit Abbas to escape. "Once the second deal was in the making," North recalled afterwards, "the Italians ordered their Carabinieri to Sigonella Air Base to prevent us from taking Abu Abbas to the U.S."

The EgyptAir jetliner had just landed when the transporters carrying a combined force of commandos from Delta and SEAL Team 6, commanded by Major General Stiner, touched down on the runway. As the Egyptian plane came to a stop and stairs were rolled toward the door by ground personnel, the black-clad U.S. commandos surrounded the jetliner. General Stiner handed his Uzi submachine gun and pistol to one of his men, and climbed he steps to the Egyptian plane. The plane's door opened, and the American general faced two Egyptian commandos, who pointed their Soviet-made AK-47s at him.

After some discussion—during which an open line to Oliver

North and the White House Situation Room was maintained—the Egyptian commandos laid down their weapons and Mohammed Abbas and the four seajackers were escorted off the aircraft toward a waiting American plane, with its engines running. Suddenly, Italian Carabinieri rushed to the parked U.S. plane and, with weapons leveled, formed a circle around the American commandos and their captives. Stiner was on the radio, describing, as it unfolded, the tense drama to North. It was at this moment, North later recalled, that he "knew it was all over. We were not going to clash with one of our allies over a terrorist."

The U.S. commandos ultimately relented, and permitted the Italians to spirit Abbas and his companions away. The Italian government then allowed Abbas to slip quietly out of Italy on a chartered Yugoslav plane, politely ignoring a U.S. request for his detention and extradition. His four companions, however, were detained by the Italian government and ultimately made to stand trial. Magid al-Molqi, the Palestinian who confessed to the actual murder of Leon Klinghoffer, was given a thirty-year sentence, and two of his confederates were given prison terms of twenty-four and fifteen years. A fourth seajacker was scheduled to be tried separately as a minor. Abbas and two deputies, Ozzudin Badratkan and Ziad el-Omar, were tried in absentia and sentenced to life imprisonment, although the gesture by the court had a hollow ring considering that the Italian government knowingly aided and abetted Abbas's escape. Members of the Klinghoffer family expressed outrage over what they perceived as the light sentences handed down to the terrorists, and the U.S. State Department, in a masterful bit of equivocation, praised the Italians for having convicted the defendants, while at the same time regretting that they were not given tougher sentences.

From the Reagan administration's point of view, the mid-air interception of the *Achille Lauro* pirates was an indisputable triumph. Throughout the nation there was a surge of pride, and the President's approval rate soared to 68 percent in the polls. For North, however, it was, at best, a mixed success. He believed that the Craxi government's cowardly capitulation to the terrorists demonstrated once again that America's European allies could not be counted on in the war against terrorism, and that ultimately the United States would be forced to take even more drastic steps to protect its citizens and property. "It was a piece of art," North reflected sadly, describing the operation. "It was a masterpiece of intelligence work, and there was smooth cooperation with some allies while others chose not to cooperate, fearing terrorist retaliation. The interception was a model of U.S. government agencies working together." He faulted the Italians for their lack of courage, and while the rest of the nation was savoring the triumph, he returned to the drawing board to plan the next U.S. blow against terrorism. Around Washington, the young Marine officer who had toiled for so long in obscurity suddenly became a celebrity of sorts when his role in the daring operation was reported in the press, although some of his critics contend that North was the source of most of the stories. Moreover, at the White House North's star was clearly on the rise; as a result of the triumph he had handed the President, he was given virtually a free hand to carry on the war against terrorists and their state sponsors with as much creativity and energy as he could muster.

"No lieutenant colonel ever had been given as much power— to rewrite U.S. counter-terrorist policy—and to have such a huge impact on our foreign policy," reflected one senior State Department official close to North, who viewed it as "a colossal mistake." In the aftermath of the *Achille Lauro* crisis, the already fragile Italian government coalition collapsed, Egypt's President Hosni Mubarak was publicly embarrassed by the disclosure that he had lied to the United States, and subsequently witnessed his regime shaken by anti-American riots over the loss of national face stemming from the takedown of the EgyptAir jetliner. Mohammed Abbas, the terrorist mastermind, became a hunted man, and has been running ever since.

"The Shores of Tripoli"

Despite North's new powers and expanded portfolio and the setback dealt to international terrorism by the daring seizure of the *Achille Lauro* pirates, terrorism was soon on the rise once again.

Terrorist organizations like Abu Nidal's Black June, Yasir Arafat's Force 17, and Hizballah were involved in a variety of new attacks and operations against Western targets, and nations such as Libya, Syria, and Iran showed little sign of reducing their support of terrorist proxies.

North believed that the only real answer was to strike at the "heart of the beast"—the terrorist-sponsoring states themselves—and make it clear that they would have to pay a significant price for supporting terrorists. Thus, he began to draft detailed contingency plans for striking directly at Libya, the most vulnerable of the state sponsors of terrorism. Unlike Syria, Libya was militarily weak and possessed only a limited air defense system; and unlike Iran, which presented real logistics problems, Libya was readily vulnerable to U.S. military power in the form of the Sixth Fleet and various NATO bases scattered across Europe. To make Libya an even more inviting target, its leader, Colonel Muammar Qaddafi, was a certifiable looney toon with little international support, even in the Islamic bloc. His repeated threats to join the Warsaw Pact had been politely brushed aside by the Soviets, who were eager to maintain some distance from the Colonel's adventurism. The late Egyptian President Anwar Sadat once described Qaddafi as "100 percent sick and possessed of the demon," and former President of Sudan Jaafar Nimeiry was even more direct. According to Nimeiry, Qaddafi has "a split personality—both evil."

North's efforts ultimately resulted in the April 15, 1986, raid on the Libyan capital of Tripoli, the first direct blow by a Western nation victimized by terrorism, other than Israel, against one of terrorism's principal state sponsors. More than two weeks before U.S. Navy and Air Force warplanes roared through the dark skies over Tripoli for 11 minutes and 30 seconds, on March 27 and March 29, 1986, Libyan couriers or classified messages were intercepted and decoded by Western intelligence. The messages originated at the Libyan intelligence headquarters in Tripoli and ordered Libyan intelligence attachés posted in the various "People's Bureaus" around the globe, in a clear and unambiguous manner, to initiate terrorist attacks on

U.S. and other Western targets. Following the interception of the second message, two operational teams were hastily assembled on March 27 at the National Security Council. The first was headed by North, as staff director for NSC counterterrorist operations, and included other NSC staffers and representatives from the CIA, State, Defense, and the FBI. The second team, headed by Deputy National Security Advisor Donald Fortier, was made up of other NSC staff members, including North, and a different set of representatives from State, Defense, and the CIA, but did not include FBI officials.

The task of the first team was to explore options designed to preempt the anticipated terrorist campaign, while the second team was charged with developing options for dealing with the Libyan problem on a long-term basis. According to North, the two teams met on a daily basis, and most of the options that were developed by the two groups were approved in short order by the President. However, few options were ever implemented because events were moving too rapidly.

"Qaddafi's orders were such," North said, "that we had to move very quickly in order to prevent a major disaster." The intercepted Libyan message stated, among other instructions, "Cause maximum casualties to U.S. citizens and other Western people." The message originated in Tripoli under Qaddafi's personal authority, and outlined operational plans for more than ten terrorist attacks.

The planned attacks were designed to be carried out by devoted Palestinian terrorist operators on Libya's payroll and, since not enough proxies could be found, by members of the Libyan intelligence community. "Qaddafi ordered his henchmen to practically go on a manhunt against U.S. citizens and people of other Western nationalities," North explained later. "Let's keep in mind that in the disco explosion, 146 Germans were wounded and the list of casualties included nine nationalities other than the U.S. servicemen and West German citizens." It was later learned that there was also substantial Syrian involvement in the plot, although what form this took is still a matter of dispute.

There was growing concern at the NSC that the Libyan terrorist attacks were imminent, and the problem for the team headed by North was to identify the specific targets before they were hit. Thus, extensive resources were directed at the Libyan People's Bureaus addressed in the intercepted communications. The messages had been sent to People's Bureaus in Europe (East Berlin, Paris, Madrid, and Lisbon), the Middle East, Africa, and the Caribbean. Subsequently, Libyan diplomats in East Berlin informed their headquarters in Tripoli that they had selected a target and were moving to carry out their mission. By Friday, April 6, the NSC team was able to piece together enough of the puzzle to ascertain that the target chosen by the Libyan operatives was a West Berlin bar, disco, or night club frequented by U.S. military personnel. Based on this conclusion, MPs were dispatched throughout West Berlin to pull American personnel out of all nightspots. Only five minutes before MPs would have arrived at the La Belle disco, a powerful bomb ripped through the establishment.

Throughout the night, North stayed in his office, in constant touch with U.S. officials on the scene. The following day, he was ready with an extensive list of counterterrorism measures for consideration by Fortier's group, which was scheduled to meet that afternoon. Present, in addition to Fortier and North, were Deputy Defense Secretary Taft, Deputy Director of Central Intelligence Robert Gates, and two other officials. In addition to reviewing the previous night's attack in West Berlin, the group was provided with conclusive data that Libyan agents were at that moment laying the groundwork for additional terrorist attacks in Paris and Madrid. According to North, it was decided to provide the data to the State Department's top antiterrorism official, Ambassador Robert Oakley, who was on his way to Europe as a Presidential emissary. He, in turn, was instructed to transmit the data secretly to the French and Spanish governments so that they could take appropriate steps. The following Sunday, the President was advised about the steps that were being taken during his regular NSC morning briefing. He approved them, and told those assembled to "try to make the world smaller for the terrorists," a message Oakley was told to convey to the Europeans on his trip.

Ironically, at this exact moment, Qaddafi—perhaps fearing that he had gone too far—initiated a desperate attempt to open secret contacts with the Reagan administration, using a series of semi-official channels and private individuals, including Italian businessmen and oil industry sources. The administration, however, had long before lost all interest in Qaddafi's unorthodox overtures to Washington. "All the messengers and well-wishers were told to lay off," North said. "They were told to tell Qaddafi that he could approach us through Belgian diplomatic channels," the only approved point of contact.

Over the years, Qaddafi had initiated a series of unusual contacts with Washington, the most notorious being through President Jimmy Carter's brother Billy. During the Reagan administration, U.S. Ambassador to the Vatican William A. Wilson, a Presidential crony, made an unauthorized trip to Libya in late March 1985 as part of an on-going private campaign to improve U.S.-Libyan relations. More than a year before, Wilson had quietly solicited Robert Keith Gray, Chairman of Washington's largest government relations firm, to meet with Libyan representatives concerning the development of a multimillion-dollar PR campaign designed to improve Libya's image in the United States. Gray had met with various Libyan emissaries since his firm had first opened its doors in 1981, but nothing had ever come of the various contacts. Wilson was ultimately forced out of the administration in May 1986, after his personal diplomatic efforts on behalf of one of the world's most notorious governments became public.

The administration rejected Qaddafi's overtures not only because it had conclusive knowledge of pending Libyan-sponsored terrorist attacks, but also because U.S. intelligence had uncovered a secret Libyan plot to "buy" American hostages in Lebanon from the Shiite terrorist group Hizballah. "We have solid intelligence that Qaddafi was trying to buy the six American hostages held in Lebanon, from Hizballah terrorists that were holding them captive," North contended. He said that Qaddafi had offered the Hizballah $100 million for the six Americans and another $50 million for the French hostages they were holding. Most of the hostages were imprisoned in a four-story building located near one of the runways at the Beirut International Airport, in cells two floors below the ground. The building also housed various Hizballah families on the upper levels. In order to block Qaddafi's offer of cash in exchange for the hostages, said North, in April 1986 "the U.S. has moved to free the hostages." He refused to elaborate on the details of the U.S. countermove at that time, but it is evident today that secret contacts with Iran were well under way and that North hoped they would deliver the American hostages from Libya's grasp.

It was evident to North and other administration planners that the La Belle disco bombing had been simply the opening salvo to the new terrorist offensive ordered by Qaddafi in late March. In terms of heading off further violence, North explained, "We were running out of time and working against the ticking terror clock." While racing to block the planned terrorist campaign, North knew that protective measures were not enough and that the time was rapidly approaching when the U.S. would have to launch preemptive military strikes against terrorists and their state sponsors like Libya.

On Wednesday, April 9, during an NSC meeting in the Oval Office, the President was provided with additional information on the planned Libyan terrorist campaign. After listening to all of the reports, the President concluded: "The evidence is irrefutable. It is conclusive. We have to move to stop them from carrying out those terror operations."

In early April, the NSC planning team was still exploring the use of Navy SEALs against selected targets in Tripoli and Benghazi. But the Joint Chiefs of Staff (JCS) rejected the idea from the very outset, raising the specter of unnecessary casualties and possible prisoners.[18] Despite North's own reservations, his team, in response, came up with the idea of using USAF B-52 bombers, or even cruise missiles, against targets in Libya. This also was rejected by the JCS, who opted, instead, for a three-carrier task force and the use of Naval air power against Qaddafi.

Although the decision had not yet been finalized as to whether air force F-111s would also be used in the raid, the decision to ferry the necessary aircraft to Britain had already been made.

North, for his part, wanted to employ surgical means to hit Qaddafi. The JCS, on the other hand, wanted simply to repeat the successful strategy employed in the March skirmishes for the Gulf of Sidra, in which U.S. warplanes attacked Libyan patrol boats and land-based radars, and the 1981 sorties in which U.S. F-14s shot down two Libyan fighter-bombers over the disputed waters. Try as he might, North also failed to win agreement on using a SEAL team to infiltrate Libya to plant or project homing devices during the raid capable of guiding the so-called "smart" bombs that would be dropped to their targets. Had one of the laser projectors been secretly positioned on the grounds of the Azzizia Barracks, where Qaddafi lived, he might not have survived the attack, and the number of civilian casualties might have been reduced. The debate over which weapons and military units to use caused a split between the JCS and the uniformed services on one side, and North and the NSC staff, buttressed by Bill Casey and the intelligence community, on the other side. After a heated exchange of views between the NSC staff and the Pentagon, the President sided with his military advisers, and the issue was put to rest.

While all this was going on, the intelligence community, under the personal direction of Bill Casey, was busy collecting the necessary data on the targets that had been selected. Satellite pictures were assembled, and intensified air reconnaissance was authorized over Libya. Armed with specific questions, U.S. intelligence agents conducted extensive debriefing sessions with Libyan exiles in the West and polled its network of anti-Qaddafi Libyan dissidents. All of the worthwhile intelligence gathered was incorporated into the operation intelligence report provided to the Air Force and Navy pilots. "The DCI [Director of Central Intelligence] is very proud of the clandestine intelligence gathering operations he was running with respect to Libya," observed North. "Those operations made the air strike possible and he has a right to be proud."

In truth, the most critical intelligence, of a real-time nature, came from another source, and it was this intelligence in the final analysis that actually permitted the raid to take place. Once again it was Oliver North who was responsible for handling this source of information and channeling the critical data to the Pentagon Situation Room, which transmitted it on to the Sixth Fleet and the F-111 pilots, already en route to their targets.

Several days before the raid, the Israelis became aware of the Sixth Fleet's high state of readiness. As North's close working relationship with Israeli intelligence had continued to grow and was being reinforced by the secret Iran Initiative, he was not surprised when a top Israeli official offered to be of assistance in providing up-to-date intelligence about Libya. At the same time, the commander of the Israeli signals monitoring service, the Israeli equivalent of the National Security Agency, suggested to NSA that it establish open secure lines between Fort Meade, NSA's headquarters, and the unit's headquarters in Israel. Although deeply concerned about possible security breaches, the United States accepted the Israeli offer.

On April 9, the Israelis offered to position their RC-135 spy plane clone over the Mediterranean, opposite the Libyan coast, for close monitoring operations. North recommended that Washington accept the offer and reluctantly NSA agreed, for it was taking the spy agency between four and ten hours to translate and evaluate the vast amount of communications data— radio signals, telephone conversations, military messages—that it was gathering from Libya. And this did not include the further delay involved in forwarding important data through intelligence channels to the Pentagon and the White House, and then on to the Sixth Fleet and other consumers.

Now responding to the semi-official request from the United States, the Israelis kept a spy plane continuously off the Libyan coast from April 10 onward. Two planes were used, operating on twelve-hour shifts. The Arabic-speaking Israeli technicians were able to listen to the Libyans and evaluate the information on the spot. It was thereupon transmitted in real time to Tel

Aviv and from there on to NSA and the White House. As it was received at Fort Meade, it was checked against intelligence the United States had collected from its own sources, and generally verified within a few hours.

Realizing that even short delays, calculated in minutes, could be critical during the actual onset of hostilities, the White House and Pentagon authorized North to approach his Israeli contacts—presumably the intelligence channel established during the TWA 847 crisis—on April 13, two days before the raid, and suggest that they transmit time-critical intelligence directly to the White House. The Israelis quickly agreed with the proposal, and opened a secure line to the White House Situation Room, where the information from the spy planes was coming in.

This proved to be a crucial bit of foresight. During the late evening hours of April 14 and early morning hours of April 15, as the F-111s were bearing down on Tripoli and the Sixth Fleet was positioning its A-6s and F/A-18s on their carrier catapults, the Pentagon asked the Israelis if the flow of data could be rushed even more. The White House Situation Room needed to know the state of alertness of the Libyan air defense systems, the whereabouts of Muammar Qaddafi, and the readiness of the Syrian MiG pilots stationed at Libyan airfields. The transmission of raw intelligence data was, by this time, pointless, since there was no time to interpret it; the White House needed precise real-time data. Once again, the Israelis readily assented to the request and opened a direct secure line from the spy plane overflying the Mediterranean to the office of their military intelligence (AMAN) chief, Major General Ehud Barak.

As data from the spy plane reached his desk, General Barak immediately passed it on to the White House or to the Israeli intelligence attaché, Colonel Moshe Zur, at Israel's embassy in Washington. Colonel Zur kept an open line to the Pentagon's war room, and would read the information to the DIA senior duty officer, who would then send it out to the Sixth Fleet and the F-111 squadron.

"The system really worked," a senior American intelligence officer later observed. Although the on-board computers on the

F-111s were already set with respect to their targets in Tripoli, the data collected by the Israelis turned out to be extremely important to the success of the raid. However, it created some internal problems within the Israeli government. Israel's Institute for Intelligence and Special Tasks (Mossad) is supposed to have sole responsibility for that country's ties to foreign intelligence services. Apparently no one in the Mossad, including its Director, Nachum Admoni, was aware of the private arrangement that General Barak had made with North and the Americans.

The April 9 NSC meeting had concluded without the issuance of an Executive Order for the Libyan air raid. The President's decision to proceed was described later by a participant in the meeting as "tentative but not decisive." The NSC meeting approved sending trouble-shooter Vernon Walters to Europe to meet with U.S. allies. He was expected to inform them that the U.S. was preparing a military operation against Libya and that the Reagan administration was determined to take decisive action.

After the NSC meeting, the two NSC staff teams met and prepared a target list. Five targets were selected and quickly approved. First on the list was the Azzizia Barracks compound, which housed command and communications centers for the Libyan military and intelligence communities. It also contained Muammar Qaddafi's personal quarters, and was where his family lived. The famous bedouin tent where Qaddafi often slept, the only heat being provided by glowing coals in the sand, was also located within the compound. The compound was protected by Qaddafi's praetorian guard.

The second target on the list was Libyan military aircraft parked at the Tripoli International Airport. Libya's Soviet-built IL-76s were used to transport troops to Chad and keep them supplied. The United States and France had been opposing Libyan designs on Chad for more than a decade. Third on the target list was the Benghazi army barracks, which provided Qaddafi with an alternative command post and praetorian guard in the Benghazi area. The fourth target was the Sidi Bilal naval port facility, the location of a naval commando center used to train Libyan and Palestinian terrorists. The Benina airfield, the base for Libya's MiG-23 interceptors that had to be neutralized for security reasons, was the final target.

With added assistance from the up-to-date intelligence being provided by the Israelis, several members of the NSC staff felt that there was a strong probability that "we will get Qaddafi himself." While there was concern that Qaddafi's death not appear as an assassination, but rather fate—being in the wrong place at the wrong time—the replacement of the Qaddafi regime was clearly the Reagan administration's chief unspoken goal in conducting the raid. Whether Qaddafi was killed in the actual raid or whether he was toppled by a coup triggered by the attack made no difference. What was important was that the Libyan government be dissuaded from using terrorism as an instrument of national policy, and if the best way to achieve that result was the removal of the existing regime in Tripoli, then so be it.

After being consulted, the Thatcher government approved the use of the U.S. Strategic Air Command base in Great Britain for the launching of the medium-range F-111 bombers, which had to be refueled en route to Libya. Prime Minister Thatcher and her top aides were apparently unenthusiastic about the raid, but went along with the U.S. request, both to repay Washington for its support during the Falklands War and because of the surprising opposition voiced by the British government to the Grenada invasion, which later turned out to have been predicated on poor intelligence and misinformation. One NSC staff source indicated that the British government had been consulted only as a courtesy. "There was no need to ask the approval of the British government," contended the source, since a secret appendix to the U.S.-British defense agreement reportedly authorizes the U.S. government to use planes stationed on British soil to defend American interests. The secret appendix was not invoked in order to lessen criticism of Mrs. Thatcher's Tory government, which was already under fire from critics for allegedly being too subservient to the Reagan administration.

On Thursday, April 10, North and various Navy and Air Force planners completed the final political and military review in advance of the raid, recommending that the attack be carried out at 2:00 A.M. Tripoli time. This decision, North later confirmed, was predicated on new intelligence information obtained from the Israelis on the readiness of Libyan air defenses. It had been learned that the last Libyan duty officer left his post at midnight, whereupon the entire Libyan air defense system was shut down. The only threat that remained came from Syrian Mig-21 pilots who manned the Libyan first interceptor squadron on a twenty-four-hour-a-day basis. The Syrian interceptors, however, were not operationally independent and therefore could not engage in an enemy attack without prior clearance. Each of their sorties had to be cleared in advance with the Libyan supreme command or with Qaddafi personally. Based on that information, said North, "We were rather sure that at 2:00 A.M. it would take the Syrians hours before they could obtain clearance for an interception sortie."

Although the actual date of the attack had not yet been set and was awaiting final Presidential action, by April 10 "everything was in place and all systems were ready to go," observed a JCS source. When the National Security Council met the following day to select a date for the raid it was decided to postpone the operation, based on recommendations from Bill Casey and North. The decision to delay action was taken mainly because of the DCI's insistence that more time be given to pull his agents—"who risked their lives for us"—out of Libya or permit them time to reach more secure locations in country. Despite the subsequent delay, not all of the CIA's agents were able to get out of Libya before the raid, although there is no evidence that any of them were later killed or captured.

For his part, North wanted to postpone the operation for a few additional days in order to obtain more exact intelligence from NSA and the Israeli spy plane concerning the targets that had been selected. In addition, North was concerned that "too many operational details were being kicked around and too many administration officials and press people were involved in irresponsible speculation" about the possibility of U.S. military action against Libya. "Those who leaked and talked publicly about sensitive intelligence and speculated about the military operation," North argued, "jeopardized the lives of U.S. servicemen and U.S. citizens overseas."

The JCS also had some second thoughts. "The Chairman, Admiral Crowe, expressed his concern for his people's ability to get in and out safely and asked for more firepower, more ships and more planes in the vicinity of the battle zone," North recalled. The JCS had originally agreed to carry out the raid with the ships and aircraft at hand, hoping to achieve tactical surprise over the Libyans. But once Crowe and his advisors became aware of the security breaches that had occurred—which, in North's words, "would have cost us the lives of too many pilots"—they insisted that the raid be postponed until certain preconditions could be met: 1) that it could be demonstrated that there had been no compromise of information relating to the timing of the raid and the list of targets, 2) that the firepower available for the mission be upgraded, and 3) that Casey's intelligence operatives in Libya were safe. Once those conditions were satisfied, Crowe and the JCS believed the operation should be launched without further delay.

On Saturday, April 12, Casey informed those gathered for a Saturday meeting at the White House, who by this time were working around the clock, that all his people were safe. It later turned out that this information was not accurate and that several CIA operatives were trapped in Libya; it took them some days to get out of the country, but all managed to do so safely. Meanwhile, the delay had worked to the advantage of the planners inasmuch as the media had begun to downplay the chances of a military strike against Libya, thus making surprise more likely. The extra time had also resulted in the collection of far more precise data regarding the targets and the exact location of Qaddafi and other senior Libyan officials. Thus, "at that Saturday meeting," North later observed, "we recommended that the air strike be carried out on Monday night, April 14, or on Tuesday morning, April 15, according to Libyan local time."

When the President returned from Camp David on Sunday

afternoon, April 13, the NSC was convened. The President was briefed by the National Security Advisor regarding preparations for the raid, following which he presented Reagan with the various options and a draft of the final operational plans. No objections came from any of the NSC members assembled. Then Admiral Crowe provided a short briefing on the final military plan of action, and the President inquired if his explicit request for a mechanism to recall the planes short of their targets had been implemented. Assured that the command post maintained the ability to abort the operation up to ten minutes before the attack was scheduled to occur, or 6:50 P.M. Eastern time, the President appeared to be satisfied with the preparations. As the final details were being discussed, Reagan instructed aides to prepare a meeting, scheduled for the following afternoon, with Congressional leaders. Around 4:00 P.M., the President gave final approval to the operation, but not before making some angry comments concerning leaks that had occurred, which he regarded as endangering the safety of the entire mission. The Executive Order drafted for the operation called for an air strike against ''terror targets inside Libya'' on Monday night, April 14, 1986, in accordance with an operational plan (code name ''El Dorado Canyon'') recommended by the NSC and the Pentagon.

Immediately after the meeting, Admiral Crowe, using a secure line, informed the Commander-in-Chief of the Sixth Fleet, Admiral Kelso, of the decision. The carrier task force thereupon initiated a series of maneuvers designed to lose the Soviet tail that is their constant shadow.

Monday, April 14, seemed to most a normal day at the White House. Only a few people sensed the tense and unusual atmosphere produced by the unfolding events. The President met with Congressional leaders at 4:15 P.M., and they were fully briefed as to the impending raid. The F-111s were already in the air and the President told the assembled members of Congress that if anyone demurred, he would recall the planes at once. No one voiced any objections, so the air strike went forward. Before they left, members of Congress were warned by the President to be extremely careful with their statements to the press. ''Whatever you say to the press outside,'' one participant recalls the

President as saying, "will affect the lives of the U.S. pilots." Despite the President's admonition, however, the Majority Leader of the House of Representatives, Jim Wright, and Senate Minority Leader Robert Byrd told the reporters that surrounded them after the meeting that the President was expected to address the nation that evening at 9:00. To anyone reading between the lines, it was clear that something big was afoot, and since Libya was the issue dominating the headlines, an unexpected Presidential address to the nation could only mean one thing. Despite the fact that the remarks by the two Congressional leaders set off a flurry of speculation in the media, the Libyans apparently did not get wind of it prior to the attack, or were unable to understand its implications.

As the meeting broke up, the White House Situation Room was already fully staffed, and members took their seats around the table. At 6:53 P.M., Eastern time, the first F-111 crossed the Libyan coastline. The F-111s were flying into the Libyan desert in order to wheel around and attack their targets from the south. At precisely 7:00 P.M., the Sixth Fleet launched its fighter-bombers. Five minutes later, CNN broadcast the first news of the attack from Tripoli, and White House spokesman Larry Speakes was directed to meet with the White House press corps in the press room. He changed his tie and dutifully rushed to the press room, where members of the media were clamoring for information and comments. At 7:11:30 P.M., the attack on Libyan targets were broken off, and all of the planes reported to be leaving the area.

The mood in the Situation Room was one of jubilation. National Security Advisor John Poindexter was moving around the room shaking hands with his staff. Upstairs in the Oval Office President Reagan was preparing his address to the nation. North, who was not participating in the Situation Room celebration, was continuing to monitor the returning warplanes, and the first reports that one of the planes might have gone down were beginning to reach him. Soon it was confirmed that one of the eighteen F-111s was unaccounted for, and North informed the President.

In retrospect, the joint Navy–Air Force military operation

aimed at removing Qaddafi from the scene and destroying key targets in Tripoli and Benghazi turned into a far more complicated mission than originally conceived. What initially was viewed by planners as a preemptive counterterrorist strike was changed by the Joint Chiefs and the Pentagon into an elaborate air raid involving the massive use of U.S. military power against highly sophisticated targets in the dead of night. While some of the Navy pilots had combat experience, none of the Air Force crews had ever engaged in combat before.

From a strictly military point of view, the main difficulties stem from the decision to carry out the attack at night, which added an additional complication to an already complex mission. The planners had settled on a night attack because they were fearful of early detection of the F-111s by Soviet satellites and submarine patrols. This forced the F-111 and A-6 and A-7 pilots to carry out their bombing runs without "eye contact with the targets," and increased the likelihood of misses and target misidentification. The decision to attack at night was also predicated on the desire to avoid combat with the Libyan Air Force during the actual bombing operation. The Libyan Air Force is notorious for its reluctance to operate at night, and the U.S. planners were confident that a night attack would minimize the chances of a direct encounter with Libyan interceptors.

The night attack also increased the demands on the electronic sweeping planes that guided the approaching warplanes to their targets, since the attacking planes were forced to maintain a fixed approach, relying solely on their flight and navigation instruments, and their laser guiding and infrared target identification systems. The decision to launch a night attack also forced the USAF to expose the extraordinary capabilities of the EF-111 Ravens to the watchful eyes of the Soviet Navy.

Other problems were a direct result of the decision to use both Navy warplanes from the Sixth Fleet and Air Force bombers based in Great Britain, involving nearly 50 planes over the target areas and another 40 tankers. The planners were therefore forced to coordinate the arrival of the F-111s, which had taken a circuitous 2,800-nautical-mile route because France and Spain had refused to grant them overflight rights, with the attacking aircraft catapulted from the heaving decks of the U.S. aircraft carriers in the Mediterranean. Instead of a quick in-out Navy air attack, the joint Navy–Air Force operation demanded split-second coordination, required the highly complicated mid-air refueling of the F-111s at night, and subjected the F-111 crews to unacceptable levels of stress and fatigue.

A daylight attack would have deployed only the carrier-launched planes from the Sixth Fleet and reduced the built-in risk of failure. So why were the F-111s employed? Sources within the Joint Chiefs of Staff admit that the decision to go for a joint operation involving both Navy and Air Force contingents can be attributed in large part to rivalries within the armed services. The Navy could have done the job, but the Air Force wanted to share the glory and test some of its newly acquired weapons systems.

In addition, Admiral Crowe had demanded more firepower and flexibility over the battle zone. Crowe's concerns were based on the fear that the situation might possibly escalate into a major confrontation that could exceed the Sixth Fleet's military capabilities. Crowe and his advisors reasoned that a scenario could develop in which Navy interceptors would be so busy defending the fleet and the returning A-6s and A-7s that the Sixth Fleet would have insufficient air power to launch a second bombing attack aimed at neutralizing the Libyan Air Force. Moreover, he warned that the initial wave of attackers might lose planes, compelling the fleet to engage in major rescue operations to save survivors. The addition of a third carrier or the introduction of different armaments on the Navy planes would provide the cushion needed, Crowe maintained.

Even given such operational considerations, the deployment of the F-111s is still difficult to defend. According to North, if the air arm of the Sixth Fleet had had better armament for the bombing mission, it could have done the job and more than likely "saved us the embarrassment of hitting many civilian targets and causing unnecessary casualties."

Despite public pronouncements by Defense Department and

other administration officials expressing satisfaction with the accuracy and results of the bombing operation, others were not so favorably impressed. After studying satellite photos, a senior intelligence official admitted that the "final results were rather poor." Few planes, it turned out, actually hit their precise targets. The Air Force planes missed the Libyan intelligence headquarters, which serves as the actual command and control center for Libyan-backed terrorist operations. Located between the Swiss and French embassies, the intelligence/state security complex was not hit, but the French embassy did sustain damage.

Another close miss was the Azzizia Barracks. The F-111s were expected to turn the military installation, where Qaddafi lives and works, "into dust," While the Air Force was instructed to assign "enough planes to the Azzizia Barracks" to turn the facility "into dust," it did not happen. While some bombs did hit the barracks, most did not, and Qaddafi escaped serious injury. Apparently the barracks was targeted by six F-111s. Three planes dropped their bomb loads on what they believed to be the Azzizia Barracks, causing the damage that was reported. Two other planes suffered from malfunctions and could not identify the target and, consequently, jettisoned their bombs over water. The sixth plane missed the target altogether.

During the many hours of meetings and the interminable planning sessions preceding the raid, the question of whether Qaddafi himself was a target came up repeatedly. Whenever the question was brought up, the answer was always the same: "We are not trying to kill Qaddafi." However, it was also frequently noted that if Qaddafi were killed during the air raid, no one would shed any tears. "We did not try to kill Qaddafi," North maintained. "There was no Executive Order to kill him, nor was there an Administrative Directive to go after him. If he was killed during the process, 'c'est la vie,' but there was no deliberate intention to kill him." In an internal document that was prepared during the many planning sessions and discussions prior to the raid, the NSC describes the rationale for targeting the Azzizia Barracks: "This facility contains command and communications centers for use in conducting terrorist attacks and other subversive activities," states the document. "The compound is heavily guarded by elite Jamahiriyah troops, Qaddafi's personal guard. The target was selected in an effort to disrupt Qaddafi's ability to stage additional terrorist attacks and to vividly demonstrate Qaddafi's limited capacity for response to his adversaries, who oppose his terrorist and subversive activities."

As a counterterrorist preemptive strike, the mission must be judged, to some extent, a failure, since neither Qaddafi nor his regime was eliminated. Despite exact intelligence and the highly sophisticated weapons used in the attack, the F-111s sent against the Azzizia Barracks either failed to drop their bombs or, for the most part, missed the target. And while there has been some diminishment of Libyan-sponsored terrorism following the raid, it probably is a result more of internal disarray than any formal decision by Libya's leadership to abandon its support of terrorism as an instrument of national policy.

Nevertheless, as a political counterterrorist operation, the raid was highly successful. The United States turned the tables on Libya's strongman: the hunter became the hunted. The raid shook the Qaddafi regime to its very foundations; and although the Libyan dictator survived, he immediately went into hiding in the Libyan desert. Qaddafi reportedly was wounded during the confusion in the wake of the air raid, but few details are known about the attack. Whether it was a disenchanted Libyan Army officer, a hired assassin, or a crazed bodyguard is still unknown, but apparently Qaddafi became so paranoid that he temporarily moved his military capital to Sabhah, some 420 miles into the Libyan desert on the edge of the Sahara.

Two days after the attack, on Wednesday, April 17, fighting was reported at two Libyan military camps, and the situation became so bad that the Libyan Air Force was called in to strafe rebellious army units. Despite the fond hopes of Bill Casey and Oliver North, the mutiny within the Libyan Army was brutally suppressed with a high loss of life. Although none of the military uprisings was successful, it was clear that Qaddafi's grip on the Libyan military and intelligence establishments had been weakened. Most important of all, the United States had proved its readiness and ability to strike, far from its own borders, at the state sponsors of terrorism—a message that surely did not go unrecognized in Tehran and Damascus, not to mention Tripoli. The American raid was also aimed at Washington's timorous European allies, as a clear demonstration that the United States was prepared to go it alone, if necessary, to protect its citizens and national interests. It was an unmistakable warning to the Europeans that the United States would consider additional military operations, wherever and against whomever it deemed appropriate, unless they began to cooperate more fully on measures for combating terrorism short of the use of force.

Aftermath of Operation "El Dorado Canyon"

Despite the fluidity of the situation in Libya during the immediate aftermath of the U.S. bombing raid, Qaddafi was able to exact a degree of revenge on the United States and Great Britain. One day after the raid, two British and one American hostage were executed in cold blood in West Beirut. According to North: "The Libyan military attaché in Damascus, Major Halifa, was personally responsible for the purchase and handling of the three hostages murdered in West Beirut on April 16." North also said that it was Halifa who actually killed the three men.

The three hostages were being held by a Hizballah splinter group controlled and financed by Qaddafi. A note found with the bodies of the slain men indicated that they had been killed in retaliation for the U.S. raid on Libya. Initially it was believed that all three men were British citizens: Leigh Douglas, a lecturer at the American University in Beirut, Philip Padfield, director of a private language school in West Beirut, and freelance journalist Alec Collett. Later, it was learned that the body believed to be Collett's was in reality the remains of American writer Peter Kilburn, a 60-year-old librarian at the American University in Beirut (AUB).

According to intelligence reports, Major Halifa received direct instructions from the Libyan intelligence headquarters in Tripoli to travel to Beirut and see to it that the three hostages were killed. Halifa made appropriate arrangements with Syrian authorities and traveled to Beirut in a two-car convoy, arriving three hours after his departure. The first car, a British-made Land Rover, was loaded with Syrian security personnel and facilitated the movement of the Libyan military attaché through Syrian-controlled territory, after which it returned to Damascus. The second car, also a Land Rover, was equipped with radio telephones, and protected by Libyan security guards, who took Major Halifa, dressed in civvies, to his destination in West Beirut.

After meeting with the Hizballah leaders, it was agreed that the executions would take place that evening on a dark, narrow, deserted street in the Shiite section, Chiyah e-Salum, of West Beirut. In order to confirm the deed to his superiors, Halifa brought a camera to the execution site so that pictures could be taken of the actual murders. After the three men were killed, their bodies were dumped on a pile of garbage, and Major Halifa traveled to offices rented by the Libyans in West Beirut to make certain that local reporters were notified of the location of the bodies. The following morning, the energetic young Libyan military attaché was on his way back to Damascus, and two days later he left Syria for Libya.

The murder of Peter Kilburn was particularly painful for North, since he had come very close to securing the release of the quiet American staff librarian from AUB. North and other U.S. officials hoped to win Kilburn's freedom with a multi-million-dollar ransom payment made with chemically treated bills that would disintegrate within approximately 72 hours, thereby denying the kidnappers any reward for their efforts. Before being sold to the Libyans, Kilburn had been held by a band of brigands whose only interest was money, not politics. The initial approach to ransom Kilburn had been made to the U.S. government by a Canadian citizen of Armenian descent, who offered to be of assistance in concluding a deal with the kidnappers. Authorities ultimately established that the Canadian was not acting as a disinterested citizen, but was part of the kid-napping ring, and therefore they made contingency plans to arrest him once the transaction had been completed. The final exchange was delayed, although the exact circumstances are not known. North blamed the CIA for not moving rapidly enough prior to the April 15 air raid on Libya.

The killings in Beirut were not the only act of revenge. In the weeks that followed, one American diplomat was shot in Aden, South Yemen, and another in Khartoum, the capital of Sudan. In the first two months following the raid, the United States experienced eleven terrorist attacks that plausibly could be linked to the action against Libya.

The American Hostages in Lebanon

The failure to rescue Kilburn was one of many setbacks in the ongoing effort to secure the release of American hostages in Lebanon. No problem consumed more of North's time during his last two years on the NSC staff, with the possible exception of the effort to keep the Contras resupplied. North generally regarded the hostages, with the exception of CIA man Buckley and those who were members of the media, as a group of addle-brained do-gooders who had failed to exercise good judgment and prudence, or wrongly believed that their "love for the Arabs" would render them secure in a city that was coming apart at the seams, and as a result found themselves in serious trouble. Moreover, it was his belief that the hostages had put their nation in an awkward position because of their egocentrism and arrogance, and he railed at the media for its willingness to portray U.S. foreign policy in the region as itself hostage to the hostage issue.

What changed North's position on the issue was the deep con-cern evinced by the President over the plight of the hostages. The families of the hostages put a great deal of pressure on the administration through the media to do something, and Reagan was touched by their pleas. Later, North would remark bitterly of attacks on the President and the administration by some of the relatives of the hostages, saying that "not a day goes by that the President does not ask about the hostages." Reagan directed the NSC to do everything in his power to secure the release of the captive Americans, and North dutifully threw himself into the task with his usual vigor. He met frequently with family members and tried to assure them that everything possible was being done, although he could not share most of the details regarding those efforts without risking security leaks. Nevertheless, Carol Weir, wife of hostage Reverend Ben Weir, later observed that North was the "most human" person she dealt with in the administration.

North explored countless channels in his quest to free the hostages, and virtually all of them were dead ends. At one point, he even set aside $2.5 million of the profits from the U.S.-Iran arms sales to fund various secret joint operations with Israel aimed at securing the release of the hostages. The funds were intended to underwrite meetings and travel, the payment of bribes, and possibly even the abduction of Hizballah terrorists who could later be traded for the hostages. So far as is known, most of the money was not spent.

Finally, North turned to Iran for assistance, since the various Shiite factions holding Western hostages in Lebanon all took direct orders from, or at least were strongly influenced by, Tehran. The secret diplomacy with Iran was already under way, involving direct links to the Iranian faction headed by Speaker of the Iranian Parliament Ali Akbar Hashemi Rafsanjani. It was by this means that North and his colleagues were ultimately able to secure the release of four hostages: Jerry Levin, Reverend Ben Weir, Father Lawrence Jenco, and David Jacobsen. There is evidence that they were on the verge of obtaining the release of Thomas Sutherland and Terry Anderson when the first reports began surfacing on the secret U.S.-Iran dialogue.

North is believed to have welcomed, and perhaps even encouraged, efforts by Church of England envoy Terry Waite to get involved in negotiations aimed at freeing the remaining hostages inasmuch as it provided a "cover story" that would explain the release of the others. Indeed, the administration was quite happy to give Waite credit for the progress that was being made, although in reality it was being purchased at the price of American arms shipments to Iran. Today, Waite himself is a hostage in Lebanon.

Olliemania

In an age that hungers for heroes, in the summer of 1987 many Americans felt that they had found one in Oliver North. Like the Biblical Daniel entering the lion's den, he stood alone, his Marine uniform bristling with decorations and battle ribbons, before a special committee of the House and Senate convened to investigate the so-called Iran/Contra matter. The Senate caucus room was packed to the rafters with spectators and reporters. Photojournalists scuttled around the witness table like crabs, jockeying for position, their cameras clicking noisily away. Blazing television lights bathed the scene in an unnatural brightness, as if seeking to chase away the shadows that had for so long cloaked the witness. As the cameras transmitted North's image to a fascinated country, the members of Congress, seated like inquisitors on a two-tiered dais, glared down at him as if he were a Mafia don instead of a former National Security Council staffer who had lost his way trying to serve his president and nation.

In the spirit of the poet Emerson, who said that his life was not an apology but a spectacle, North told his story, what he described as "the good, the bad, and the ugly," rarely mincing words, at turns riveting, melodramatic, contrite, humorous, and spellbinding. Prior to his testimony, the TV networks and most national publications had already written his political obituary. *Time* called it "Hanging Ollie Out to Dry." A week later North was on the cover of *Time,* and this time the headline said it all: "Ollie Takes the Hill: The Fall Guy Becomes a Folk Hero." His picture was also featured on the covers of *Newsweek* and *U.S. News & World Report,* making it a clean sweep of the news magazines, and within days at least three special publications devoted solely to North and his testimony were on newsstands across the nation. In the wake of his dramatic testimony, the *National Enquirer* reported that 52,912 readers called the tabloid's "900" telephone number in response to the question "Would you vote for Oliver North for President?" and said "yes" by a landslide 15-to-1 margin. Olliemania swept across America. "Ollieluja: Keep North and Fire the Congress," read one bumper sticker.

The *Washington Post*'s Mary McGrory demanded to know, "Who'll Break the Colonel's Spell?" During his testimony, Capitol Hill was inundated with more than 150,000 telegrams of support, the second largest response to a public event in modern times. By July 23, his defense fund had soared to $1.276 million in voluntary contributions. And by early December 1987, it had reached $3.1 million, with a thousand letters a week still pouring in.

No public relations creation, Oliver North was "the real thing," and whether one viewed him as a hero or a villain, it was clear in the aftermath of his testimony that he was assuming larger-than-life proportions. Today he is an icon of our popular culture, one of those overnight sensations that come along every so often in America. So pervasive is his notoriety that he has even become grist for popular comic strips. He has been satirized in "Doonesbury" and in Berke Breathed's "Bloom County," where character Steve Dallas "talks like Ollie North" to get his woman in the mood for lovemaking.

Oliver North tee-shirts were, for a while, a staple of street vendors, right up there with the Pope John Paul II tee-shirts and ashtrays, and are still advertised in the classified sections of some magazines. There is even an $80 Oliver North commemorative coin. Two Washington entrepreneurs, moreover, report that they sold 1,500 buttons, for $3 each, bearing the Colonel's picture and the legend: "An American hero. Duty, honor, country." One of the orders they received was from North's devoted secretary, Fawn Hall. Speaking of Fawn, her picture adorns another button with the caption: "Secretary for the Defense of Lt/Col Oliver North."[19]

People magazine gave North's picture—along with those of other notables like David Letterman, Diane Sawyer, and the presidential busts on Mt. Rushmore—a Tammy Faye Bakker makeover, complete with false eyelashes, heavy mascara, and face powder. North's face was also fair game in another *People* magazine piece where a celebrity dentist from Beverly Hills volunteered his solution to the pressing national problem of the gaps between his teeth. And if further testimony of North's star status was needed, impressionist Rich Little does his own version of Oliver North on his latest record album.

North was even invited to give a send-off speech to the Super Bowl–bound Washington Redskin football team in January 1988. He told the team: "The only thing that man or God could ask of you is to do your very best and you'll be proud of yourself."[20] For their part, the team responded with a chant of, "Ollie, Ollie."

North was satirized in 1987 at Washington's venerable Gridiron Club dinner. To the tune of "Hello, Dolly," the chorus sang:

> Hello, Ollie
> Well, hello Ollie
> It's so nice to have you here where you belong
> You're looking swell, Ollie.

And North replies:

> I'm no Nero, I'm a hero,
> I did nothing wrong.
> I found these nice mullahs
> Paying top dullahs,
> Read a line from Reagan's
> Scripture now and then.
> Piece of cake, fellas
> Just for Freedom's sake, fellas,
> I would love to do it all again.

To which the chorus responds:

> Oh, no, Ollie,
> Oh, no, no, Ollie,
> That is not what we had in mind.
> So take the stand, Ollie
> Tell the story of your glory
> Cov'ring your behind.

Every detail of North's life has been ferreted out in an avalanche of newspaper articles and magazine profiles, and throughout much of 1987 his picture regularly graced the cover of the *National Enquirer* and the other supermarket "rags," right up there with Sly Stallone and Elizabeth Taylor. The *Enquirer* also traced his family roots, and even did a six-page spread on him at one point covering such dramatic topics as "We Used to Razz Him—He Was Too Shy to Ask the Girls Out," "Fearless Ollie Won 2 Medals—He Led His Men Through Hell & Back," and "Ollie Could Make $35 Million if He Cashed in on His Fame." The *Enquirer* even held an "Oliver North look-alike contest." In case you were wondering, the contest was won by an ex-Marine from Hull, Massachusetts, who described his selection as "an honor." *Life,* not to be outdone, scooped all of its rivals by printing the first photograph of Oliver North getting a haircut.

With respect to North's future, *Advertising Age,* the top publication of the ad industry, speculated on North's value as a product pitchman, concluding tongue-in-cheek that he was ideal for Gillette Co.'s Dry Idea deodorant, cole slaw "shredders," and "contra-ceptives." A Wells, Rich, Green executive ruled out Jockey shorts: not enough credibility.[21] A number of television and radio commercials based on the Iran/Contra hearings and featuring North look-alikes/sound-alikes hawked everything from cars to pizzas and records.

In Washington, D.C., you could be photographed standing next to a life-size cardboard cutout of North for five bucks, and the vendor reported that business was brisk. Conservative groups searched through their files for pictures of North that could be recycled in fund-raising pitches, and even the Republican National Committee sought to capitalize on his public appeal in a letter, signed by GOP Chairman Frank J. Fahrenkopf, calling for funds to underwrite a massive lobbying campaign for Contra aid. A flap ensued when Republican Senator Warren B. Rudman, a member of the congressional Iran/Contra panels and one of North's chief antagonists, protested the letter. Fahrenkopf, however, stood his ground, and a GOP spokesman later said that response to the letter had been "very positive."[22]

The Emergency Committee to Support Colonel North's Freedom Fight, a Washington-based group, offers contributors a videotape that "takes you through Oliver North's life from his boyhood in Philmont, N.Y., to his service in Vietnam, to the now famous battle on Capitol Hill." Bold letters invite contributors to "See: The slide show Congress wouldn't let you see. Hear: From the people who know Oliver North best. Vietnam veterans and close friends talk about North's leadership, patriotism and heroism. Feel: The emotion of Col. North's appeal to stop the Soviet Union's attempt to establish a terrorist base in Nicaragua." The offering closes with the assurance that: "This special documentary will be a treasure that your family and friends will cherish for years to come."

On the just plain silly side, North was also the subject of a number of Christmas cards, including one produced by a Chicago company showing North in a stocking cap and captioned, " 'Tis the season to be Ollie." Inside, the card read: "Do not shred until after December 25."

Counterattack

As 1987 drew to a close, North's critics struck back. North and former NSC Advisor John Poindexter won the annual "doublespeak" award from the National Council of Teachers of English, which bestows the award on public figures judged guilty of misusing the English language. North was described as a "Full Metal Jackass" in *Esquire*'s popular "Dubious Achievement Awards" for defending the diversion of money for the Iranian arms sales to the Contras as "a neat idea." The *Washington Post*, frustrated by its inability to lay a hand on the charismatic colonel, gave him an award in its magazine section for the "Best Public Dialogue on the Issue of Lying." This was followed in January 1988 by a *Post* article, illustrated with North's photo, regarding the tenth Joint Service Conference on Professional Ethics, held at the National Defense University. According to the article, the military officers in attendance spent much of their time discussing North's conduct at the NSC, although without reaching any consensus.

A handwriting expert, after examining a page of North's appointment book, concluded "North's handwriting suggests that while he may show toughness, courage, and loyalty, he is devoid of warmth, charity, kindness or love."[23] He went on to suggest that, while North may be "a perfect soldier," he is perhaps "very disturbed." On the other hand, the handwriting expert said that the way North writes his "g's" indicates that he is "not a philanderer . . . He's no Gary Hart."

Conservative "gonzo" journalist P.J. O'Rourke joined the year-end effort to trash North in his reflections on 1987 in *Rolling Stone* magazine. "Ollie North," wrote O'Rourke, "almost got away with destroying America's foreign policy because of his ditzy cuteness and chestful of pretty medals." Even *People* magazine, which had gotten so much mileage from North earlier, delivered up a backhanded compliment by naming him one of "The 25 Most Intriguing People of '87," and then explaining that he was a "one-minute hero . . . whose defiance in a dubious cause finally left an unpleasant aftertaste."[24] Perhaps the unkindest cut of all occurred when the San Francisco firm that manufactured Ollie North dolls announced that it was converting its unsold stock to Mikhail Gorbachev dolls by slapping a new head on the body and replacing the Marine uniform with a well-cut Italian suit.

A number of critical studies of North have appeared, including Ben Bradlee Jr.'s *Guts and Glory: The Rise and Fall of Oliver North,* which was made into a television miniseries. Such books have called into question North's propensity to exaggerate and even lie about himself and his activities, and there is little doubt but that his reputation has been damaged.

North even became a 1988 presidential campaign issue, and candidates—especially Republicans—were challenged by reporters to express their views about him. Wary of the strong public sentiments North still aroused, most waffled, as in the case of 1988 GOP contender Bob Dole, who described North as "a patriot'' but ''not a hero.'' ''I think once he started dealing maybe as an agent for the president,'' said Dole, ''then he over-stepped his bounds, he didn't serve the president well.''[25] Vice President George Bush, whose campaign was haunted by the Iran/Contra issue, continued to praise North as national hero, since ''he stood up there, took the heat.''

Judgment of History

Like all of those who climb too far too fast, Oliver North's fall was made even more poignant because of how far he had come. In the best American tradition, North was a small-town boy from Philmont, New York, who—through a combination of luck, derring-do, and a seemingly limitless capacity for work— had found himself at the seat of American power, the White House, and had made the most of it. He became a modern-day warlord, deftly manipulating the levers of power, the de facto commander of guerrilla armies and the hunter of terrorists, who relished slugging it out with this nation's adversaries in the ''dirty little wars'' and military engagements that dominate this nation's conflict landscape. In retrospect, what is most amazing about North is just how much he was able to accomplish with so few resources. Whether one regards him as a dedicated patriot or a one-man wrecking crew, North clearly was a man of action, not of reflection, who had little patience for endless political debates concerning policy and nuance. To North, the United States is, after all, ''a nation at risk in a dangerous world.''

As to what his future holds, no one can be certain. He was indicted and later convicted on three relatively minor charges as a result of the investigation conducted by Special Counsel Lawrence Walsh and forced to endure a protracted public trial that once again catapulted him back into the limelight. North's supporters regard his prosecution as nothing short of a ''witch hunt,'' and even former President Reagan indi cated publicly that he doesn't believe North did anything wrong (although once again he modified his remarks later). North's courier, Rob Owen, has despaired over the efforts to prosecute North and others for doing what they believed right and in the national interest, and holding their actions up to ridicule and contempt. "I see all that is good being portrayed as bad," said Owen, "and all that is bad being viewed as good and right."[26]

Evidence made public by North's defense team during the trial has made it clear that he was more of a guided missile than a loose cannon. Both Ronald Reagan and George Bush appear to have been far more involved in the Iran/Contra matter, and in efforts to raise funds for the Contras, than previously acknowledged. Moreover, while North admitted to lying to Congress and to altering key documents, new evidence seems to support his claim that he did so with the full knowledge of his superiors, Admiral John Poindexter and former NSC advisor Robert C. McFarlane.

Had North been sentenced to prison, it would have been one of the most politically divisive acts in recent U.S. history, and might have produced enormous pressure for a presidential pardon. However, a presidential pardon for North would have been even more controversial than Gerald Ford's pardon of Richard Nixon in the aftermath of Watergate.

If North's conviction is overturned on appeal, the possibilities open to him are limitless. There is talk of his moving to the West and running for the Senate or becoming a televangelist, a profession sorely in need of public rehabilitation. Should he ever decide to write his memoirs, literary agents say the manuscript will fetch a $3 to $5 million advance, thus eliminating any financial worries for the remainder of his days providing he invests the money prudently.

Oliver North is a relatively young man, and we have not heard the last of him yet. There is still a fire burning inside of Oliver North. You cannot see the flames or smell the smoke, but it is there. It is an all-consuming fire, fed by his patriotism, hatred of terrorism, and fervent anticommunism. North will never be content to remain quietly on the sidelines; there is too much left to do, and he is the quintessential believer that one man, with right on his side, can make a difference.

As to history's judgment, North has repeatedly told friends: "When it's all over, I will be found on the side of the angels."

8

Counterterrorist Commandos: The New Samurai

> There's a difference between a soldier and a warrior.
>
> —Delta Force operator

SOME have called them the "modern Ninja," others the "new Samurai." They are a special breed of men, living testimony to the difference between mere soldiers and warriors. They boast nicknames like "Chainsaw," and "C.D." (Certain Death), and "Black Jack," and their universal self-assurance, fighting skills, and splendid physical conditioning set them apart from all the rest. Some are the kind of men who need "the fur shaved off of them in the morning before they put their clothes on"; others are reflective warrior-philosophers as comfortable with a book as a submachine gun.

They are the members of the world's antiterrorist commando units, and when a plane is hijacked or an embassy seized by terrorists, they are usually the ones called in to resolve the situation. Such units are among the most elite military and law enforcement organizations in the world. They operate in secrecy, and many of their actions are cloaked in mystery. Their failures are often front page news, while their successes often remain classified or attributed to other military units in order to preserve their anonymity. The chief counterterrorist units of the West have developed their own special mystique and rituals. They form a unique military/law enforcement fraternity that trains together, carries out joint operations, and even holds an annual "Counterterrorist Olympics" where their respective skills can be pitted against each other. Some of the units put stock in smart uniforms, berets, and insignia, while other units revel in their very anonymity, wearing the uniforms and insignia of regular military units, known to each other only by personal recognition and closely held passwords.

The Best of the Best

What makes a top-notch antiterrorist unit? According to former DOD official Noel Koch, the three most important criteria are 1) trust, 2) independence, and 3) training.[1] In other words, the unit—its officers, men, and capabilities—must be trusted by the political leadership, who will ultimately decide whether or not to deploy the unit and will mandate the rules of engagement. Secondly, the unit's leadership needs to be free of political and other outside interference to the greatest degree possible. Many observers blamed the failure of the U.S. rescue mission in Iran on too many White House restraints and excessive concern over Iranian casualties.[2] Finally, there is no substitute for training or, for that matter, actual experience. The units generally viewed as the best in the world have had the opportunity to hone their skills to precision.

Asked to name the three best counterterrorist (CT) units in the world, without hesitation Koch names the British SAS, the West German GSG-9, and the French GIGN. His conclusions are echoed by Leroy Thompson in his book *The Rescuers: The World's Top Anti-Terrorist Units,* and by most other informed observers.[3] While rating units can be both arbitrary and subjective, Thompson establishes six criteria for measuring the relative competency of CT units: command and control, training, personnel/selection, weapons/equipment, intelligence/research, and versatility/resourcefulness. He assigns a value of 1 to 5 to each unit in each respective category, with 5 being the highest score possible. Only the SAS is accorded a perfect total score of 30, with GSG-9 coming in a close second with 29, and the

GIGN placing third with 27. The U.S. Delta Force ranks sixth in the world, with a combined total of 25, right behind the Israeli Sayaret Matkal, which comes in fifth with 26. Delta scores lowest on Thompson's index in the category of command and control, the problem that contributed most to the failure at Desert One. According to Koch, when he first examined the issue of command and control in mid-1981, "This government didn't have its shit together."[4] While the situation has improved substantially in recent years, Koch and others believe that things are still far from optimal. "There are still serious management problems that have to be corrected," he maintains.

By the same token, Koch believes that the Israelis are over-rated and still trading on their past triumphs. "They're just not that impressive," says Koch.[5] In support of Koch's contention, it should be noted that the Israelis, as a consequence of their previous successes, do not get as much practical experience dealing with conventional terrorism as they used to. The Palestinians have, for the most part, graduated from terrorism to guerrilla warfare, with an emphasis on border incursions and small unit attacks on Israel.

On the other hand, the nearly universal accolades accorded the SAS may stem, in large measure, from the unit's role in dealing with the protracted terrorist conflict in Northern Ireland and the threat of IRA attacks throughout the United Kingdom. In practical terms, no other unit in the world has as much actual experience as the SAS. Unlike the overbureaucratized command structure in the United States, says Koch, communications between the SAS and the British leadership "do not have to pass through forty-seven mattresses."[6] Even more important, Prime Minister Margaret Thatcher has actually drilled with the SAS as a part of British crisis planning, and therefore possesses first-hand knowledge of the unit and its capabilities.

Other excellent counterterrorist units include the Italian GIS (Groupe Interventional Speciale) and NOCS (Nucleo Operativo Centrale di Sicurezza), both of which are constantly underrated; the Australian SAS (which Thompson contends is the fourth best unit in the world); Spain's UEI (Unidad Especial de Intervention), which gets plenty of operational experience contending with the Basque ETA; the Royal Dutch Marines; and the FBI's hostage response team (classified by Thompson as the eighth best unit in the world). In addition to the world's top units, virtually every major Western nation, and an increasing number of Third World countries, today maintains some kind of counterterrorism unit that can be deployed in the event of a serious terrorist threat. The quality of such units is consistently improving, and knowledgeable observers say there are probably three dozen good to excellent units in the world, and another three dozen mediocre to poor units, some of which probably are as much of a threat to hostages and innocent civilians as they are to terrorists.

Genesis of a New Breed

The modern wave of terrorism from which the world has suffered for the past two decades can be traced in large measure to two events in the late 1960s: 1) the defeat of the Arab armies in the Six Day War, and 2) the rise of the Provisional Wing of the Irish Republican Army (IRA). The first event convinced stateless Palestinians that their destiny lay in their own hands, and not with the often-contentious and bickering Arab governments. The second event reinvigorated the moribund IRA and embroiled Great Britain in a major, protracted conflict within its own borders. These two events were subsequently augmented by the outbreak of sectarian warfare in Lebanon (and the disintegration of the Lebanese state), the emergence of an alienated and violent European youth movement, and the rise of Shiite fundamentalism, all of which spawned other formidable terrorist challenges.

At first, most Western governments believed that terrorism was a transitory problem, and not a significant threat to their stability, values, or national institutions. Others held that it was predominantly an Israeli or British problem that need not concern other governments. But as the level of violence increased, the attacks spilled over national frontiers, and the violence became internationalized, some observers began to have second thoughts about the Western posture of essentially ignoring the problem and wishing it away with good intentions.

No event contributed more to jolting Western governments out of their apathy than the "Munich Massacre" of 1972. Just before dawn on the morning of July 18, 1972, Black September terrorists slipped into the Olympic Village and made their way to an apartment block at Connollystrasse 31, where the Israeli Olympic team was quartered. The terrorists, led by a Libyan named Mohammed Masalhad, forced their way into the apartments occupied by the Israelis, killing two team members—a coach and a weightlifter—in the process. Nine Israelis were taken hostage, and in exchange for their safety the terrorists demanded the release of 234 Arab prisoners incarcerated by the Israeli government and West German terrorist leaders Andreas Baader and Ulrike Meinhof, who had recently been captured and imprisoned in a Frankfurt jail.

What had been dubbed by the West German government as the "Games of Peace and Joy" had suddenly been transformed into a nightmare reminiscent of the nation's Nazi past. Jews were once again locked in a drama for survival on German soil. Ironically, the West German government intentionally had minimized security in Munich in order to avoid comparisons to the 1936 Berlin Olympics, dubbed "Hitler's Games," which had been characterized by military pageantry and omnipresent security. Now they were paying the price for their well-intentioned, but ill-considered, decision to downplay security at the XX Olympiad.

The seventeen-hour standoff between the authorities and the terrorists rapidly became a media extravaganza without modern parallel. More than a half-billion people reportedly tuned in on their television sets to watch the real-life drama unfolding at the Olympics. Without question, the most powerful and enduring image of the Games was that of the ski-masked Black September terrorist on the balcony of the squat concrete apartment block at Connollystrasse 31, which forever changed the popular image of a Palestinian from a "refugee" to a "terrorist."

The Israeli government refused to accede to the Black Septembrists' demands and informed the West Germans that they would hold Chancellor Willy Brandt's government entirely responsible for the successful resolution of the crisis. The Israelis did indicate, however, that they would not object if the West Germans offered the terrorists safe passage to an Arab country in exchange for the release of the hostages. But the Israelis were adamant that under no condition should the hostages be permitted to leave West Germany while still under the control of the Arab terrorists.

The West German government initially favored giving in to the terrorists' demands, but in view of Israeli intransigence, Chancellor Brandt and his advisors opted to mount a rescue operation as the terrorists' "final deadline" approached. The Black Septembrists, meanwhile, told the West German negotiator, Interior Minister Bruno Merk, that they wanted a plane to fly to Cairo with their hostages. Merk agreed to their demand, and an ambush was prepared for the terrorists at the German airbase at Furstenfeldbruck, fifteen miles away.

The terrorists and their hostages were transported to Furstenfeldbruck by helicopter, where an unoccupied Lufthansa Boeing 727 was positioned, as if waiting to take the terrorists to Cairo. The first of the two helicopters touched down at 10:30 P.M., the other arrived five minutes later. The Germans, however, inexplicably underestimated the number of terrorists, and had only five marksmen positioned at the airfield to take out eight terrorists. The light was poor, and the Bavarian police marksmen were using bolt-action rifles. It was a makeshift ambush, without the benefit of rehearsal or operational experience.

At 10:44 P.M., a shot shattered the stillness as one of the snipers tried to hit Mohammed, the terrorist leader, as he returned across the tarmac after inspecting the 727. The shot missed, and all hell broke loose. It took more than an hour to bring the situation under control, but by that time all nine Israeli hostages, and five of the terrorists, were dead.[7]

Ironically, the crack Israeli commando unit, the 269 General Headquarters Reconnaissance Unit, had been dispatched to

West Germany to assist in the rescue operation, but the Germans had refused to let it land. According to some reports, it was circling over West German territory when the firefight at Furstenfeldbruck commenced. Had the Israelis, with their superior equipment and training, been involved in the rescue operation, the outcome may well have been different. The Germans had, however, permitted a second plane, bearing Zvi Zamir, the chief of the Mossad, his operations director, and other Mossad officials, to land, and they watched the debacle from the control tower, sick with frustration and outrage over the German ineptitude.

The Munich disaster humiliated the West German government as no other event had since its founding in the aftermath of World War II. Bonn moved quickly to correct the deficiencies evident at Furstenfeldbruck and created an elite counterterrorist unit within the Federal Border Guard called the Grenzschutz-gruppe-9 (GSG-9). Other Western European governments, like the French, cognizant of their own vulnerabilities, also established new units to combat terrorism. For their part, the British government assigned the responsibility to the Special Air Service (SAS), which created a Counter Revolutionary Warfare (CRW) unit dedicated to defeating terrorists in an urban environment.

The Israeli Tradition

Many of the newly formed units, including the German GSG-9, looked to the Israelis for inspiration and specialized antiterrorist training and skills. The Israelis, after all, had been fighting terrorism longer than any other Western power and had established a reputation for both efficiency and ruthlessness. The first commander of the German GSG-9, General Ulrich Wegener, told an Israeli correspondent: "We learned a lot from your methods and tactics, and we are carefully studying all of your operations." Indeed, when the German unit was first established in 1972, Wegener and his senior officers were guests at the headquarters of the Sayaret Matkal. Although the depth of

Israeli-German cooperation has never been fully revealed, it is known to have been extensive, and includes the comprehensive exchange of intelligence information. In the words of former Prime Minister Menachem Begin's military attaché, Brigadier General Ephraim Poran, "We gave the Germans all the information they needed. All the intelligence they wanted was transmitted to them. Our cooperation is not a secret. We are ready to help any country in the world which is willing to fight terrorism."

The 269 General Headquarters Reconnaissance Unit (it recently was given a different numerical designation), the chief Israeli special operations arm against terrorism, was a successor organization to Unit 101, which had been created in 1948 and headed by former Major General Arik Sharon. After charges that the unit was out of control and behaving as little more than a death squad in some areas, it was disbanded and its functions transferred in 1953 to the newly created 269 General Headquarters Reconnaissance Unit, known also as the Sayaret Matkal. Tasked with conducting secret operations behind enemy lines, the Sayaret Matkal became Israel's most legendary and daring military unit.

In one of its most dramatic operations, in 1955 the unit infiltrated Syria and established a tap on the communications lines between Damascus and the Golan Heights, then Syria's military "front" with Israel. A decade later, members of the Sayaret Matkal drove to Beirut disguised as United Nations observers to deliver $9 million in cash to former president Camille Chamoun to bankroll his party in national elections. Members of the unit also wore U.N. uniforms on a mission during the mid-1960s to conduct reconnaissance of Iraqi Air Force capabilities. On December 28, 1968, Sayaret Matkal commandos blew up fourteen aircraft on the ground at Beirut airport in retaliation for Popular Front for the Liberation of Palestine (PFLP) hijackings of Israeli jetliners.

A year later, on December 26, 1969, members of the Sayaret Matkal carried out a bold raid on the Gulf of Suez and brought back an entire Soviet-made P-12 radar station never before seen in the West. In May 1972 the unit executed the first successful rescue of a hostage jetliner after a Sabena passenger jet was hijacked to Israel by members of Black September. After negotiating with the terrorists for 48 hours, the Israeli negotiators informed the Black Septembrists that the Israeli cabinet had decided to accept their demands, including the release of jailed terrorists. As a deception, Israeli soldiers dressed in prison uniforms were brought to the airport some distance from the hostage jetliner, and an old TWA airliner was pulled onto the runway to give the skyjackers the impression that the plane that was to take the prisoners to Cairo had arrived. Then, some twenty Israeli "technicians" but actually members of the Sayaret Matkal, moved out to "service" the Sabena plane. Using explosives, they smashed through the doors of the plane, shouting to the passengers to hit the floor before they opened fire on the terrorists. Using flares to stun and blind the terrorists, and low-velocity bullets, they killed two of the terrorists and wounded two others. Only one passenger—who had ignored orders to get down—died in the operation, which demonstrated to the world that the West did not have to sit back and simply absorb terrorist outrages. General Wegener and his unit studied the Israeli Sabena operation very carefully in planning their successful rescue of a Lufthansa jetliner at Mogadishu five years later.

In April 1973, approximately thirty members of the Sayaret Matkal left Israeli fast patrol boats in Zodiac rafts and landed on a beach near Beirut. There, they were met by eight Mossad agents who had infiltrated into the city earlier and rented seven vehicles from Avis. Splitting into three groups, each struck at a different target. The first group went to the apartment house where Black September leader Abu Youssef lived, and shot Youssef and his deputy Kemel Adwan to death. The second group of Israeli commandos blew up the headquarters of the Democratic Front for the Liberation of Palestine (DFLP), and the third team destroyed a Black September ordnance center, which included a car-bomb workshop. The commandos—all dressed in civilian clothes—ran into trouble as they made their way back to the rafts, and the Israeli government was forced to acknowledge its complicity in the raid by sending in helicopters to delay the pursuers with cannon fire and by dropping spikes (caltrops) on the streets behind the fleeing commandos. The commandos abandoned the rental cars on the beach, and were able to make their way back to the waiting patrol boats in the rafts. The Israelis suffered two dead and two wounded in the raid, but in addition to the casualties and damage they inflicted on their terrorist enemies, they seized a treasure trove of secret documents and intelligence material. As a footnote, the Israelis paid Avis only after the rental car company "raised hell" and confronted the Israeli government with the unpaid bill.

The unit's most daring unpublished mission was the killing of a top terrorist on the outskirts of Damascus. Members of the Sayaret Matkal also attempted to assassinate the late PFLP leader Wadia Haddad in the early 1970s by firing bazookas at his apartment while he was making love to the Palestinian sky-jacker Leila Khaled. The two Palestinian terrorists received only minor injuries in the attack, which presumably gave new meaning to the term "coitus interruptus."

Although it was essentially a Mossad-run operation, elements of the Sayaret Matkal played a major role in the remarkable rescue of the passengers of an Air France jetliner to Entebbe, Uganda, on July 4, 1976. The overall on-site commander was Brigadier General Dan Shomron. The force commander, Lt. Colonel Jonathan Netanyahu, was the only Israeli to die in the expertly executed mission, which marked a turning point in the West's war against terrorism. The fact was, however, that members of the Mossad, who had earlier infiltrated Uganda from London, had already engaged the terrorists and the Ugandan soldiers at the airport when commandos of the Sayaret Matkal burst from the lead C-130 that landed in the darkness, along with a black Mercedes that resembled that of Ugandan dictator Idi Amin, designed to momentarily confuse the Ugandan soldiers.[8] In case a rescue operation had to be mounted, three additional Israeli aircraft loaded with troops circled overhead, but were not needed. The Mossad let the Sayaret Matkal take all of the credit in order to preserve its legendary anonymity.

The Entebbe mission required extraordinary planning and execution, not to mention a great deal of luck. It was the most audacious, though not the most difficult, operation ever attempted against terrorists and their state sponsors. In addition to the men and women directly involved, credit should be given to Israel's political leadership, especially Prime Minister Yitzhak Rabin and Defense Minister Shimon Peres, for having the courage to order the rescue operation. There is little question but that Israel's Labor government would have fallen if the mission had turned into a debacle.

Until the mid-1970s the Sayaret Matkal was the only Israeli military unit capable of carrying out unique unconventional operations against terrorists. But this was to change after the disaster at Ma'alot on May 15, 1974. After killing five civilians, Palestinian terrorists seized an Israeli school in the Israeli border community of Ma'alot, taking four teachers and one hundred children hostage. After negotiations broke down, the Sayaret Matkal was ordered to assault the building. Although all three terrorists were killed, 22 children died in the rescue operation, and approximately 60 were injured. The public outcry in Israel over what was perceived as the heavy-handed tactics of the Sayaret Matkal led to the creation of two new units: 1) Yamam (YMM), an element of the border police that emphasizes hostage rescue skills, and 2) Shal-dag (which comes from the Hebrew word for a bird that snaps fish out of the water), a battalion-sized unit (600 to 800) that is more technically oriented than its counterparts and concentrates on the employment of precise weapons systems against Israel's adversaries.

Thus, today the Israeli government has three highly skilled and effective antiterrorist units to draw upon in times of crisis, plus the very formidable skills of the Mossad. Despite the problems at Ma'alot, the Sayaret Matkal remains Israel's most distinguished antiterrorism unit. Two of its former commanders, Generals Ehud Barak and Dov Tamari, are among Israel's most decorated military men. Tamari has won Israel's highest award, the Medal of Heroism (equivalent to the U.S. Medal of Honor), five times, and Barak twice—a very impressive feat since, unlike the United States, the Israelis are rather stingy with military decorations. The commander of the Sayaret Matkal can still walk into the Israeli Prime Minister's office at any time of the day or night without an appointment, thus eliminating the chain of command and ensuring operational flexibility.

Three Israeli units have first priority when it comes to selecting from new recruits called to military service: the Sayaret Matkal, the Air Force (candidates for pilot training), and the naval commando (frogmen) unit. Of these, Sayaret Matkal officers get first pick, thus making the unit the most selective in the Israeli military. All recruits must be volunteers, and before being selected they must undergo extensive psychological testing. They subsequently must earn their airborne wings (paratrooper) before they are admitted to the Sayaret Matkal for six months of intensive training. They undergo rigorous physical conditioning and are schooled in weapons, explosives, hand-to-hand combat, communications, aggressive driving techniques, and even navigation. Every recruit is given sniper training and, in addition to all Israeli weapons, must be totally familiar with enemy weapons. They learn to become killers, skilled in both individual and small-group operations. They are trained to "achieve their mission and survive even if they have to carry on alone," explains one former commander. Indeed, every private is trained to show initiative and take over the unit in the event that his officers and non-coms are removed from action. An "almost religious devotion to achieving the target" is drummed into all members of the unit, says a former officer of the Sayaret Matkal. Former Prime Minister Golda Meir once described the men of the unit as "highly motivated young Israelis . . . who know that each of them may one day carry the fate of the whole country" on their shoulders. For members of the unit, training never really stops, and every man works continuously to upgrade his skills.

Like the U.S. Delta Force, Sayaret Matkal commandos wear no special insignia and keep a very low profile. Members of the unit are never deliberately photographed, and Israeli censors keep a close watch for unauthorized pictures that might expose the identity of any Sayaret Matkal commando. Nearly all members have international experience, and most speak fluent Arabic. The unit continues to emphasize ingenuity and improvision over doctrine, and generally makes do with far less high-tech equipment than its Western counterparts. While men and officers generally operate on an informal first-name basis, there is nothing casual or laid-back about the Sayaret Matkal, and with the exception of the Ma'alot massacre, the unit boasts more than a quarter century of operational successes against terrorists and their state sponsors.[9]

West Germany's GSG-9

If the Israelis emphasize boldness and daring, West Germany's GSG-9 (Grenzschutzgruppe-9) places a premium on sophisticated technology and rigorous training. This is not to say that the Germans are not bold; rather, it is a tribute to the fact that GSG-9 may have taken a more scientific approach to the problem of terrorism than any other elite unit. Moreover, the unit has been lavishly supported by the West German government and seems to want for very little.

Since its inception, the GSG-9 has been deployed against Red Army Faction (RAF) terrorists in West Germany; traveled undercover with West German athletes to both the winter and summer Olympic games, as well as to other athletic events; provided executive protection to top German government officials; conducted secret reconnaissance and, reportedly, strike missions against foreign terrorists; and assisted in the protection of threatened West German embassies in Beirut, Tehran, and other cities. The unit's most famous and dramatic mission, however, was the rescue of a hostage Lufthansa jetliner at Mogadishu, Somalia, in 1977. The Boeing 737, with 86 passengers and a crew of five on board, was hijacked on October 13 by four Palestinian terrorists while en route from Majorca to Frankfurt. The GSG-9 was immediately ordered into action (Operation ''Magic Fire''), and took up pursuit of the captive jetliner at once in another aircraft, shadowing the Lufthansa 737 around the Mediterranean (Rome, Cyprus, Bahrain, Dubai, Aden, and Somalia) as the terrorists negotiated with West German authorities for the release of imprisoned RAF and Palestinian terrorists and a $15 million ransom. After a five-day odyssey, during which the pilot of the aircraft was murdered and his body pitched out on the tarmac, the GSG-9 detachment, accompanied by two British SAS operators, stormed the jetliner, killing three of the four terrorists and giving the West—little more than a year after Entebbe—another significant victory against international terrorism.

GSG-9's current strength is 219 men, and candidates for the unit must already be members of the Federal Border Guard service. About 150 men apply to join the GSG-9's select ranks each year. Of these, few more than thirty actually make it all the way through the testing and training phase to become members of the unit, entitled to wear GSG-9's distinctive forest-green beret and eagle badge. The training is among the most rigorous in the world, and lasts for nine months. The unit relies heavily on technology—during combat-shooting training and exercises, for example, shooters are outfitted with electronic devices that measure each man's reaction times, in seconds and fractions of seconds, as he responds to various stimuli. One test measures the ability of a man, standing with his back to a target, to draw his weapon on cue, turn, fire, and hit the center bulls-eye. Reaction times of under a second have been observed.[10]

In addition to an exotic array of weapons and other equipment, which will be described later in this chapter, the unit maintains a stable of high-speed cars and helicopters to transport it to the scene of trouble. In one of GSG-9's most dramatic training exercises, the unit's operators, armed with assault rifles and riding in a helicopter, pursue a full-size target mockup of a terrorist escape vehicle. As the Bell UH-1D chopper flies by the car, shooters—depending on their instructions—must either pick off the terrorist in the backseat holding a gun to the head of the driver, or hit the vehicle's engine block. Shooters generally score a hit more than 85 percent of the time.[11]

The unit's original commander, Lt. Colonel (later Brig. General) Ulrich Wegener, who led the Mogadishu rescue mission, is a tall, spare man who speaks fluent English. He is known as an outstanding trainer and leader of men, and, like so many other special operations officers, he also has a reputation for impatience with bureaucracy and red tape and for not mincing words, even when addressing superiors.

The GSG-9 has provided technical and training assistance to many other CT units, including the U.S. Delta Force. Prior to the attempted 1980 rescue of U.S. hostages in Iran, for example, Wegener offered to infiltrate a team of GSG-9 operators into Tehran disguised as a television camera crew in order to obtain up-to-date intelligence needed in planning the raid, but the offer was politely turned down for reasons that are still a mystery. GSG-9 operators have been on the scene to advise many other CT units, such as the Royal Dutch Marines in 1977 during the South Moluccan train seizure at Assen, Holland. GSG-9 even provided counterterrorist training to six Georgia state troopers in preparation for the 1988 Democratic convention, held in Atlanta. Indeed, there is an extraordinary amount of interaction and cooperation between the globe's major CT units, and many strong personal relationships exist between operators from different nations. This friendship and sense of fraternity is also fostered through friendly competition, thanks to the annual Combat Team Competition, otherwise known as the Counterterrorist Olympics, one of Wegener's brainstorms. At the first competition, held in 1983, twenty-two different units were represented. Each nation that participates currently has the option of sending two five-man teams. The various teams compete to determine who has the best shooting and endurance skills (obstacle course, rappelling, fast-roping, etc.), and GSG-9 has dominated the competition to date.

One exception to the normally warm relations that exist between the counterterrorist units of different nations reportedly is long-standing animosity between the British SAS and their Israeli counterparts. Most liaising generally is done via the

GSG-9 due to the letter bomb murder of a former SAS officer's brother by Jewish terrorists during the conflict that led to the creation of the state of Israel.

The British SAS

As noted at the beginning of the chapter, there is general agreement among knowledgeable observers that the finest counterterrorism unit in the world is the CRW (Counter Revolutionary Warfare) unit of the British 22nd SAS (Special Air Service) Regiment. When he was asked to create the U.S. Delta Force, it was to the SAS that Lt. Colonel Charles "Chargin' Charlie" Beckwith looked as a model. Indeed, Beckwith had spent a tour with the SAS during the early 1960s as an exchange officer, an experience that made an indelible impression on him. Initially shocked by their sloppy barracks and disdain of military formalities, or what he called their "freebooting" style, Beckwith soon came to realize that it was performance, and not appearance, that was emphasized, and that the SAS had men who loved being warriors but hated being soldiers.

The SAS had originally been founded during World War II by a Scots Guard Lieutenant named David Sterling who, while recovering from parachuting injuries in a Cairo hospital, came up with the idea of establishing an elite commando organization that could operate behind enemy lines, engaging, principally, in sabotage operations. It was, in his mind, the ideal force multiplier wherein small groups of commandos, no more than four or five in number, could wreak a great deal of havoc on a much larger force and compel the enemy to tie down large numbers of troops protecting its rear. In what has now become a favorite part of SAS lore, Sterling vowed to present his idea directly to the British Commander-in-Chief of the Middle East at his headquarters.

Realizing, however, that as a junior officer he would never be given an appointment with the C-in-C, Sterling decided to surreptitiously infiltrate the headquarters compound and drop in unannounced for a face-to-face chat. Although he was still on crutches, he scaled a tall wire fence and painfully limped into the main administrative building. His presence was soon detected, and just before he was caught, he barged into the deputy C-in-C's office, saluted, and thrust the concept paper he had composed at Lt. General Neil Ritchie. Ritchie was impressed, and a short time later Sterling was promoted to captain and authorized to set up a sixty-six–man unit that was to evolve into the modern SAS.

Over the years that followed the SAS was to serve with distinction wherever British interests were on the line: from Malaya to Borneo, Oman, Northern Ireland, and the Falklands, to cite only a few examples. Although not conceived as a counterterrorist unit, during the mid-1970s a full squadron (78 men) of the 22nd SAS Regiment was designated as the Counter Revolutionary Warfare squadron called the SP (Special Projects Team) within the SAS, and was permitted to devote its full attention to counterterrorist training and operations.

Selection and training for the SAS is among the most rigorous in the world. There is a good deal of give-and-take between officers and men, and the atmosphere is sometimes described as a collegial one. Nevertheless, woe to any man who does not maintain his skills at a peak level or who lets some detail escape his attention—he will not last long. Indeed, the SAS is more a state of mind than anything else, and requires even more mental toughness than physical toughness, which is remarkable considering that the unit's physical conditioning standards are unsurpassed. One way that mental toughness is instilled in volunteers during the training phase is by constantly throwing up new challenges that prevent the attainment of some goal and test their ingenuity and ability to deal with adversity. For example, volunteers may be ordered on a fifteen-mile forced march over rough terrain and, when they reach the point where they are supposed to rendezvous with their transport back to the base, they see the trucks drive away and are told that they must complete another ten-mile march.

Over the years, the SAS has been regarded with distrust and suspicion by the British left, perhaps in part because of David

Sterling's outspoken anti–Labour Party comments and his suggestion that a paramilitary civilian strikebreaker force be created to intervene in domestic labor unrest. Others see it as a vestige of the British colonial past and the days of Empire, a tool of intervention used to "suppress freedom fighters and other progressive peoples." If Prime Minister Margaret Thatcher has a praetorian guard in spirit, if not in fact, it is the SAS, which closely identifies with her muscular foreign policy and determination to use military force when necessary. On the other hand, for an organization that has always prided itself on being the first to volunteer for action abroad, the SAS has never relished its role in Northern Ireland, which many view as transcending its normal military mission for one of garrison duty and activities more tailored to police units.

The SAS feels far more comfortable undertaking missions like "Operation Nimrod" at Princes Gate, accompanying the GSG-9 at Mogadishu, or parachuting onto the deck of the QE II in mid-ocean in 1972 when there was reason to believe that a powerful bomb had been hidden aboard the luxury liner.

France's GIGN and RAID

Although it has never received the public acclaim or attention accorded to other elite counterterrorism units, France's GIGN (Groupement D'Intervention de la Gendarmerie Nationale) was actually successfully deployed five months before the Israeli raid at Entebbe. On February 3, 1976, Somali terrorists from a group known as the Front for the Liberation of the Coast of Somalia (F.L.C.S.) seized a school bus in Djibouti containing thirty children, all of them sons and daughters of French military personnel, including the Foreign Legion. Intelligence indicated that the F.L.C.S was a Somali-backed terrorist organization that hoped to drive the French out of Djibouti so that it could be annexed by Somalia. Ten men from GIGN, under the command of Lt. Christian Prouteau, were dispatched to Djibouti to deal with the situation, since it was felt that the

Legion elements stationed in the country did not have either the training or the subtle technique that the situation required.

There were six terrorists on board the bus, and, armed with sniper rifles, Prouteau and his men took up positions around it to await an opportunity to simultaneously shoot all of the terrorists. Food sent to the children was drugged to induce sleep, so that they would be less likely to jump up or panic at the moment of the attack, and to reduce their profiles in front of the bus windows. Hours passed before the opportunity to strike came; at this moment there were four terrorists on board the bus and two outside. Prouteau's men killed five of the terrorists outright, but one was able to reboard the bus when Somali border units opened fire on the GIGN men and support elements from the Legion. Prouteau and two of his men braved the withering Somali fire to reach the bus and eliminate the final terrorist; however, they were too late to save one little girl. The Foreign Legion was outraged by the Somali complicity in the incident and for nearly ten hours pounded Somali border positions with artillery and small arms fire, inflicting dozens of casualties on the Somalis. "The massive retaliation on the Somali border post by the 2nd REP and GIGN, which accounted for the death of a possible East German or Soviet 'advisor' to the terrorists as well as numerous Somali troops," writes Leroy Thompson, "was an excellent object lesson to states which choose to support terrorism."[12]

Known as "the men in black," GIGN was founded in 1973. It was initially conceived of as a unit to back up police when things got out of hand, especially in hostage-barricade incidents. Although part of the French gendarmerie, the paramilitary police controlled by the Ministry of Defense, for the most part the GIGN operates in a parallel fashion to regular military units like the SAS, the GSG-9, and the American Delta Force. Nevertheless, unlike most other CT units, its members also have arrest powers and in the past have, on rare occasions, been deployed against criminals.

The GIGN is headquartered at the unit's modern new facility on a military base outside Paris, which houses administrative offices, a large garage where the unit's vans and pursuit cars (some with 2.5-liter engines) are kept and maintained, equipment storage areas, an indoor shooting range, physical training and exercise rooms, a "shooting room," and dormitory facilities. There is also a rappelling tower outside and, in back, a dog kennel, since GIGN is the only major counterterrorist commando group to use dogs in its operations. The dogs, mostly German shepherds, are employed to distract and to take down adversaries. Consistent with gendarmerie practice, the men of GIGN and their families live at the unit's nearby compound. It takes less than thirty minutes to assemble twenty combat-ready GIGN commandos at any hour of the day or night. There is also an airfield close by, where the unit's helicopters and executive jet stand by to transport the men of GIGN to the scene of the next crisis.

The unit is composed of 80 men, who were selected only after passing rigorous intelligence, psychological, and physical examinations and extensive background checks. Although they sometimes change into black coveralls for missions, when not deployed the unit's members generally wear jogging suits instead of uniforms. Each man has the option of footgear, and nearly all choose running shoes over combat boots. While most elite CT units have an upper age limit, the GIGN does not enforce an arbitrary age cutoff: so long as a man can pass the physical and other tests, he can qualify for the GIGN. Since the GIGN is exclusively a crisis intervention unit, members of the unit train constantly between missions. The goal of the training is to produce jacks-of-all-trades with well-honed skills rather than specialists. Every man is required to master skills such as mountaineering, scuba diving, hand-to-hand combat, aggressive/evasive driving, marksmanship, and parachuting.

Every CT unit places an emphasis on certain skills or procedures that set it apart from other units, and GIGN is no exception. Perhaps GIGN's most unique signature skill is precision parachuting onto rooftops as a means of gaining access to hostage buildings, by contrast to the fast-roping or rappelling techniques emphasized by nearly every other CT unit. Also, in contrast to other units, GIGN's weapon of choice is the .357 Magnum revolver, which can be outfitted with a silencer, folding stock, and scope. The philosophy of the unit can be summed up in the oft-repeated maxim "one shot to do the job." The GIGN operator is taught to pick his shot with extreme care and to wait for just the right shot, thereby reducing the risk to hostages or innocent bystanders by bringing the situation under control with a minimum of force. Members of the unit are taught not to kill for the sake of killing, but only as a means of stopping the enemy; they are expected to kill only on precise orders from their superiors or in self-defense.

All GIGN training is conducted with live ammo, and one of the unit's most dramatic exercises involves a simulated hostage scene where two "terrorists" emerge from the unit's garage with a hostage in tow. In reality, they are both GIGN operators. Each "terrorist" is wearing body armor and a rope necklace with a clay disc the size of a teacup saucer suspended from it, over the center of his chest like a target. Indeed, the clay discs *are* targets. Dangling from a rope on the rappelling tower a hundred yards away is a GIGN operator with a .357 Magnum. As the terrorists advance toward their "getaway vehicle," a dog breaks from concealment and races toward one of the "terrorists," taking him down in an instant. Simultaneously, the clay disc on the other "terrorist" explodes from a perfectly placed .357 round, knocking the "terrorist" from his feet despite the protective body armor. It is all over in a matter of seconds: the "hostage" is safe, one "terrorist" is "dead" and the other in custody.

France's other elite counterterrorist unit is RAID (Recherche Assistance Intervention Dissuasion), which serves as a kind of national police SWAT team. As one approaches the unit's unmarked headquarters on a seventy-acre estate outside of Paris, there is nothing, other than the large number of vehicles parked next to the main structure, to suggest that the occupants of the secluded chateau are anything but ordinary country gentry. The chateau houses the unit's offices, dormitories, training areas, and the National Command Center for Terrorism. From the

Command Center, RAID stays in constant communication with police around the country. Should a crisis occur, elements from the unit can be rapidly airlifted to the trouble spot from a nearby airport, using Interior Ministry helicopters.

Created on June 1, 1985, and fully operational by December 1 of the same year, RAID differs from GIGN in that it is a law enforcement unit that is employed not only against terrorists, but also against formidable criminals such as drug dealers and organized crime bosses. Recent interviews with top French officials suggest that while RAID's mission is still evolving, it is envisioned as the primary response force in the event of terrorist incidents in France itself, something like the FBI hostage rescue unit in the United States. Just as regular military forces are not deployed on U.S. territory, French authorities came to believe that the use of the GIGN might signal either panic or overreaction on the part of the government, and they desired the creation of a unit that was exclusively law enforcement, rather than military, in its orientation. Moreover, because it is a police unit, RAID can also conduct investigations and engage in the kind of police work that normally is critical to apprehending terrorists. GIGN, by contrast, because of its highly military character and operational style, will be used chiefly outside of metropolitan France in rescue operations.

All members of RAID are experienced police officers who apply from their local departments. It is envisioned that rank-and-file members of RAID will only spend a couple of years with the unit, and then rotate back to their regular police assignments, carrying with them the skills and training they have acquired during this period. More than 1,200 men applied for the original 75 positions with RAID, and those selected received intensive training, including karate, boxing, marksmanship, and evasive/aggressive driving skills, but as the unit's first commander, Robert Broussard, explained, the most important instruction "you don't find in books. It comes from our experience."[13] Much of the physical training is conducted in the old chapel connected to the chateau. Brilliant-colored light streams through the stained-glass windows as lean, athletic men work out or practice hand-to-hand combat on large gray mats.

The unit's philosophy is one of "swift, smooth surprise," and to this end a great premium is placed on being able to operate surreptitiously and undercover. Members of the unit do not wear uniforms, but rather ordinary street clothes, and use identifying insignia only when deployed during hostage/barricade and similar situations. For pursuit and surveillance the unit maintains unmarked souped-up Peugeots capable of top speeds of more than 205 kilometers per hour. In order not to tip off suspects, even the radio antennae of the cars are built into the window frames and their two-way radio speakers are hidden in the pull-out ashtrays. There is an element of humor in observing a RAID officer speak into his ashtray, but the camouflage works very effectively. The nondescript exterior appearance of RAID's cars assists in tailing suspects and permits them to blend into traffic so that they can choose the opportune moment to make their move. Because of the nation's traffic congestion, motorcycles are often employed for maintaining close-in contact with a suspect's car; the RAID man on the motorcycle hands off to the pursuit car only at the last minute.

When this author visited the RAID headquarters, most driving maneuvers were taught in the parking area abutting the chateau, but Broussard indicated that he hoped to get funds for a paved racetrack on the estate where there would be more room for teaching evasive/aggressive driving skills. He also said that he wanted to build a much more sophisticated firing range, where his men could practice their marksmanship skills.

Broussard, Directeur Central des Polices Urbides, was widely regarded as "France's toughest cop" when he was asked to form RAID. A stocky, bearded man with a direct, no-nonsense manner, Broussard made his reputation as the top law enforcement officer in Corsica, seat of France's toughest organized crime syndicates. Stories about Broussard's courage are legion and include an incident in which he and his men surrounded a house in Corsica where a wanted crime boss and his henchmen had taken refuge. Because he had superior firepower and numbers, Broussard knew that he would ultimately prevail, but he also was concerned that many lives, on both sides, would be lost in the fight. So he approached the house and asked to talk to the crime boss, a former parachutist like himself, "para to para." The crime boss acceded and opened a bottle of wine. While the standoff continued, Broussard and the crime boss finished the first bottle and went on to another, regaling each other with military reminiscences. Finally, after many hours, the crime boss agreed to surrender to a fellow "para," and left the house arm-in-arm with Broussard, followed by the rest of the criminal gang, who had laid down their arms.

Broussard's appointment was a clear signal of a tough new attitude toward terrorism in France on the part of the Chirac government, especially Interior Minister Charles Pasqua and his deputy, Internal Security Minister Robert Pandraud, who were referred to in some leftist circles as the "Tontons Macoutes."

The former number-two man in RAID, and now its commander, is Ange Mancini. By contrast to the taciturn and disheveled Broussard, Mancini is good-looking and nattily attired, and if Broussard is sometimes referred to as "the Clint Eastwood of France," then Mancini is surely the Sonny Crockett of "Miami Vice" fame. Mancini is gregarious and something of a showboat, but he has a reputation for fearlessness and daring that equals his predecessor's. Mancini is a Corsican, and nearly 80 percent of the original members of his unit are Corsican; some even boast gold inlaid maps of the island in their pistol grips.

Much of France's recent success, both against the French terrorist group Action Directe and foreign terrorists operating on its territory, can be attributed to the excellent police work of RAID.

The U.S. Delta Force

The U.S. Joint Special Operations Command (JSOC), which was established at Fort Bragg, North Carolina, in 1981 to coordinate various U.S. military counterterrorist and hostage-rescue elements, is extremely secretive and provides no official description of its components or their activities. However, it is known that the chief component units are the Army's Delta Force, Navy SEAL (Sea, Air, Land) Team 6, and the "Night Stalkers," a unique helicopter unit that is part of the 106th Aviation Group.[14]

The creation of the U.S. counterterrorist Delta Force resulted, in part, from the confluence of a man and an event. Ever since serving with the SAS in the early 1960s, a Special Forces officer by the name of Charles "Chargin' Charlie" Beckwith had lobbied the Pentagon regarding the need for a special operations unit patterned on the SAS. The U.S. military establishment, however, has long resisted the notion of "elite" units, and for years Beckwith was regarded as something of an eccentric, although everyone who came into contact with him described him as a superb leader and motivator of men. Nevertheless, in a Pentagon where the "bean counters" are in the driver's seat, the notion of establishing an elite special operations unit like the one proposed by Beckwith was viewed with suspicion and distrust.

In the wake of the successful rescue of the hostage Lufthansa jetliner at Mogadishu by GSG-9, the Carter White House inquired of the Joint Chiefs about U.S. antiterrorist capabilities. Despite considerable opposition and interservice bickering, the Joint Chiefs reluctantly authorized the establishment of an elite counterterrorist force known as Delta, and Beckwith was selected as its first commander. Delta ultimately superseded an existing parallel unit known as "Blue Light," a makeshift interim force drawn chiefly from the 5th Special Forces Group. The designator "Blue Light" was a derivative of the "Green Light" units that carry U.S. backpack nuclear weapons. Blue Light, which was disbanded in August 1978, had a larger mandate, whereas Beckwith saw Delta as essentially a hostage rescue unit.

But where Blue Light had been formed from a basic nucleus of men, the cornerstone of Delta was a rigorous selection process designed by Beckwith, and drawing heavily upon the SAS recruitment profile. Just to try out for Delta, a volunteer had to:

> perform at top efficiency his MOS (Military Occupation Specialty); the recruit needed to be at least a Grade 5 on his second enlistment; have no limiting physical profile; be at least twenty-two years old and an American citizen; have a GT score of 110 or higher; be able to pass a Modified Special Forces Physical Training Test and a physical examination; be airborne-qualified or volunteer for airborne training; have no recurring disciplinary offenses on his record; (and) have two years active service remaining after assignment.[15]

Initially, all the prerequisites desired were fed into a computer, which identified the names of military personnel who fit the profile. Each individual on the list received a letter that basically said: "Congratulations. You have been chosen to attend the Delta Force selection course, which will be held on [date]. Should you be interested, take this to your personnel manager. If you are not interested, don't reply back."

"What's this Delta Force?" one of the recipients, a Special Forces non-com based in Alaska, asked his military friends. No one knew, but they told him it was reputed to be a very tough organization, and that nearly everyone flunked out of the selection course. That was enough for him: he decided to give it a try. His selection class started with approximately 160 men; only nine made it, and he was one of them.

"As a child, all I wanted to be was a soldier," he recalled, describing his reasons for volunteering for the selection course. "That's what my father was and that's what I wanted to be. I first joined the paras because they was the tough boys and I liked 'em. It was exciting. Then I found out that the Rangers is supposed to be even tougher, so I immediately progressed to the Rangers. After I got into the Rangers, they said, 'Boy, them Green Berets is what's going on. You ought to be a Green Beret.' " To him, Delta was just part of a natural progression to find the roughest, toughest unit in the entire U.S. military establishment.

The extraordinary psychological (especially stress), physical, mental, and aptitude tests that Beckwith had devised meant that very few volunteers made it through the selection course. Beckwith, therefore, was forced to send recruiters around to U.S. Army bases in this country and abroad in order to interest men in Delta. It ultimately took "two years to find individuals who were unusually inquisitive, sensitive, resourceful, and imaginative. Two years to find people who could be at times extremely patient and at other times extremely aggressive; who could operate under unusually restrictive constraints at one moment and be audacious, freethinking individuals the next; operate with orders and operate without them; be able to lead and to follow; withstand prolonged physical and mental activity and endure extended monotony."[16]

During the nineteen-week Operators Course at Fort Bragg, Delta recruits honed their weapons skills and were taught navigation, explosives, communications, climbing and rappelling, fast-rope techniques, evasive and aggressive driving, hand-to-hand combat, HALO and HAHO parachuting, combat medicine, room clearing, and how to manage hostage situations. The Delta curriculum also involved teaching certain criminal skills such as lock picking, car theft, and weapons improvisation. One deficiency that instructors rapidly spotted was that most of the men lacked communications skills, so an instructor was hired from a local college to teach remedial English.

Initially, no one in the unit possessed evasive/aggressive driving skills, so Beckwith sent several members of the unit to a driving school in California operated by a former Grand Prix driver. The idea was that when they completed the course, they would return to the unit and train everyone else. They didn't have any vehicles to train with, however, so Beckwith sent fifteen men in civilian clothes out to the rental car agencies in the Fayetteville area with instructions to lease one car each. They took the cars out to an abandoned airstrip and practiced spinouts, reverse

180s, bootleggers' turns, panic stops, and a host of other techniques. At the end of the day, as they prepared to return the cars, someone noticed that the tires had taken a real beating: some were nearly flat, on others the lining was visible and whole chunks of tread were missing. They asked Beckwith what to do, and he issued a check and sent them out to buy new tires. Buying new tires became a regular part of the routine each time Delta held a driving practice session, and one of the great mysteries throughout the car rental agencies in the Fayetteville area concerned the mysterious appearance of spanking new tires on rental cars. Little did they realize the ordeal to which the cars were being subjected. "I'll tell you," says a former Delta operator. "I'd never buy a used rental car from the Fayetteville area."

Several cars were also banged up in training accidents. On one occasion, the car "rolled over two or three times." They towed the wrecked car from the deserted airstrip out to a public road and reported it as a normal accident. "It was interesting trying to be covert and hiding these things," recalls former Delta Force Master Sergeant J.D. Roberts, "since most of our equipment was coming from rental agencies."

Delta borrowed or rented virtually every type of transportation conveyance that could possibly be, or ever had been, hijacked by terrorists, and practiced "rescuing" it for hours on end. Posing as police, "we'd go and get a Greyhound bus and park it somewhere, keep it the whole day, and just attack that thing from every single angle." Similarly, Amtrak loaned the unit a train, which was placed on a remote spur, so that the 1977 seizure of a train by South Moluccan terrorists in the Netherlands, and its recovery by Royal Dutch Marines, could be recreated. It was, ironically, the unit's namesake, Delta Airlines, that was regarded as "our best friend." Delta operators would spend up to a week at a stretch training on planes provided by the airline at its headquarters in Atlanta, doing endless rehearsals and mock assaults, until the unit's skill at rescuing hostage aircraft was perfected to an art form.[17] Most often, the men of the unit would rest during daylight hours and receive classroom instruction in an old hangar, so that at night, under the cover of darkness, they could practice their "takedown" techniques on every possible type and configuration of jetliner.

Perhaps no skill is more important in hostage rescue operations than marksmanship, since success often will depend on the ability of the Hostage Republic Unit (HRU) to isolate and neutralize the terrorists without causing harm to any hostages. As a result, Delta operators generally shoot several thousand rounds a week in practice, and are expected to master pistols, submachine guns, assault rifles, combat shotguns, and sniper rifles. According to standards set down by Beckwith, the unit's snipers had to hit targets at 600 yards 100 percent of the time, and targets at 1,000 yards 90 percent of the time.[18] When pitted against other elite U.S. law enforcement and military organizations in shooting matches, the Delta operators nearly always win, losing only to the Secret Service snipers on some occasions.

Delta is regarded as the best "room clearing" unit in the U.S. military inventory; that is, the best unit for forcibly accessing a room or building, neutralizing all hostile elements, and rescuing any hostages that are being held. To hone such skills, Beckwith had a "shooting house" constructed at a cost of $90,000. Nicknamed the "House of Horrors," it was patterned after the SAS "Killing House" (Close Quarter Battle House) at Hereford. Virtually every hostage rescue unit in the world trains on such a facility. Delta's "House of Horrors" has four rooms, employing a variety of silhouette, pop-up and video-projected targets that test the operator's ability to burst into a room and shoot all of the terrorists without hitting any hostages or bystanders. One of the rooms is dedicated to night shooting, and members of the unit generally wear night-vision goggles during training. Another room is configured like the cabin of an airliner.

To be successful, the operator must not only be an excellent marksman, but must also make a number of correct, and virtually instantaneous, judgments as to who are the good guys and who are the bad guys in the room. It must be done, in Beckwith's words, "quickly and violently."[19] On one occasion, a target figure may be holding a weapon in its hand when it pops up or pivots toward the operator, on the next it may simply be pointing or holding a benign object in its hand. The Delta operator may have to sort out the intentions of a half dozen or more people in a room in the flick of an eye; and, as Beckwith has written, there is no room for anything less than perfection every time. "No one can ever have a bad day," members of the unit remember Beckwith drumming into them.

Beckwith could be notoriously short-tempered, and rarely displayed much patience for officials from Washington, especially if he believed their presence was disrupting the unit's training schedule. Irritated by what seemed to be a continuous stream of visitors from the nation's capital, each group requiring a "performance" of the unit's skills, Beckwith finally resolved to do something about it. When the next delegation arrived, he seated the four men, unbeknownst to them, in one of the rooms of the shooting house. Suddenly the door blew open, and a team of Delta operators burst into the room, firing at the targets which had popped up only inches from the seated visitors. All four visitors were terrified by the demonstration of room-clearing skills, and one man reportedly even wet his pants, but despite their later anger, none protested Beckwith's action out of fear of having their courage questioned. Word of the incident in the shooting room got around, though, and the number of Washington visitors dropped off precipitously.

Most of Delta's operators were young non-coms with little advanced education or experience beyond their military service. Thus, to round out their training and provide them with some international seasoning and savoir faire, Beckwith decided to send as many men as he could abroad for a week or two, mostly to Europe, to familiarize them with foreign travel (on their own as opposed to traveling in groups), hotels and restaurants, foreign exchange, crossing borders, and operating undercover. One Delta operator was dispatched to Brussels, told to register at a particular hotel, and instructed to buy a copy of the *International Herald Tribune* the next day. He was to locate his code name in the "personals" section and follow the instructions. He rose bright and early, according to habit, and waited for the paper to reach the newsstands. When, at last, it arrived, he found an ad that read: "Mike. I missed you in Madrid, but will call you at (hotel name) in Paris on Tuesday. Love, Cynthia." He made his way to the designated hotel in Paris and bought another copy of the *International Herald Tribune,* only to find another coded message sending him to a rendezvous in another country. At each of five or six designations, he picked up some item that established that he was in the appropriate city at the appropriate time, such as a theater ticket stub or a café check.

Deployment

Delta operators have been present at or in the close vicinity of every major hostage rescue attempt during the past decade. Indeed, cooperation between Western counterterrorist units has become so extensive that on-site observers from brother units are the rule rather than the exception. Some units have even carried out joint operations. In late 1975, for example, there was agreement on a joint U.S.-French rescue operation in Lebanon designed to free all of both nations' hostages. Unfortunately, just before the operation was to get under way, some of the hostages were once again moved by the terrorists, and a precise fix on their new location could not be obtained. It had already been decided that the mission would not go forward unless there was reasonable certainty that *all* of the hostages could be freed.

The Germans and the French have carried out joint operations against Hizballah and Action Directe, and in 1985 the British SBS (Special Boat Squadron) provided advice to the U.S. Navy SEALs in conjunction with the *Achille Lauro* seajacking.

Although Delta operators participated in several still-secret operations to rescue hostage jetliners in the Caribbean, and have provided support and on-the-ground assistance to a number of allied units, they have yet to carry out an operation totally on their own to save hostage Americans. They nearly got their chance during the TWA 847 hijacking in 1985, while the hostage aircraft was on the ground in Algiers, but the Algerian government refused to grant permission for the rescue to go forward. The TWA jetliner was soon on its way back to Beirut, and Delta subsequently spent two weeks on Cyprus waiting for an opportunity to go into action in Beirut. U.S. intelligence, however, could never pinpoint the exact location of all of the hostages at the same moment, and the situation was settled via diplomacy.

Ironically, the existence of the Delta Force first became generally known to the American public as a result of the failed 1980 attempt ("Operation Eagle Claw") to rescue American hostages held in Iran. Although he had initially ruled out any use of force to resolve the crisis, President Jimmy Carter, cognizant of the approaching presidential election and frustrated by the failure to achieve a diplomatic resolution of the problem, finally authorized Delta to attempt a rescue effort in late April 1980.

The unit had been activated in the first days following the November 4, 1979, seizure of the embassy and those inside. Beckwith's first challenge had been to secretly move his men to Fort Peary, Virginia, near Williamsburg, the CIA's training facility known as the "farm," which would serve as a secure training and preparation site. Once again, Beckwith sent his men out to Fayetteville's rental car agencies to lease a variety of vehicles for the trip north. The men of A Squadron and a handful of support personnel were then broken up into small groups, and each group assigned a vehicle. The trunks of each car were loaded with weapons and ammunition, and each group given an ATF (Bureau of Alcohol, Tobacco and Firearms) emergency number in case they were stopped by authorities or had an accident.

Delta's B Squadron was engaged in winter training exercises—principally learning to ski—at Breckinridge, Colorado, when Beckwith ordered them back to the East Coast. They were told that it was of utmost importance that they not attract any attention that would suggest that Delta had been activated. On the way back to Denver, the rental truck with all of their equipment broke down. B Squadron arrived at Denver's Stapleton Airport in seven station wagons full of hard-looking, athletically built men, all dressed in similar clothing. Each vehicle was piled high with gear, including large black military lockers with green military straps on top. There was also a small truck that had been hastily leased.

The plane that was supposed to pick them up was late, so they were forced to wait on the edge of the tarmac in their vehicles, heaters running, trying to stay warm. Finally, the chartered 727 arrived and the ground crew immediately began refueling it. However, after opening one of the wing tanks on the jet, the crewmen disappeared. Meanwhile, another crewman opened the fuel tank on the other wing and started pumping fuel in. The transfer valves apparently were open, and as the men of Delta watched from the shadows, the fuel going in one wing began spilling out onto the tarmac from the open tank on the opposite wing. Soon there was fuel all over the tarmac, and fire engines were called in to foam the area and clean up the spill. This, in turn, attracted a local television crew, which began filming the incident.

The arrival of the TV crew produced universal consternation among the Delta commandos, who had been ordered to keep their activation absolutely secret. While the TV crew filmed the scene on the tarmac, the seven cars and one truck began quietly and inconspicuously backing around the corner of one of the hangars. Had the TV crew turned around, they surely would have spotted the Delta men and possibly scooped one of the biggest stories of the year. But as it was, they finished their filming and departed, permitting the commandos to board the plane, no one being the wiser.

The members of Delta spent nearly half a year on the "farm," living in Quonset huts and training for the raid on Tehran. Their movements outside were carefully timed to avoid Soviet satellite pass-overs. Initially, members of B Squadron were not told where they were being sent, but several commandos did a recon of the area the second night in all-black gear and quickly discovered that they were on a CIA reservation. While life on the "farm" was confining, with little liberty, there was an abundant population of white-tailed deer at Fort Peary. To the consternation of the CIA, Beckwith permitted his men to hunt the deer, and they often dined on venison.

Desert One

During the night of April 24/25, 1980, at a site designated "Desert One" deep within Iran, an American rescue party was to assemble for a final thrust into Tehran, some 265 nautical miles to the northwest, as part of a plan to rescue 52 American hostages nearing their seventh month of captivity by the revolutionary regime of the Ayatollah Khomeini. Eight U.S. Navy Sea Stallion helicopters, flown from Masirah Island off the coast of Oman, would rendezvous with six C-130 transports, loaded with men, fuel, and equipment, at Desert One. Once refueled, the Sea Stallions would transport the ground elements of the rescue party, mostly Delta Force operators, to another site, known as Desert Two, about fifty miles from Tehran. They would remain at Desert Two until nightfall, and then be transported in vehicles assembled by an advance party with the help of Iranian "friendlies" into Tehran, where they would simultaneously hit the U.S. embassy, where most of the hostages were being held, and the Iranian Foreign Ministry building, where the U.S. Chargé d'Affaires and two other Americans were being detained. Once they had freed the hostages, both teams would meet at a nearby soccer stadium and be airlifted out by the Sea Stallions. In the event of trouble, U.S. warplanes would prevent the Iranians from launching their own aircraft and AC-130 Spectre gunships would "hose" the streets of Tehran with Gatling gun fire.

Unfortunately, three of the Sea Stallions experienced mechanical problems en route to Desert One, which left one less than the absolute minimum number needed to complete the mission, and Beckwith made the decision to abort the operation. However, hopes of being able to slip out of Iran undetected and repeating the operation sometime thereafter with a full complement of helicopters were dashed when—at approximately 2:40 A.M. on the 25th—one of the choppers, during refueling in preparation for withdrawing, struck a C-130, causing it to explode. The ensuing fire left eight American servicemen, and allegedly one "civilian," dead, and a number severely burned and injured. At that point, the rest of the helicopters were abandoned, and the rescue party made a hasty retreat from Iran.

The debacle at Desert One was a sad and heart-wrenching setback to the men of Delta; for them, it remains what the poet has described as the "darkest altar of our heartbreak."[20] Few can doubt their courage, or their readiness to sacrifice their lives, if necessary, to rescue their fellow countrymen from the clutches of the Ayatollah and his acolytes. No one was more distraught over the failure of the mission than Charlie Beckwith, but there is little question that he made the right decision not to proceed without an adequate number of operational helicopters. The planning of the raid, however, can be faulted on many counts.

It is clear today that the planners of the mission failed to build in the redundancies necessary to insulate "Operation Eagle Claw" from the kind of unexpected mechanical failures that occurred. So worried were planners over White House concerns that a minimum amount of force be utilized that they failed to commit enough resources to the operation to do the job. Indeed, it is a universally accepted military axiom that the unexpected always must be anticipated and planned for.

Another problem was excessive secrecy. In preparation for the raid, the Atlantic Fleet commander had been told that there was a need for some of his Sea Stallion helicopters. When he asked why they were needed, the response was "for training." Thus, he gave them his "clunkers" rather than his best choppers.[21]

Like the later Grenada invasion, the Iranian rescue mission was a monument to poor planning and poor coordination. It suffered from an obsession with secrecy, the involvement of too many government agencies and military organizations, the failure to conduct a "dry run" with all of the elements, confusion regarding command and control, and just plain bad luck. In defense of the operation, however, it should be noted that it was a far riskier and more complex undertaking that either the Entebbe raid or the German rescue mission at Mogadishu. If everything had gone without a hitch, it stood a reasonable chance of success; however, President Carter and the Joint

Chiefs were living in a fool's paradise if they really believed that the rescue party and hostages could get out of Iran without the probable commitment of additional military assets and a high loss of Iranian, and possibly even American, life. Had things soured in Tehran, instead of at Desert One, nothing less than a massive and ruthless use of American military power would have saved the day.

On April 27, 1980, President Carter and National Security Advisor, Zbigniew Brzezinski, flew down to Fort Peary to greet the disheartened men of Delta. Carter wanted to express his personal gratitude for the effort, however unsuccessful, they had made. Ninety-six men were assembled in a hangar near one of the black runways on the "farm" to greet the President. It was a poignant moment, of both sorrow and anger. Carter wanted to shake each man's hand, and he began moving down the line. But as he did so, each Delta man tried to crush the President's hand in order to show his contempt for him and what they perceived, rightly or wrongly, as his policy of weakness. After the first dozen or so handshakes, one of the escort officers quickly perceived what was happening and moved in front of the President. "Lighten up, guys," he whispered as he moved along the line. "Like shit," responded on the commandos. "He nearly killed us."

Grenada

It was largely because of the unit's expertise as "room clearers" that Delta was used in Grenada as part of Operation "Urgent Fury." Many Grenadian political prisoners were being held in the prison on Richmond Hill, overlooking the capital of St. George, and it was assumed that once the invasion started they would all be killed. It was, therefore, decided to send Delta's B Squadron to rescue the prisoners, and other Delta elements were assigned to secure the Point Salines airfield. The SEALs were given the task of spiriting the Governor General, Sir Paul Scoon, who was under house arrest, off the island to safety; capturing the island's major radio station; and running reconnaissance of the landing strip at Pearls Airport and the beach where the Marines were expected to come ashore.

Delta's A Squadron, which had parachuted in the pre-dawn hours onto the airfield at Point Salines, was immediately pinned down by stiff Cuban and Grenadian resistance, and suffered six dead and sixteen wounded before a C-130 Spectre gunship could provide the unit with air support after sunrise.

The mission against the Richmond Hill prison was scheduled to take place under the cover of darkness, and Delta operators were outfitted with night-vision goggles and pack 4's. They were to be transported to the island on UH-60 Blackhawk helicopters flown to Barbados on C-5A transports and reassembled there. However, for reasons still not fully explained, the sun had already risen by the time the operation got under way. The plan called for two helicopters to take out the guard towers while four hovered over the prison courtyard and the Delta operators fast-roped down to the ground. But they never got the opportunity even to get the ropes out because the choppers came under fire from an anti-aircraft battery on a nearby ridge, which the Air Force was supposed to have taken out, and from prison guards who opened up with machine guns and small arms.

As they pulled out of the cross fire, the lead chopper's communications gear was knocked out and a second chopper began smoking badly; all but one of the choppers had wounded on board. As the choppers came back for a second pass, the craft that was smoking faltered and, according to one of the Delta operators, "the back blew out . . . and it went in." The pilot rotored into the ground, but the terrain was steep and the chopper rolled over twice and caught fire.

Driven off by the murderous fire, the other choppers hovered over the ocean, near the coast, while awaiting clearance to go to the aid of their comrades that had been shot down. Because of confusion at the command level it took over fifteen minutes for the clearance to come through, during which time those not injured in the crash had pulled their companions free of the wreckage and taken cover. Only the pilot was dead, having taken a .50-caliber round in the chest, but several of the survivors were seriously injured. When the other choppers returned, they found there was no place to land, so the men fast-roped down over the burning wreckage and set up a defensive perimeter to return fire. More than two hours passed, however, before the Navy sent in choppers to evacuate the casualties. The Richmond Hill prison was subsequently abandoned by the enemy, without a further shot being fired.

After it was all over, one of the men counted twenty-eight holes in the Blackhawk that had hovered over the wreckage. "The Blackhawks are worth their money," he said later, "I can tell you that. When we got back they were all shot to shit."

The SEALs, meanwhile, were faring little better than their Delta counterparts. The team sent to take control of Radio Free Grenada had been ambushed, with two dead and two wounded—half of the assault force. The team that was supposed to reconnoiter the beach and landing strip at Pearls airport also had met with disaster, with half of its number drowning as they executed a low-altitude jump from a C-130 transport. On the other hand, the Governor General's residence, along with Scoon and his staff, was soon in the hands of the SEAL contingent sent to secure it. However, before they could evacuate the Governor General, several enemy armored personnel carriers (APCs) pulled up outside. The lightly armed SEALs knew they were in real trouble but could not contact the command ship *Guam* for help since their primary communications gear had been left behind in one of the helicopters. They broke out another com set, set to a different frequency, and sent out a distress call, which was picked up by the Delta contingent near the Richmond Hill prison. "Hey, Sarge, your backpack is squawking," a Delta operator remembers saying to one of his companions. They patched the SEALs through to the *Guam,* and several choppers were sent to their aid, including two Cobra gunships shot down by anti-aircraft batteries. One of the SEALs at the Governor General's residence, however, turned out to have brought along two LAAWS rockets, one of which he fired at the APCs, forcing them to pull back and forgo an assault out of fear that the SEALs were better armed than they actually were.

Other U.S Counterterrorist Units

The activities of U.S. Navy SEAL (Sea, Air, Land) teams can be divided into two categories: 1) special operations/unconventional warfare and 2) counterterrorism. Only SEAL Team 6, however, is principally trained and deployed in counterterrorist operations. SEAL Team 6 has been involved in a number of major operations, including the *Achille Lauro* incident. Other SEAL teams, by contrast, are skilled in such things as the sabotage of enemy targets, limpet-mining enemy shipping, reconnaissance of amphibious landing areas and the destruction of obstacles, counterinsurgency, and deep penetration operations designed to collect intelligence about the enemy. SEAL units, for example, regularly conduct operations on Soviet territory, especially against Soviet naval facilities near Murmansk. Indeed, one SEAL unit narrowly escaped being captured on Soviet territory in recent years. The SEALs have also conducted missions designed to place taps on Soviet undersea communications cables.

In addition to military units, there are a variety of both local and federal law enforcement organizations that have counterterrorist capabilities. First and foremost is the 50-man FBI Hostage Response Team (HRT), based at Quantico, Virginia, the chief civilian CT team available to the President. The FBI HRT trains with the SEALs, Marines, 82nd Airborne, and Delta. Indeed, the FBI HRT and Delta engage in a spirited rivalry to see which can "take down" a hostage plane quicker and more efficiently in training exercises. The FBI HRT, in turn, passes on counterterrorist training, including instruction for hostage negotiators, to local law enforcement agencies. The FBI also maintains regional HRTs as well, which are composed of field agents who come together for special training and exercises. Incidentally, it should be noted that the FBI's role in combating terrorism is expanding overseas due to new statutes that make attacks on Americans overseas punishable in U.S. courts.

As in the case of Delta, the British SAS has had a strong influence on the FBI HRT, which has copied many of the British unit's training procedures and adopted its all-black garb and balaclavas to hide the identity of its operators.

In addition to the FBI capability, a number of other federal agencies maintain CT units, including the U.S. Park Service. Perhaps the most secretive specialized unit drilled and prepared to engage terrorists is the Department of Energy's Nuclear Emergency Search Team (NEST), based in Germantown, Maryland. NEST is tasked with the protection of nuclear facilities and shipments and the recovery of nuclear material diverted by criminals or terrorists. It is not dependent on any other federal agency, and maintains special aircraft, ground vehicles, and radiation-detection equipment designed to identify and locate the radiological "signature" of stolen fissionable material or clandestine bombs. Given the gravity of any potential threat involving fissionable material, the unit's Rules of Engagement (ROE) are said to be the most sweeping and unrestricted in the federal government.

Several U.S. Secret Service officers were recently disciplined for having humorous badges made up with the legend: "You elect 'em, we protect 'em." The Secret Service's role, nevertheless, in combating terrorism cannot be underestimated. It is the front-line agency charged with the protection of the President and Vice President and their immediate families, as well as the President-elect, the Vice President-elect, former presidents and their wives, minor children of former presidents, presidential candidates, various other U.S. officials (at the President's direction), visiting foreign leaders, and certain other distinguished foreign visitors. Given the increasing sophistication of foreign terrorists, the Secret Service trains with U.S. counterterrorism units and has developed formidable capabilities of its own.

Several units have also been created, known as "black hat" teams, to challenge the security of U.S. military bases, other top-secret government facilities, nuclear facilities, and even the White House, to see how well personnel and procedures would measure up in the event of a real terrorist threat. One of the best of these teams is the U.S. Navy's Security and Coordination team, known as the "Red Cell," which was originally set up as part of SEAL Team 6. To date, the unit—which is supported by an outside government contractor and composed of SEALs and other special operators—has been responsible for more than 270 terrorism awareness exercises at U.S. Navy bases, piers, and other facilities around the globe.

The exercises are conducted under tightly controlled conditions and in very limited time windows, and involve, according to one secret report, "penetrating base outer perimeters by climbing fencelines at day or night, using false ID at gates, commandeering gates, or running them. Terrorist tactics enacted on bases included the bombing of personnel, support assets, and critical strategic assets, and the taking of hostages and barricading within facilities on base." The realism that the Red Cell strives for during its exercises also has its pitfalls. For example, an exercise where a hostage was taken at a U.S. Navy facility in California reportedly got out of hand and resulted in injury to the "hostage," and is currently the subject of litigation.

According to the secret report, "Navy antiterrorism specialists demonstrated the vulnerability of installations to terrorist tactics" at fourteen U.S. Navy bases around the world. In one instance, despite the fact that the target base was at a high state of threat readiness, a Red Cell "terrorist" team was able to get past perimeter defenses simply by riding through the main gate hidden in the trunks of taxicabs.

Corruption Probes

In recent years, virtually all of the U.S. special operations/counterterrorist units have been touched by scandal. There are charges that some of the units have lived high off the hog, buying Mercedes-Benz, Rolls Royce, and Porsche automobiles; traveling first class and globe-trotting on private jets; setting up expensive "front" corporations and renting penthouses; double-billing the government for expenses and pocketing the money; and even acquiring a hot-air balloon from DEA (Drug Enforcement Administration). Critics allege that some of the counterterrorist units operated as a law unto themselves, and that even the Secretary of Defense and his principal deputies did not know what they were up to. There are also allegations of missions that got out of hand and resulted in injuries to innocent people.

Delta Force, SEAL Team 6, ISA (Intelligence Support Activity), and other units are all currently, or recently have been, under investigation for financial irregularities and other abuses. The problems involving Delta were so pervasive, in fact, that the unit was reorganized following allegations that more than $200,000 in false vouchers were filed by members of the unit.

ISA was a secret Army intelligence unit that grew out of the Iran hostage rescue mission and provided support to Delta and various counterterrorist operations, including the hunt for kidnapped U.S. General James Dozier in Italy. By 1985, it reportedly had 283 agents spread around the world. More than a dozen officers connected with ISA have been investigated for financial improprieties, and Lt. Colonel Dale Duncan, one of ISA's top men, was convicted in 1985 of fraud involving nearly $90,000 in missing funds. Among other accusations, Duncan allegedly double-billed the unit for airline tickets and bought his wife a red Porsche sports car with some of the missing money. Former Special Operations boss Colonel James Longhofer, who has seven decorations for bravery in combat, subsequently was court martialed for not conducting a thorough investigation of Duncan and accusations related to others in the unit. He was sentenced to two years in prison and fined $24,000, which he is appealing.

In the mid-1980s, 85 members of Delta were reprimanded or court martialed for filing false travel and lodging vouchers in conjunction with the operation of overseas protective details, mostly involving the protection of U.S. ambassadors in places like Beirut. The Delta operators served as part of the embassy staff, under official cover, and argue that the double-billing procedure was necessary in order to survive, especially in expensive international cities. Many, including some of the original members of the unit, resigned in disgust rather than accept reprimands. They contend that the Pentagon brass knew that the false vouchers were being filed and tacitly gave it their approval since it was clear to all concerned that the men were not receiving enough money to take care of their food and lodging needs.

A number of members of SEAL Team 6 have been convicted and are currently serving prison sentences for such things as submitting false purchasing claims and filing false vouchers. Commander Richard Marcinko, the unit's highly respected first Commanding Officer, who established SEAL Team 6 in 1980, had his name removed from the selection list for promotion to captain, and is currently under investigation for a variety of financial and other abuses. According to reports, the unit purchased Mercedes-Benz cars, to be used in undercover operations, outside of normal procurement channels, and individual members have been charged with the theft of scuba gear, for setting up a system that overpaid travel claims, and for forging receipts for cash advances. Discipline was said to be lax, and members of the unit reportedly were involved in dozens of brawls, speeding and drunk driving incidents, and even such things as pit bull fighting and procuring rental cars for "demolition derbies."

As if this were not enough already, seven members of the Red Cell Team, established as a part of SEAL Team 6 to test security awareness and preparations at Naval and other military installations, and a civilian contractor, Essex Corporation, have been sued in Los Angeles federal court for $6.2 million in connection with an incident during a security exercise. On March 19, 1986, Ron Sheridan, the security director of the Naval Weapons Station at Seal Beach, California, was kidnapped by Red Team members at his home in suburban Los Angeles. Sheridan's wife, Marge, witnessed the abduction. She grabbed a pistol, and could have shot the "assailants," but they whispered something to Sheridan about it being an "exercise," and he waved her off.

Sheridan was pushed into a waiting vehicle and driven to an undisclosed location, where he was beaten, had his head shoved in a toilet bowl, and stripped of his clothes. He sustained multiple cuts, abrasions on the face and back, a rib dislocation, and internal muscle trauma during the ordeal.[22] After more than thirty hours of captivity he was finally released. Essex Corporation representatives on the scene, themselves former SEALs, who were monitoring the entire exercise on film as part of their company's contract with the Navy, allegedly made no attempt to assist Sheridan and, therefore, were also named in the suit.

Some say it is the secrecy that such units use to shield their activities that accounts for such problems; secrecy that contributes to too little administrative and financial oversight. Others believe that there is too much temptation, that some special operators have lived too long under prosperous "legends," or cover, and cannot easily revert back to the routine and relatively low pay of the military. One former SEAL Team 6 member blames it on the "unconventional mentality" that is part of the job. "You learn to cheat, only don't get caught," he says. 'Why were you late?,' someone asks, and you make up some bullshit excuse: 'We didn't want to leave without everybody and somebody had the runs, and you tell a funny story and they love it." Still others maintain that the problem is the conventional military, those disparagingly called "the clean boys." They "don't understand what we are all about," says one special operator. "A lot of our problems are because the military brass don't think in an unconventional manner. They're used to deploying large numbers of people and don't think small unit tactics and operations." This has led to a Pentagon vendetta against special operations units like Delta and the SEAL Team 6, say champions of those units. Much of the support for such units comes from the Congress, and conspiratorialists maintain that the Joint Chiefs and other top Pentagon officials deliberately gave some of the special operations units "too much rope, knowing that they would hang themselves. Then they could go back to the Congress and say, 'See, we told you this would happen.' " Indeed, there is evidence that the Pentagon did not insist on any real checks or oversight for a long time, and then established new guidelines and applied them retroactively.

Whatever the reasons, U.S. special operations/counterterrorist capabilities have been damaged by fraud, waste, and abuse problems, real and alleged. The Pentagon has set up new oversight procedures to maintain closer financial accountability, which hopefully will prevent a repeat of past difficulties without jeopardizing the flexibility, security, and sometimes unusual needs of such units. As the former head of one covert unit used to tell his operators, "Always get a receipt. Even if you get someone laid, get a receipt. We can argue later over whether it was in the national interest that you got someone laid, but at least you'll have a receipt and no one can accuse you afterwards of pocketing the money." He adds: "It's the accountants that always get you."

Allegations of poor discipline and unprofessional behavior may be harder to address. Special operations units attract an unusual breed of men who, by their very nature, "have to be used," says a former SEAL. "SEALs don't just 'exist' well," he continues, maintaining that boredom and down time are the real enemies of any special operations unit. "SEALs are an operational asset, not an administrative asset. They're not like ships sitting off the coast. They should be used more, like Soviet *spetsnaz,* if for no other reason than to keep their proficiency up and to get them used to operating under cover." If the U.S. employed Delta and SEAL Team 6 more, he contends, there would be far fewer attitudinal and other problems associated with the units.

By contrast, former DOD special operations chief Noel Koch maintains that, generally speaking, "Special operations forces have no role in fighting terrorism."[23] While counterterrorist units are largely derived from the special operations forces community, continues Koch, they are really just reaction forces. The problem, therefore, is to find other ways to employ them when they are not reacting to specific challenges.

Profile of a CT Operator

Just what kind of man becomes a member of an elite counterterrorist military or law enforcement unit? In addition generally to being superbly conditioned physical specimens with above-

average intelligence, most of those who volunteer for elite counterterrorist units have what has been described as "unconventional personalities." As one ex-Delta man put it, "I have never
been a conformist, you see. As a child I wasn't. In school, I
wasn't." This is just the opposite of the standard Marine profile, where one conforms to the system or is out. This theme is
echoed by a former assault team leader of SEAL Team 6 when
he was asked why he became a SEAL.

> I was in Navy ROTC, but I was never very big at drilling and
> all of the routine madness. So when I was reviewed in my junior
> year to see if you are going to stay in or not, they asked, "Why
> do you do so well in summer when you're out on cruise and then
> you come back here and don't do anything? I said it's because
> a lot of what you're doing here is Mickey Mouse bullshit that has
> nothing to do with the Navy and its mission. Well, a Marine
> Corps Lt. Colonel was there and he blew up. But the CO of the
> unit was an Airdale captain and he called me outside and took
> me down to his office and said, "I'm going to recommend you
> for the place I think you'd fit best in the Navy."

The following year he was on his way to BUD/S (Basic Under-
water Demolition/SEAL) training.

   According to psychiatrists involved in screening the original
Delta applications, most of those selected had psychological profiles that were most often associated with criminal behavior. As
one former Delta operator quipped, "Don't send Delta in to rescue the plane if they've already paid the ransom because you'll
never see the ransom again. They'll take down the plane and
just keep going." The sense that every special operator has a little bit of larceny in his character can also be glimpsed in the
story of the Delta operators who were tasked, as part of an exercise, with planning the robbery of Fort Knox. Other operators
kept close watch on one member of the unit, who kept on repeating, with undisguised enthusiasm, "Man, this will work. This
will really work." In many respects the men of Delta were, and

remain, misfits, mavericks, unsuited to the demands and requirements of a peacetime military. "They are the kind of guys you can't housebreak," says one observer. A former Air Force officer reflected the disdain with which most regular military men view special operations forces: "It's too bad that you can't just put them to sleep between wars."

While a few give the impression that they howl at the moon at night, the vast majority of CT operators are quiet professionals and not very colorful, says Noel Koch. "Most Delta guys are older," explains Koch, "top ranking NCOs."[24] Although a few develop a bad case of what is sometimes called the "for realies," the quality most valued in a counterterrorist operator is steadiness, says a former member of SEAL Team 6. The best operators are solid, dependable, and bold without being reckless. They are also men who have mastered a unique range of difficult skills, from extraordinary marksmanship to exiting out the back of a low-flying aircraft at night into the sea in a Zodiac raft. There are probably not ten thousand men at any one time in the United States, a nation of 240 million, qualified to be active-duty members of Delta Force or SEAL Team 6.

Despite an outwardly tranquil appearance, CT operators are a different breed of men. Not only are they men who hunger for adventure, but many CT operators just plain like to fight. They are never so alive or happy as when they are in the midst of a mission, "running the tables" on the bad guys, no matter the risks involved. If it were not for the risks, another veteran special operator contends, it "wouldn't be any fun. It's defying the odds that makes it worth doing."

CT operators not only work extremely hard, but they play very hard as well, and much of their play involves thrill-seeking and risk taking. Like pilots, CT operators seem to have a penchant for fast cars and motorcycles, as the parking lot of any CT unit compound will attest. Skiing, scuba diving, flying, sport parachuting, mountain climbing, and hunting are all frequently mentioned by CT operators as favorite pastimes. With the exceptions of U.S. football or soccer, there is little interest in watching sports on television; CT operators, it seems, do not want to get their thrills vicariously.

Every unit has a bar or pub that it favors in proximity to its base, and the brawls that occur are the stuff of legend. One special operations man, before going to his favorite hangout, straps a fighting knife to his ankle, slips another in the small of his back, and wraps piano wire—that can be used as a garrote— around his waist. "Is all that stuff really necessary?" asked a newcomer to the unit. "Sure," he responded. "You never know what might happen."

Another member of a special operations unit periodically used to get tanked up at the local pub, pull out a knife, and jam it into the top of the bar. He would then challenge anyone in the house to arm-wrestle him. If he lost, the winner got to stick him with the knife in his arm; if he won he got to stick the loser.

The SEALs maintain a private club near their Little Creek, Virginia, facility which, unlike other area bars, does not close at 2.00 A.M., but stays open all night. Good-looking women who want to party (known as "frog chasers," as in frogmen), are always welcome, but those who don't meet the grade are turned away with the admonition that the place is "too full." Because it is exclusively a SEALs preserve, there is not the usual friction with outsiders that leads to problems. And if that is not enough of a disincentive, a huge former Medal of Honor winner tends bar and personally expels troublemakers.

Becoming a member of a CT unit is one of the ultimate macho experiences. Women have not been admitted to any of the leading CT units in the world, and one of the great attractions of the CT units is the camaraderie, the feeling of a special bond that exists between members of the unit—the "all for one, one for all" attitude. "You're very loyal to your people and what you're doing," says a former member of SEAL Team 6. "They stress that all the way through: no one does anything alone. It's a team." There is no room for error when carrying out a counterterrorist mission, and each member has to have complete trust in his fellow team members and officers. This sense of loyalty to other members of the team transcends everything else. "You do anything for a teammate," says one former CT operator. "And you never leave one behind; that's unthinkable." This sense that one's first loyalty belongs to the unit is often cited by CT operators as an explanation for the high divorce rate typical of their units. "It's hard on a wife and kids," says a former Delta man. "Sometimes you get a call in the middle of the night and just walk out the door. You can't say where you're going or when you'll be coming back . . . or if you'll ever be coming back. It's the nature of the business."

Some men join CT units for what they perceive as the glamour and mystique attached to being a counterterrorist commando, but the glamour does not last very long. "What it's all about doesn't sink in until you see some people die," observes a former SEAL Team 6 operator soberly, who says he witnessed nearly a dozen SEALs die during the five-and-a-half years he was a member of the unit. "That's when you realize it's for real. Up till then I think a lot of people got caught up in the glamour of it. They don't realize it's not a pretty game. It's not a sport. It's very real, and it's cruel."

Weapons and Equipment

Counterterrorist commandos and law enforcement units are constantly seeking new weapons that will give them an edge in the close-in combat characteristic of most engagements with terrorists. In this way they hope to lessen the danger to themselves and increase it for the terrorist enemy.

Few counterterrorist units are armed with assault rifles, being predisposed to more compact weapons suitable for use in tight spots and in close-quarters fighting. Several Israeli special operations units are exceptions to this rule inasmuch as they regularly use a folding-stock version of the Galil assault rifle, although Uzi submachine guns, including the tiny mini-Uzi, are also employed on some missions. Similarly, the Italian NOCS (Nucleo Operativo Centrale di Sicurezza) unit is armed with

H&K assault rifles. For the most part, however, assault rifles and combat shotguns are used for blasting locks and hinges rather than engaging the enemy.

Men of the 22nd regiment of the British SAS (SP Team), by contrast, are normally armed with the 14-shot Browning Hi-Power 9-mm pistol, carried in a holster on the right hip, and the 9-mm Heckler & Koch MP5-series submachine gun, often described as "the Cadillac of submachine guns," or a silenced Sterling SMG. The H&K MP5 was used for the first time by the SAS in an actual mission during the 1980 incident at Princes Gate. The MP5 has also been adopted by the West German GSG-9, the U.S. Delta Force, France's RAID, and the Italian NOCS, to name but a few CT units. The U.S. Delta Force was equipped with two variants of the weapon, MP5A2s and MP5A3s (telescoping-stock), on the ill-fated 1980 mission to rescue the U.S. hostages in Tehran.[25]

The MP5K, which has a short barrel and no stock, is a superbly crafted weapon and can be fired fully automatic, in bursts, or in a single-shot mode. It boasts excellent open sights and has a reputation for being perhaps the most accurate of all submachine guns, an important factor in engagements where innocent bystanders or hostages could be struck by wild shots. Several extremely effective suppressors, or silencers, can be married to the weapon, and an ultra-short version known as the MP5KA4 is also available.

The SAS reportedly also has a number of MP5KA4s concealed inside attaché cases that fire through a port in the end of the case. The shooter operates the concealed MP5KA4 by pressing a "trigger" in the handle of the attaché case, which activates a laser aiming-spot indicator and fires the weapon. Another variant on the same theme is a silenced .22-caliber American 180 built into an attaché case, with a 180-round drum magazine. It also uses a laser sighting system and is fired by pressing a "trigger" in the handle. Because it is silenced and the empty shell casings are ejected within the case, it could be fired in a crowd without anyone knowing where the attack is coming from. In addition to covert counterterrorist operations, either weapon would also have great utility to terrorists. In 1981 a German working for the Libyans but purporting to be employed by the Saudis sought to purchase five attaché cases with the built-in MP5KA4s, but the arms dealer reported the overture to British intelligence.

Other submachine guns commonly used by counterterrorist commandos include the Italian Beretta M12, which comes with a folding stock, the British Sterling, the Swedish K, and the Israeli-made Uzi. Designed in 1949 by Uzi Gal, an elfin and engaging Israeli who now lives in Pennsylvania, the Uzi is a relatively unsophisticated but extraordinarily reliable weapon, and remains extremely popular with some CT units.

Submachine guns like the 9-inch-long Ingram Model 10 occasionally have been used by CT units, such as the Israeli commandos at Entebbe and some police SWAT teams in the United States, but the weapon has a tendency to jam and is generally considered too inaccurate for counterterrorist operations. Without its famous "whispering death" silencer, which makes the weapon more than twice as long but adds weight to the front of the SMG where it is needed, the Ingram "rises" dramatically and must be held down with a strap on the front. Weapons like the Ingram find more acceptance today by Miami drug dealers and criminals than law enforcement and counterterrorist professionals.

Given the need for extraordinary accuracy and surgical placement of shots, especially during hostage rescue missions, the submachine gun is a realistic option only for the world's top CT units. In most units, major emphasis is placed on developing handgun skills. The most popular handguns are the Browning Hi-Power, the Beretta 92SBF, the Smith & Wesson 459, the Heckler & Koch P7M8 and P9S, and the SIG-Sauer P-226. The German GSG-9 operator carries an H&K P7 9-mm automatic pistol, which has a revolutionary squeeze cocker that means that the weapon is ready to fire as soon as it is gripped. According to Leroy Thompson, "With all but the most highly-trained HRU [Hostage Rescue Units], the handgun may actually be the best assault weapon because the operative must consciously pull the trigger each time he fires, thereby countering any tendency to fire wildly and forcing target selection."[26] Handguns, moreover, can be easily concealed and therefore are ideal for undercover work or for commandos sneaking up on a hostage aircraft disguised as mechanics or ground personnel.

Recalling the disaster at the XX Munich Olympics, every major counterterrorist unit regards sniping skills as absolutely essential. The origin of sniping can be traced back to the eighteenth century when rival armies tried to pick off enemy officers to sow confusion among enemy troops. Most CT units favor bolt-action sniper's rifles with extremely sophisticated optical sights, although, as Thompson notes, "many HRUs are switching over to highly accurate self-loading rifles which allow more rapid target acquisition should the sniper have to deal with multiple targets."[27] Snipers generally work in two-man teams in which one man serves as the observer and the other as the shooter. Top choices among the sniper's rifles available today include the SIG/Sauer SSG 2000, the Steyr SSG PII, the Mauser 66, the Galil Sniper, the WA 2000, the M40-A1, the FN Sniper, the M21, the H&K models PSG1 and G3SG/1, and the Remington Model 700 (used by the U.S. Marine Corps). Although the GSG-9 originally adopted the Mauser 66, in recent years it has largely changed over to the Heckler & Koch PSG1, a semi-automatic 7.62 NATO rifle. The PSG1 is in service with the military forces of over fifty nations. One recent innovation on the market is called "Synco-Fire," described in its promotional literature as "a powerful new tool for aggressively dealing with criminal and terrorist violence," which electronically links all CT marksmen together under the control of one commander and ensures that they will all fire simultaneously.

Sound suppressors (silencers) are utilized by most units for clandestine work or so as not to give away the position of the shooter. In recent years, however, some U.S. government officials, betraying remarkable ignorance, have viewed silencers as "assassination tools." During the Carter administration, the U.S. State Department actually prohibited the export of suppressors to Great Britain on the grounds that they had no real military application and likely would be misused in Northern Ireland. Carter's ambassador to El Salvador, Robert White, mandated that his security guards, some of them Delta operators, could not use or even bring suppressors into the country. As one Delta man recalls, "He treated his security detail like the enemy."

Both because of their stopping power and since terrorists are increasingly wearing body armor, some CT commandos are employing Teflon-coated Glaser Safety Slugs and armor-piercing rounds. Such ammo is less likely to richochet, but may overpenetrate. Some units are also experimenting with low-velocity rounds that can be fired in close-quarters engagements with less fear of penetrating airline hulls.

Perhaps the most famous SAS contribution to the counterterrorist arsenal is the stun or concussion grenade, sometimes known as "flash-bangs." The magnesium-based grenades have a blinding flash and thunderclap report (200 + decibels) designed to disorient adversaries and permit CT commandos to get the drop on them. Since "flash-bangs" do not spew shrapnel like combat grenades, there is little threat of permanent injury to hostages or other innocent bystanders. The major problem associated with "flash-bangs" is the potential of fire. "Flash-bangs" were first employed during the German GSG-9 operation to rescue a captive jetliner at Mogadishu. Two British SAS operators, Major Alastair Morrison and Sergeant Barry Davies, accompanied the Germans and tossed "flash-bangs" inside the aircraft as the doors over the wings were breached. The GSG-9 subsequently developed its own DT11B1 stun grenade.

Most CT commandos are skilled in the use of combat knives, and some experiment with weapons like bows and crossbows that fire medal darts and wicked-looking steel-tipped arrows. CT units have tool chests full of custom-made equipment tailored to their unique needs, such as bolt cutters, bomb blankets, lightweight ladders, climbing spikes, sledgehammers, and rappelling gear. In order to gather intelligence on their adversaries, CT units also boast thermal imaging systems, "spike" mikes, directional microphones, and a variety of other eavesdropping devices. The Royal Dutch Marines counterterrorist unit even has a former acrobat as an operator whose specialty is reconnaissance and getting close enough, undetected, to a target to place spike mikes and eavesdropping equipment where they can be most effective. Since rapid door and barrier breaching is often critical and explosive charges are not always appropriate, most CT units employ various kinds of thermal and high-speed cutting torches, including a monstrous circular power saw developed in the United States that will cut through steel doors in a matter of seconds.

Many CT units have their own equipment and surveillance vans, four-wheel-drive vehicles, souped-up cars and motor-cycles, helicopters, and even executive jets. Some of the hardened 280 SE Mercedes-Benz pursuit sedans employed by the German GSG-9 are capable of speeds in excess of 130 miles an hour, and have gun ports in their bullet-proof windshields so that commandos can fire at the vehicles they are chasing. A few units have also experimented with all-terrain fast-attack vehicles based on dune buggy designs and cigarette-type speedboats.

A U.S Navy nuclear attack submarine has been refitted to carry Navy SEALs on covert missions, and fifteen two- and six-man minisubs have been built for transporting SEALs in and out of hostile territory. Delta Force, by contrast, will be transported by the Army's 160th helicopter unit, known as the "Night Stalkers." The unit's motto is "Death Waits in the Dark," and its pilots are among the "hottest" and most daring to be found anywhere. They fly the MH-6, known as the "killer egg," one of the swiftest, quietest choppers ever built, outfitted with night-vision equipment and navigation systems that permit them to be operated in total darkness.

The SAS, the GSG-9, and a number of other units use remote-control track vehicles, like the British-manufactured Wheelbarrow MK8, for handling bombs and for surveillance, and weapons can even be mounted on the vehicle's mechanical arm. Some of the radio-operated vehicles can actually climb stairs.

When fully dressed out for combat, most counterterrorist operators look like apparitions from another world. Virtually all of their clothing is black or of dark color, which allows them to blend in with the shadows or nighttime darkness, when most missions are carried out. Indeed, GIGN commandos are even referred to as "the men in black." The style of clothing varies from unit to unit, but nearly all CT operators wear some kind of overalls or "utilities," assault vests made of ballistic armor, and balaclavas or flash hoods. Ballistic helmets are achieving greater acceptance because of the protection they afford and because communications systems can be built into them; however, many CT operators still favor berets and less confining headgear. GSG-9 commandos generally wear a titanium safety helmet, equipped with a two-way radio, that "will resist any normal-calibre bullet."[28] The Swiss make an even tougher titanium helmet, the PSH-77, that is so strong it can absorb repeated direct hits from a 9-mm Uzi submachine gun.[29] If not using respirators, CT operators will wear safety goggles to protect their eyes from the flash of stun grenades, or ski masks to hide their features.

Footgear is extremely varied, and ranges from traditional military combat boots to ultra-soft athletic shoes that permit commandos to approach a target with great stealth or to creep along the fuselage of a hostage jetliner without making any noise.

When operating covertly, CT units often have to shed their special clothing and elaborate equipment in order to blend into the local population. On the Iran rescue mission, for example, Delta operators dressed like many of the Iranian students and Revolutionary Guards: blue jeans, combat boots (especially "Chippewa" climbing boots), M1965 field jackets dyed black, dark-colored shirts, and a wool navy watch cap.[30] Each man had a tape-covered American flag on his shoulder so that the Delta commandos could not later be accused of being spies. Instead of tape-covered flags, today many units have a small

Velcro patch on their shoulders to which a Velcro-backed flag easily can be affixed.

Risks and Prospects

On November 24, 1985, an Egyptian commando team attempted to rescue an EgyptAir jetliner being held by terrorists on Malta. The poorly trained commandos jumped the gun and launched their assault forty-five minutes before Maltese troops were supposed to initiate a diversion. In addition to blowing the main door and the over-wing hatches, the Egyptian commandos hoped to gain access to the passenger cabin by blasting a small hole through the roof of the rear cargo hatch. Unfortunately, one of the inexperienced commandos used more than a kilo of C4 plastic explosive to do a job requiring a shaped charge only a fraction that size. The resulting explosion took out six rows of seats, killing at least six passengers and setting off a roaring fire that swept through the plane. Forty-five more passengers died of toxic fumes and smoke inhalation, or were shot by the commandos as they fled the burning aircraft.

Less than a year later, there was to be a tragic replay of the Malta debacle at Karachi, Pakistan, when Pan Am flight 073 was hijacked by Arab terrorists reportedly under the command of Abu Nidal. The hijackers seized the jumbo jetliner with 374 passengers and 15 crew members on the ground shortly after the flight had arrived from Bombay, India. After sixteen hours of negotiations, the four terrorists apparently panicked when the lights in the plane went out and opened fire on their hostages. Pakistani commandos on the scene failed to react promptly and it was not until passengers began fleeing from the slaughter inside the aircraft that they mounted their own assault, which was clumsy and confused. When it was all over, twenty-one passengers were dead and as many as a hundred injured. The terrorists, one of whom was badly wounded, were taken into custody after surrendering.

There was even highly unusual public criticism in the Soviet news media of an assault by a Russian police unit on a hostage jetliner in March 1988. Nine people, five of them terrorists, died in the attack and at least twenty were wounded. According to reports in the West, the police officers fired willy-nilly through the underside of the aircraft after their presence was discovered by the hijackers. The aircraft, a Soviet-built Tu 154, also was reportedly rocked by an explosion and gutted by the subsequent fire. It is not known whether the terrorists were carrying a bomb or if the explosion was caused by the police in an effort to breach the fuselage.

The disasters at Malta, Karachi, and Leningrad underscore the problems inherent in trying to rescue hostage jetliners. Moreover, they are clear evidence that extremely precise skills and training are required to successfully carry out such missions, and that an improperly equipped, trained, and led force may represent more of a threat to the hostages than to the hijackers. Counterterrorist operations are not an exact science, nor are they for the indecisive or faint of heart: they require well-honed procedures, split-second timing, and an ability to improvise according to the conditions since no two hijackings are identical. Even crack Western CT units generally require more than a little luck in order to carry out a rescue operation. Finally, one of the great heresies in circulation today is that such missions can be accomplished without casualties. The fact remains that nearly every rescue operation to date involving a jetliner has resulted in some loss of innocent human life.

It also must be noted that counterterrorist units of the kind described in this chapter are not a panacea, and have only limited utility in the war against terrorism. They represent a reactive response to specific terrorist incidents rather than a proactive measure designed to address the problem in all of its permutations. Prevention will always remain the first goal of antiterrorism efforts. However, the very fact that such units exist serves as a deterrent and keeps terrorists continually on their guard with respect to their plans and operations. It is hoped that CT units may be deployed in the future in a more proactive or preemptive fashion; that is to say, in advance of an actual terrorist attack rather than after it is already under way.

9

Off the Reservation

Haven't we worked in the same sewers?
—One special operator to another

IN 1984 John Wayne Hearn and Paul Englett, two ex-Marines who had "bounced around" a great deal and held down a series of dead-end jobs, decided to make a drastic career move: they would become hired guns, counterterrorists, mercenaries, security specialists, whatever there was a market for. But the first obstacle confronting them was how to make their talents known to prospective clients. Why not advertise, they decided. But where?

Murder for Hire

The two men decided to place an ad in *Soldier of Fortune* magazine in the summer of 1984, which would appear in the September issue: "EX-MARINES—67–69 Nam Vets," read the classified ad. "Ex-DI. weapons specialist–jungle warfare. pilot. M.E. high-risk assignments. U.S. or overseas. [phone number]." Shortly after the ad appeared, Englett dropped out of the partnership for personal reasons. In the meantime, Hearn received a number of responses to the ad, including one from Bob Black of Bryan, Texas, located near College Station. Black, who was supported largely by his wife and had a history of psychiatric problems, was not looking to hire someone but rather for a job himself. Although an electrician by training, in his later confession to police he described himself as a "professional killer." He told Hearn that he wanted to link up with him and perform the same kind of services. Hearn apparently thanked him for his interest and told Black to stay in touch.

Hearn also got a call from a young woman named Debbie Banister, who singled out his ad because of its local area code. She explained that her sister was having child custody problems with her ex-husband and that she needed some help. Hearn met with Banister and they soon became romantically involved. Ultimately, Debbie convinced him to kill her sister's ex-husband, and, while he was at it, her ex-husband as well.

After committing both murders, Hearn heard from Black once again, who said that he had some guns for sale. Hearn went to Texas to meet with Black, but did not buy any guns. Instead, Black offered him $10,000 to kill his wife, saying that he had been turned down by three other people already. It later turned out that he was having an affair with another woman and had purchased a $150,000 life insurance policy on his wife. Hearn declined Black's entreaty and left. When he got to Houston, he called Debbie and told her what had happened. She blew up, telling him they could use the money, and reminding him that he'd killed two other people already, so what difference did a third person make? Chastised by Debbie, he returned to Bryan and murdered Black's wife on February 21, 1985.

Back in Georgia, police investigators queried Debbie about Hearn, who had been photographed with her at the funeral of her late former husband. She identified him as a cousin, but further investigation revealed that she was lying. As part of their investigation, detectives reviewed Hearn's long-distance phone records, including the calls to Bryan, Texas. They subsequently called the Bryan police and learned about the unsolved murder of Black's wife, which bore a remarkable similarity to their own cases, and soon a murder warrant was issued for Hearn.

Hearn fled town one step ahead of the law and headed for Boulder, Colorado, in his car. He intended to approach *Soldier of Fortune* publisher Bob Brown about his offer to pay $1 million for the first Nicaraguan pilot to defect with a Mi-24 (HIND) helicopter, presumably to see if Brown would finance an effort to steal one of the gunships, thereby setting himself up for life someplace beyond the reach of U.S. authorities. Hearn, however, got cold feet en route and called the Bryan police to turn himself in.

Hearn turned State's evidence and was ultimately convicted of the three murders, for which he received three life terms. On the basis of Hearn's testimony, Black was convicted of murder and is currently on death row in Texas. Debbie Banister and her sister were also convicted of participating in the murders of their former husbands and were given long jail terms. The murders also spawned litigation against *Soldier of Fortune* magazine, which was sued for $22.5 million by Mrs. Black's survivors for having run Hearn's original classified ad.

On March 3, 1988, a jury in Houston, Texas, ordered *Soldier of Fortune* to pay $9.4 million in actual and punitive damages to Mrs. Black's mother and son. It was the first time a publication had been held liable for a crime facilitated by a classified ad. Attorneys for Mrs. Black's survivors argued that the magazine was negligent in printing the ads. However, attorney for the plaintiffs Ronald Franklin, who drove a baby blue Ferrari to the courthouse every day and was described by one SOF associate editor as "the kind of kid guys like us used to beat up when we were young," demonstrated a deep-seated animosity toward the magazine. "We brought this case to get *Soldier of Fortune* off the magazine rack," he told CBS News on the courthouse steps after the verdict was announced, "and I hope we've done that."[1] SOF publisher Bob Brown is appealing the verdict. According to Brown: "This means that every publisher is going to have to look at every ad he publishes and make a determination . . . try and look into the minds of those individuals that put those ads in, and that's just an impossibility."[2] The case raises major First Amendment issues and is likely to go all the way to the Supreme Court, especially since additional litigation against SOF flowing from more than two dozen other crimes in nineteen states allegedly linked to classified ads published in the magazine.

As an editorial in the *Los Angeles Times* observed, "it is hard to escape the conclusion that it [*Soldier of Fortune*] was sued by Mrs. Black's son and mother because, of all the parties to this tragedy, *Soldier of Fortune* was the only one with any resources." The editorial goes on to say, "If a publication is to be held liable for the criminal acts undertaken by its readers, using products or services advertised on its pages, then what about those menacing ads for steak knives? And ant poison? And gin?"[3] Another editorial maintained that SOF "was no more culpable in the terrible crime than was the mailman who delivered *Soldier of Fortune*. Freedom of the press lost Round One. Almost certainly higher courts will reverse this ruling."[4]

The Hearn case also raises serious questions about former spooks, special operators, and military veterans who decide to make their special skills available to the highest bidder, even for illegal endeavors. Before the liability issue was raised, magazines like *Soldier of Fortune* ran dozens of classified ads offering "mercs for hire." "Don't get mad, get even," suggests one ad. "Work alone, short term, discreet, confidential." "MECHANIC," reads another. "Short term, high risk contracts." A third ad seeks employment opportunities for "TOP RISK ACTION GROUP. Contracts with individuals, organizations and governments. Recovery, rescue, defense, intrusion training and strategic consulting internationally. No reds."

Other classified ads offer up the services of "Two Dutch shocktroopers for military job," "Six year USAF—S.E. Asia Vet," "Qualified literate rational experienced professional with diverse background seeks high-risk, high paying position," "HUNTER: HIGH RISK CONTRACTS," "Former military-intelligence member. Specializes in rescue from cults, street pimps," and "SAVANT FOR HIRE: Professional investigator, body guard, armed escort, bondsman, and bounty-hunter. Also have knowledge of military and counter-terrorism."

In retrospect, most of those who read the ads dismissed them as the work of losers, Walter Mittys, or guys trying to impress their girlfriends. Moreover, there was a certain humorous and self-parodying quality about them. Surely no self-respecting mercenary or private-sector special operator would really advertise for work, especially not in *Soldier of Fortune* or the other adventure magazines likely to be monitored by law enforcement authorities. The ads had run for the better part of a decade before it became clear that they were actually facilitating the commission of illegal acts, including murder and mayhem. To the credit of the editors of *Soldier of Fortune,* they pulled the ads as soon as they learned what was happening.

Hearn and the other "mercs" described above are, for all intents and purposes, amateurs, the flotsam and jetsam of past wars and a bitter present, frustrated by unfulfilled lives, without status or steady work, desperately seeking the approbation of others and a chance to make a "real score." No one is likely to take them seriously, least of all someone actually in the market for men of special martial talents and capabilities. The bozos who find work end up in jail or in the grave, like the hapless American "mercenary" Daniel Gearhart, who was executed by the Angolan government after answering an ad for mercenaries in a California newspaper.

But what happens, by contrast, when a real badass "goes off the reservation"—an ex–Delta operator or CIA warlord, someone who can apply all of his cunning and formidable training to the commission of crimes or acts of terrorism? When the counterterrorist is seduced "by the dark side" and becomes a terrorist? Indeed, several terrorist groups currently operate as "Third Force" organizations, available to the highest bidder, and a number of former Basque ETA terrorists currently provide security to Colombian drug lords. Thus, if terrorists can be seduced by the prospect of easy money and new thrills, why should it come as a surprise that a few Western counterterrorist commandos, skilled in the "black arts," might not also choose the same path? After all, many Delta operators with twenty years in the service can expect little more than $800 or $900 a month for a pension. Says one observer, "All you need is one of these guys to go in the wrong direction because they're so well trained."

It is hard to get a handle on renegade operators, but there are rumors of an ex–Delta man nicknamed "Dirtball" working for the antigovernment guerrillas in El Salvador. Another former Delta operator is said to have joined the Sandinistas to avenge his father, who had been killed by Somoza.

The most celebrated case to date, however, involves former CIA contract officers Edwin P. Wilson and Frank Terpil, along with a score of other Americans, who—for lucrative contracts—supplied military technology and training to Libyan dictator Muammar Qaddafi. Today Wilson is serving 52 years in the federal pen for various crimes, while Terpil is still on the loose. Recent intelligence reports place Terpil in Bulgaria and Syria, engaged in the sale of arms and drugs and the provision of other services to international terrorists.

The Strange Odyssey of Ed Wilson

He was a soul-possessing man, a larger-than-life figure with shoulders that would fill a doorway. A poor boy from Nampa, Idaho, Edwin P. Wilson's life seemed to be a testament to the "American dream." In his heyday he cast a long shadow, living on a $5 million estate in the horse country near Upperville, Virginia, lavishly entertaining congressmen and senators, inviting presidential aides to hunt on his property, traveling the world, always on the move. He owned property in several states and half a dozen nations, and maintained an apartment in Geneva with a spectacular view of the lake. By his own admission, his net worth was at least $14 million. He dreamed, at different times, of becoming assistant secretary of defense for security affairs or even director of central intelligence.

Then, the man who had lived in the shadows all his adult life suddenly became the subject of international speculation and publicity, and his carefully constructed world began to crumble around him. His life and activities became grist for television and publications on every continent. It was darkly alluded that he was a modern incarnation of the "Old Man of the Mountain," the fabled master assassin who presided over a school of the dark arts, accused of everything from involvement in the Bay of Pigs to Francis Gary Powers's shootdown, the overthrow of the Allende government in Chile and the assassination of Orlando Letelier, and with arming and training Muammar Qaddafi's international terrorist brigades. Death has dogged his heels. At least five of his former employees and associates have met untimely deaths, and more than a score have been imprisoned or ruined because of their association with him.

Wilson is a man of paradox. The walls of his Washington office were decorated with only two signed photographs: one of Libya's Colonel Qaddafi, the other of Hubert H. Humphrey. While he was described variously as "a brilliant guy" and "one hell of a good mind," he surrounded himself with a motley assortment of men and women who possessed substantially more modest gifts: thugs, ex-cons, losers, mean-spirited men like arms dealer Frank Terpil, whose business partner George Korkola was fond of telling potential customers, "It will cost you more [for weapons] if you are communists. And it will cost you even more if they will be used to kill Americans." Men like John "the Dutchman" Dutcher, described by one former associate as "the deadliest man with his hands I've ever seen." Men like Douglas Schlachter, a former gas station employee who became, in time, Wilson's right arm in Libya. Wilson was a man's man who loved a good fist fight and a stiff drink, who never backed away from trouble, yet his closest associate was a woman. And then there was the greatest mystery of all: how could a man described as "absolutely loyal to his country" and "a super patriot" apparently sell out the United States in a dizzy succession of business deals that provided arms, training, and technology to international terrorists?

Beginning in 1976, Wilson became the number-one target of the U.S. Attorney General's Office Major Crimes Division in Washington, D.C. Every director of central intelligence from Schlesinger to Casey received a special briefing on Wilson's activities. He was the subject of special briefings presented to every president from Nixon through Reagan. His arrest and subsequent trials and convictions made headlines around the world. In a strange twist, a number of his former associates resurfaced as major players in the recent Iran/Contra affair.

Ed Wilson traveled far from the dusty little farm community of Nampa, Idaho. Today, however, he is locked in a tiny cell in solitary confinement at the federal prison in Marion, Illinois. But despite millions of words in the media devoted to him and his exploits, associates, public trials, and alleged crimes, the mystery remains. Who is Edwin P. Wilson? What were his crimes? Why did he become an agent of international terrorism?

The Education of a Special Operator

Like so much of his career, the early years of Edwin P. Wilson remain shrouded in mystery. Little is known of his youth except that he was raised on a farm near Nampa, Idaho. A strapping lad with a build like a lumberjack, he attended the University of Portland, graduating in 1951 with a degree in business administration. His graduate studies in industrial management were interrupted by the Korean War, and he joined the Marines, leaving the Northwest for the wider world that beckoned. "He didn't dwell on the past too much," recalled a former associate who said that Wilson almost never spoke of his youth or Idaho roots; but at least one person who knew him well said that he traveled back to Idaho occasionally, and there is some suggestion that he kept a bank account in Lewiston, Idaho, as recently as eight years ago.

After the Korean War, Wilson used his Marine explosives and logistics experience to, in his words, "wrangle a job from the CIA." And thus began a career that would take him to the heart of darkness and back again. One of his first assignments with the CIA was in the Office of Security, and he was one of those who provided security for the supersecret U-2 spy plane, first at the Nevada test site and later in California. He accompanied the planes to West Germany and Turkey, and was stationed in Turkey at the time Powers was shot down. With the demise of the U-2 project, he was transferred to the CIA's international organizations unit, an assignment that was to shape the rest of Wilson's professional career.

In the mid-1950s, the U.S. government was deeply concerned about communist penetration into the American labor movement, especially the maritime unions. To counteract this influence, the Agency set up operations to monitor communist activities and to help noncommunist members withstand efforts to subvert their unions. It was against this backdrop and the tensions of the cold war that Ed Wilson was assigned to penetrate the Seafarers International Union (SIU) and become the Agency's "man inside." According to Wilson, he was able to "find a job on my own without any help from the Agency," beginning as a "bone breaker," or enforcer, and quickly rising to become the union's international representative in Europe. As the union's international representative, Wilson traveled extensively, recruiting contacts and setting up a small clandestine network to monitor arms and munitions shipments by the Soviet Union and European nations, especially to revolutionaries in Cuba and Latin America.

As part of his activities to stem the influence of Communist party members in European trade unions, Wilson allied himself with various radical trade union factions and, after having won their trust, encouraged them to call unpopular and destructive strikes. His real motive was to give post-war European governments a pretext to crack down on communist influence in maritime trade unions. As a result of the efforts of Wilson and others, there was a marked reduction of Communist party influence in the stevedore, longshoremen's, and international seafarer's unions throughout Western Europe and the Mediterranean. Wilson also was active in England, where he helped undermine the radical London docker's leader, Jack Dash.

It was during this period, say friends, that Wilson acquired a taste for the good life, and developed the free-wheeling operational style that later would lead to his downfall. Nevertheless, years after Wilson left the Seafarers Union, several of the contacts and informants he recruited during this period were still passing along vital information on arms and munitions shipments by the Soviet Union to the Central Intelligence Agency.

After his wife and two sons were detained in Belgium for suspected currency violations, Wilson was called home by the union which, still unaware of his CIA connections, assigned him to the AFL-CIO headquarters in Washington. Wilson recalls: "George Meany, at that time, wanted someone to work for him in international activities in the Far East." At the behest of the AFL-CIO, Wilson made a three- or four-month tour of the Far East, in which he established many of the contacts who were later to serve him well both in Vietnam and in his business operations.

Using experience gained through the SIU, Wilson was instrumental in the Bay of Pigs operation during the 1960 gear-up for the overthrow of Castro. While still on the SIU payroll, Wilson recruited and supplied many of the exiled Cuban and South American mercenaries involved in the Bay of Pigs operation. Using his numerous contacts, and operating out of the Miami station, code name "J.M. Wave," Wilson procured arms and many of the small boats used in the initial training and ultimately the landing. He also provided logistical support to a number of operations designed to harass Castro both before and after the invasion. One of the men who worked most closely with Wilson during this time was E. Howard Hunt, later of Watergate fame. Hunt, who at the time was in charge of the CIA's liaison with the Frente Revolucionario Democratico (FRD) in Mexico, an organization of anti-Castro Cuban exiles, worked as Wilson's paymaster throughout the Bay of Pigs operation.

King of the Proprietaries

It was during this period that Wilson was first called upon to set up front companies to mask an intelligence operation, in this case the rapidly expanding preparations for the invasion. For the rest of his intelligence career, Wilson would be identified with so-called "proprietary" activities, that is, companies operated clandestinely by the CIA to provide unofficial cover for its agents and operations.

Perhaps the most famous proprietary companies run by the Agency in the post-war period were its airlines: Air America, described during the war in Southeast Asia as "the largest unscheduled airline in the world"; Air Asia; Southern Air Transport; and Civil Air Transport (CAT). At one time the combined assets of the CIA's air proprietaries were in excess of $50 million. The companies operated by Wilson were on a far more modest scale, but no less important to the success of various intelligence operations. Most of the companies provided cover for the activities of agents and the acquisition of goods and services needed in CIA operations. Occasionally a company would be used to launder funds. Most had only a handful, if any, real employees, and few ever turned a profit. But then profits were not the purpose of such companies. Like surplus assets at the conclusion of an operation, profits were generally viewed as a nuisance and complication, hard to dispose of and easy to trace. This is the reason why later, as the U.S. effort against Castro began to wind down, many proprietaries and leftover assets were sold off at "public" auction, usually held at 2:00 in the morning. Such "midnight" fire sales provided Agency employees with prime real estate at bargain-basement prices.

It was in Miami that Wilson developed several important relationships that were to last throughout his CIA career, most notably with Theodore "Ted" Shackley, known as "the Ghost," one of the most distinguished, but controversial, intelligence officers in the Agency's history. Shackley, the boy wonder of the clandestine services, took over J.M. Wave and the Miami station in February 1962—ten months after the Bay of Pigs disaster—at the age of 34. The Miami station was to become the largest CIA station in the world, with over 700 Agency personnel and a budget in excess of $500 million. Shackley had worked for the legendary Bill Harvey during the construction of the Berlin tunnel, and had been recalled to headquarters to head a team making a vulnerability study of the Castro regime. He was to go on to serve as Chief of Station in Laos and Saigon.

Wilson came into the picture once again when the CIA decided to restructure the dummy corporations and proprietaries that provided cover employment and commercial disguises for Operation Mongoose, the post–Bay of Pigs plan ordered by President Kennedy to get rid of Castro. When Wilson arrived on the scene there were at least 55 such companies operating in conjunction with Mongoose, running the gamut from travel agencies to consulting firms, gem stores, boat rental and repair shops, fishing operations, and investment firms. These included the Caribbean Research and Marketing Corporation; the Dodge Corporation; PARAGON Air Service, which recruited and provided cover for Operation Mongoose pilots; and Ace Cartography, Inc., which operated a fleet of specially modified boats based at Homestead Marina. The reorganization of some of the companies was simply a matter of changing the letterhead and the names on the office doors of various cover organizations established for the Bay of Pigs invasion. Often the players were the same, only the names changed. For example, Ace Cartography listed W.A. Robertson, Jr., and Grayson L. Lynch as registered agents. They were "Rip" and "Gracie" of Mineral Carriers Ltd., the first two Americans ashore at the Bay of Pigs.

Wilson's logistics skills and maritime connections made him the perfect man for the job. Working closely with Shackley, Wilson served as paymaster, recruiter, and manager of the proprietary companies and more than 500 safe houses in and around the Miami area. It was during this period that Wilson met some of the Cuban exiles who would later betray him to the authorities.

All during this time Wilson remained active in union activities in Washington, and this provided him access to many well-known politicians and public figures, especially in the Democratic party. In 1964, he became involved in politics, serving as an advance man for Vice Presidential candidate Hubert H. Humphrey in the fall campaign. He subsequently maintained an occasional friendship with Humphrey, though there is no evidence that Humphrey ever knew of Wilson's real identity and activities. One curious fact, however, is that it is reliably reported that Humphrey often used the CIA fleet of Gulfstream jets for campaign travel during his 1968 run for the presidency.

Despite Wilson's direct involvement in domestic politics while on the CIA's payroll, after the November election, which saw Humphrey elected to the second-highest office in the land, the Agency assigned him to organize a Washington-based proprietary. In early 1965, Wilson established a maritime consulting concern called, appropriately enough, Maritime Consulting Associates, Inc. Little is known of the actual activities of this firm except that it specialized in a number of things Wilson had become acquainted with during his Seafarer's tour, principally the monitoring of international shipping and trafficking in high-technology goods and services. The firm's chief monitoring target was the Soviet Union.

Three years later, in 1968, another company, called Charles Seifried and Company, was incorporated in the District of Columbia. The company ostensibly operated as a steamship broker and agent. Three months later the name of the company was changed to Consultants International Inc., and it was CI that was to become, over time, Wilson's chief base of operations in subsequent years.

Working for "Mona"

In 1971, Wilson joined Task Force 157, one of the most successful and unusual intelligence ventures in the nation's history. TF 157 was a U.S. Navy, not a CIA, intelligence operation, and those who worked for it would joke that they worked for "Mona," which was short for "Mother Navy." By contrast to some reports, Wilson did not "run" TF 157, nor was he one of the principal players. Rather, he performed his specialized function: the establishment and operation of business "fronts" that provided non-official cover to 157's agents and operations.

In an era of growing reliance on technologically gathered intelligence collection, 157 was the classic HUMINT operation, that is, intelligence collection by humans. HUMINT complements the other "INTS," which include COMINT (communications intelligence), ACINT (acoustic intelligence), NUCINT (nuclear intelligence), PHOTINT (photographic intelligence), SIGINT (signals intelligence), and ELINT (electronic intelligence). In recent years a storm of controversy has swirled around HUMINT operations. Critics charged that HUMINT operations are expensive, unreliable, and hard to control. They point to men like Ed Wilson and other rogue agents accused of "going off the reservation" as evidence of the difficulties involved in relying on the talents of the often resourceful, but frequently individualistic, ruthless, and exotic HUMINT operators. Not only are such operations, especially inserting agents in enemy territory, unnecessarily dangerous, charge critics, but HUMINT functions can be performed more efficiently and less expensively by technological means. More than 90 percent of all intelligence collection today is technologically gathered, they note, and therefore HUMINT has become a dangerous anachronism capable of bringing discredit on the intelligence establishment, as it did during the Church Committee hearings in the mid-1970s and subsequent allegations of CIA wrongdoing.

Supporters of HUMINT, by contrast, argue that those who would rely exclusively on technologically gathered intelligence are essentially bureaucratic personalities, grown soft and content to push paper in air-conditioned offices but afraid to ply their skills in the field. They point to the fact that the Soviets are still strong advocates of HUMINT, and note that the rise of anti-HUMINT sentiment within the intelligence community paralleled the decline of national confidence that witnessed America shrinking back from seeking to control and influence world events and instead becoming simply a passive player in world affairs. While acknowledging occasional control problems and the fact that disclosure of certain HUMINT operations could be detrimental to the national interest, advocates maintain that HUMINT collection is often critical to "the success of special operations such as direct action raids, antiterrorist operations and hostage rescue operations." Moreover, there are other kinds of intelligence that can only be collected through human means. As one long-time spook put it: "Electronic and other kinds of intelligence will tell you how many Russians can dance on the head of a pin, or how many missile silos there are, but *not* what they're going to do with those missiles. HUMINT will tell you what they are going to do with them."

Navy Field Operations Support Group came into being in 1965, and its charter was signed by Secretary of the Navy Paul Nitze on December 7, Pearl Harbor Day. For communications purposes it was designated Task Force 157. The creation of 157 coincided with the beginning of the dramatic expansion of the Soviet navy witnessed during the past quarter century.

According to one of its former commanders, the Navy needed HUMINT "more than any of the other services because they are further out, the most exposed." 157's primary mission was to gather intelligence on Soviet and East bloc naval and merchant marine movements. Beginning with its first installation at Guantanamo Bay, 157 gradually expanded to encompass twenty-four offices scattered around the globe. Eventually it covered all of the major maritime choke points in the world: the Bosporus, Suez Canal, Danish Straits, Panama Canal, Gibraltar, and the Straits of Malacca. Soviet Mediterranean anchorages were monitored utilizing innocent-appearing fishing boats, and East bloc merchant seamen were probed for information in ports of call.

TF 157 operatives prowled the seamy bars along the waterfronts of the world, ever alert to recruit a merchant seaman from a communist country as an observer, courier, or recruiter of others. A photo and first-hand description of a Chinese, Soviet, or East bloc port could provide invaluable insights into the activities and interests of those nations. One of those recruited was the proprietor of a little nightclub in Naples along Via Mergellena, overlooking the bay. The club, located in the basement of an old apartment house, had three small whitewashed stucco rooms. One room was furnished as a piano bar and the other two as the dining room and dance floor. The small tables scattered about the place were covered with red-checkered tablecloths and illuminated by candles stuck in Chianti bottles. The little club was a favorite of the officers from various merchant ships, and the proprietor was constantly on the lookout for travelers or merchant seamen with access to the Soviet Black Sea ports or other areas denied to Western eyes.

One of the most important activities of 157 was to monitor Soviet vessels for the existence of nuclear weapons on board. It was often impossible to gather such information by airborne means, and so 157 operatives—sometimes at great personal risk—were dispatched to take readings, sometimes in heavy seas and bad weather. 157's greatest coup occurred during the October 1973 Middle East War when its agents learned that the Soviet Union had shipped nuclear weapons to Egypt.

Owing to its network of agents and informants, 157 began to pick up an even wider circle of information, including intelligence on terrorist activities. In one case, a 157 case officer learned in advance of plans by the Popular Front for the Liberation of Palestine (PFLP) to hijack a number of jetliners in September 1970 in an effort to obtain hostages to trade for imprisoned PFLP members and other Palestinian terrorists. Five days later, terrorists managed to seize four airliners, having been thwarted in an attempt to take over a fifth. After prolonged negotiations and the release of a number of terrorists held in Europe, all of the hostages were released and the planes destroyed by explosive charges. Why warnings from 157 were not heeded remains a mystery to this day.

TF 157 established a particularly effective presence in the People's Republic of China using both resident agents and port caller operations. When Henry Kissinger made his famous secret journey to Beijing in July 1971, which ultimately led to U.S.-Chinese rapprochement, 157 provided a secure communications channel for him.

At its peak, 157's budget was said to be about the same as the cost of "operating a destroyer for about a year," or $5 million. This did not include certain other logistics and support costs buried in the Navy budget.

The first commanding officer of 157 was a former enlisted man and Daddy Warbucks look-alike named Thomas J. Duval, known as "Big Smoke" for his bald pate, six-foot-four, 280-pound physique, and the enormous cigars that were his trademark. Duval remembers being contacted by the CIA about Wilson. "We've got a guy that's got some maritime cover companies," he was told. "You ought to look at him because we'd like to turn him over to you. He's got a big pair of balls and he doesn't mind getting out working." But the recommendation came with a word of caution: "He's hard to handle," Duval was warned. "You've got to keep really good control because Ed will tend to go running off in all directions."[5]

Duval was impressed by Wilson's experience in setting up marine proprietaries, and a deal was struck. The CIA transferred several maritime operations to 157 and ostensibly retired Wilson, giving him a $25,000 separation bonus. Wilson was also given written permission to keep Consultants International and several other proprietary companies he had set up for the Agency. The transfer of stock was completed in April 1971, and Wilson became president of Consultants International. Consultants International thereupon became a front for Naval Intelligence instead of the CIA. The main cover for 157, however, was called Pierce Morgan Associates, Inc., located at 4660 Kenmore Avenue in Alexandria, the Seminary Plaza Professional Building. Wilson also formed World Marine Incorporated and was able to secure the use of Aeromaritime and Aeromaritime International as covers for 157 operations. By 1975, Wilson boasted that he had established more than 100 cover companies during the previous five years. One of the other companies created was a freight forwarding service, based in Washington and later in Houston, known as Aroundworld Shipping and Chartering, which later was the vehicle for the shipment of illegal explosives to Libya.

Wilson traveled extensively during the early 1970s—Libya, the Middle East, Australia, New Zealand, Indonesia, the Philippines, Hong Kong, Chile, Brazil—maintaining the scores of contacts that were always his stock-in-trade.

In addition to setting up cover companies, Wilson also engaged in procurement activities on behalf of 157, purchasing boats, electronic gear, scuba equipment, and other matériel used in its operations. Despite Wilson's independence and excessive secretiveness, his former colleagues from 157 generally have only praise for him. Recalls one former chief of 157: "I like Ed. He was always very straight with me. I never had any problems." In response to accusations of financial misdealings by Wilson while employed by 157, Duval asserts that Wilson "never had any access to money. I like to tell people I'd give Ed a dollar to go buy coffee and he'd always bring me back the change."[6]

Former 157 members bridle at suggestions that their unit somehow became a "rogue elephant" engaged in all kinds of unauthorized skullduggery, from engineering the overthrow of the Allende government in Chile and the fall of Prime Minister Gough Whitlam in Australia to laundering drug money and selling arms. Defenders of the unit point to the fact that 157 had "more controls and audits than any other organization in the Navy. There was not a penny spent without proper audits." Evidence suggests that 157 was "run by the book," its activities thoroughly coordinated with the Director of Central Intelligence and personally approved in every case by the Director of Navy Intelligence.

While Wilson kept a desk at 157 headquarters, he divided most of his time between Pierce Morgan Associates and Consultants International. On a normal day he would leave his house by 6:00 A.M. and not return until 8:00 or 9:00 P.M., and sometimes not before midnight. Usually he would stop first at Pierce Morgan and then make the rounds of his various businesses, arriving at Consultants International sometime before noon. Once at Consultants International he would spend most of his time on the phone or engrossed in meetings. He was not a reflective man, nor was he comfortable putting his thoughts down on paper. In fact, his inability to communicate by means of the written word is well known. Wilson was a shoot-from-the-hip kind of guy who made intuitive decisions and was at home in the midst of the pandemonium that usually characterized his businesses. Not a detail man, he always relied on others to "take care of the fine print."

In addition to performing services for 157, Wilson and others at Consultants International engaged in various side deals and private entrepreneurial activities. Gradually it became impossible to distinguish between Wilson's work as a private businessman and his work for 157. Weapons, agricultural commodities, electronic surveillance equipment, jeeps, tents, boats and other naval matériel all moved through the firm at one time or another, and, with the profits, Wilson began to indulge in his passion for real estate.

Real Estate Mogul

Prior to the early 1970s Wilson had dabbled in the purchase and sale of property, buying up mortgages from servicemen and CIA employees transferred away from the Washington area. On April 15, 1967, personal financial statements put Wilson's net worth at approximately $200,000, chiefly from real estate holdings. His first major real estate transaction had been a sixteen-acre farm on Leesburg Pike in Virginia, which he and his wife, Barbara, fixed up. They also bought the house across the street from it, a pattern he was to repeat several times.

Shortly after joining 157, Wilson made a $60,000 down payment on a 500-acre farm in Upperville, Virginia. Over the years this farm grew to more than 3,000 acres, including once again the land across the road. According to Barbara Wilson, this was to "ensure that no one spoils the view." Others recall that Wilson always feared that he was under surveillance, variously by the KGB, the Israelis, the CIA, the media, or later, the Justice Department. Thus, it is likely that he sought to ensure that no one built a house on the property that could be used to monitor his comings and goings.

At the time of his arrest, Wilson owned an office building in Rosslyn, Virginia; two farms in England, complete with manor houses, valued at more than $1.5 million; a fashionable row house in London; several townhouses in downtown Washington; and an assortment of other holdings in North Carolina, Switzerland, Malta, Lebanon, and Mexico.

The Friends of Ed Wilson

Wilson was known for his easy style with people, being as comfortable with a day laborer working on his farm as with a U.S. senator at the National Democratic Club. "He was the kind of guy that gave a lift to hitchhikers," recalls one former associate.

A first meeting with Ed Wilson was an experience few people ever forgot: his towering size, strong voice and direct manner, the handshake that felt like it would leave your hand in a cast. Wilson never lacked presence. But though he clearly enjoyed other people, he took pains, in the words of former associate Don Lowers, not to "cultivate real close friendships."[7] Indeed, Wilson once boasted to a colleague that "he never had a friend for more than two years." The only exception to his rule was his love affair with Roberta "Bobbi" Barnes, who went to work for him as a bookkeeper and ultimately ended up as his closest confidante, mistress, and, like Ed, a fugitive. A dusky blonde divorcée in her late twenties with a young son, Bobbi, according to those who knew her best, was "probably the most intelligent person Wilson surrounded himself with." It was Bobbi who was the keeper of the gate, the person one had to get past in order to see Wilson. Wilson trusted her with the books and financial records, and in his absence she could speak for him. Wilson's relationship with Barbara, his wife and mother of his two sons, was described by those who knew them as a "close friendship" instead of a love match, characterized by congeniality, not passion. Although not given to public displays of affection, Wilson seemed to delight in Bobbi and, as the world began closing around him, it was Bobbi who gave him strength and kept his spirits up. Wilson had always been something of a womanizer, in a discreet, low-key sort of way. The offices of Consultants International were located near Washington's infamous 14th Street strip, where hookers and junkies plied their wares, and Wilson occasionally sent the chauffeur from the Hill & Knowlton public relations firm office, located in the same building, to solicit whores for him, always tipping generously for the service. But once his affair with Bobbi blossomed, Wilson seemed to settle down and forget about other women.

Bobbi Barnes easily stood out in comparison to many of the other people Wilson drew around him. Indeed, he was considered by most who knew him to be an extremely poor judge of character. "He was like somebody who picked up stray cats," one of Wilson's former colleagues remembers. "He'd come up with some of the damndest people, and after a few weeks he'd say, 'You're right, they're screwing me.'" Perhaps his most notorious associate was Frank Terpil, described by one former intelligence agent as "the darkest man I ever knew." It was Terpil who first introduced Wilson to Libya.

Terpil was a streetwise kid from Brooklyn, the son of a ne'er-do-well father and a mother who worked hard to raise him and two sisters. His first brush with the law occurred when he was only fifteen, and was a precursor of things to come. He was arrested for selling a Thompson submachine gun he had acquired from a New York City policeman to the son of his high school science teacher. Less than three decades later, the same offense, compounded by orders of magnitude, would net him a sentence of 53 years in prison.

Terpil was introduced to Wilson a short time after being "released" from the CIA as a result of being caught "flagrante delicto" speculating in currency exchange rate differences between Afghanistan and India. Stranded in Afghanistan by the outbreak of hostilities between India and Pakistan, he was discovered to be absent, without authorization, from his post in New Delhi, where he tinkered with and repaired encryption and code-breaking equipment for the Agency. Reassigned to headquarters, he "walked the halls" until he got the message and left. "They have this euphemism there of 'walking the halls,'" he later explained to a PBS reporter. "You're not given a desk. You don't have an assignment. And consequently you usually wind up going to the cafeteria every day, in which you see other people in this position. So you form a little Cafeteria Club or 'Walk the Halls' Club or whatever you call it."[8]

Terpil is described by several who knew him well as a modern-day pirate: amoral, cunning, and vicious. Throughout his life he demonstrated a total disregard for rules and regulations, believing that rules were made to be broken. Likewise, he refused to let his life be governed by clocks and watches; former associates remember that he was always late. He railed against all convention and seemed to delight in shocking those around him with outrageous table manners and rude behavior. Though stocky, with a receding hairline and a droopy unkempt moustache, he fancied himself as a ladies' man.

Although it might seem out of character for an international arms merchant and advisor to terrorists and their state patrons, Terpil was a henpecked husband. His wife Marilyn constantly nagged him and would call up his business colleagues and associates at 2:00 A.M. saying, "I haven't seen Frank since 6:00 P.M. Do you know where he is?" More likely than not, Terpil was shacked up with a bimbo in a hotel room someplace, dreading the thought of going home. Many believe that Marilyn was one of the reasons he traveled so much.

After he became a supplier of arms and torture equipment to Ugandan dictator Idi "Big Daddy" Amin, Terpil used to travel to Kampala with a black girlfriend. "He showed her off to indicate how much he liked blacks," says a former associate. Apparently she became pregnant at one point and Terpil got her an abortion in New York City. Marilyn once went looking for Frank and his girlfriend in London armed with a .38, but, fortunately for Terpil, she did not find him.

He idolized former CIA contract agent Mitch WerBell, and affected the dress code of a mercenary, sometimes boarding commercial flights in full camouflage attire. It was Terpil's showy behavior and tendency to grandstand that most disturbed many of those who knew him. He also had a reputation for rarely telling the truth, even when it came to mundane matters; he was viewed by many as a "pathological liar" and a "real bullshit artist." Terpil constantly told "war stories," most either invented or second-hand, which were designed to make him look either like a real tough guy or a mover and shaker, depending on his mood. Don Lowers, a former Wilson employee, maintains that "Terpil was such a bullshitter that you just let it go in one ear and out the other."⁹ Another former colleague blames Terpil's penchant for exaggeration and his endless stream of war stories as the reason he attracted so much attention by federal prosecutors. "I think they're [the war stories] the main reason this whole thing has been blown so far out of proportion," the man, a former business partner of Terpil's in

Uganda, contends. "Now they're paying the price for their bull-shitting." He cites, in particular, a story told by Terpil and another former partner, Gary Korkola, about poisoning an innocent diner's soup in a Beirut restaurant to demonstrate the lethality of a poisonous substance that they were selling. "It didn't happen," says the former colleague. "They heard it from someone else and simply adopted it as their own story."

After meeting Terpil and Kevin Mulcahy for the first time at a party held at Wilson's Upperville estate, Duval took him aside and told him, "I don't know where you find these goddamn flakes but these guys are going to get you in trouble. Both of 'em are as full of shit as a Christmas turkey." Reflecting on the conversation, Duval added with bitterness: "Terpil's trying to convince me what a hot man he is, and he's nothing but a goddamn teletype repairman. Mulcahy said he'd lost his foot in Vietnam, but I know he really crashed his motorcycle while looped on drugs."[10] Several years later Wilson recalled the conversation to Duval. "You were right about Terpil," Wilson told him. "I'm getting away from him."[11]

Another Wilson associate was Douglas M. Schlachter, who was working near Wilson's farm at the Crossways Texaco service station, owned by his brother Hank, when they first met. Schlachter was a high school dropout from New York who had no military service or covert experience, although he was an avid hunter and outdoorsman. He was also a poacher who would hunt deer in the Virginia countryside at night with a bright spotlight that would blind the deer, causing them to freeze in their tracks while he picked them off. Later, with Frank Terpil, Schlachter would take up poaching again in Uganda, both for sport and ivory.

Wilson took a shine to the gas station jockey and hired him to manage his Upperville estate. By all accounts, he was very good with machinery, worked hard, and served Wilson with dog-like devotion. Short, stocky, and affable, Schlachter rapidly made himself indispensable to Wilson, and Wilson ultimately repaid his loyalty by setting him up in business.

Schlachter subsequently tried to emulate Wilson in all things, from purchasing a gentleman's farm on the Rappahannock River in Virginia's hunt country to entertaining and traveling lavishly, and drawing around him his own set of retainers and hangers-on. Schlachter's secluded three-story fieldstone house, at the end of a long dirt road, was beautiful and expansive, and became home to his wife and three children. He called it, pretentiously, "Warrenton Stud Farm," and the name appeared on his personal stationery. But try as he might, he could never transcend his background; the grease from the service station remained forever under his fingernails. This only served to frustrate him and make him try harder to impress those he came into contact with. He became flashy and flamboyant, driving a metallic pink Cadillac, adorning his fingers with diamond rings, wearing expensive—but tasteless—double-knit suits and matching ties over an omnipresent shoulder holster and gun. He liked throwing money around, tipping generously, and flashing a wad of hundred dollar bills at places like Elan (now defunct) on K Street and the Crystal City Club. He cultivated, with only limited success, an air of intrigue as if he "really had heavy-duty things going down," recalls a former friend. Schlachter's brother Hank, who owned the service station, used to whisper to visitors: "You know, he's [Doug] working for the CIA."

Schlachter also loved gaudy jewelry, and reportedly spent a quarter of a million dollars on precious stones and gold jewelry while he was riding high, buying much of it at inflated prices. The last time this author saw Schlachter was in the dimly lit lounge at the Key Bridge Marriott shortly before he became a fugitive. He took a small black presentation case from his coat, glanced furtively in both directions, and placed it on the table. He slowly opened the case, revealing a matched set of six perfect one- or two-carat diamonds, each a different color. He claimed it was a jeweler's grading case that had originally been presented to French Emperor Napoleon III. Schlachter explained that he was leaving the country and needed to sell the stones for cash.

Schlachter developed a weakness for Chivas Regal scotch and had been drinking heavily, often became abusive. Like Wilson and Terpil, he also chased women, employing several of his girlfriends at the offices of Delex International in suburban Virginia. Delex had been set up by Wilson to take the place of Inter-Technology, which had been presided over by Terpil and Mulcahy as the conduit for illegal military sales to Libya. At one point, Schlachter got a call from a Democratic congressman who was reportedly sleeping, separately, with two sisters, both of whom were on his congressional staff. He asked Schlachter to take one of them off his hands and Doug, ever eager to curry favor with the powerful, especially when the favor was providing a job to an attractive woman, readily agreed. The woman who came over to Delex was ultimately to become his mistress and partner during his subsequent days as a fugitive.

Off the Reservation

Whether Wilson gradually went bad or whether he was always bad is a matter still debated among his former friends and associates, journalists, and even federal prosecutors. What is known is that after Wilson left TF 157 on April 30, 1976, taking with him some of the proprietaries that he had created, he began scrambling for business opportunities, tapping former colleagues for leads and favors, putting out feelers. His net worth had increased tenfold during the time he had worked for 157, all through real estate speculation and the appreciation of his holdings, and, while he was certainly not poor, his overhead was high. Besides, he wanted to be a "mover and shaker" in Washington, a big-bucks businessman and wheeler-dealer, hoping to buy his way into some future Democratic administration as a top political appointee. Prior to a front-page *Washington Post* story linking him to the assassination of former Chilean Foreign Minister Orlando Letelier, who died in a bomb blast on Washington's embassy row while commuting to work, Ed Wilson lobbied to get a high-level government post.

Wilson's colleagues say that his firms were generating very little business: Delex International was showing only a modest profit, and OSI (Operational Systems Inc.), Aroundworld Shipping and Chartering, and the farm were all losing money.

According to one of his key associates, nothing in the United States was producing "close to the money he required." Nevertheless, Wilson remained confident that things would begin to take off. "Ed figured if you kept enough balls in the air," says Lowers, "something would pay off."[12] Then he met Frank Terpil; some say it was at a cocktail party, others claim it was through a mutual friend, Joe Sands, in London.

Terpil became Wilson's entrée into the Libyan market, a market Wilson had wanted to enter for several years, even while working for 157. Terpil apparently had a number of contacts in Tripoli. It has never been established exactly why Wilson was intrigued with doing business in Libya, especially in view of the North African country's strident opposition to the United States and Qaddafi's reputation for having a screw loose.

One of the ironies associated with Wilson's decision to actively target Libya as a market for weapons, training, and technical services was his business relationship with retired Brig. General Joseph J. Cappucci, who had once been stationed at Wheelus Air Force Base in Tripoli, before the Americans were kicked out by Qaddafi. Cappucci, a diminutive and easy-going Air Force careerist whose last position before retirement had been as head of the Defense Investigative Service (DIS), worked for one of Wilson's companies, OSI, and was about to leave to take a job with Northrop Corporation. Instead, Wilson dispatched Don Lowers to meet with Cappucci and offer to help set him up in business as a private security firm. Wilson reportedly never actually owned stock in Joseph J. Cappucci Associates, but rather only an option to purchase 40 percent of the stock. He loaned Cappucci the money to get started, however, and Lowers moved over to the new company to look after the books and day-to-day management. Cappucci set up shop in an elegant townhouse owned by Wilson off Washington Circle in the nation's capital. Wilson, Terpil, and Schlachter also did some business from the townhouse, and used the fully furnished apartment in the basement for clandestine meetings as well as trysts with their respective mistresses. The downstairs reception desk was run by an attractive and very perky former Wilson employee, who had once done secretarial work for the legendary head of counter-intelligence at the CIA, James Jesus Angelton. Bobbi Barnes was also located in the townhouse, on the third floor.

During the coup that brought Qaddafi to power in 1969, Cappucci had helped Yehia Omar, an influential official in the government of Libya's deposed King Idris, to flee the country via Wheelus Air Force Base. When Cappucci opened shop, his first customer was Omar, who remembered his debt to the General. Omar even moved his personal attorney, a former counsel to President Ford, into the townhouse. During this period, Omar was listed as a diplomat with the nation of Oman, but in reality he was a top financial advisor to Sultan Qaboos, and reputedly Anwar Sadat's "bag man." He also had extremely close ties to the CIA. Omar, whose worth was estimated to be close to a billion dollars, maintained a luxurious Washington apartment, which encompassed nearly a full floor of one of Washington's most expensive apartment buildings. The only other apartment on the floor, which was much smaller but still commodious, belonged to the CIA's former top Middle East operative, who had retired.

Qaddafi had threatened to kill Omar, allegedly the top foreign target on Libya's "hit list," and Cappucci's firm was one of those that provided security services to him. One of those hired to look after Omar was Cuban-born former CIA operative Felix Rodriguez, who later would become one of the principal figures in the Contra resupply operation headed by Oliver North. Felix was recommended by Thomas G. Clines, a friend of Wilson's and a former senior CIA covert operator who had once run the secret CIA base at Long Tieng in Laos. Cappucci's firm was also given a contract, arranged through Omar and cleared by the CIA, to train Sadat's security detail in Egypt.

Thus, at the very moment that Wilson and his confederates began doing business with the Qaddafi regime, one of Wilson's affiliated firms, located under the same roof, was providing protection to one of Qaddafi's most outspoken opponents, and helping to upgrade security for Qaddafi's sworn enemy, Egyptian President Anwar Sadat.

Cappucci's relationship with Omar ultimately led to a break with Wilson. It was Wilson, however, who ultimately asked Cappucci and his company to vacate the townhouse, apparently because he feared the Libyan intelligence would discover Cappucci's relationship to Omar. Although Wilson had ample opportunity to have Omar "hit," he never did. According to Cappucci, the only suspicious thing Wilson ever did regarding Omar was to ask for the address of his apartment in Washington.[13] Cappucci gave him a false address, and never heard anything more about it.

In a period of eighteen months after leaving TF 157, Wilson transformed the nearly moribund proprietaries he had taken with him into a global business network with dozens of employees and tens of millions of dollars in sales. But for all intents and purposes, he only had one client: the government of Libya. As author Joseph Goulden has written, next to the foreign oil companies Wilson "became the West's leading trader in Libya."[14] He also became one of the chief quartermasters of international terrorism, providing Libyan military and intelligence organizations with arms, tons of explosives, surveillance technology, aviation parts, contract pilots, night-vision equipment, and training. The Libyans, in turn, transferred much of the technology and training on to some of the more than forty international terrorist groups that Libya has aided and abetted over the years.

In 1976 Wilson and his colleagues provided the Libyan government with thousands of explosives timers, which were still appearing in Arab terrorist bombs as late as 1988, and 40,000 pounds of C4 plastic explosive. According to some reports, he made an estimated profit of $32.5 million from the deal. Wilson also set up a bomb factory in a former palace about twenty miles from Tripoli, importing explosives experts to teach the Libyans how to design and fabricate bombs and to manufacture a variety of boobytraps and assassination devices that could be used to kill Qaddafi's opponents. He brought over a number of active and retired U.S. Army Special Forces advisors to train the Libyans in covert and special operations skills, skills that were readily applicable to terrorist operations. He even tried to hire former CIA contract killers to assassinate enemies of the Libyan government. There are also reports that he tried to buy a variety of munitions for the revolutionary government in Iran.

As but one illustration of the impact of Wilson's operations, American intelligence experts contend that without the British, American, and French contract pilots assembled by Wilson to man Qaddafi's C-130s and helicopters, Libyan operations in Chad would have been impossible. There are reports that some of his pilots even flew combat sorties. Wilson is also accused of attempting to sell sensitive technology to the Soviet Union, including a sophisticated computer program used to analyze and interpret aerial reconnaissance information.

Wilson "hated Libya with a passion" and described it to colleagues as "the asshole of the world." Nor did he think much of Qaddafi. But the money was flowing in and no one seemed to care: not the Americans, or the Israelis, or any other Western intelligence service. Wilson made little attempt to hide the fact that he was doing business with Libya, and maintained contact with a number of his old Agency buddies. On occasion, he would debrief people both at State and the CIA when he returned from Libya, and no one raised any objection to what he was doing. While he was not totally candid about his operations, a number of former employees, including Kevin Mulcahy and ex-CIA operative John "I.W." Harper, had approached federal authorities about Wilson's activities, but received a cold shoulder. Most of those who viewed Wilson's activities with trepidation, however, simply convinced themselves that "it had to be an Agency operation." Wilson had so many friends in the government, so many Agency ties, recalled Don Lowers, "that you couldn't help but feel that somehow the Agency was involved."[15]

Meanwhile, Terpil and Wilson had a falling out, and by mid-1977 Terpil was spending most of his time working for Ugandan dictator Idi Amin. In September of 1976, perhaps at Qaddafi's suggestion, Terpil met in Kampala with Robert Astles, Amin's British-born security advisor; Wadia Haddad, operational chief of the Palestine Liberation Front (PLF) until his death in 1978; and, allegedly, Carlos "the Jackal." (Terpil's claim that Carlos was present, however, seems like another of his exaggerations, thrown in to embellish the story.) Following the meeting, Terpil began supplying the Ugandans with sophisticated torture and security equipment and the necessary training to operate and maintain it. Ultimately, Terpil was actually given an office in the dreaded State Research Bureau, the headquarters of Amin's secret police and the site of their torture chambers. He described it as "a one-way gate." On several occasions, Terpil boasted to colleagues, as well as to federal undercover agents, of torture techniques used by the Ugandans and the murder plots he had been involved in on their behalf.

During this same period, Doug Schlachter became Wilson's operational chief in Libya. Schlachter was very pro-Libyan and openly anti-Semitic. He spoke constantly to colleagues about how the Libyans "could be brought into the Western fold if handled properly," and he tried to convince Wilson to take a more activist role in "patching up differences between the U.S. and Qaddafi." What the Libyans needed, maintained Schlachter, was a big PR campaign in the United States. Wilson, however, thought Schlachter was "wasting his time." Several of Schlachter's former associates believe that the reason he got along so well with the Libyans was that he "was basically a peasant like them. He had a peasant mentality, and didn't look down on them like Wilson and the others."

In a sealed grand jury indictment handed down in July 1980, Schlachter was accused not only of participating in the transfer of illegal explosives and gun running to Libya, but also of actually recruiting, on Wilson's behalf, many of the Americans engaged in training Libyan commandos in terrorist tactics and in supervising their instruction. In addition, he reportedly arranged for martial arts training for Qaddafi's bodyguards.

Sometime in 1979, Wilson became angered that Schlachter was becoming too independent, and had made an "unauthorized" trip back to the United States. Schlachter finally broke with his old mentor and, with his girlfriend Tina, departed for the African nation of Burundi and set up a freight-forwarding operation. After his whereabouts were discoverd by federal prosecutors, he cut a deal with Assistant U.S. Attorney E. Lawrence Barcella, Jr., and returned to the United States, where he became a government witness against Wilson and the others.

After his indictment in 1980, Wilson jumped bail and returned to Libya, where he began drinking heavily, mostly imbibing a locally distilled moonshine known as "flash," since Libya is officially "dry." Nevertheless, he would occasionally call up old friends and colleagues in the United States, often waking them up in the middle of the night, to offer them a "chance to make big money" doing such things as training Qaddafi's praetorian guard.

Wilson was growing increasingly isolated. On December 21, 1981, his mistress, Bobbi Barnes, was picked up entering the United States to spend Christmas with her sister and her family in Austin. Her name had popped up on a computerized "lookout" list when she went through immigration, and she had been detained. She subsequently agreed to cooperate with Assistant U.S. Attorney Barcella.

In June 1982 Wilson, who had been a fugitive for almost two years, was lured from Libya and detained, by prior arrangement with the U.S. government, in the Dominican Republic. After informing Wilson that his papers were not in order, the Dominicans put him on the first plane for New York, where federal agents were waiting for him. In subsequent trials, Wilson was convicted of smuggling arms and explosives to Libya and of attempting to induce two convicts to murder his wife, Barbara, prosecutors Larry Barcella and Carol Bruce, and a number of witnesses who had testified against him. He was sentenced to a combined total of 52 years in prison, with little chance of parole before the year 2000.

During Wilson's various trials, he and his attorneys tried to argue that he was actually working for the CIA, and that all of his actions had been sanctioned by senior intelligence officials. However, no proof was ever put forward to justify his claim. According to a former member of the House Intelligence Committee, there was "no paper trail, no written trail at CIA. No one officially knew." Wilson was to maintain that he was double-crossed by two former officials of the clandestine arm of the CIA, Ted Shackley and Tom Clines, but even he had to admit that his official contact with Shackley had ended in 1977. Wilson had loaned Clines money on a number of occasions, including $500,000, which he used to set up a company that handled U.S. shipments of arms transferred to Egypt. Clines later pled guilty to defrauding the U.S. government with inflated invoices.

Another Iran/Contra figure damaged by association with Wilson and his colleagues was Major General Richard Secord, who was identified by Doug Schlachter as involved in sales of military equipment to Iran at a time when Secord was still an active-duty military officer. Although he was later exonerated, Secord never received his promotion to three-star rank, and decided to retire, thus setting into motion the chain of events that would ultimately lead him to Oliver North's door. Interestingly, Wilson, Secord, Shackley, Terpil, Schlachter, and other Wilson associates all resurface in conjunction with the Nugan-Hand Bank scandal in Australia. The Nugan-Hand Bank allegedly laundered intelligence and drug money until it collapsed in 1980, following the death (some say murder) of founder Frank Nugan. Nevertheless, one should not read too much into the fact that the same set of players has reappeared over and over again, from the secret war in Laos to the Iran/Contra affair. The special operations/intelligence community, after all, is very small and, to a certain degree, incestuous. It is an "old boy" network, and the involvement of one individual in the network usually leads to the involvement of others.

In 1984 Wilson called an acquaintance (collect) from the federal penitentiary in Marion, Illinois, and asked him to recommend a Washington-area real estate agent. He gave Wilson the name of a very attractive young real estate agent by the name of Sally Ward, and Wilson called her a number of times in subsequent months. During one of the calls Wilson asked her how old she was, and Sally responded that she was thirty. "That's great," responded Wilson, ever the optimist. "You'll still be young when I get out and I want to meet you then."

Preventing "Rogue" Counterterrorists

Ironically, there were no federal laws that prohibited Americans from providing support and training to terrorist organizations, unless they engaged in the sale of illegal weapons and explosives. Similarly, no laws prevented former U.S. intelligence operatives and commandos from transferring their knowledge of the "craft" to foreign governments, and even to terrorists. Legislation was introduced in Congress, known as the "Prohibition of Training and Support for Terrorism Act of 1984," which would make it a crime for U.S. citizens to manufacture, sell, or export military weapons, equipment, and technology, or to provide training and expertise to other nations or individuals for the purpose of aiding and abetting international terrorism. However, the legislation, called by some the "Ed Wilson bill," failed to pass Congress because of problems some members raised over the definition of a terrorist group, and whether or not such a law represents an abridgement of a citizen's First Amendment right to free expression. Members of the House Foreign Affairs Committee, in particular, became hopelessly bogged down in ACLU (American Civil Liberties Union) concerns and lost sight of their paramount obligation to protect the American public. Rather than sit down and redraft objectionable language, the shortsighted members of the Foreign Affairs Committee scuttled the legislation.

To deal with the unresolved problem of U.S. citizens aiding and abetting international terrorism, the Reagan administration moved to tighten existing laws by means of administrative changes in the International Traffic in Arms Regulations (ITAR) and the inclusion of "murder for hire" provisions in the Omnibus Crime Bill of 1984. However, various categories of criminal behavior are still not covered by existing law, especially the training of foreign terrorists and certain forms of conspiracy to provide logistics and other support to terrorists and their state supporters.

According to former Deputy Director of the State Department's Office for Combatting Terrorism, Terrell A. Arnold, one of the difficulties in developing legislation is that the problem of special operators going off the reservation is "larger than the Wilson/Terpil case. It's not the ideal example on which to build generic legislation," says Arnold.[16] The potential for abuse of counterterrorism skills and technology is so great that serious policymakers are alarmed, believing that the cases that will dominate tomorrow's headlines are already in the process of happening today. Virtually every covert intelligence organization and elite counterterrorist unit has one or two anecdotal stories about ex-operators who have "gone bad" or "over to the other side." However, hard information is hard to come by and guarded like "the family jewels," lest it become public and bring discredit on the whole unit. There are even one or two unverifiable stories floating around the community about units sending their own men out to kill those who have gone off the reservation before they can do too much harm.

10

Hunting the Hunters

The body of a dead enemy always smells sweet.
　　　　　　　　　　　　　　　　—Aulus Vitellius

I T WAS called the "Boudia barbecue." Mohammed Boudia
was a dapper Palestinian living in Paris, using a forged
Algerian passport. Spending most of his time with artists and
theater people while seducing attractive women, he was thought
to be an affable, but inconsequential, man. The reality, however, was far different. Boudia was the "foreign minister" of the
Palestinian terrorist organization known as Black September,
which had carried out the massacre of Israeli athletes at the
Munich Olympics the year before.

His assignment was to mold the various European terrorist
groups into a coherent, unified organization. He dreamed of a
global network of terrorists—from the Basque ETA to the Japanese Red Army and Black Septembrists—that could exchange
weapons, intelligence, and logistical support, and ultimately
stage joint operations, attacking simultaneously in different
parts of the world.

Early in the morning on June 28, 1973, after spending the
night with a French girlfriend, Boudia climbed into his white
Renault 16 sedan parked on the rue des Fosses St. Berhard. An
explosive charge placed behind the driver's seat went off, taking
Boudia with it. Some three hundred feet down the street sat a
small VW "bug," its rear windows covered with black masking

tape. Peering out through two slits in the tape were two agents of the Israeli "Mossad." Boudia's funeral pyre brought smiles to their faces.

An Eye for an Eye

The attack on Boudia was carried out by an Israeli hit team set up in the aftermath of the Munich massacre. The rise of the Palestinian terrorist organization Black September, which was more formidable than any terrorist opponent the Israelis had yet faced, presented the Israeli government with a unique challenge. Established by Yasir Arafat and the PLO as a "deniable" action unit, Black September was responsible not only for the murder of the Israeli athletes at Munich but also for attacks on Israeli diplomats and supporters of Israel throughout the world. The success and viciousness of the attacks convinced the Israelis that their current antiterrorism strategies weren't working. They needed new answers, new methods of fighting back, Prime Minister Golda Meir's advisors told her. According to General Zvi Zamir, head of the Mossad, and General Aharon Yariv, her personal advisor on terrorist activities, Israel needed to carry the war to the terrorists, using the same tactics and weapons employed by Black September against them. They proposed to the Prime Minister the creation of an assassination squad which, if it were to stop Black September terrorism, had to "eliminate not just one leader but the entire leadership. The life of an Arab terrorist chief must become so perilous," relates David Tinnin, "that . . . no replacements would dare to volunteer."[1]

After a period of agonizing soul searching, Meir summoned Yariv and Zamir and told them, "Send forth the boys."[2]

The Israeli hit squad called itself "The Wrath of God," and despite efforts to distance it from the Israeli government, there is little doubt that it was wholly controlled and tasked by the Israeli intelligence agency, the Mossad.

Their number-one target was the operational chief of Black September, Ali Hassan Salameh, a darkly handsome, rakish man who, before his death, would marry Georgina Rizak, a former Miss Universe. He was given the code name "The Red Prince" and hunted relentlessly until his death at the hands of the Mossad in 1979.

The first to die, however, was Wael Zwaiter, a cousin of Yasir Arafat and the head of Black September's operations in Rome. Zwaiter was shot a dozen times on a Rome street by two Israeli gunmen. Less than two months later, Dr. Mahmoud Hamshari, Black September's number-two man in France, answered the telephone at his flat one evening. After the caller was assured that he was speaking to Hamshari, he activated a high-pitched tone that detonated a powerful shrapnel-filled bomb secreted beneath Hamshari's phone stand. Hamshari died a few days later in a Paris hospital. Events had now come full circle since Hamshari had plotted former Israeli Prime Minister David Ben-Gurion's death in 1969.

In the weeks and months that followed, a dozen top members of Black September were murdered by the Israeli hit team, and Black September operations virtually came to a standstill. But it was Salameh who the Israelis wanted most of all, and he kept eluding their grasp. Finally, word came that Salameh was traveling to Scandinavia, purportedly to meet with the leadership of other terrorist groups that used Stockholm as a safe haven. However, it was in the city of Lillehammer, Norway, that the Israelis caught up with and killed a man believed to be Salameh as he was walking along a suburban street with his pregnant Norwegian wife. The killers shot the unarmed man twenty-two times. Later it was learned that they had murdered a Moroccan waiter named Ahmed Bouchiki, and not Salameh. An Israeli magazine carried the headline, "Sorry, Wrong Man!"[3]

Six members of the hit team, all of whom had support roles, were arrested by Norwegian authorities before they could flee the country. Although the Israeli government continued to deny any involvement in the incident, several of those captured were amateurs who had been recruited by the Mossad, and they readily broke under interrogation. Five of the six were convicted of participating in Bouchiki's murder and sentenced to jail terms.

However, not one of the five served his full sentence—each was quietly paroled and allowed to leave the country.

To this day many questions remain unanswered about the Lillehammer debacle. Were the Israelis set up and purposely led to the young Moroccan waiter, who bore a physical resemblance to Salameh, by Black September operatives, confident that the Israelis would kill the wrong man, thereby exposing their secret war and holding them up to ridicule and censure in the eyes of the world? Or, conversely, were the Israelis just incompetent? There is some evidence that the best and most capable members of the Wrath of God were "burned out" physically and mentally and had been allowed to take time off. Rather than postpone new operations until its chief operatives were back on the job, the Mossad leadership had made the mistake of assembling a backup hit team without the necessary skills and training. In retrospect, both explanations probably contain elements of truth.

Shortly after Bouchiki's death, Israel "leaked" reports to the media indicating that the Wrath of God had been disbanded. Even if the reports had been accurate, which they were not, Black September was, for all intents and purposes, finished. Its leadership had been decimated and the Israelis had proved to Arafat and his lieutenants that they could be just as ruthless as their Palestinian adversaries. It was clear to the Palestinian leadership that there was nothing to be gained from perpetuating the clandestine war.

The Mossad, nevertheless, continued to hunt Salameh and those responsible for the Munich massacre. In January 1979, Salameh met a fiery end on the rue Madame Curie in Beirut, while on the way to visit his mother. A Volkswagen packed with explosives detonated as Salameh's Chevrolet station wagon and a Land Rover carrying his bodyguards passed by. The station wagon was ripped to pieces and set on fire by the blast, which also killed those in the Land Rover. Salameh's broken body was transported to the American University Hospital, where he died on the operating table.

And the Mossad continues to hunt.

War without Limits?

The methods used by the Israelis to combat terrorism are the harshest of any Western democracy, reflecting its precarious place in the world and the threat it feels from many of its neighbors. Terrorist attacks, like the seizure of a bus in the Negev desert by three Arab gunmen in March 1988, during which three Israelis were killed, resulted in retaliatory Israeli air strikes on targets in southern Lebanon, part of a cycle of terror and counterterror that has gone on for decades in the Middle East.

To date the other Western democracies have eschewed the kind of reflexive military retaliation favored by Israel in the aftermath of terrorist attacks, and none, with the possible exception of Great Britain and Spain, have felt their own interests sufficiently threatened to dispatch hit squads to selectively target their terrorist enemies the way the Wrath of God did. Nevertheless, in recent years the nations of the West have, with some notable exceptions, demonstrated much greater resolve with respect to taking forceful action to control and suppress terrorism.

Publicly most nations still shrink from using force against terrorists and their state sponsors, except to rescue hostages, the 1986 U.S. raid against Libya being a notable exception. On the other hand, there is a nasty war going on in the shadows, witnessing, on occasion, nations like Great Britain, France, and West Germany striking back at terrorists with little regard for the niceties of law or due process.

The French, for example, have carried out general bombing raids on terrorist camps in the Bekaa Valley in retaliation for Iranian-sponsored acts of terrorism against French soldiers and civilians. They also attempted to place a vehicle full of explosives in front of the Iranian embassy in Beirut, but the vehicle was discovered and the bomb defused. The French have carried out other covert retaliatory acts against Iran and its proxies. By contrast to the French government's public criticism of the U.S. raid on Libya, French intelligence operatives tried at least twice to kill Qaddafi in the mid-1980s. And, as the French are quick to point out, they battled Qaddafi's forces in Chad for more than a decade. French military and intelligence units routinely engaged in operations against the Libyans and their Chadian proxies. French advisors served with the central government's forces during both training and combat, and operated ground-to-air missiles against Libyan aircraft. Sabotage missions by French agents deep within Libya temporarily crippled elements of the nation's infrastructure, and Libyan ships were targeted on the high seas.

The British government, despite its public denials, also has moved into a much more proactive posture regarding its protracted conflict with the Irish Republican Army. James Bond's "licence to kill" apparently has been given to some British counterterrorists. Under new and more liberal rules of engagement, IRA terrorists have been gunned down without any attempt to take them alive. In some cases, the British government simply has attributed the deaths to problems arising from "antiterrorist confrontations," in other instances there is little effort to mask the real nature of their actions. In March 1988, for example, three known IRA terrorists, intent on leaving a car with 500 pounds of explosives in a public area on Gibraltar, were shot to death by British undercover agents, purportedly members of the SAS. The three IRA terrorists, two men and a woman, were unarmed. British Foreign Secretary Sir Geoffrey Howe explained the British action by saying, "They [the IRA terrorists] made movements which led the military personnel, operating in support of the Gibraltar police, to conclude that their own lives and the lives of others were under threat. In the light of this response, they were shot dead."[4]

The British are also engaged in a deadly effort to cultivate suspicion and dissension within the IRA itself by spreading false rumors and misinformation in what amounts to the framing of various IRA members so that they will be killed or neutralized by their own comrades. In other instances, efforts have been made to deliberately detonate IRA bombs and explosives prematurely, so that from all outward appearances the deaths of the

IRA bomb makers will simply be attributed to accidents or poor technical skills.

Similarly, the British-backed Royal Ulster Constabulary (RUC) has also been accused of having an unofficial "shoot to kill" policy in Northern Ireland, which has resulted in the deaths of a number of IRA terrorists and sympathizers in recent years. But even prominent critics of the RUC believe that the killings are not so much sanctioned by higher authority as reflective of a general attitude on the part of some frustrated police officers, who have seen too many comrades killed by the IRA, not to take prisoners "if no one is looking."

It has also long been suggested that West Germany ran out of patience in 1977 and took extraordinary steps to destroy the leadership of the so-called Baader-Meinhof Gang of the Red Army Faction/Rote Armee Fraktion (RAF). Trouble began in 1972 with the arrest and incarceration of the RAF's top leadership, which simply served as an impetus for new acts of terrorism by their compatriots designed to win their leaders' freedom. Although a number of terrorist actions by the RAF had failed in this regard, the West German government made a serious tactical blunder in 1975, trading five RAF members for a prominent Christian Democrat politician who had been kidnapped by the terrorists. This gave new hope to the RAF that continued terrorist actions could put enough pressure on the government in Bonn to ultimately secure the freedom of their comrades.

Such hopes were dashed, however, when GSG-9 commandos rescued a hostage jetliner at Mogadishu, Somalia, in 1977, killing three of the four terrorists. So despondent were the imprisoned terrorists over the failure of the hijacking to spring them that three of the top leaders of the RAF—Andreas Baader, Ulrike Meinhof, and Gudrun Ensslin—allegedly "committed suicide," simultaneously and in separate cells, in Stammheim prison. In all likelihood, however, they were murdered by West German agents, hopeful of sparing innocent lives in the future by eliminating the RAF's founders.

The strategy worked. Although the RAF has continued its

campaign of terror, it has never recovered from the loss of its most gifted and ruthless leaders. It took several years for new leadership to emerge, and these new leaders have turned out to be less capable and more vulnerable than their predecessors. While the RAF is still active today, it is much smaller, and its activities more circumscribed than before.

Can the United States Kill Terrorists?

Contrary to popular fiction and films, not to mention unsubstantiated allegations by left-wing organizations, the United States does not engage in the individual targeting of terrorists or in any activity that could be interpreted as assassination. There are no statutory prohibitions against assassination, and the United States clearly possesses the capability to carry out so-called "wet" operations. However, all U.S. presidents since Gerald Ford have, in one form or another, voluntarily renounced the use of assassination as a matter of national policy. Executive Order No. 11,905, signed by President Ford, limited the ban to "political" assassinations.[5] The ban was expanded and made more comprehensive under President Carter. Carter's Executive Order No. 12,036 drops the word "political" and states that "no person employed by or acting on behalf of the United States Government shall engage in, or conspire to engage in, assassination." President Reagan's Executive Order No. 12,333 maintained the Carter language. At the time of this writing (May 1989), President Bush has not signed a new executive order nor has the White House ordered one prepared for his signature. It can be surmised, nevertheless, that he feels bound by his predecessor's executive order and that the ban on "assassination" is still in effect.

The problems with all of the executive orders banning assassination is that none of them actually defines assassination. As the United States begins to take more aggressive counterterrorist measures, the meaning of the word "assassination" has become an issue. Does, for example, the ban on assassinations apply to counterterrorist actions carried out by U.S. military forces acting under lawful orders? To what extent could the U.S. bombing raid on Libya in April 1986 be construed as an attempt to "assassinate" Muammar Qaddafi? From a Rules of Engagement (ROE) perspective, what constitutes appropriate force in resolving terrorist incidents? Moreover, where does the legitimate use of force end and assassination begin?

Assassination is often defined as "treacherous murder," and the term is generally applied to the killing of a prominent political personage (a "protected" person) or to a murder carried out for political reasons. Obviously, terrorists should be regarded as neither "protected" persons nor immune from military retaliation. Many observers also believe that the term "assassination" should not apply to acts by American military and other duly constituted forces, operating outside the boundaries of the United States, that result in the death of terrorists. Such actions, they say, can be justified as attempts to preempt—invoking the doctrine of anticipatory self-defense—future illegal acts on the part of terrorists.

While the temptation to liquidate terrorists will always be great, especially in the aftermath of some particularly violent or reprehensible terrorist attack, it should never be done promiscuously or without clear sanction from higher authorities, who can be held accountable for their decisions. In this connection, appropriate procedures will have to be found to give counterterrorist forces the freedom of action needed to successfully engage terrorists any place on earth while still safeguarding the basic values of those societies that they are charged with protecting.

The debate over assassination is illustrative of the fact that there are no neat, clean, uncontroversial answers to fighting terrorism. It is an ugly kind of warfare and there is nothing tender about it. The question today is just how the United States should combat terrorism. What options are available to policymakers, and what are the various moral, legal, and political considerations associated with each?

Small Doses of Force

Just as this nation's strategic nuclear policy is based on the doctrine of "flexible response," so too should our policy regarding low-intensity warfare be predicated on the notion of "flexible response." This means having and using the right tool for the job. In this connection, the problem today for most Western governments, with their vast nuclear and conventional arsenals, is dealing out small doses of force. In the absence of effective Western cooperation against terrorists and their state sponsors, the United States will have to rely on its right of self-defense in addressing the problems of terrorism, and this was confirmed in the preamble to National Security Decision Directive 138 (NSDD 138). But the question remains: what constitutes self-defense? What limits, if any, should be placed on antiterrorist actions? Are all means acceptable in defending ourselves?

"Keep running after a dog," goes the old saying, "and he will never bite you." So it is with terrorism. Terrorists must be placed permanently on the defensive by means of constant, unrelenting preemptive actions and operations designed to isolate, reform, and even topple terrorist-sponsoring states. As part of this program, consideration should be given to targeting individual terrorists and their organizations, using both law enforcement and military measures to hold them accountable for their actions. To carry this out, it will often be necessary to engage terrorists, one on one, in a return to the ancient rhythms of warfare where every adversary had a name and a face. There is nothing impersonal about this kind of warfare. Moreover, it is a nasty business, and requires that Western societies overcome their squeamishness about elite counterterrorist and intelligence units and the kinds of operations necessary to protect Western societies from terrorist outrages.

In the final analysis, the counterterrorist is the ideal tool for dealing out small doses of force against terrorists. He is the West's new paladin, ready and eager, as one special operator put it, to "duke it out with the scumbags of the earth" in defense of our citizens, institutions, and values. In an age that hungers for heroes, the counterterrorist is "the real thing," doing what other men and women only read about or imagine in their daydreams. No play actor or pale imitation created by a PR man and a press kit, the modern counterterrorist is engaged in the ultimate contest of skill, daring, and will in the contemporary world, a zero-sum game against the most formidable adversary on earth. In a world threatened by terrorist opponents who reject the very institutions and principles that we are striving to defend, the counterterrorist may be all that stands between us and the abyss.

Notes

1. Counterterrorism Hype

1. Andy Lightbody, *The Terrorism Survival Guide: 101 Travel Tips on How Not to Become a Victim* (New York: Dell, 1987).
2. On March 1, 1954, four members of the Puerto Rican Nationalist Party, led by Lolita Le Bron, entered the Visitors Gallery in the U.S. House of Representatives while it was in session and fired a fusillade of shots at the crowded House floor. Although there were 243 members in the chamber at the time of the attack, remarkably, no one was killed, and only five were wounded.
3. "Capitol Police Seize 1,162 Weapons in '87," *Roll Call*, March 20, 1988, p. 1.
4. Gar Wilson, *Phoenix Force* (Toronto: Worldwide, 1987), back cover.
5. Dick Stivers, *Able Team* (Toronto: Worldwide, 1987), back cover.
6. J. Bowyer Bell, conversation with author, February 1, 1988.
7. Sign in gun shop.
8. "As Rambo Goes, So Goes the Nation," *Washington Post Magazine*, September 13, 1987, pp. 17–18.
9. Ibid.
10. *Far Eastern Economic Review*, April 9, 1987, p. 35.
11. Jack Anderson, "CIA Discovers Terrorists Have 'Invisible Bomb,' " *Washington Post*, August 8, 1983, p. C14.
12. Jerome Greer Chandler, "Plastic Terror: Is There A Defense?" *American Legion Magazine* (June, 1986), p. 20.
13. "The Backpack Nuke," *Time*, June 3, 1985.
14. "PLO Said Developing Fighter Plane," *Washington Times*, October 19, 1984, p. 6.
15. See "Sunni Suicide Bomber Uses Mule," *Washington Post*, August 7, 1985, and "Coconut Bomb is Exploded," *Washington Post*, November 4, 1982.

16. John Minnery, *How to Kill*, vol. 4 (Boulder, CO: Paladin Press, 1979), p. 2.

17. This author has identified more than a dozen different ways of spelling the Libyan dictator's name, the most common being Qaddafi (*New York Times, Washington Times,* and *The Economist*), Qadhafi (*U.S. News & World Report* and *Defense & Foreign Affairs*), Gadaffi, Gaddafi (*Intelligence Digest* and *Time*), Gadhafi (*Washington Post* and *The Wall Street Journal*), Kaddafi (*Newsweek*), Kadafi (*Los Angeles Times* and *Baltimore Sun*), Khadaffi (*Soldier of Fortune*), Al-Qadhafi, El-Qaddafi, Khadafy (*Atlanta Constitution*), and Qadhdhafi (*The Middle East Journal*), to cite only a few variations. There are some that believe that the first step in fighting Qaddafi is to reach some consensus on how to spell his name. For the purposes of this study, however, the Libyan "Duce" will be referred to as Muammar Qaddafi.

18. See "When Would You Use U.S. Military Might? The Democrats Waffle," *Wall Street Journal*, January 15, 1988, p. 1.

19. "David Letterman Show," March 17, 1988.

20. "Doctors Learn from Ulster Violence," *New York Times*, August 18, 1987.

21. Guillermo Sevilla Sacasa, letter to member of the U.S. Congress, June 25, 1977.

22. "Castro Calls Reagan 'Liar,' 'Worst Terrorist,' " *Washington Post*, July 10, 1987.

23. "Nicaraguan Accuses U.S. of State Terrorism," *Washington Post*, July 20, 1985, p. A16.

24. "Libyan Aide Denies Country Aids Terrorism but Differs on Definition," *Washington Post*, May 30, 1981, p. A22.

25. Jonathan Kozol, *Rachel and Her Children* (New York: Crown, 1988).

26. "Hijacking Defendants Deny They're Terrorists," *Washington Times*, July 8, 1986.

27. See "Weinberger Suggests Turning to the U.N. with Terrorist Woes," *New York Times*, June 26, 1984, p. A14.

28. Italics reproduced as in the original document.

29. Allan Gerson, "Linguistic Subterfuge: Terrorism By Any Other Name is Still Terrorism," *Congress Monthly* (January/February, 1984), p. 9.

30. Sander Vanocur, speech, "The Role of the Media," The Fletcher School of Law and Diplomacy, Tufts University, April 18, 1985.

31. I am grateful to Terrell E. Arnold, former Deputy Director of the State Department's Office for Combatting Terrorism, for his insights with respect to defining terrorism.

32. Associated Press, "Once Again, Detroit in Line to Top Major Cities' Homicide List," January 1, 1988.

33. President Ronald Reagan, quoted in "The Presidential Band Wagon; Reagan Salutes 007 in TV Promotion," *Washington Post,* June 29, 1983.
34. A Black September terrorist pumped five bullets into Jordanian Prime Minister Wasfi Tell in the foyer of the Sheraton Hotel in Cairo on November 28, 1971. Tell tried to draw his own gun but collapsed, mortally wounded, on the floor, and his assassin knelt down and lapped his blood. Fusako Shigenobu, the notorious "Auntie," queen of the Japanese Red Army, was once told by a journalist that the JRA was regarded by most of the world as "a plague." "If that is so," she is alleged to have responded, "we might infect the whole world. I am the germ of that plague." For the Shigenobu quote, see Albert Parry, *Terrorism: From Robespierre to Arafat* (New York: Vanguard Press, 1976), p. 437.
35. "How We See Each Other: The View From America," *New York Times,* November 10, 1985.
36. James Traub, "The Law and the Prophet," *Mother Jones* (February/March, 1988), p. 48.
37. Michael T. Klare and Peter Kornbluh, eds., *Low Intensity Warfare; Counterinsurgency, Proinsurgency, and Antiterrorism in the Eighties* (New York: Pantheon, 1987), p. 14.

2. The Fear Industry

1. E.J. Criscuoli, interview, September 11, 1987, Rosslyn, VA.
2. Ibid.
3. "The Best Small Companies," *Business Week,* May 25, 1987.
4. Richard W. Kobetz, interview, June 12, 1987, Berryville, VA.
5. Criscuoli interview.
6. R. James Woolsey, statement to author, December, 1987, Center for Strategic and International Studies, Washington, D.C.
7. "Film-Studio 'Cop' Acts to Foil Latin Pirates of U.S. Hit Movies," *Wall Street Journal,* September 2, 1987.
8. The study was based on one dozen countries in Europe: the Netherlands, Spain, Italy, Norway, Sweden, Switzerland, the United Kingdom, Austria, Belgium, France, Denmark, and West Germany.
9. Tony Geraghty, *Inside the SAS* (Nashville, TN: Battery Press, 1980), p. 81.
10. Ross Perot, quoted by Richard Shenkman in "Rescue by the Private Sector," *National Review,* May 30, 1980, p. 655.
11. Jim McAdams, quoted in "Smooth Operator," *Rolling Stone,* April 24, 1986.
12. Jordan's name appears as Bob McKenna, also a "nom de guerre," in

The Elite: The Story of the Rhodesian Special Air Service, by Barbara Cole (South Africa: Three Knights Publishing, 1984).

13. Bob Jordan, interview, January 19, 1988, Washington, DC.
14. Jordan interview.
15. Jordan interview.
16. Sam Hall, *Counter-Terrorist* (New York: Donald I. Fine, 1987).
17. Rob Owen, conversation, March 12, 1988, Washington, DC.
18. Hall, *Counter-Terrorist,* p. 189.
19. Hall, *Counter-Terrorist,* p. 252.
20. Hall, *Counter-Terrorist,* p. 50.
21. "Apology to Control Risks Group," *Sunday Times,* July 13, 1986, p. 1.
22. "Corporate Gumshoes Spy on Competitors," *Washington Post,* March 30, 1986, p. F1.
23. Lt. Colonel Oliver North, *Taking the Stand: The Testimony of Lieutenant Colonel Oliver L. North* (New York: Pocket Books, 1987), p. 181.
24. North, *Taking the Stand,* p. 182.
25. Victor Colucci, statement to author, 1987.
26. Criscuoli interview.
27. "20-20 . . . The Magic Number for 1987's First Resident Class," *ESI Update* (March/April, 1987), p. 1.
28. See "A School for Aspiring Bodyguards," *Insight,* December 22, 1986, p. 22.
29. Richard W. Kobetz & Associates, *Training Programs 1986–1987,* brochure (Berryville, VA: Richard W. Kobetz & Associates, Ltd., 1986).
30. Kobetz interview.
31. See Richard W. Kobetz & Associates, *Appearance, Dress, Etiquette, Dining, Manners, Protocol and Personal Conduct* (Berryville, VA: Richard W. Kobetz & Associates, Ltd., 1985).
32. Kobetz interview.
33. "Alabama Long Popular With Mercenaries," *Atlanta Journal & Constitution,* July 7, 1985, p. 1.
34. See James A. Nathan, "The New Feudalism," *Foreign Policy* (Spring, 1981), p. 156.
35. North, *Taking the Stand,* p. 12.
36. Nathan, "The New Feudalism," p. 156.
37. Jim Hougan, *Spooks* (New York: William Morrow, 1978), p. 9.
38. See Peter J. Brown and Terrell E. Arnold, "Terrorism as Enterprise: The New Private Sector," in *Beyond the Iran/Contra Crisis: The Shape of U.S. Anti-Terrorism Policy in the Post-Reagan Era,* Neil C. Livinstone and Terrell E. Arnold, eds., (Lexington, MA: Lexington Books, 1988), p. 196.
39. "Md. Hospital in Uproar Over Camera Hidden in Locker Room," *Washington Post,* March 26, 1987, p. B1.

40. Criscuoli interview.
41. Like Anderson, former hostages Jeremy Levin of CNN and Charles Glass of ABC had legitimate reasons for being in Lebanon, that is, to report the news.
42. Contrary to some impressions, however, the Soviet Union is not totally devoid of terrorism, as a recent incident illustrates. In March 1988 a woman and eleven members of her family, some of whom were part of a family jazz ensemble called the Seven Simeons, tried to hijack a Soviet jetliner with weapons smuggled aboard in musical instrument cases. According to Soviet press reports, they demanded that the plane be diverted to "a capitalist country." During a refueling stop at an airfield near Leningrad, Soviet commandos stormed the plane. At least nine people, including five of the hijackers, were killed in the ensuing gun battle. Further, there is so much terrorism against the Soviet Union in the Afghan capital of Kabul that Western correspondents generally avoid cafés, which are frequently bombed, and wear their national flags sewn to their jackets so they are not mistaken for being Russians.

3. Rescue American Style

1. All of the interviews in this chapter were conducted over a several month period during 1988 with Don Feeney, Dave Chatellier, J.D. Roberts, Jim Hatfield, Cathy Mahone, Frank Baker, and several sources who will remain anonymous.

4. High-Tech Counterterrorism

1. Neil Smit, interview, August 12, 1987, Washington, DC.
2. E.J. Criscuoli, interview, September 11, 1987, Rosslyn, VA.
3. Criscuoli interview.
4. Terrorists not only are becoming ever smarter with respect to the tactics of their opponents, but also more sophisticated at avoiding operational pitfalls. The Japanese Red Army (JRA), for example, went so far as to create a course for its members on preventing emotional involvement with their victims.
5. The munitions seized by the French were: 20 SAM-7 missiles; 975 AK-47 assault rifles; 16 12/7-mm heavy machine guns; 12 82-mm MP41 mortars; 10 RPG-7s; 320,000 rounds of ammunition of different calibers; 984 mortar shells; 4274 AK-47 magazines; 8 Herstal assault rifles; 194,000 rounds of 7.62 ammunition; 782 7-kilo packages of Semtex (Czechoslovakian) plastic explosive; and 1,976 electric detonators.

6. Scott A. Boorman and Paul R. Levitt, "Deadly Bugs," *Chicago Tribune,* May 3, 1987, p. 19.
7. Richard W. Kobetz, interview, June 6, 1987, Berryville, VA.
8. David Blundy and Andrew Lycett, *Qaddafi and the Libyan Revolution* (Boston: Little, Brown, 1987), p. 177.
9. Criscuoli interview.
10. "U.S. Companies Pay Increasing Attention to Destroying Files," *Wall Street Journal,* September 2, 1987.
11. "Top Crimestopper in Europe? TV, Says Study of Security," Frost & Sullivan press release, 1987.
12. Brian Jenkins, speech, International Seminar on Aviation Security, Feb. 8, 1989, Herzlia, Israel.
13. U.S. Government, *Report of the DOD Commission on Beirut International Airport Terrorist Act,* copy of the final draft (Washington, DC: December 20, 1983), pp. 3–4.
14. I am indebted to security engineering consultant Kenneth O. Gray for sharing his outstanding work in this field. See Kenneth O. Gray, "Vehicle Access Control as Related to Countermeasures Against High Speed Car-Bombing Attack," presented to the Securing Installations Against Car-Bomb Attack conference sponsored by the Defense Research Institute, Washington, DC, May 15–17, 1986.
15. Sewell Whitney, "Dressed to Live," *Counterterrorism & Security* (November/December, 1986), p. 11.
16. "Bulletproofing People at Risk," *International Combat Arms* (January 1988), p. 10.
17. "Technology and Terror," *Nature,* May 20, 1987, p. 814.
18. Ibid.

5. Writing Terrorism to Death

1. J. Bowyer Bell, *A Time of Terror* (New York: Basic Books, 1978), p. 94.
2. J. Bowyer Bell, statement to author, 1984.
3. Gayle Rivers, *The Specialist: Revelations of a Counterterrorist* (New York: Stein and Day, 1985), p. 1.
4. Ibid.
5. Rivers, *The Specialist,* p. 2.
6. Rivers, *The Specialist,* p. 8.
7. Rivers, *The Specialist,* p. 19.
8. Rivers, *The Specialist,* p. 206.
9. Ibid.
10. J. Bowyer Bell, conversation with author, February 1, 1988.

11. "Soviet Influence in Wester Press?" *Disinformation,* No. 6 (Summer 1987), p. 4.
12. Ibid.
13. "Soviet Influence," p. 5.
14. For an excellent survey of terrorism as it is portrayed in contemporary literature and film, see Walter Laqueur, "The Image of the Terrorist: Literature and the Cinema," in his *The Age of Terrorism* (Boston: Little, Brown, 1987), pp. 174–202.
15. Michael Ledeen, interview, May 13, 1987, Washington, DC.
16. Bob Woodward, *Veil: The Secret Wars of the CIA 1981–1987* (New York: Simon and Schuster, 1987), p. 125.
17. Fred Landis, "Disinformationgate," *Covert Action Information Bulletin,* No. 27 (Spring 1987), p. 72.
18. Ledeen interview.
19. Ledeen interview.
20. Ledeen interview.
21. Ledeen interview.
22. Ledeen interview.
23. Ledeen interview.
24. Michael Ledeen, quoted in *Washington Jewish Week,* June 18, 1987, p. 35.
25. Ledeen interview.
26. 'Ex-NSC Aide Ledeen Says Advice Ignored on Arms-for-Hostages," *Washington Times,* September 29, 1987, p. 4.
27. Ledeen interview.
28. "Key Iran-Contra Figure Ledeen Might Not Testify," *Washington Post,* July 5, 1987, p. A16.
29. Ledeen interview.
30. Michael Ledeen, "How the Iran Initiative Went Wrong," *Wall Street Journal,* August 10, 1987.
31. Ibid.
32. Michael A. Ledeen, *Perilous Statecraft: An Insider's Account of the Iran-Contra Affair* (New York: Scribner's, 1988).
33. Ledeen interview.
34. For more information regarding Woodward's allegations re. Casey, see David Halevy and Neil C. Livingstone, "The Last Days of Bill Casey," *Washingtonian* (December, 1987), pp. 175–245.
35. Alan Hart, *Arafat: Terrorist or Peacemaker?* (London: Sidgwick & Jackson, 1984), p. 349.
36. Edward F. Mickolus, *The Literature of Terrorism* (Westport, CT: Greenwood Press, 1980), p. 145.
37. Michael T. Klare and Peter Kornbluh, eds., *Low Intensity Warfare* (New York: Pantheon, 1988), p. 13.

38. William Powell, *The Anarchist Cookbook,* 23rd printing (Secaucus, NJ: Lyle Stuart, 1971), p. 9.
39. Powell, *Anarchist Cookbook,* p. 12.
40. J. Flores Publications (Rosemead, CA: 1987), p. 12.
41. Peder Lund, interview, 1987, Boulder, CO.
42. Kurt Saxon, *The Poor Man's James Bond* (Harrison, AR: Atlan Formularies, 1972), title page.
43. Kurt Saxon, *The Poor Man's James Bond* (Eureka, CA: Atlan Formularies, 1972), title page.
44. Arcco catalogue, 1987–1988. The firm describes itself as: "A world class military supply store" (see p. 38).
45. Saxon, *Poor Man's James Bond* (Harrison edition), p. 2.
46. Clips from the interview with Saxon can be seen on "Textbooks for Terror," ABC "20/20," March 27, 1986.
47. Saxon, *Poor Man's James Bond* (Harrison edition), p. 20.
48. Saxon, *Poor Man's James Bond* (Harrison edition), p. 22.
49. Saxon, *Poor Man's James Bond* (Harrison edition), p. 18.
50. Kurt Saxon, interview, 1987, Boulder, CO.
51. "City Folk 'Subhuman,' Says Author of 'Killer's Book,' " *Courier-Democrat* (Russellville, Arkansas), October 17, 1982.
52. Ibid.
53. Saxon, *Poor Man's James Bond* (Harrison edition), p. 3.
54. Saxon, *Poor Man's James Bond* (Harrison edition), p. 1.
55. Saxon interview.
56. Saxon, *Poor Man's James Bond* (Harrison edition), back cover.
57. Saxon interview.
58. John Minnery, *How to Kill,* Vol. 1 (Boulder, CO: Paladin, 1973), preface.
59. Minnery, *How to Kill,* Vol. 1, p. 51.
60. John Minnery, *How to Kill,* Vol. 4 (Boulder, CO: Paladin, 1979), p. 84.
61. Minnery, *How to Kill,* Vol. 1, preface.
62. John Minnery, *How to Kill,* Vol. 3 (Boulder, CO: Paladin, 1979), p. 35.
63. Minnery, *How to Kill,* Vol. 1, p. 57.
64. Ibid.
65. Interestingly, during the early 1960s the U.S. intelligence community was tasked by President Kennedy "to get rid of" Fidel Castro. One of the potential assassination techniques they investigated was to rig up one of Castro's microphones to electrocute him. It seems that U.S. operatives had noticed Castro's habit of tapping his microphones in order to emphasize particular points he was trying to make. It was decided that by hooking up one of the microphones directly to a power source, they could "fry" him in front of a large crowd, and it would appear that one of his technicians was to blame.
66. John Minnery, interview, 1987, Brantford, Ontario.

6. *Soldier of Fortune* and the Armchair Counterterrorist

1. Robert K. Brown, interview, July 1, 1987, Boulder, CO.
2. Robert K. Brown, "A Slow Boat to a Slow War," *Soldier of Fortune* (August, 1987).
3. Brown interview, July 1, 1987.
4. Brown interview, July 1, 1987.
5. Jay Mallin and Robert K. Brown, *Merc: American Soldiers of Fortune* (New York: Macmillan, 1979), p. 27.
6. Brown interview, July 1, 1987.
7. Brown interview, July 1, 1987.
8. Brown interview, July 1, 1987.
9. Gary Crouse, interview, August 19, 1987, Boulder, CO.
10. "The Soldier of Fortune Story: A March to Success," brochure for advertisers (Boulder, CO: Omega Group Ltd., no date), p. 2.
11. Jim Graves, interview, July 1, 1987, Boulder, CO.
12. Fred Reed, "Playing Soldier," *Playboy* (November 1986), pp. 90–154. See also Fred Reed, "Kill Them All and Let God Sort Them Out," *Washington Post Magazine,* Dec. 7, 1986, pp. 26–34.
13. Brown interview, July 1, 1987.
14. Conversation with Bob Miller, February 23, 1988, Houston, TX.
15. Graves interview, July 1, 1987.
16. Brown interview, July 1, 1987.
17. "The Soldier of Fortune Story: A March to Success."
18. Graves interview, July 1, 1987.
19. Brown related this incident in the July 1, 1987, interview. All statements by Brown referring to it are from this interview.
20. Robert K. Brown, interview, November 11, 1987, Boulder, CO.
21. Gary Crouse, interview, August 20, 1987, Washington, DC.
22. Crouse interview, August 20, 1987.
23. Crouse interview, August 20, 1987.
24. Jim Graves, interview, June 30, 1987, Boulder, CO.
25. Brown interview, July 1, 1987.
26. Graves interview, June 30, 1987.
27. Robin Wright, statement to author, 1988, Washington, DC.
28. Derry Gallagher, telephone conversation, June 20, 1987.
29. Graves interview, June 30, 1987.
30. Brown interview, July 1, 1987.
31. James Harrer, "Editor-Publisher Linked to Murder," *Spotlight,* March 9, 1988.
32. Graves interview, June 30, 1987.
33. Robert K. Brown, statement, July 1, 1987, Boulder, CO.

7. Oliver North's Passionate War against Terrorism

1. Ronald Reagan, *Public Papers of the Presidents of the United States* (Washington, DC: U.S. Government Printing Office, 1981), p. 3. Carter, by contrast, had publicly ruled out the use of force at the outset of the hostage crisis.
2. Alexander Haig, "Secretary Haig's News Conference of January 28," *Department of State Bulletin* (February, 1981), p. J.
3. "Gates Denies Slant Given CIA Reports," *Washington Times,* September 30, 1987, p. 3.
4. Robert Chapman, statement to author, 1981, Washington, DC.
5. Lt. Colonel Oliver North, "Resume," dated March, 1986.
6. Other attendees included Robert M. Sayre, Director of the State Department's Office for Combatting Terrorism; Stephen S. Trott, Assistant Attorney General of the Criminal Division; Major Gen. W.H. "Duff" Rice, Director of the Joint Special Operations Agency at the Department of Defense; Noel Koch, Principal Deputy Assistant Secretary of Defense, International Security Affairs; Deputy Secretary of State Kenneth Dam; Under Secretary of State for Political Affairs Lawrence S. Eagleburger; Admiral John Poindexter, Deputy Assistant to the President for National Security Affairs; Ronald I. Spiers, Under Secretary of State for Management; Robert E. Lamb, Assistant Secretary of State for Administration; Langhorne A. Motley, Assistant Secretary of State for Inter-American Affairs; Richard W. Murphy, Assistant Secretary of State for Near Eastern and South Asian Affairs; John H. Kelly, Deputy Assistant Secretary of State for European and Canadian Affairs; and Terrell E. Arnold, Deputy Director of the State Department's Office for Combatting Terrorism. The five outside "experts" were Brian Jenkins, Sam C. Serkesian, Joseph Rosetti, Harry L. Pizer, and this author. Robert C. McFarlane, the President's National Security Advisor, was supposed to attend but could not make it.
7. Secretary of State George Shultz, "Terrorism and the Modern World," speech to Park Avenue Synagogue, New York, October 25, 1984, p. 23.
8. Noel Koch, interview, April 30, 1987, Arlington, VA.
9. See Neil C. Livingstone and Terrell E. Arnold, *Fighting Back: Winning the War Against Terrorism* (Lexington, MA: Lexington Books, 1985).
10. David Halevy, interview, February 28, 1988, Washington, DC.
11. I am indebted to David Halevy for his assistance regarding North's years at the NSC. Some material in this chapter appeared in "The Ollie We Knew," by David Halevy and Neil C. Livingstone, *The Washingtonian* (July 1987), pp. 77–158.
12. Lt. Colonel Oliver North, conversation with author, November 14, 1986, Washington, DC.
13. Amir Taheri, *Holy Terror* (Bethesda, MD: Adler & Adler, 1987), p. 85.

14. See Bob Woodward, *Veil: The Secret Wars of the CIA 1981–1987* (New York: Simon and Schuster, 1987), p. 397.
15. Ibid.
16. William Casey, speech to the Fletcher School of Law and Diplomacy, Fourteenth Annual International Security Studies Conference, Cambridge, MA, April 17, 1985.
17. The interviews and conversations with Oliver North quoted in this chapter were conducted by Neil C. Livingstone and David Halevy over a three-year period from 1984 to 1986. Most took place in Washington, DC.
18. For six months following the raid, however, SEAL teams carried out regular landings on the Libyan coast designed to harass, deceive, and intimidate Qaddafi.
19. Fawn, unfortunately, had the misfortune of becoming a public figure in the same year that Gary Hart's paramour, Donna Rice, and TV evangelist Jim Bakker's illicit lover, Jessica Hahn, burst into the national consciousness, and she was immediately stuck with the label ''bimbo,'' and lumped in with the other two women. Fawn's only commonality with either Rice or Hahn is that she is both young and attractive. Unlike the other women, while working with North she was tireless, dedicated, patriotic, smart, and extremely competent. No one who knows Fawn Hall ever believed that her relationship with North was anything but professional, and the innuendo and tittering that accompany her name today are unwarranted and wholly inappropriate.
20. Jeff Bostic, quoted in ''Redskins Get Super Sendoff From North,'' *Washington Post*, January 24, 1988, p. D9.
21. Leonore Skenazy, ''Ollie's Follies Could be Ad Hit,'' *Advertising Age*, July 20, 1987.
22. ''Two Republicans Protest Use of North Name to Raise Funds,'' *Washington Post*, August 27, 1987.
23. ''People,'' *Washington Post*, August 27, 1987.
24. P.J. O'Rourke, ''The Year That Fell to Earth,'' *Rolling Stone*, December 17–31, 1987, p. 123.
25. ''Dole Shares Views on Reagan, North and Iran Affair,'' *Washington Post*, January 1, 1988.
26. Robert W. Owen, statement to author, February, 1987.

8. Counterterrorist Commandos: The New Samurai

1. Noel Koch, interview, April 30, 1987, Arlington, VA.
2. See Paul B. Ryan, *The Iranian Rescue Mission: Why it Failed* (Annapolis, MD: Naval Institute Press, 1985), pp. 59–61.

3. See Leroy Thompson, *The Rescuers: The World's Top Anti-Terrorist Units* (Boulder, CO: Paladin Press, 1986).

4. Koch interview.

5. Koch interview.

6. Koch interview.

7. It was later learned that two of the sharpshooters who had terrorists in their sights had "frozen" at the crucial moment and not pulled their triggers. As the first commander of the U.S. Delta Force, Charlie Beckwith, later observed: "Their marksmanship had been assessed. Their resolve had not." See Col. Charlie A. Beckwith and Donald Knox, *Delta Force* (New York: Harcourt Brace Jovanovich, 1983), p. 131.

8. The crew of the first C-130 used infrared sighting devices stripped from tanks in order to land in the inky blackness. By the time the second aircraft hit the ground, however, the Mossad had managed to get the runway lights working.

9. I am indebted to David Halevy for his insights into Israel's counterterrorism capabilities.

10. Rolf Tophoven, *GSG-9: German Response to Terrorism* (West Germany: Bernard & Graefe Verlag Koblenz, 1984), p. 32.

11. Tophoven, *GSG-9*, pp. 58–59.

12. Thompson, *The Rescuers*, p. 23.

13. Robert Broussard, interview, RAID headquarters near Paris, France, 1986.

14. See John M. Collins, *Green Berets, SEALs & Spetsnaz* (London: Pergamon-Brassey's, 1987), p. 21.

15. Beckwith and Knox, *Delta Force*, p. 127.

16. Beckwith and Knox, *Delta Force*, p. 132.

17. The unit also conducted extensive training on an aircraft in a TWA hangar at New York's Kennedy Airport.

18. Beckwith and Knox, *Delta Force*, p. 143.

19. Beckwith and Knox, *Delta Force*, p. 144.

20. George Baker, *Sacred Elegy V.*

21. Harry Summers, seminar on low-intensity conflict, November 22, 1986, Georgetown University, Washington, DC.

22. "Navy SEALs under Fire for Acting Warlike," *San Diego Union*, August 19, 1987, p. 1.

23. Koch interview.

24. Koch interview.

25. Some U.S. commandos also carried XM177E2 and M3A1 submachine guns on the Iranian operation as well.

26. Thompson, *The Rescuers*, p. 172.

27. Thompson, *The Rescuers*, p. 182.

28. Rolf Tophoven, Bernard Verlag, and Graefe Verlag, *GSG-9: German*

Response to Terrorism (Oldenburg, West Germany: Neue Stalling GmbH, 1984), p. 48.

29. Michael Dewar, *Weapons & Equipment of Counter-Terrorism* (London: Arms and Armour Press, 1987), p. 143.

30. See Gordon L. Rottman, *U.S. Army Special Forces 1952–84* (London: Osprey Publishing, 1985), pp. 56–57.

9. Off the Reservation

1. "CBS Evening News", March 3, 1988.
2. Ibid.
3. "Soldier of Misfortune," editorial, *Los Angeles Times,* March 9, 1988.
4. "Magazine Innocent of Murder," editorial, *Gazette Telegraph* (Colorado Springs), March 8, 1988, p. B6.
5. Thomas Duval, interview, Washington, DC.
6. Duval interview.
7. Don Lowers, interview, Washington, DC.
8. "FRANK TERPIL: Confessions of a Dangerous Man," WGBH Transcript, 1982.
9. Lowers interview.
10. Duval interview.
11. Duval interview.
12. Lowers interview.
13. Joseph J. Cappucci, interview, Washington, DC.
14. Joseph C. Goulden, with Alexander W. Raffio, *The Death Merchant: The Rise and Fall of Edwin P. Wilson* (New York: Simon and Schuster, 1984), p. 179.
15. Lowers interview.
16. Terrell E. Arnold, telephone interview, March 22, 1988.

10. Hunting the Hunters

1. David B. Tinnin, with Dag Christensen, *The Hit Team* (Boston: Little, Brown, 1976), p. 47.
2. Michael Bar-Zohar and Eitan Haber, *The Quest for the Red Prince* (New York: William Morrow, 1983), p. 144.
3. Tinnon, *The Hit Team,* p. 174.
4. Sir Geoffrey Howe, quoted by the *Washington Post,* "British Amend Account of Killing of 3 in Gibraltar," March 8, 1988, p. A7.
5. "No employee of the United States Government shall engage in, or conspire to engage in, political assassination." See Executive Order No. 11,905.

Select Bibliography

Adams, James. *Secret Armies*. London: Hutchinson, 1988.

Asencio, Diego. *Our Man is Inside*. Boston: Little, Brown, 1982.

Barnett, Frank R., B. Hugh Tovar, and Richard H. Shultz, eds. *Special Operations in US Strategy*. Washington, DC: National Defense University, 1984.

Beckwith, Col. Charlie A. *Delta Force*. New York: Harcourt Brace Jovanovich, 1983.

Bradlee, Ben Jr. *Guts and Glory: The Rise and Fall of Oliver North*. New York: Donald I. Fine, 1988.

Clutterbuck, Richard. *Kidnap, Hijack and Extortion*. London: Macmillan, 1987.

Collins, John M. *Green Berets, SEALs & Spetsnaz*. London: Pergamon-Brassey's, 1987.

Dewar, Michael. *Weapons & Equipment of Counter-Terrorism*. London: Arms and Armour Press, 1987.

Eshel, David. *Elite Fighting Units*. New York: Arco Publishing, 1984.

Garrett, Richard. *The Raiders*. New York: Van Nostrand Reinhold, 1980.

Geraghty, Tony. *Inside the SAS*. Nashville: The Battery Press, 1981.

————. *This is the SAS*. New York: Arco Publishing, 1983.

Mallin, Jay, and Robert K. Brown. *Merc: American Soliders of Fortune*. New York: Macmillan, 1979.

Martin, David C., and John Walcott. *Best Laid Plans: The Inside Story of America's War Against Terrorism*. New York: Harper & Row, 1988.

Mickolus, Edward F., *Transnational Terrorism: A Chronology of Events, 1968–1979*. Westport, CT: Greenwood Press, 1980.

Mickolus, Edward F., Todd Sandler, and Jean M. Murdock. *International Terrorism in the 1980s: A Chronology of Events, 1980–1983*. Ames: Iowa State University Press, 1989.

Scotti, Anthony J. *Executive Safety & International Terrorism*. Englewood Cliffs, NJ: Prentice-Hall, 1986.

————. *Police Driving Techniques*. Englewood Cliffs, NJ: Prentice-Hall, 1988.

Sterling, Claire. *The Terror Network*. New York: Holt, Rinehart and Winston, 1981.

Thompson, Leroy, and Michael Chappell. *Uniforms of the Elite Forces*. Poole: Blandford Press, 1982.

Tophoven, Rolf, Bernard Verlag, and Graefe Verlag. *GSG-9: German Response to Terrorism*. Olenburg: Neue Stalling GmbH, 1984.

Index

About the Author

N EIL C. LIVINGSTONE is an author, lecturer, and frequent media commentator on terrorism and national security issues. He advises major governments and corporations on security matters and crisis management. Formerly a senior executive in an international security company, today Mr. Livingstone serves as an adjunct professor in Georgetown University's National Security Studies program, as consulting editor to the Lexington Books *Issues in Low-Intensity Conflict* series, and as president of the Institute on Terrorism and Subnational Conflict. Mr. Livingstone has served on advisory panels to the secretary of state and the chief of naval operations and has also appeared before the vice president's Task Force for Combating Terrorism. He is a former consultant to the ABC News show "20/20" and CBS's "The Equalizer."

Mr. Livingstone has written five books on national security topics and more than 60 articles, monographs, and chapters in books. He has delivered some 140 major speeches and appeared on more than 130 television programs, including "Nightline," the "Today" show, "Good Morning America," "Crossfire," the "MacNeil-Lehrer Newshour," and all three evening network news programs.

Mr. Livingstone's 1987 article (with David Halevy) "The Ollie We Knew," which was published in *The Washingtonian* and syndicated by *The New York Times,* was named by the 1988 *Media Guide* as "One of the 10 best stories of the year from the print media."